MONSTERS OF THE GÉVAUDAN

MONSTERS

of the

GÉVAUDAN

The Making of a Beast

Jay M. Smith

HARVARD UNIVERSITY PRESS

Cambridge, Massachusetts
London, England

2011

Library of Congress Cataloging-in-Publication Data

Smith, Jay M.
Monsters of the Gévaudan : the making of a beast / Jay M. Smith.
p.   cm.
Includes bibliographical references and index.
ISBN 978-0-674-04716-7 (alk. paper)
1. Gévaudan (France)—Social life and customs—18th century.
2. Popular culture—France—Gévaudan—History—18th century.
3. Beast of Gévaudan—History.
4. Wolf attacks—France—Gévaudan—History—18th century.
5. Wolves—France—Gévaudan—Folklore.
6. Monsters—France—Gévaudan—Folklore.
7. Narration (Rhetoric)—Social aspects—France—History.
8. Discourse analysis, Narrative.
I. Title
DC611.G4S64   2011
599.7730944′81—dc22   2010044994

For my mother and father, in loving memory

Contents

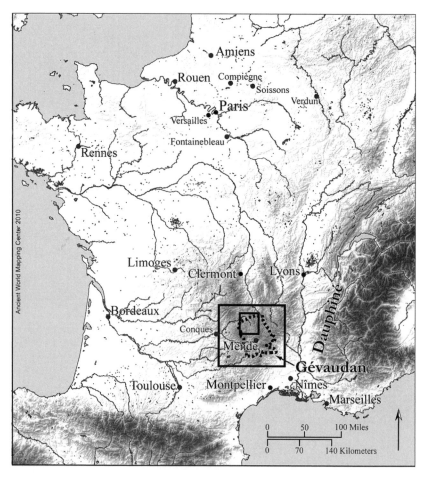

France, showing the Gévaudan region in the south. *Maps on pp. viii and ix by Richard Talbert and Brian Turner, Ancient World Mapping Center, University of North Carolina, Chapel Hill*

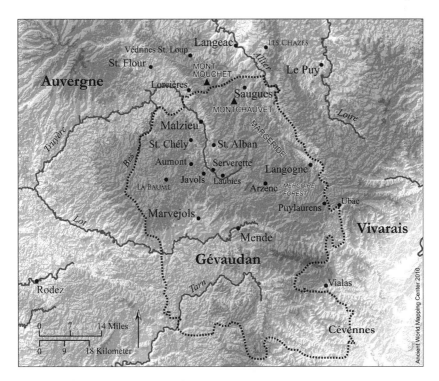

The Gévaudan, in northern Languedoc.

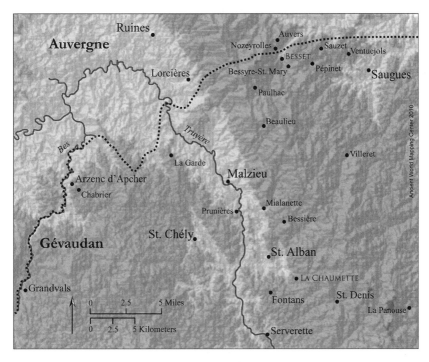

The highest concentration of attacks occurred in the northern Gévaudan.

MONSTERS OF THE GÉVAUDAN

Introduction

The Beast and Its World

In the winter of 1765, reading and listening audiences all across France were horrified and enthralled by stories of a "wild beast" *(bête féroce)* that terrorized inhabitants of the Massif Central. With a physical description that defied belief, and the ability to strike quickly, evade detection, and confound its pursuers, the mysterious beast had attacked and killed dozens of people in and around the remote mountainous region of the Gévaudan in the southern province of Languedoc. The victims, virtually all of them women and children attacked while tending their small flocks of sheep or cattle, died grisly deaths. According to many accounts, the "beast of the Gévaudan" lunged deliberately for the neck, delivering fatal wounds and quenching its thirst for human blood before feasting on the bodies of its peasant victims. Several of the unfortunates were decapitated, and at least one skull—separated from the rest of the body and found at the edge of a wood some distance from the other remains—was cracked open like a nutshell.[1] Reports of new assaults came with alarming frequency, and by the end of 1765 the beast would claim sixty victims. As northern Languedoc and neighboring Auvergne descended into mass panic, the growing legend of the beast captured the attention of France and much of Europe. The air of mystery hovering over the Gévaudan would attract commentary from such luminaries as Voltaire, Immanuel Kant, Frederick the Great, and the English novelist Horace Walpole.

The beast of the Gévaudan aroused anxieties and exercised imaginations in France until the fall of 1765, when the king's gun-bearer *(porte-arquebuse)* François Antoine brought an end to the craze by tracking and killing a large wolf on the grounds of the royal abbey of Les Chazes in southern Auvergne. After embalming the animal in compliance with royal wishes, officials quickly dispatched it to the king's court where Antoine's son presented it to Louis XV and other dignitaries. Public interest in the killings in the Gévaudan (which actually resumed after a brief respite) went into sudden decline after the younger Antoine's triumphal march to Versailles, but it is no exaggeration to say that in the year between November 1764 and November 1765 the exploits of the beast, with its "long tail and enormous talons," constituted a national and international phenomenon that held the attention of many thousands of people.[2]

The story of the beast of the Gévaudan lives on in French popular culture. The subject has produced a stream of television shows, *bandes dessinées,* novels, and films in intermittent bursts since the 1930s. The popular 2001 film *Le Pacte des Loups* (translated as *Brotherhood of the Wolf)* became one of the great blockbusters in French cinematic history, despite its tenuous connections to historical reality.[3] The film's success in France is explained, at least in part, by its knowing incorporation of familiar narrative signposts. The film introduced its own bizarre features to the story, but it gave stunning visual expression to a familiar myth that had passed into folklore in the course of the nineteenth century. Since the early years of the Third Republic (1870–1940), when the legend of the beast enjoyed a renaissance after a period of benign neglect, the basic storyline has been set in amber, with names, dates, and events reappearing in only slightly varied shape and order with each new telling of the tale.

Unlike other books written on the microhistorical scale, *Monsters of the Gévaudan* does not unearth a forgotten or hitherto unknown story.[4] On the contrary, this book revisits and seeks to rend several long-established narrative patterns. The story of the beast has been told so often and according to such familiar formulas that it demands to be told afresh, with new purposes in mind. Over the years a great number of historical accounts have been written, almost all of them penned by local historians drawn to the tale because of its enduring regional resonance.[5] Their books and articles, and the websites that have grown up around them, have fleshed out useful aspects of the general narrative, often in minute detail, and they have helped to maintain public interest in a fascinating mystery.[6]

Virtually all of the research represented by this large body of literature, however, has been carried out in response to, and in perpetual support of, a narrow and trivializing framework of analysis that has shaped discussions of the beast since the late nineteenth century. In 1889 the abbé Pierre Pourcher reignited interest in the story of the beast of the Gévaudan by publishing an enormous tome in which he argued that the beast acted as an agent of divine will; writing on the beast has been shaped by that proposition, in one way or another, ever since. A devoted student of the tale, Pourcher performed a great service by sampling from a huge trove of documents found in the departmental archives in Montpellier and other repositories, and he hardly deserves exclusive blame for the peculiarly narrow frame of analysis that has defined the subject of the beast in modern times.

Suffice it to say, however, that ever since 1889 the story's aficionados have followed Pourcher's lead by focusing their attention on the nature of the beast itself. Beyond establishing basic timelines for the killings and describing the seemingly endless hunts that went on until the summer of 1767, writers have used their evidence to advance one or another theory of the beast's identity: the beast had to be a wolf or a wolf-dog hybrid, it had to have supernatural qualities, it had to be a psychotic human being or an animal trained by said psychotic, it had to be a surviving remnant from the prehistoric era, and so on.[7] Because the sources for the story have been deployed for narrow purposes—eyewitness accounts, assessments of animal tracks, and descriptions of victims' bodies have been especially prized—they have been torn from the social, cultural, and intellectual webs in which they first found meaning. They have become the raw material for a seemingly timeless "whodunit" (or "whatdunit").[8]

I approach the story from a new angle by shifting attention away from the beast itself. The identity of the beast presents a less compelling historical subject than the attitudes, assumptions, motives, and frustrations of the human beings who struggled to understand and defeat the lethal enemy in their midst. To probe these cultural and psychological depths, we must map the mental environment of the times. What were the interactions among mid-eighteenth-century popular beliefs, scientific thought, religious tensions, media markets, aristocratic culture, local criminality, and postwar French politics that created this mental environment? How did this environment condition human reactions to news of the beast?

The full richness of the large documentary record arising from the actions of the beast has gone unrecognized because of the narrow definition of the subject in modern times. Multifaceted documents that glisten with insight have been read selectively or reduced to single meanings. Some critical sources—perhaps most notably the correspondence of a key player, the hunter and dragoon captain Jean-Baptiste Duhamel—have been underexploited because so much attention has been paid to those sources that seem to throw light on the identity of the beast.[9] I examine all of the available sources in close detail in order to break through the ossified discourses that have long surrounded the beast's tale, placing the voices behind the documents in active dialogue with one another. Thus a clearer picture emerges of how the beast came to be "made"—that is, how the beast took on the dimensions it acquired, how its activities impressed contemporary imaginations, and how the suspenseful story of the hunt expressed and magnified issues that shaped the culture of the times.

The story of the beast of the Gévaudan is dramatic and absorbing, and its unfolding reveals human responses to crisis in all their many facets: fear, urgency, courage, humor, compassion, cynicism, desperation, confusion. This book introduces the story to an audience of readers that should have become acquainted with this intriguing monster long ago.[10] Although the outlines of the tale of the beast of the Gévaudan are familiar in France, it has received little attention from historians worldwide. In truth, it has been consigned to a ghettoized space even in French historical understanding. This gripping episode, filled with heartbreak and heroism, deserves wider and closer attention.

While investigating the human dimensions of the story, I also seek to return the beast to its historical birthplace, to highlight the connections between the phenomenon of the beast of the Gévaudan and the larger currents that carried all who were touched by the events. Few if any written accounts of the events in the Gévaudan describe in detail this wider historical setting, even though the region's terrible trial transpired within a web of developments that proved crucial to France's future.[11] The suddenness of the beast's rise to prominence and its equally sudden vanishing from public consciousness at the end of 1765 suggest that the resonance of its story owed much to the turbulent conditions of the moment. Thanks to the growing fashion for natural history in the culture of the Enlightenment, the spiritual tensions that arose from the religious clashes of the late 1750s and early 1760s, the exciting but newly disruptive influence of "publicity" on politics and public space, and a heightened sense of national vulnerability in the wake of the Seven Years' War, the deeds of the beast invited the attention and nervous projections of a society poised on the threshold of revolutionary transformations. The anxieties that attended this set of transformations, I argue, distilled the curiosities, fears, and hopes of a wide cross section of the French population, creating an atmosphere in which many—the elite and the lowly, the learned and the unlearned—could accept, and even expect, the presence of a monster.

The contrast between the lived episode and the event as remembered and narrated, a contrast already becoming visible by the late 1760s, also exposes the seams that connect the largely premodern world of 1765 to the forms of public reason thought characteristic of the "disenchanted" culture of the postrevolutionary era. In following changing definitions of the "thinkable" in the later eighteenth and early nineteenth centuries, I show the progressive naturalization of the oppositions that would come to underlie the myth of modernity in France: elite versus popular, urban versus rural, public versus secret, rational versus superstitious, national versus regional (and royal), secular versus religious, official truths versus underground rumors, science versus magic. The beast emerges as a sign of, and a powerful stimulant for, the conceptual winnowing that necessarily informed the construction of "modern" consciousness and the definition of a "traditional" past.

The fate of the beast's story in modern times becomes the focus of the last chapter of the book. Victimized by strategic forgetfulness just as France was passing into modernity, and later revived amid the polarized political environment and scholarly ferment of the Third Republic, the story of the beast of the Gévaudan arrived in the contemporary era shorn of most of its relevant history. Close-up appreciation for the event as it was apprehended in the moment, combined with analysis of the contrast between the event and its successive narrative constructions, helps to delineate the layers of forgetfulness and psychological distancing that obscured the original meanings of the beast and, by the early years of the twentieth century, had turned it into a one-dimensional object of timeless speculation.

We will march through the highlights of the story in more or less chronological order, with several side journeys through meaningful contexts. Access to the events that make up the narrative comes chiefly through the experiences of important individuals who helped drive the action and whose thoughts and behavior exemplified the forces at work in the making of the beast. In the course of our investigation, which delineates at least seven distinct phases in the beast's making, many monsters of the Gévaudan will reveal themselves.

By the story's end, the beast's actual identity should look much less important, and less intriguing, than the various individuals and historical forces responsible for the creation of the monsters to which "the beast" gave form. The imaginative work of the beast's creators not only reflected the times in which they lived but also proved vital to the construction of a powerful legend that would survive in one form or another for more than two hundred years. When discussing the creature or creatures responsible for the tragedies these human actors confronted, I refer consistently to "the beast," even though the singular form is inescapably misleading. The term was the one most favored in the eighteenth century—it usually appeared in capitalized form as *la Bête* —and its evocative qualities convey well the aura of mystery that enveloped the principals engaged in this story. The actual killings likely resulted from the work of a number of wolves, or even a succession of packs of wolves that moved through the region over a period of years. But the singular identifier anchors the reader in the atmosphere that prevailed in that dreadful year of 1764–1765. It evokes a culture in which the hunt for "the beast" remained pregnant with meaning and resonated in a recognizably premodern key. In more ways than one, I seek to restore *that* beast—and the forces that made it—to the historical record of France's *ancien régime*.

1

Sounding the Alarm

The beast's rampage began without fanfare. On the last day of June in 1764, just beyond the eastern edge of the Gévaudan in the lush hills of the Vivarais, a fourteen-year-old girl named Jeanne Boulet was attacked and killed, apparently as she watched over a small number of sheep or cattle.[1] Little is known about the incident, which escaped the attention of authorities and left no documentary traces other than the burial notice composed by the parish priest. Given the circumstances of the event, however, one can assume that Boulet's neighbors in her village of Ubac probably accepted her loss as a horrible but natural occurrence. The sheep and cattle that dotted the hillsides of northern Languedoc occasionally attracted predators, and the locals understood that sheepherding involved risks. Indeed, the language used by the curé in the burial notice suggests that the culprit had already been spotted roaming the area in the weeks before the attack.[2] Jeanne Boulet's age and gender may have increased her vulnerability to whatever ravenous animals prowled the fields, but the women and adolescent children of rural France led flocks or herds to pasture as part of their normal domestic routines. Her family and neighbors would have been justified in assuming that she had been the unlucky victim of a tragic but random accident.

Events would soon show that the region had more to fear than bad luck.

On 8 August a fifteen-year-old girl died in the parish of Puylaurens in the Gévaudan itself, and at the end of that month, a sixteen-year-old boy succumbed to a violent attack while working in the fields between Langogne and the Mercoire forest. Then, between 1 and 26 September a string of four deadly attacks signaled the onset of a crisis in the Gévaudan.[3] One of these attacks claimed the first adult victim of the rampage, a thirty-six-year-old woman in the parish of Arzenc who fell to her assailant at sunset only a few steps removed from the safety of her door.[4] Anxious communities began to mobilize in self-defense.

Not all of the relevant correspondence survives, so the exact point at which provincial authorities began to monitor the developing crisis remains unclear. Surely by September, bands of armed locals, led by concerned seigneurs, had begun to "beat the bushes" in the forests around Langogne in the eastern Gévaudan, where the early attacks were concentrated. The dragoon captain Jean-Baptiste Duhamel, whose company was then stationed in that city, participated in at least some of these early hunts, apparently on the orders of the military commandant of the province. In any case, the steady activity of the locals around Langogne was probably responsible for the event that galvanized the authorities. In the first week of October, the beast—or the terrifying phenomenon contemporaries identified by that name—moved northwest toward the mountains of the Margeride and began to terrorize the environs of Saint-Chély, Saint-Alban, and Malzieu. With the entire breadth of the old *comté* of the Gévaudan now put at risk by the assaults, word passed from local to provincial officials that the developing situation required attention and resources.[5]

The individual most likely to have set the machinery of government in motion was Etienne Lafont, whose calming presence and quiet competence would prove invaluable throughout the ordeal. France in the 1760s was divided into large administrative districts called *généralités*—fiscal units that corresponded roughly to the geography of already-existing provinces. The *généralités* were governed by royal agents known as intendants. These members of the so-called "robe" nobility had been appointed to their posts after having proven themselves first as judges and then as masters of requests in the king's council.[6] The intendant shared power with a provincial governor, who always came from the highest reaches of the titled nobility, and he negotiated with a wide range of institutions and dignitaries whose prerogatives could either help or hinder execution of his designs.

To navigate the web of rival authorities with whom he had to contend, the intendant relied on a small corps of subdelegates who did his bidding in the localities throughout the province. Often nominated by local power brokers with close ties to the intendant, the subdelegates tended to be selected for their knowledge of local affairs and their reputations for honesty and efficiency. From his administrative base in Montpellier, the intendant Marie-Joseph-Emmanuel de Guignard de Saint-Priest needed trusted local figures to represent his will and to keep him apprised of events across the length and breadth of the province. For the Parisian-born Saint-Priest, the need was especially acute in the relatively inaccessible northern reaches of Languedoc.

Fortunately for Saint-Priest, his subdelegate in the Gévaudan was Etienne Lafont, and Lafont's knowledge of the region ran deep. Lafont had secured a foothold in the world of provincial respectability by serving as an attorney in the *parlement* of Toulouse (an exalted "sovereign" court) in the 1740s, but ties of family and clientage kept him rooted in the Gévaudan throughout his life. Born in the small town of Chirac near Marvejols, where his father had made a modest fortune in banking, Lafont eventually attracted the appreciative attention of the powerful bishop of Mende, who probably encountered the capable young lawyer on one of his many official visits to Toulouse.[7] When the office of syndic (administrative manager) of the diocese fell vacant in 1749, the bishop recruited Lafont for the position, and the lawyer happily returned to his native region and its capital in Mende. Because the syndic of the diocese generally served also as subdelegate to the provincial intendant, Lafont quickly became acquainted with Saint-Priest and his father (who had preceded Marie-Joseph in the intendant's post), and he retained their firm trust to the end of his life.

Perceptive, empathetic, and conscientious, Lafont kept his ear close to the ground from the beginning of the beast's ravages, communicating frequently with parish priests, village consuls, and local notables, who could provide details of each new attack. Few would have had a more natural ability to translate between the concerns of a frightened population and the intentions of those in power. A native who had spent time in the provincial capital, Lafont understood the patois of the peasantry but spoke the official French that had been the lingua franca of elite society since the seventeenth century.[8] The kind of dual citizenship he possessed—a local product, he nevertheless enjoyed the confidence and patronage of powerful elites with connections at Versailles—enabled him to function effectively as the face of provincial authority in the Gévaudan. Scion of a respectable family of bourgeois notables who craved but did not possess noble status, descendant of Protestant Hugue-nots and loyal servant of the Catholic church, Lafont's background gave him a unique capacity to mediate between different worlds. In 1764–1765, he would use that capacity to the fullest. Almost alone among the principal players in the ordeal, Lafont would survive the vicissitudes of the long drama with his reputation fully intact, having made no enemies and many new admirers. He would even earn personal nobility in 1766—in part, no doubt, because of his steadiness during the episode of the beast.[9]

Lafont was thus well suited to coordinate the official response to the de-veloping crisis in the Gévaudan. By early October if not sooner, he had con-tacted Saint-Priest as well as local seigneurs whose social standing made them likely leaders of local efforts to root out the beast. Working closely with Jean-François Charles de La Molette, comte de Morangiès, whose lands around Saint-Alban were already affected by the menace, Lafont took the lead in facilitating hunts and assisting the shaken communities in and around the Margeride. As he explained in one letter to the intendant, he had sought to establish in each parish a "permanent hunt" with eight to ten local inhabitants moving about on constant patrol, but he had been disappointed to find that most villagers were too "timid" to venture far afield except in large groups led by experienced hunters.[10] Lafont authorized payment of twenty sous per day to those peasants willing to take time away from the fields to assist local ef-forts, but he also began to discuss with his superiors the possibility of asking for professional soldiers to lead the chase for the beast.[11] The fateful decision to bring in the professionals would be taken before the first of November.

Perceiving the Unusual

In the wake of the bloody month of September, the beast grew in stature. "Ev-eryone is on guard," Lafont would write, and in the minds of those anxious to defeat it, the enemy took on extraordinary proportions.[12] The change is reflected in the language officials used to talk about the threat. The letters of the comte de Morangiès, for example, show a generic *bête féroce* turning into the famously imposing *Bête.* But the word *bête,* an everyday term that could be applied to all animals, did not adequately capture the anxieties aroused by the creature in the Gévaudan. On 14 October, the military commandant of Languedoc, Jean Baptiste de Marin, comte de Moncan, ordered all officers

of the local police *(maréchaussées)* to provide Captain Duhamel with any assistance he required in the effort to eliminate the "monster" *(monstre)* that
roamed the mountains of the Vivarais and the Gévaudan.[13] Two weeks later,
Morangiès informed Lafont of his intent to rid the region of "the monster
that ravages it."[14] Duhamel asked Lafont to keep him apprised of any sightings, so that he could immediately dispatch troops to "finally destroy this
monster."[15]

The term *monster* conventionally referred to any human or animal with a
"shape contrary to the order of nature." The *Dictionary of the French Academy*
listed as illustrative definitions the terms *horrible, frightening, terrifying,* and
hideous. In addition, though, the word referred to a being—usually a person
—that displayed unnatural cruelty.[16] In the context of the happenings in the
Gévaudan, those who used the word *monstre* seem to have had both connotations in mind. They sought to identify an unnatural creature with unusually
cruel habits. By November, when the *Courrier d'Avignon* published its first
reports about the events, the species and character of the evil animal had become an object of wide speculation, and many had become convinced that
the phenomenon of the beast of the Gévaudan constituted a unique encounter with the unknown.[17] Hypotheses about the beast's provenance, identity,
and characteristics came from all corners, and authorities on site showed signs
of desperation. As the eminent French historian Emmanuel Le Roy Ladurie
has noted, the beast generated apocalyptic fears at a level "unheard of" on the
national stage.[18]

From the vantage point of the twenty-first century, the fact that the beast
attracted such feverish attention seems unremarkable. Public alarm, even hysteria, in the face of gruesome killings, a parade of innocent victims, and officials' inability to stop the carnage would seem to require no explanation at
all. In the modern world, persistent threats to public safety are guaranteed
to provoke outcry and to create anxiety. In the context of the early modern
French experience, however, the public's fixation on the events in the Gévaudan counts as something of a mystery. On the one hand, a unified "public"
did not yet have the self-awareness or the political habits to hold accountable
a "government" that had a specific responsibility to insure public safety. The
functional division between government and public (or civil society), and
the form of official accountability it implied, would not really emerge before
the end of the eighteenth century, even though the middle decades of the century provided signs of a growing self-consciousness among a critical French

public and a new willingness to direct concentrated criticism toward the crown.[19] On the other hand, the beast's ability to generate such agitated attention in 1764 also requires explanation because the violence in the Gévaudan conformed to long-established patterns. Death by wolf attack did not count as an unusual occurrence in the eighteenth-century French experience.

The rural historian Jean-Marc Moriceau has documented thousands of deadly wolf attacks across the French realm from the late sixteenth through early nineteenth centuries, and a wealth of evidence shows that in especially dire decades such as the 1590s or 1690s the human victims may have numbered in the thousands.[20] In times of war and human devastation, such as the Wars of Religion of the late sixteenth century or the Nine Years' War at the end of the seventeenth century, the incidence of wolf attacks may have increased because of widespread bloodletting. For the typical rural locality, however, the risk that a man-eating wolf or wolves might show up to wreak havoc and disrupt the peace remained high from one end of the period to the other. The threat was ubiquitous. Rabies-infected wolves claimed well over a thousand French lives in the early modern centuries, and in spite of the modern "dogma" that healthy wolves never attack humans, man-eating wolves unhampered by disease killed at least 1,857 people in these same years. Because of huge gaps in the administrative records before the nineteenth century, Moriceau is inclined to put the true number of human fatalities in the early modern period closer to a staggering 9,000.[21]

Mountains and forested regions were especially vulnerable to lupine predation, and each year the danger to humans rose in the warm spring and summer months, when agricultural laborers spent more time working outdoors. The Parisian glazier Jacques-Louis Ménétra, passing through the Cévennes in the spring of 1761 en route from Montpellier to Lyon, reported an encounter with a threatening "legion" of wolves that had to be scattered with a shot from his pistol. He thought they "were coming to eat me."[22] The small, the frail, and the isolated—the adolescent shepherdess exemplifies the type—always stood out as the predators' most likely targets. Charles Perrault's 1697 version of *Little Red Riding Hood* may have specifically reflected enduring legends about werewolves in the author's native Touraine, but the wide and lasting resonance of his tale attests to the fear of wolves that marked the oral culture he so memorably translated to print.[23]

In the century before the crisis in the Gévaudan many other regions had experienced panic-inducing assaults from ravenous wolves. Localized emergencies involving infamous "beasts" took their toll in the Gâtinais (1650s), the Limousin (1690s), the Touraine (1690s and again in the 1740s), and the Auxerrois (1730s). Dozens of victims in these regions fell to fanged predators over an extended period of time, causing anxieties similar to those that washed over the Gévaudan. The terrifying habits and profile of that later killer, including its alarming preference for women and children, its propensity to decapitate, and its alleged supernatural abilities and malevolent designs, all had ample precedent in French rural experience.[24] The 1690s had been especially horrific, but events occurring within recent memory had also provided a grisly chronicle of human carnage. Operating from the forests of the lower Limousin in 1744, one ferocious wolf had claimed at least twenty victims, devouring "every child it encountered, especially girls," before it was finally eliminated. In 1754, wolves had killed between ten and twenty shepherds in the Lyonnais.[25] In January of 1764, near the city of Thiers in Auvergne, a wolf infected by rabies had attacked forty-three people, many of whom died agonizing deaths—some of them affectingly described by the intendant Simon-Charles baron de Ballainvilliers, who would be centrally involved in the events in the Gévaudan.[26] These many scattered incidents point to a distinctive pattern of violence that left a deep imprint on rural life throughout the early modern era. Moriceau estimates that in the thirteen years between 1743 and 1756 the annual average of human deaths by wolf attack throughout French territory topped one hundred; the risks to the peasantry would decline steadily, but still only slowly, over the course of the next sixty years.[27] We might expect knowledge about earlier episodes to have counteracted impulses toward hysteria or reckless speculation, both among the locals and among distant observers of the events in the Gévaudan.

And yet, once the reality of the peril sank in, imaginations ran wild. Why? For Le Roy Ladurie, the whole phenomenon can be explained as a fortuitous convergence of peasant superstition and a newly created "national market for news and information." Once the gazettes recognized the news value of the story, he suggests, the beast of the Gévaudan evolved into something unprecedented: a legendary local werewolf made national by "mass media."[28] Christophe Pincemaille provides a similarly straightforward explanation for the fears aroused by the events in the Gévaudan. Wild speculation about the beast, in his estimation, grew out of a "peasant mentality" shaped by "ancestral fears" and primitive myths. The "popular portrait" of the creature, given a public platform by the rhetorical flourishes of the bishop of Mende, came to be widely disseminated. Thus a supernatural legend became lodged in the col-lective consciousness "in spite of the efforts of the authorities."[29]

The role of newspapers and broadsheets in fanning the flames of fear and anxiety was undeniably important, and popular beliefs about werewolves, witches, and demons informed public speculation about the nature of the beast of the Gévaudan, as we shall see. But the idea that the irrational excesses surrounding the phenomenon of the beast emanated from the misconcep-tions of the uncultivated is rooted in modern prejudice. Similarly anachronis-tic is the notion that those misconceptions came to be magnified and nation-alized through a sort of media accident that wiser authorities proved powerless to stop. Context explains much about the reactions to the news emerging from the fields of the Gévaudan, but that context included much more than peasant lore and the coincidental growth of print media in the middle decades of the eighteenth century.

Careful dissection of the behavior and motivations of the characters that populated the story of the beast uncovers the workings of a bountiful mental universe. The interpretive dispositions favored by that mental universe would not have been identical for everyone, needless to say, but evidence shows that they were shaped by a variety of forces arising from the intellectual, political, and religious history of France, forces typically beyond the control of the peas-antry. Deliberate reconstruction of the narrative reveals that "authorities" and other elites had their own reasons for allowing the beast of the Gévaudan to achieve outsized importance. Those who ultimately attempted to play down the nature of the threat did so for reasons that cannot simply be credited to the superior rationality of France's governing classes.

A survey of developments from October through December of 1764 shows that the emergence of the beast's legend can be traced to many sources, including the culture and laboring practices of the peasants of the Gévaudan, the swelling currents of eighteenth-century science, contemporary appetite for exotica, and the religious debates of the age. In light of the social and cultural forces prevailing in France in 1764, one might even say that the beast of the Gévaudan unwittingly anticipated—on the darker side of the cultural register—the spirit of Voltaire's famous quip about God, to wit, that if he did not exist, it would be necessary to invent him.[30] The first fruitful interactions between imagination and reality occurred, of course, over the fields of the af-flicted territory.

A Monstrous Habitat

The people of the Gévaudan had good reasons to suppose that they faced an exceptionally foul creature. The early attacks, from Ubac to Arzenc, had occurred some twenty miles apart, and the beast's range had begun to expand ominously. Seven victims had fallen over the course of the summer, and in early October stomach-turning brutality became characteristic of the attacks. The first victim in the Margeride, a twenty-year-old woman from the village of Apcher, near Prunières, was decapitated on 7 October; the woman's skull would be found only after a week had passed. In the days that followed the assault in Apcher, six adolescents would suffer attacks, with each absorbing serious wounds on the face, neck, or head. Four of the afflicted would actually survive the attacks, but just south of Aumont on 15 October the beast completed a devilish week's work by severing the head of a ten-year-old boy, whose torso was savagely shredded.[31] The pattern established in these early October assaults served to justify journalists' consistent representation of the beast as a bloodthirsty creature that preferred to "seize its unfortunate victims by the nape of the neck, choke the life out of them and drink their blood before separating the head from the trunk of the body."[32] After the atrocities of early October, Lafont began warning villagers that women and children should always be accompanied by armed men when they went to their pastures. He expressed dismay that so many continued to take "imprudent" risks.[33]

As Lafont surely understood, economic necessity lay behind the imprudent risk-taking. Like their counterparts all across France, the peasants of the Gévaudan were enmeshed in an exploitative and still-feudal agrarian system that funneled most of the profits of the soil to landlords and left most families facing hunger when the grain supply dwindled in the months before the fall harvest. French peasants who worked the fecund lands north of the Loire river could be subject to occasional grain shortages because of the constant pressure to keep Paris provisioned with bread, and the sun-baked valleys of the Mediterranean basin, dedicated to the cultivation of wine and olives, were vulnerable to intermittent bouts of harsh weather and blight. But features peculiar to this region—well captured in Le Roy Ladurie's characterization of "the sad misery of the Massif Central"—made life especially tenuous in the Gévaudan.[34]

The rugged highlands of the Gévaudan, with altitudes generally ranging between three and four thousand feet, consisted of steep and forested slopes, limestone plateaus, rolling meadows, treacherous moors, and large outcroppings of granite, in roughly equal proportion. Such land was poorly suited to agriculture. This was the chief reason the area had so few inhabitants. With a population of no more than 120,000 in the 1760s, a number that "correlates not at all with its size," according to one contemporary official, the former province of the Gévaudan was, as it remains today, one of the most sparsely settled regions in all of France. The largest city of the old county, Saugues, had no more than about 3,000 inhabitants, and all other municipalities of significant size (Mende, Saint-Alban, Langogne, Marvejols, Saint-Chély, Malzieu, Florac) had small populations of between 1,500 and 2,500. More than 80 percent of the region's inhabitants were scattered across some 200 rural parishes varying in size from a thousand or so to fewer than one hundred residents.[35]

In this land of widely dispersed village communities, few of them with any tradition of organizational solidarity, seigneurial power, and the seigneur's share of the annual produce, weighed heavily.[36] Worse, peasants and lords competed over the output of generally weak harvests. Here there were few large and productive farms. Instead the inhabitants of the region worked small parcels with poor soil. According to one estimate, between one-third and one-half of the land available for farming was made up of dense woods and unclearable marshlands. The peasants of the Gévaudan who managed to survive these difficult conditions supplemented their daily staple of rye bread with barley gruel, carrots, turnips, chestnuts, and whatever onions and herbs they could gather from their modest household gardens.[37]

Given their uneasy relationship to the land, the peasants' firm attachment to the modest stock of sheep and draft animals they owned or controlled is not surprising. The livestock were vital to the life of the region in more ways than one. For the most humble, the animals provided needed warmth in winter, wandering freely between the stables and the adjoining cooking or sleeping quarters of their masters. They helped to blunt the bitter chill that permeated the stone walls and slate roofs of the cramped, squat homes of the peasantry. In spring, the fertilizer the animals deposited on the fields made it more likely that the harvest of the coming fall would be merely inadequate rather than disastrous and life threatening. Cows and sheep also added meager amounts of milk and cheese to a regional diet that left the poor of the Gévaudan exceptionally malnourished.[38]

Sheep proved critical to the economy of the Gévaudan in other ways. Because the land alone could not insure a family's subsistence, even the smallest households engaged in cottage industry of one kind or another, and most specialized in the production of rough woolen cloth known as *cadis*. In the 1780s, the intendant in Montpellier would casually say of the Gévaudanois, "all of the inhabitants of town and country are weavers," spinning and carding in their homes whenever their time could not be used "more profitably."[39] This indispensable regional industry entered a period of decline in the 1760s because of new competition from cotton spinners in Lyons and other cities and because the growing taste for luxury items in the course of the century called for fancier, more finished woolen products.[40] Responding to signs of stagnation, the Estates of the Gévaudan would allocate 5,000 livres in the spring of 1765 for the purchase of new spinning wheels and the services of a master spinster willing to "spend the time necessary to teach the new methods" of dyeing and finishing to area residents.[41]

Even with the textiles trade in relative decline, however, sheepherding remained central to the everyday lives of the peasantry. Whether raising sheep for sale at one of the weekly markets in Saint-Flour, Aumont, or Marvejols, spinning raw wool to sell to itinerant merchants or commercial establishments in Mende or Saint-Chély, or laboring in the fields for a wealthy landed proprietor with large flocks in need of care—or most likely, some combination of these activities—the cultivators of the Gévaudan cared for sheep as part of their livelihoods. For the young and able-bodied, moreover, opportunities to farm out one's labor increased in the spring and summer months, when large migrant flocks from the south made their way to the cooler elevations of the Massif Central for midyear grazing.[42]

Few peasants, then, would have been inclined to heed Lafont's initial warnings about the dangers lurking in the pastures. While men tilled the furrows, gathered wood, or took to the road in search of work, women and children cared for the herds and spun their wool. In any event, how many actually heard the dire warnings or recognized the seriousness of the threat they faced? Word of recent wolf infestations in the lower Limousin or the Lyonnais would not have been likely to penetrate the natural barriers thrown up by the imposing hills of the Massif. Except for groups of the devout who crossed the well-worn pilgrimage path from Le Puy to Conques to Santiago de Compostella, and who stopped at inns in Saugues or Malzieu to rest their weary feet, the outside world entered into the Gévaudan only infrequently. As the intendant would later write, builders of major roadways would have faced "insurmountable difficulties" here because of the great quantity of "mountains, rapids, and escarpments."[43] Most of the existing roads were in poor condition, "impractical for man and beast" alike, according to the hunter Antoine.[44] News passed slowly from one community to the next, and even urgent warnings were unlikely to reach all concerned. Simple inertia kept many peasants heading into their fields each day.

In communities made aware of the heightened risks—one can assume that the news had penetrated far by late fall of 1764—the women and children whose duties carried them into the pastures may have felt a profound sense of foreboding. Even in the best of times, the inhabitants of this undulating land, most of them physically gaunt and undersized, lived in constant combat against the forces of nature. The climate was famously harsh and fickle. The nutrient-starved soil held unusually high levels of moisture, and although the widespread saturation made the pastures ideally suited to grazing, the water underground also turned the earth into an unpredictable entity. Beneath the fern- and heather-covered surface lay pockets of earthen muck that drew in stray animals and their keepers, with sometimes dangerous consequences.

The rock formations, too, held their terrors. Irrupting from the earth in all shapes and sizes, often at odd angles, they gave the impression of having been strewn about by giants. Local legends held that Gargantua himself had passed through the area, carpeting the landscape with discarded rock; one megalith near Marvejols was popularly known as "the tomb of the giants."[45] Some of the outcroppings were so large and so menacing in appearance that they were thought to harbor fairies or monsters. One such formation, known in the local patois as "del Cougobre," was said to have sheltered a monstrous serpent that had terrorized the town of Javols in the distant past.[46] The perceived risk of encountering such fantastic creatures also ran high because of the multitude of dense forests. In the Gévaudan, as elsewhere throughout Europe, forests figured in the imagination as zones of mystery that lay beyond the bounds of society's rules.[47] Fear of the unexpected, and of the mysteries hidden within the trees, would only have grown as sunset approached, for in this remote region the night arrived with a "roaring blackness" that discouraged even hardy natives from venturing outdoors.[48]

That some of the afflicted communities would respond to news of the beast's predation by invoking fantastic and "ancestral" explanations of natural phenomena is therefore not surprising. Not having experienced a prolonged and deadly wolf rampage in their lifetimes, inhabitants of the region would

The hilly terrain of the Gévaudan features densely grouped and sometimes menacing outcroppings of granite, as in this area between Saugues and Langeac. *Author photo*

understandably imagine enemies, and seek explanations for misfortune, commensurate with the ghastliness of the events they now endured. In 1764 as in earlier times, blind fear and adrenaline often led to exaggerated physical descriptions of suspected wolves and to the visualization of other creatures rendered all the more terrifying by displacement from their natural habitats: lions, bears, leopards, tigers, as well as shape-shifting amalgams of the same.[49] Peasants also customarily accounted for terrible deeds by attributing unpredictable or violent acts to the presence of an enchanter or enchantress. Many of the surprising attributes that would be credited to the beast of the Gévaudan—the ability to walk on its hind legs, the impermeability of its hide, a will to mock the dogs and hunters who sought to bring it down—belonged to a rich stock of characteristics associated with enchanted animals and the sorcerers and fairies believed to consort with them.

Supernatural events did not always require the presence of witches or fairies, however. According to legend, wolves had a built-in capacity to cast spells on the unfortunates who met their gaze. In 1765 the *Courrier d'Avignon* would relay a local report about a boy who had "contracted a fever" after the beast looked him in the eyes.[50] The *loup-cervier* (a European lynx) was also widely assumed to be endowed with a quasi-magical aura. Hares, too, allegedly had a large bag of tricks at their disposal, which they often used for playful purposes.[51]

Perhaps most frightening of all were the creatures thought to combine qualities of the human, the animal, and the supernatural: werewolves *(loups-garous)*. The beast's evident preference for children would have aroused strong suspicions among the local populace, for werewolves had a notoriously strong taste for the fat of the young.[52] According to both popular lore and learned discourses of earlier centuries, the fat of young Christians, when mixed with other unlikely products of nature, accounted for the very existence of the werewolf. Humans' ability to effect physical transformation was thought to depend on the bodily application of "infernal and diabolical compositions" provided by agents of the devil or Satan himself.[53] In 1599 Jean Beauvoys de Chauvincourt had reported on a man recently brought to trial for lycanthropy in the city of Angers. Coated in pungent devil's grease, Jacques Rollet had given off a telling odor so "stinking and rotten *(puant et infecte)* that no man of this world could approach him." In 1765, a broadsheet reporting details from the scene would similarly note that one young girl who had encountered the beast of the Gévaudan had been practically knocked over by breath that was "stinking rotten" *(d'une puanteur infecte)*.[54]

Among the learned, belief in werewolves, or at least the open and official acceptance of their existence, had waned along with the incidence of witchcraft trials in the course of the seventeenth century. Chauvincourt in 1599 was already drawing on both Aristotelian and Christian arguments to suggest that lycanthropy consisted only in an ability to make others perceive the wolflike form.[55] In the eighteenth-century French countryside, however, few doubted the reality of the werewolf. Physical features remarked by those who had allegedly laid eyes on the beast—including not only the stench, but also long claws, unusually large teeth and, at times, an erect stature—showed a frightening consistency with the enduring popular image of the malevolent wolf-man.[56] Reports about the beast's eyes, often described as glowing or "sparkling" *(étincelants)*, would have added to peasant fears. The naturalist Georges-Louis Leclerc, comte de Buffon, had described wolves as having that trait, but haunting eyes were also thought to be one of the distinctive physical characteristics manifested by the *loup-garou*.[57] As one expert had reported in 1610, people who assumed the figure of the wolf displayed "terrifying and sparkling eyes like wolves."[58] The published literature about the events in the Gévaudan frequently reported on these various telltale signs of the werewolf, sometimes suggesting without explicitly mentioning the suspected presence of the *loup-garou*.

Superstitious explanations for frightening events thus lay ready at hand, and social and topographic conditions in the Gévaudan would have provided ample space for the expansion of native fears and the myths of enchantment they engendered. The low population density of the region often left villagers feeling isolated. A nineteenth-century traveler was struck by the sight of the "naked cottages and bleak fields" that greeted him on the Gévaudan side of the Allier river, and the unrelenting variability of the landscape ensured that pastures and streams frequently lay at a considerable distance from human settlement.[59] Shepherds and shepherdesses thus found themselves face to face with nature for great expanses of time. While watching their herds and flocks they stood alone with their thoughts, save for the sights and sounds emanating from the rivers, fields, and forests that bounded the movement of their grazing sheep and cattle. In those cases where herds grazed in common, and two or more shepherds shared time in one place, they would inevitably pass the time by exchanging rumors about the ravenous creatures that surrounded them, now concealed from view. Latent anxieties would add fuel to the powers of the imagination, creating filters for the perception of the monstrous.

In such conditions, the general absence of firearms would surely have contributed to feelings of helplessness and unease. Ownership of guns had long been an exclusive privilege of the aristocracy. Like the nobles' special rights to brandish a sword in public, to enjoy exemption from certain taxes, to hunt game and maintain dovecotes, and to serve as officers in the military, their ownership of firearms symbolized aristocratic superiority and helpfully restrained any inclination to insolence among the nobles' social inferiors. The law therefore prohibited peasant tenants from possessing firearms.[60] The comte de Morangiès mentioned in one of his letters to Lafont that, among the few residents of Saint-Alban who actually owned a firearm, "few would want to reveal them," probably because of the legal risks involved.[61] Moncan, the military commandant, made an exceptional announcement permitting "all inhabitants to arm themselves" in October 1764, but fears of rising criminality, seigneurial reticence, and a general lack of resources in this impoverished region combined to restrict access to guns throughout the next year.[62] In the following spring, Lafont redoubled his efforts to have firearms supplied to rural communities, but he was rebuffed by the cautious intendant.[63] Antoine still complained about the problem in August.[64] For their self-defense peasants were generally forced to rely on staffs, or *bâtons,* sometimes fitted with bayonets. These basic implements at least had the advantage of being common and familiar, though one subdelegate would later complain that the ubiquity of the ineffective *bâton* and peasants' general inexperience in handling arms served as notable barriers "to the destruction of this beast."[65]

Suspicions about the true nature of the monster they faced and an awareness of being ill-equipped to engage in a lethal struggle with a dangerous killer probably lay behind the widespread peasant timidity noted by Lafont. But the general sense of insecurity also provided occasions for admirable bravery tempered by common sense. On the Auvergne side of the Gévaudan's northwestern border, a handful of parishioners set out one day in October to clear brush and to search for the beast, accompanied by several hounds but armed only with pickaxes and spades. When the dogs suddenly gave chase to a creature spotted in the woods, the startled men tossed their "weapons" in the air and began to holler wildly "like Scottish mountaineers," according to witnesses who arrived at the scene. After regaining their composure, the men joined in pursuit of the animal—the prey was indeed a wolf—and eventually forced it to take refuge on a small outcrop in the middle of a lake. After a protracted struggle whose details provided endless amusement to the local subdelegate (he reported that, after some debate, the men had slowly waded into water up to their chests, coaxing the dogs to follow), the hunters finally defeated their opponent. After first attempting to stone it to death, they completed the job when one of the men delivered a fatal blow to the animal's head with the sharp end of a shovel. They presented the ears of their foe as proof of their labors and courage, and although subsequent events would show that the real beast remained alive and well, the appreciative intendant granted each of the intrepid hunters a reward of six livres.[66]

Such tales of rustic courage and resourcefulness suggest that it would be unfair and inaccurate to see the beast's exploding public presence in late 1764 as a sign of the fearfulness of a local peasantry following its benighted instincts into fantasy. In a report sent to the intendant of Auvergne in December, one subdelegate even made a point of praising the peasants of his region for their fearlessness.[67] Evidence of superstition and curious popular beliefs is certainly available in the rich annals of the beast of the Gévaudan, but the sensational image of the beast owed its existence to many creators, both high and low.

The beast's sheer persistence clearly surprised everyone involved. The intendant Saint-Priest, for example, informed the royal minister Louis Phélypeaux, comte de Saint-Florentin, that "there is no more room to doubt the reality of this affliction" after learning of the death of two more children in late October. The beast would not move on, and that seemingly unusual fact became the chief premise underlying the wide speculation about its mysterious identity.[68] Curiously, among the first conclusions drawn from the beast's evident attachment to the territory of the Gévaudan, a conclusion that would go largely unchallenged for months, was that it acted alone. Even the experience of the "Scottish mountaineers" had underlined the presence of multiple wolves in the region, and subsequent events would show beyond doubt that the area suffered from a heavy infestation of wolves, an affliction that would not subside before the late 1760s. Yet in the face of anecdotal evidence and the reporting of their own senses, the Gévaudanois and the many outsiders who arrived to help them consistently regarded the killings as the work of a single destructive creature, not as a telling symptom of an overgrown wolf population. The modern commentators who would dismiss the tale of the beast as superstitious nonsense have generally credited the peasantry with this particular error, citing the popular belief in werewolves.

In fact, however, from the earliest stages of the story a nearly universal consensus held that the beast was to be thought of as a single monstrous entity. The military commandant Moncan had already come to think of the beast as a "monster or leopard" by the middle of October.[69] The eminently sensible Lafont remained open to the possibility that numerous wolves shared responsibility for the deaths in the Gévaudan. Nevertheless, in a letter written to the intendant at the end of October, he also expressed the emerging consensus. Because Langogne to the east had suffered no depredations since the western hunts had begun, he wrote, the evidence of migration "makes me presume that a single beast is responsible for all the disorders."[70] Most seem to have been prepared, or inclined, to believe that the cruelties visited on the Gévaudan were the work of a uniquely destructive malefactor.

The beast's refusal to go away quietly had heightened the sensitivities of peasants, curés, and local officials, preparing all to witness the unexpected and to account for the extraordinary. As eyewitness and secondhand reports were spread, the killings continued apace, and a self-perpetuating cycle of exaggeration, speculation, and seeming confirmation of singularity pointed to the existence of a foul and unnatural being. A syndic from the Vivarais named Lachadenède reported in late October that "all who have written to me regarding the size of this animal agree that it is larger than a wolf." The beast possessed a massive head and an extremely long tail; "some say it is a hyena, others a panther, still others a *loup-cervier;* this is all I know for certain about this terrible animal."[71] A woman who survived an attack in December described for Captain Duhamel the beast's "powerful" paws, "with six talons," its "wide and pointy" fangs, and its "large and sparkling" eyes.[72] The *Courrier d'Avignon,* claiming to relay information reported from the scene, added to the portrait. "Its countenance is so frightening that it would take a Hercules to face up to it. No one doubts this in the region where it roams, for among those who have tried to muster their courage, some could not even bring themselves to fire on it, no matter how safe the distance, and others have fired wildly with hands trembling."[73]

As the *Courrier's* report suggests, the travails of hunters in the field testified to the unusual nature of the beast of the Gévaudan. Each new failure functioned as an elixir to the growing legend, showcasing both the terror-stricken state of those forced to contend with the creature and the beast's seemingly supernatural ability to elude its enemies. The *Courrier* report may have expressed a slightly distorted version of an incident that occurred in late October, fully described by a troubled Lafont in a dispatch to the intendant. Over a hundred peasants had gathered to assist the designated leader of the hunt, an innkeeper from Mende named Mercier, in the parish of Saint-Alban, where the beast had been tracked. The men who carried arms were instructed to surround a forest thought to serve as the beast's lair. The others marched into the interior to beat the bushes and flush out the enemy. Aroused by this small army of invaders, a frightening animal emerged and passed before two of the hunters.

> The first fired from about ten paces. [The beast] fell from the force of the blow but picked itself up; the second then fired from the same distance and it fell again. The two hunters and several peasants rushed forward, believing the beast to be dead, but it recovered once again and fled toward the woods, moving with a faltering gait and more slowly than before, yet still faster than its pursuers. It absorbed yet another shot as it entered the woods, though this blow did not bring it down. When it reemerged, a hunter fired again from about fifty paces. Again the beast went down, but recovered as before and retreated into the woods. [The party] searched until nightfall without managing to find it again.

The beast had survived two shots from point-blank range and the hunters claimed to have made contact at least two other times, and yet it lived to attack several more children two days later in the nearby parish of Fontans. The whole event would help to encourage the local myth, later noted by a fascinated Parisian observer, that the beast had the capacity to "charm" firearms, making it "impervious to lead."[74] Whether the subdelegate accepted the hunters' account at face value is not clear. Later in his report he speculated that the muskets may have been improperly loaded. He might also have mentioned the difficulty of firing with accuracy. Smoothbore muskets were the weapon of choice for soldiers and most huntsmen, and although the muskets of the 1760s had become marginally more reliable than those of previous generations, they were still notoriously untrustworthy at long range and would have performed erratically in the hands of the fearful.[75] In any case, there is more than a hint of suspicion in Lafont's observation that the wounded animal still managed to run "faster than its pursuers." The subdelegate acknowledged that this painful missed opportunity, together with the paralyzing fear that began to overtake the region, convinced him of the need "to engage the support of troops."[76]

Local authorities close to the action in the Gévaudan—Lafont, Duhamel, Morangiès, and others—consistently credited reports that described a single creature possessing unfamiliar, if not extraordinary, qualities. Their receptivity to this idea, in turn, fueled a cycle of speculation that quickly acquired national dimensions. The *Courrier,* evoking ancient myths from the age of the Punic Wars, would soon be comparing the savagery of "this terrible quadruped" to "the famous serpent that Regulus had to combat in Africa."[77]

Why would local authorities and their peasant compatriots ignore conventional wisdom regarding the dangers of wolves and embrace, however provisionally, an emerging hypothesis about a mysterious creature—a monster—with fearsome abilities? The psychologically disorienting effect of living through a killing spree cannot be discounted, and the sense of anxiety prevailing among the beast's opponents undoubtedly created a space where wild suspicions could flourish. The absence of a fixed, reliable representation of the attacker or attackers not only encouraged the mind's conflation of different incidents into one frightening phenomenon but also placed more weight on the terrified testimonies of individuals who had had fleeting encounters with a dangerous predator. Exaggerated descriptions and traditional popular explanations for strange events—leopards, *loups-cerviers,* sorcery, werewolves—rapidly filled the informational void the authorities confronted. Moreover, the possibility that a new breed of wolf with an unaccustomed physical appearance had appeared in the area is not entirely out of the question, even though the presence of an unfamiliar breed could hardly account for the attribution of quasi-magical qualities to the offending specimen.[78] For all these reasons Duhamel, Lafont, and the inhabitants of the region can be excused for entertaining, at least momentarily, theories that deviated from their own quotidian understanding of the natural world. As we shall see, the authorities' suspension of disbelief would be sustained by other forces that transcended local conditions and individual psychologies.

2

Monsters Real and Imagined

Local circumstances in the Gévaudan certainly help to account for the origins of a myth that would soon be broadcast to all corners of Europe. But distinctive features of the broad intellectual environment of the age also help to explain why the beast instantly assumed exotic form and arrested the attention of people far removed from the events. By the middle decades of the eighteenth century, uncertainties exposed and interrogated through scientific discourses, theological debates, and boisterous public squares had prepared the faithful, the religiously skeptical, and everyone in between to embrace with fascination all evidence of the monstrous. The first stories of the beast fell on ears well primed to receive them.

Nature's Monsters

To understand why tales of the extraordinary could take such firm hold of the imagination, and resonate far and wide for months on end, one needs to place the phenomenon of the beast of the Gévaudan within the broad context of the eighteenth century's understanding of nature's possibilities. To recapture the outlines of that vanished mental ecosystem the reader must set aside the enduring but potentially misleading assumption that Europe in the eighteenth

century served as the birthplace of the modern world. According to the typical cardboard account of the Age of Enlightenment (or *lumières*), courageous
skeptics, innovative philosophers, and experimental scientists, all suffused by
the inquisitive spirit conveyed by Kant's motto, "dare to know," finally succeeded in establishing a sound epistemological basis for the evaluation and
dissemination of knowledge of the world.[1] With the assistance of sympathetic
publishers, indulgent censors, leaders of salons, and, after about 1720, a newly
robust reading market that rewarded the purveyors of new ideas, they finally
dispersed the mists of doubt and ignorance that had held mankind in a sorry
state of intellectual dotage since the Middle Ages.

There is some truth to this picture. The Enlightenment, born of the experimental scientific culture that coalesced in the course of the seventeenth
century, did mark an important break in the timeline of western history. One
can even argue that the decade of the 1760s represented the high-water mark
of the age, especially in France.[2] But signs of a growing appetite for new ideas
in and around the 1760s should not be regarded as proof of the displacement,
withering, or eradication of older ideas. As Herbert Butterfield argued in a
memorable essay, and as historians of the Enlightenment have affirmed repeatedly in recent years, a "whiggish" perspective on human progress inevitably distorts historical reality and misrepresents both the pace and nature of
cultural change.[3] Despite its transformative effects and the triumphalist manner in which the successes of the philosophes have been represented ever since
the end of the eighteenth century, the changes made possible by the Enlightenment resulted less from climactic conflicts between forces of light and darkness than from protracted negotiation and collective rumination. The Enlightenment was not a reformist program pushed by an intellectual vanguard
but a multifaceted process of inquiry riven with contradictions—contradictions actually magnified by the explosion in publishing that transformed civic
life beginning in the 1720s. A mental posture specific to the age—curiosity
and adventurousness, on the one hand, combined with intellectual inertia and
generalized uncertainty, on the other—helped to shape the reception and interpretation of the beast of the Gévaudan.

Contemporary perceptions of nature illustrate well the fluid and un-
bounded character of the eighteenth century's world of ideas. Natural philosophers working in fields now referred to as chemistry, botany, entomology,
and zoology made discoveries and devised explanations of natural phenomena
that would forever change scientific thought and practice. But through the

1760s and beyond, the technically detailed explorations of nature carried out by the likes of Herman Boerhaave, Antoine Lavoisier, and René Antoine Ferchault de Réaumur existed alongside ideas that recalled the fascination for natural "wonders" expressed in medieval literature.[4] The abbé Jean-Antoine Nollet, who occupied France's first chair in experimental physics (established in 1753 at the Collège de Navarre), called the "marvelous" a "seductive poison that even the best minds have trouble resisting."[5] Nollet would have known of the risks firsthand, since he frequently gave "theatrical" demonstrations designed to strike the senses. More than once he delighted audiences by using an electrified boy—suspended by silk ropes in a darkened room—to produce sparks from an "electric kiss." (Jean-Jacques Rousseau would accuse Nollet himself of constructing a "laboratory of magic.")[6]

Examples of the "seductive" effects of the marvelous are easy to find. At the dawn of the Enlightenment, in the closing decades of the seventeenth century, Nicolas Malebranche sought to moderate Descartes' powerful but rigidly mechanistic account of human physiology by recycling a medieval argument about the power of the imagination—specifically the maternal imagination—and its ability to produce physical effects.[7] For proof of the phenomenon he pointed to the birth of a deformed child whose mother had witnessed, and evidently suffered psychic scars from, a convicted criminal's public breaking on the wheel. Malebranche's unverifiable hypothesis generated little public discussion in the decades that followed, but as late as 1756 the respected naturalist Johann Eller, director of Berlin's Academy of Sciences, actually expanded on Malebranche's speculations. He recorded the imagination's adverse effects on a barnyard dog that, after having been harassed repeatedly by an agitated turkey, gave birth to a pup whose head eerily resembled that of the mother's tormenter. For Eller the event offered compelling evidence that "women should not flatter themselves that they hold the exclusive power to create monsters from the strength of their imaginations."[8]

That natural philosophers would be tempted to speculate about the mysterious powers of invisible, or occult, forces is understandable. Belief in such powers underlay the appeal not only of charlatans like Frédéric-Antoine Mesmer, who in the 1780s claimed to manipulate the therapeutic forces of "animal magnetism," but also converted Newtonians such as Voltaire and Pierre-Louis Maupertuis, who eagerly explained gravity and the intangible laws of celestial mechanics to a curious readership.[9] But invisible forces were not the only creative source for ideas that today would be regarded as outlandish. Eighteenth-

century practitioners of science also speculated about purportedly visible creatures that had simply not yet revealed themselves sufficiently to the scientific
gaze. A wide range of strange entities came under discussion.[10]

Benjamin Martin, a Newtonian designer of microscopes whose overview of "experimental physiology" went through successful French translations in 1741 and 1764, expressed appropriate skepticism over the existence
of griffins, satyrs, dragons, and unicorns, but he refused to rule out their
possibility. Belief in the reality of mermaids and mermen is widely attested
throughout the eighteenth century, and Benoît de Maillet's visionary geological work *Telliamed* (1748) offered startling proto-evolutionary hypotheses that
prominently featured fish-men. Maillet even cited eyewitness accounts of men
"covered with scales" from the late seventeenth century. In 1769 Gabriel-
François Coyer, citing for support the ideas of Maupertuis, insisted that the
"natural history" of the alleged giants of Patagonia deserved the same attention "as the shells and butterflies that fill our fashionable curiosity cabinets."[11]
Claude-Nicolas Le Cat, a celebrated surgeon of Rouen who corresponded
with Voltaire and helped to found his city's Academy of Sciences in 1744,
wrote a 1755 treatise in which he casually asserted that animals were sometimes
found "living in the middle of solid bodies." The *Mercure de France* discussed
the possibility, and the respected *Journal Encyclopédique* referred to the phenomenon as an established reality as late as 1762.[12]

Speculation about freakish or preposterous products of nature took place,
moreover, not on the margins of scientific inquiry but at its very center. From
the late seventeenth century through the 1730s, the French Academy of Sciences showed an almost obsessive interest in monsters, those creatures defined
as "contrary to the order of nature." Bernard le Bovier de Fontenelle was already complaining in 1712 about the "infinite" discussion devoted to the subject, but monsters' central place in the scientific discourse of the time is easy
enough to understand.[13] The existence of living beings whose forms deviated
from what John Locke called "the established course of nature" challenged
the venerable idea that God had created an orderly and harmonious universe,
comprising a great chain of being that reflected the eternal design of a providential deity.[14] Discussion of the character of the monster had overlapped
with metaphysics in earlier centuries, but in France the founding of the royal
Academy of Sciences in the 1660s suddenly made the problem of the monstrous an urgent empirical issue. As clinical dissection of deformed human
specimens came to occupy a greater proportion of the time and energy of

leading members of the Academy, the boundary separating the divine will from natural processes became a site of constant skirmishing between advocates of Christian orthodoxy and proponents of one or another form of naturalism. Monsters, in other words, became entangled in one of the principal questions that underlay the various domains of Enlightenment thought. To what degree should the natural world be understood as operating autonomously from the mind and purposes of God?

Even before the Academy's debates on monsters had erupted, the sober skepticism that had settled over the continent following the witch hunts and the calamitous religious wars of the sixteenth and seventeenth centuries had greatly reduced the supposed range of divine or demonic action in the affairs of this world.[15] Still, naturalists recognized a need to reconcile the evident logic of God's creation with the presence of creatures that defied or subverted that logic—humans born without limbs or sexual organs, pigeons with two heads, conjoined twins. The need became only more pressing over time, as accumulating fossil evidence in the eighteenth century continued to reveal an unsuspected natural history of unfamiliar beings.

Confronting this growing body of evidence, the natural philosophers of the first third of the eighteenth century generally opted for one of two explanations. The dominant position held that all organisms, no matter how seemingly unusual or short-lived, resulted from the flowering of "preexisting germs," or seeds, present since Creation and activated by the ever-inscrutable will of God. This explanation came to be associated with the physician and anatomist Guichard Joseph Duverney, who achieved wide fame for his public dissections at the king's botanical garden in Paris, and whose collected anatomical observations would be published posthumously in 1761.[16] The opposing view, also avowedly orthodox but less reliant on the mysteries of the divine will, held that the very monstrosity of monsters proved they were the products of "accidents" occurring sometime after implantation of the seed. The physician Louis Lémery, for example, held that the formation of conjoined twins likely resulted from a violent collision between two normal eggs.[17]

Fixed on the narrow issue of God's responsibility for the monstrous, the proponents of these two perspectives took for granted the exceptionality of the monster and therefore saw no need to theorize the relationship of the monster to other creatures of the animal kingdom. Others began to move beyond this dichotomous framework by the 1730s. Gottfried Wilhelm Leibniz had already suggested that monsters of past and present might be seen as "me-

diating species" that filled gaps in the great chain of being, and later naturalists extrapolated from Leibniz's insight and used the category of the monster
to explore the nature, meaning, and taxonomic features of the "species." The
new imperative to carry on simultaneous examinations of the monstrous and
the seemingly normal would be captured succinctly by Voltaire in 1768, in his
own commentary on "monsters and diverse races." How can we agree on the
origin of monsters, he asked, "if we still do not understand the formation of
regular animals?"[18]

The polymath Maupertuis, among the few scientists of the eighteenth
century who seem to have glimpsed the possibility of evolution, suggested
that monsters could be seen as nature's own experiments—the prototypes of
species-to-be. He therefore encouraged the *savants* and crowned heads of Europe to create menageries that would be dedicated to the study of these "bizarre" creatures.[19] The Swedish botanist and naturalist Carl Linnaeus, whose
classificatory scheme for the natural order provided the foundation for the
binomial nomenclature used today, flatly rejected biological fluidity of the
sort that Maupertuis envisioned. He was no less fascinated by the epistemological challenges posed by the existence of monsters, however. The very first
edition of his *System of Nature* (1735) addressed the problem of the monster by
categorizing and labeling famous exemplars (for example, the satyr and the
phoenix) in an effort to naturalize and demystify them. The twelfth edition
of this influential work, published in 1766, actually created a distinct species
called *Homo monstrosus,* to which were relegated the many vexing examples
(some of doubtful existence) of morphological anomaly among humans.[20]

Others remained unsatisfied by Linnaeus' taxonomical solution to the
problem of the monster, and experimental naturalists continued to test and
interrogate the lines delimiting biological variation. In 1764, for example, the
surgeon Le Cat conducted a detailed autopsy of a "monstrous fetus" born to a
woman of Normandy. His published report focused on the anatomical oddities of this singular specimen, but Le Cat actually exploited the abnormalities
of the monster—it lacked a heart as well as other major organs—to demonstrate a physiological principle applicable to all humans, namely, the circulation of blood between mother and fetus.[21]

Le Cat, like other anatomists, focused on concrete anomalies in his appreciative investigations of the monstrous. Jean-Baptiste Robinet found a
more theoretical way of explaining the contiguity of normal and monstrous
bodies. He reprised and elaborated the insights of both Leibniz and Mauper-

tuis in a 1768 essay examining the "natural gradations of the forms of being." In it he argued that "bizarre forms" shared fundamental characteristics with normal "neighboring forms" and also prepared the way for "new combinations to come."[22] Robinet here anticipated the spirit of Diderot's *Dream of D'Alembert* (1769), which effectively obliterated the distinction between the monstrous and the normal by defining organic abnormality as the chance result of missed developmental connections occurring within a complex "bundle of threads."[23]

This tendency to naturalize the monster—that is, to assimilate monstrous forms to the general order of nature—is perhaps best captured by the work of Buffon, the naturalist whose fame and influence towered above all others in the second half of the eighteenth century. Buffon had been appointed the director of the king's botanical gardens in 1739. His *Natural History* (1749–1767), the first three volumes of which appeared in 1749, became a surprise bestseller, the third most popular work in all of French literature in the second half of the eighteenth century.[24] The text had popular appeal because of its handsome illustrations and elegant presentation, but it attracted wide attention also because it offered a new theory of nature. Rejecting the manmade categories of Linnaeus, which focused narrowly on the individual's physical characteristics, Buffon favored an open-ended approach that sought out the many affinities—such as habitat, diet, and especially, behavior—which connected species, or groups of species, to one another. This horizontal orientation to the study of natural forms and Buffon's conviction that the "prodigious" number of nature's products could not be contained by artificial classificatory schemes made him exceptionally open to discovering and making sense of the unusual. As he declared in 1755, "it is necessary to see nothing as impossible, to expect anything, and to suppose that all that can be is. Ambiguous species, irregular productions, anomalous beings will from now on cease to astonish us."[25]

Buffon's desire to expand and probe the margins of normality explains the intensity of his interest in hybrids, an interest widely shared by naturalists and their readers from the 1750s through the 1770s. Hybridity seemed to hold the key both to the definition of species and to the mysteries of reproduction, and Buffon and his various collaborators and rivals therefore engaged in a wide range of experiments intending to produce new hybrid products—crosses between dogs and foxes, sheep and goats, wolves and dogs. Buffon, whose own experiments proved unsuccessful despite his optimal position as

Naturalist of international renown, member of the French Academy, friend of philosophes, recipient of royal favors, George-Louis Leclerc de Buffon may have been the most esteemed man of letters in France by the time of his death in 1788. From a series depicting "illustrious Frenchmen," this image shows the naturalist surrounded by the objects of his curiosity. *Bibliothèque Nationale de France, N 2, Buffon*

head of the king's natural history cabinet, eagerly followed the news of a dog-fox hybridization in 1764, and in 1766 wrote his first important theoretical statement on the processes underlying hybridity, "On the Degeneration of Animals."[26] Buffon's Swiss rival Charles Bonnet, whose much-read *Contemplation of Nature* (1764) effectively reconstituted the great chain of being, would later encourage cross-breeding between dogs and wolves. Surely those species promised better results than the infamous hen-rabbit experiments of the abbé Louis-François de Fontenu, which had been discussed in Réaumur's seminal treatise on the breeding of birds in 1749, and which spawned the rumor (accepted by Linnaeus) that Fontenu had succeeded in producing chickens covered with fur.[27]

Naturalists had their own reasons for investigating hybridity and the boundaries of species. They struggled to understand the mechanisms of what would eventually come to be called heredity, genetics, and speciation. Their interest almost surely reflected Europe's sustained exposure to the environments of the New World and its experience with human "intermixing" and creolization.[28] The Jesuit missionary Joseph-François Lafitau, whose *Morals of the American Savages compared to the Morals of Primitive Times* (1724) had sparked interest in the mysterious American continent, had even been inspired to use the alleged existence of a headless race of humans, legends of which circulated widely in the French New World, to argue for the essential monogenetic unity of the human species.[29]

Whatever the origins of their interests, one result of naturalists' open-ended investigations was to fuel public fascination for strange beings of all kinds. Buffon's own multi-volume *Natural History* played an especially notable role in stimulating interest in the unusual. Buffon reached unprecedented numbers of readers by employing an accessible writing style. An admiring reviewer noted in 1772 that "everyone has read, reads, and re-reads the *Natural History*."[30] The naturalist's evocative descriptions of animals and minerals from the Old and New Worlds made natural history exciting and alluring to a vast audience that would have struggled to understand Réaumur or Maupertuis. In sparking what Louise E. Robbins has called a "midcentury fad for natural history," Buffon gave definitive shape to a growing public hunger to understand the exotic.[31] After all, many other contemporary forces whetted consumers' appetites for stories, theories, and artifacts involving strange or ambiguous creatures. The publication of travel literature depicting faraway lands, the rapid expansion of overseas commerce, French military engagement in the wilds of America, Rousseau-inspired discussions of the respective virtues and characteristics of the natural and civilized worlds: all of these developments made the French eager to pursue both the natural and the unfamiliar.

Symptoms of a growing curiosity about nature are evident up and down the social and political hierarchy. The royal menagerie, established at Versailles in the 1660s, accumulated new specimens throughout the later seventeenth and eighteenth centuries, and many of the king's acquisitions—like the zebra imported in 1760, stuffed and prominently displayed in a glass case after its death—became tourist attractions of the moment. Nor were animals the only objects of royal fascination. In the spring of 1765, the minister Saint-Florentin worked diligently to acquire on Louis XV's behalf the skeleton of the dwarf Bébé, the exotic and recently deceased guest of the exiled king of Poland, Stanislas Leczinski. After arranging the transfer of the dwarf's remains, Saint-Florentin made a point of reassuring Leczinski's secretary that "the box containing the skeleton will be opened only by M. de Buffon," the king's servant who by then had become the most renowned naturalist of the day.[32]

In the course of the eighteenth century, as Robbins has shown, merchants directed a growing stream of exotic animals (especially parrots and monkeys) to Parisian pet-owners who had an appetite for nature or a desire to engage in an exciting new form of conspicuous consumption. Formerly restricted to wealthy aristocrats, the possession of exotic animals soon became just another sign of the leveling effects of the marketplace.[33] Striving to satisfy the popular demand for the strange and the bizarre, entertainers and exhibitors at Parisian street fairs aggressively advertised the living oddities and foreign species they incorporated into their shows and displays. The entertainment at these often raucous public spectacles included contortionists, acrobats, and tightrope walkers, but also exotic animals from France or foreign lands. The English traveler Thomas Pennant, passing through Paris in March of 1765, reported his visit to the always magnificent Saint-Germain fair, where he marveled at the sight of "a Chamois, a horned cock, a bottle nosed Whale, a fine striped Tiger cat, a Porcupine, and a Cassowary."[34] In 1749, the Saint-Germain fair had been host to perhaps "the greatest sensation of the age"—the display of an Asian rhinoceros, thought to be the first of its kind ever to set foot in France. "Much resorted to by all ranks of people," as Pennant observed, Saint-Germain and the other street fairs became such magnets of the exotic that even naturalists, including Buffon, attended them with notebooks in hand.[35] No wonder the editor of the *Courrier d'Avignon* dreamed, in April of 1765, that the beast of the Gévaudan itself would eventually be displayed at the Saint-Germain fair.[36]

Amid this rich panoply of the exotic, however, hybrids or suspected hybrids held a special place in the popular imagination. The continuing belief in the existence of mermaids, griffins, and satyrs (and wolfmen) has been mentioned. The reality of such mythical creatures seemed to be supported, moreover, by strange and observable examples of hybridity in the contemporary world, tales of which circulated through both polite *salons* and rowdy cabarets. The street fairs, for example, often featured exotic creatures alleged to be hybrids, including one in 1748 said to possess the characteristics of at least six different species.[37] The so-called "porcupine man," Edward Lambert, aroused learned discussion in London and Paris in the 1750s, causing some to fear that Lambert and his scaly epidermis represented "a different species of mankind." The "philosopher of nature" Jean-Baptiste-Claude Delisle de Sales claimed to have seen in his youth a girl with the head and feet of a monkey, and he remembered reports of an exhibit of a wolf-child in Lyons in the 1750s.[38]

Voltaire, in a 1768 essay, "The Singularities of Nature," expressed his own belief that "monstrous unions" between different species were not uncommon in warm climates. He even coyly suggested to his largely urban readers that examples of such monstrous offspring, though "unknown in our cities," could almost certainly be found in the countryside.[39] Intrigued readers could only hope that such monstrous hybrids bore no resemblance to the odd creature depicted in Parisian broadsheets in early 1784. In January of that year, as Robert Darnton has noted, journals excitedly reported the discovery of a bizarre animal from one of the corners of Peru, a terrible monster that had developed the nocturnal habit of devouring "the swine, cows, and bulls of the area." With the face of a man, the horns of a bull, the ears of an ass, the wings of a bat, and the scales of a fish, the captured animal's alleged figure became the talk of Paris. The *Courrier de l'Europe* saw the creature as proof of the existence of harpies, "heretofore considered legendary."[40]

In the eighteenth century, French conceptions of the natural world were more capacious than our own. The Renaissance collectors who had inaugurated the early modern tradition of natural history in the sixteenth and seventeenth centuries saw themselves engaging in "the pursuit of wonder." They conceived of the information they collected as belonging to an "infinitely permeable" continuum of knowledge that included artifacts "from the imaginary to the exotic to the ordinary."[41] These assumptions about the infinite mystery of natural knowledge, far from simply fading into oblivion after 1700, actually found new outlets in a generation that became obsessed by nature's explanatory potential. In learned milieus of the early eighteenth century, one certainly finds evidence of a newly dismissive attitude toward forms of "wonder" that inspired only paralyzing awe; that fearful disposition, which elites increasingly associated with the uncultivated, seemed to stifle the active pursuit of knowledge.[42] But naturalists of the eighteenth century devoted unremitting effort to defining the boundaries between the natural, the supernatural, and the preternatural (a characterization applied to the rare and marvelous artifact that nevertheless belonged to the natural order.)[43] In carrying out this work, by which they also "tried to map the territory of the monstrous," they continued to yield fantastic new evidence of the mysteries held by the natural world. The gradual downgrading of awesome "wonder" no doubt resulted, in part, from habits of discrimination called into being by the bewildering variety of scientific knowledge placed on offer in both private and public settings in the eighteenth century.[44] In the cities, elite and popular audiences hungered for knowledge about nature after mid-century—public lecturers turned the boulevards of Paris into "schools of physics"—and few who attended public spectacles or hosted experiments by Nollet and his imitators had yet to develop a firm instinct for separating the illuminating from the "amazing."[45]

Confronted and excited by the discoveries and writings of Buffon, Linnaeus, and the Encyclopedists, many wise denizens of the age of Enlightenment still retained an interest, and a provisional belief, in creatures that defied classification. Exposure to arresting ideas provided new stimulus to forms of curiosity with deep roots in Europe's religious, literary, and cultural history, as well as new sources with which to confront and understand a still-enchanting world. In this particular intellectual and cultural milieu, on the cusp of dispassionate rationalism but still informed by a rich tradition of wonder and mystery, the task of separating real from imagined monsters posed cognitive challenges at all levels of the social hierarchy.

Visualizing the Predator

When eyewitnesses and newspaper reports began to suggest in the fall of 1764 that the beast of the Gévaudan had something of the monstrous about it, and that the species of the creature remained open to speculation, they obviously drank from the same wellspring of curiosity and anxiety that had supplied Paris and other French urban centers for years. In the minds of all those affected by the events, the mere strangeness of the experience was enough to conjure a well-established repertoire of monstrous associations. When those associations then passed through the Parisian rumor mill or found their way into print, they were greeted by a receptive audience of readers and curiosity-seekers who had been taught by Buffon and his collaborators "to expect anything" from nature's realm.

Tellingly, the earliest descriptions of the beast of the Gévaudan shared two features consistently. All agreed that the beast's species had yet to be determined. Most also suggested that the characteristics displayed by the beast were likely to prolong the mystery indefinitely. The first reports from the *Courrier d'Avignon* emphasized the beast's mysterious identity and speculated that the creature was a panther that had "escaped from the hands of its trainer"; only a week later the editor backed away from the theory, admitting that the beast had come "from who knows where."[46] The *Courrier* had not been wrong to suggest, though, that concerned eyes turned to the keepers of private menageries in the early months of the story. One of the most assiduous followers of the beast's exploits would later recall that the nature-loving king Charles Emmanuel III of Piedmont-Sardinia, with his capital in nearby Turin, fell under suspicion for a time.[47]

The mystery of the beast's identity was sustained by the conflicting descriptions provided by witnesses or those who reported their accounts. The *Courrier* highlighted the uncertainties. "There is much debate over [the beast's] figure and species. An innkeeper of Langogne who saw it, and who was made seriously ill by the terror it caused him, described it as long, squat, having a rusty color and a black stripe down its back, with a long tail and enormous talons. A curé who hunted [the beast] with his parishioners, and who claims to have seen it three times, described it as long, thick as a calf, having the same color with the same black stripe, and the muzzle of a pig. Several peasants have described it similarly, the one difference being that they give it a head more like that of a cat, which of course has no resemblance to a pig." The picture was further obscured in the newspaper's next issue, which reported that the beast was "almost three feet in height and very long," with a "dull gray" color on its back, a light red chest, and a short and bristly coat.[48] The paper's Parisian correspondent looked forward to the moment, after the beast had been conquered, when the mystery would finally be dispelled. Then "it will be easy, especially for those who have frequented menageries, to determine its species."[49]

In the meantime, however, the twin propensity to apply to the beast a mélange of characteristics associated with different animals and to speculate about its exotic origins became only more pronounced. As the *Courrier* noted, "if it is still unidentified, it's not for lack of names; they give it too many."[50] Suggestions of hybridity, which reflected and reinforced not only popular suspicions about werewolves but also a general scientific interest in species-mixing, proliferated. Lafont's initial description of the beast—probably based on the recollections of the unlucky hunters whose October encounter with the creature has been discussed—relied on a series of differentiating compari-

"Ferocious Beast that Ravaged the Gévaudan in the year 1764." Uncertainty about the identity of the beast of the Gévaudan in late 1764 and early 1765 led to speculation about all sorts of exotic creatures, including lions. *Bibliothèque Nationale de France, Qb1 1764*

sons to other animal types. "It is much larger than a lynx and has the height and nearly the shape of a large wolf; its muzzle is similar to that of a calf."[51] Duhamel, after later sending an engraved image of the beast to the intendant Ballainvilliers in Auvergne, expressed confidence that "you will believe, as I do, that this animal is a monster sired by a lion but with a mother of undetermined species."[52] The *Gazette d'Amsterdam* reported that the creature shared characteristics with both the bear and the boar, while still others saw in the beast "a monstrous product of a cross between a bear and a female wolf."[53] The *Gazette de France,* in its first account, invoked characteristics of both the fox and the greyhound, while also noting that the creature, "much larger than a wolf," had hornlike ears and teeth as sharp as a razor[54] A broadsheet published in January of 1765 described the beast as having a mouth like a lion, defensive tusks like those of a boar, and a back like that of a fish, "covered with scales that finish in a point."[55] These endless speculations about the hybrid nature of the beast might help to explain the widespread assumption, even among the educated, that the monster acted alone; it was the consensus of naturalists that hybrids could not reproduce.[56] A hybrid would have a higher than normal probability of being a one-of-a-kind creature.

Unadulterated species of exotic origin nevertheless also attracted attention. In a dispatch from the end of November, after listing the animals most often mentioned in connection with the beast's atrocities (leopard, tiger, hyena, lynx), the *Courrier* added a new possibility to the mix: a monkey. "This sentiment has been expressed by an American woman who married someone in the region. She affirms that in her country, there are monkeys matching this description, and they are most formidable." The *Courrier* gave credence to the theory because it helped to account for the apparent savagery of the beast's fighting style, and anecdotal evidence from other lands seemed to add weight to the hypothesis. "In the first volume of the memoirs of the comte de Forbin, one finds that [Forbin], returning from Siam via the straits of Malaga [sic], and engaged in a hunt, killed a monkey that had been on the verge of attacking him, and whose figure—as he described it—bore a striking resemblance to the animal in question."[57]

The memoirs of Claude, comte de Forbin, which detailed his naval exploits and his travels to Asia and other foreign lands, had been published in 1729 and went through multiple editions in the 1730s and 1740s. The *Courrier*'s citing of this one relatively minor episode from Forbin's lengthy travel narrative underlines the extent to which readers of this period were drawn to

FIGURE

DE LA BÉTE

FAROUCHE

ET EXTRAORDINAIRE, QUI DÉVORE LES FILLES
Dans la Province de Gévaudan, & qui s'échappe avec tant de
vîtesse, qu'en très-peu de tems on la voit à deux ou trois lieues
de distance, & qu'on ne peut l'attraper ni la tuer.

EXPLICATION.

ON écrit de Marvejols, dans la Province de Gévaudan, par une Lettre en date du premier Novembre mil sept cent soixante-quatre ; que depuis deux mois il paroît aux environs de Langogne, & de la Forêt de Mercoire une Bête farouche qui répand la consternation dans toutes les Campagnes. Elle a déja dévoré une vingtaine de Personnes sur-tout des Enfans & particulièrement des Filles. Il n'y a guére de jours qui ne soient marqués par quelques nouveaux désastres. La frayeur qu'elle inspire empêche les Bucherons d'aller dans les Forêts, ce qui rend le bois fort rare & fort cher.

Ce n'est que depuis huit jours qu'on a pu parvenir à voir de près cet Animal redoutable. Il est beaucoup plus haut qu'un Loup : il est bas du devant, & ses pattes sont armées de griffes. Il a le poil rougeâtre ; la tête fort grosse, longue, & finissant en museau de Lévrier; les oreilles petites, droites comme des cornes ; le poitrail large & un peu gris ; le dos rayé de noir & une gueule énorme ; armée de dents si tranchantes, qu'il a séparé plusieurs têtes du corps, comme pourroit le faire un razoir. Il a le pas assez lent, & il court en bondissant. Il est d'une agilité & d'une vîtesse extrêmes : dans un intervalle de tems fort court on le voit à deux ou trois lieues de distance. Il se dresse sur ses pieds de derriere, & s'élance sur sa proie, qu'il attaque toujours au cou, par derriere, ou par le côté. Il craint les Bœufs, qui le mettent en fuite. L'allarme est universelle dans ce Canton ; on vient de faire des Priéres publiques ; on a rassemblé quatre cens Paysans pour donner la chasse à cet Animal féroce ; mais on n'a pu encore l'atteindre.

Vû par moi Censeur pour la Police.
Vû l'Approbation, permis d'Imprimer à la charge d'enregistrement à la Chambre Syndicale. Ce 24 Novembre 1764.
DE SARTINE.
Régistré sur le Régistre N° 16. de la Communauté des Libraires & Imprimeurs, page 197.

Se vend AUX ASSOCIÉS. Chez F.-G. DESCHAMPS, Libraire, rue Saint-Jacques.

the strangeness and the danger of the more exotic forms of nature. Forbin's recounting of his experience would indeed have resonated for those attuned to the recent events in the Gévaudan, and it had the added attraction of portraying both steely resolve in the face of peril and a quick and happy ending. As Forbin remembered it, strong winds in the straits of Malacca had forced his ship to take temporary refuge on the Malaysian coast during his return home from Siam in 1687. To kill time, he and his comrades probed the interior of the country in search of wild game native to the region. Forbin got more than he bargained for when, "in the time it took to glance from one side to the other, I saw a monstrous monkey coming toward me. It advanced with sparkling eyes and an air of assurance that would have frightened me had I not been armed. I went toward it, and when we were ten paces apart I fired, striking it cold dead." The monkey had apparently achieved impressive dimensions. "This was a terrifying animal. Its tail was long, like a lion's. It stood more than two and a half feet high, and stretched eight feet long from head to tail, with a long, wide face covered in splotches recalling the appearance of a drunkard." When he showed the specimen to the other men on the ship, "they confessed that they had never seen a monkey so large in all the Indies."[58]

The characteristics of Forbin's monkey overlapped with the emerging profile of the beast—the tail, the elongated figure, the "sparkling" eyes (the rich semantic field of the adjective *étincelant* clearly straddled the realms of natural history and sorcery). But other features of the story, including the animal's strange visage and its singularly ineffective plan of attack, set it apart from the experience in the Gévaudan. Despite the considerable commercial traffic clogging French ports such as Bordeaux and Marseilles in the eighteenth century, most of it propelled by overseas trade, few readers of this dispatch would have been prompted to speculate that the killings in the Gévaudan were the work of an escaped simian import from Malaysia. Nor was that really the intention behind this literary reference. Forbin's adventure merited a mention because it added to the stock of terms that could usefully signify the

---

opposite page: "Figure of the Ferocious Beast." One of the first depictions of the beast, this image appeared on a broadsheet produced in late November of 1764. The description of the demonlike "figure of the ferocious beast," with its "paws armed with talons" and its teeth "like a razor," closely followed the text of the *Gazette de France,* which had run its first notice on the story of the beast just one day before the print's date of publication. *Bibliothèque Nationale de France, Qb1 1764*

exotic, the unusual, and the unknown. In a single brief report the *Courrier's* editor had employed a coded vocabulary that managed to evoke a whole world of the untamed: tiger, leopard, hyena, lynx, monkey, America, Siam, Malaga.

Among the many exotic animals and points of origin bandied about in private and public discussions of the beast's identity, a favored image emerged over the course of autumn, 1764: the African hyena. Several recent developments had encouraged this line of thinking. A hypothetical linkage between the hyena and a puzzling rash of killings in the Lyonnais had already been considered and ultimately discounted by a naturalist of that region in 1756, and when the ninth volume of Buffon's *Natural History* appeared in 1761 it contained a menacing image and a full description of the hyena's habits, disposition, and physical make-up.[59] The hyena's characteristics aligned in surprising ways with the evidence and rumors accumulating in the Gévaudan. As Buffon described it, the hyena operated as a sulking and "solitary animal," and it possessed an uncommonly foul temperament. It inhabited "the caverns of mountains" and the "clefts of rocks" in Africa and Asia, and it preyed on many of the same animals favored by wolves. The hyena differed from the wolf in at least one significant way, however. The hyena "is stronger and has a more aggressive demeanor," exhibiting so much determination that, at night, it was known to "break down the doors of stables and the fences around sheep pens." This "extremely ferocious" creature had "no fear of panthers," it bravely "defends itself against the lion," and it "sometimes attacks men." When hungry, the creature was known to frequent graves where it "uses its paws to tear to shreds the bodies of animals and men." The hyena, Buffon ominously inscribed, was "untameable."[60]

This account of the manners and morals of the hyena would have sounded hauntingly familiar to the frightened inhabitants of the Gévaudan. The physical portrait that Buffon provided would only have added to the plausibility of the hyena hypothesis. According to the naturalist's description, the hyena reached "about the size of a wolf, and it seems related to this animal in the general shape of its head and body." Other aspects of its appearance differed from the wolf, however. The tail was bushy and the animal's coat was described as coarse and long (a subject on which there had been conflicting reports in the Gévaudan). The distinctive mane, "running the length of its body from head to tail" and giving "the appearance of a mixed color of black and grey," seemed to square with the repeated assertions that the beast had a multihued coat and sported a black stripe down the length of its back. Most eyewitness descriptions also converged on the beast's strange countenance and the odd shape of its head. Here, too, Buffon supplied corroborating evidence. The untameable hyena had "long, sharp, pointed, naked ears" that were more or less wolflike in appearance, but the muzzle was shorter and the head markedly wider. Most striking, the hyena's "eyes shine in the dark," and some even said that it could see "better at night than in day."[61]

For a time, speculation about the hyena generated surprisingly close attention to the shape of the beast's legs and paws—Buffon having specified that the hyena had four fingers per paw. In Marvejols the author of an anonymous letter of 26 January, published in the *Année Littéraire*, worried that "it is still unknown whether this beast has four fingers on its front paws, though it is clear that it has only that many on its rear [paws], with a marked talon serving as a fifth." If it could be verified that four was the correct number, the correspondent suggested, "there is little doubt that we are battling a true hyena." Captain Duhamel himself would later reject this theory—he disputed the number of fingers and talons—and he seems to have relied on Etienne Lafont, his frequent ally, to take his case to the public.[62]

The intriguing correspondences between Buffon's description and the murky details emerging from the woods of the Gévaudan help to explain why the image of the beast-as-hyena remained lodged in readers' consciousness long after hunters on the scene had ruled out the possibility. As late as 1782, a tobacco merchant in Paris sold stuffed hyenas to "curious naturalists" of the city, advertising them as "animals of the Gévaudan."[63] In a memoir of 1779, Gilbert du Motier, marquis de Lafayette remembered the "mischief" caused by the beast in his native Auvergne. "The hope of meeting it," he recalled of his experience as an eight-year-old boy, "made my walks exciting." Feverish rumors clearly made an impression on the future hero of two worlds, because many years later Lafayette was still identifying this specter of his youth as a "hyena."[64]

Buffon's *Natural History* ran through dozens of full or partial editions from the 1760s to the end of the century. The publication of the first volumes of a sprawling duodecimo edition in 1752 would have made at least some of Buffon's text available to readers of relatively modest means.[65] Whatever the format, however, we know that Etienne Lafont had access to a copy of the *Natural History.* In his first serious description of the beast—the one in which he also invoked the images of the wolf, calf, and lynx—he remarked on the beast's "long coat," typical of the hyena, "at least as it is represented in one of the plates in volume nine of the natural history of Buffon."[66] In turning to Buffon for assistance, moreover, Lafont hardly stood out among the crowd. The intendant of Auvergne, Ballainvilliers, would later cite Buffon in a letter to officials at court. Various newspapers invoked the naturalist's authority, or surreptitiously borrowed language from his text, in their reporting on the mystery.[67] The comte de Morangiès probably also had Buffon in mind when he struck a rare chord of optimism as snow began to fall on the Gévaudan at the end of October 1764. "If this animal was born in Africa, as seems likely, I believe he will suffer greatly in the dead of winter. . . May we trust in providence."[68] When he delivered his annual report to the Estates of the Gévaudan in March of 1765, Etienne Lafont represented the considered opinion of all

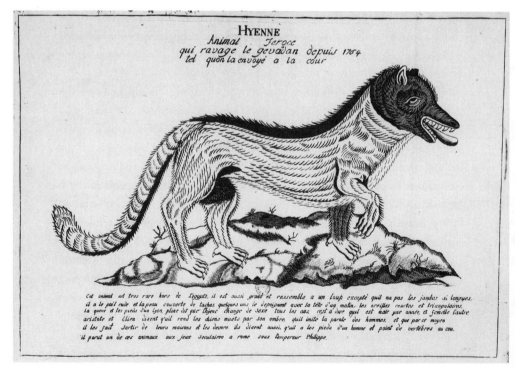

"Hyena." For several months between late 1764 and the middle of 1765, many people suspected that the beast was a hyena escaped from a menagerie or smuggled into France aboard a merchant vessel. The rumors circulated so widely and lasted so long that perceptions remained clouded even in the face of clear evidence to the contrary.
Bibliothèque Nationale de France, Qb1 1764, collection Hennin

who had expended their time and effort over the previous months in the mad-
deningly fruitless hunt: "some assumed it to be a hyena; others a wolf, the animal to which it now seems, judging all the evidence, to have the closest resemblance; and others, finally, a monster."[69]

Lafont's succinct summary of the bewilderment that clouded minds in
the first months of the affliction and his forthright admission that some regarded the beast as an indefinable "monster" points up the existence of the
two sets of variables that authorities struggled to process—variables that Buffon, with his acute interest in animal behavior, at least came close to encom-
passing. First, the conflicting and inconsistent physical descriptions of the
beast made it difficult to produce a stable visual image that could be associated with a single known species. Perhaps more frustrating, and chilling, was
the fact that the beast's physical singularity seemed to coincide with a set of
behaviors regarded as alien and extraordinary, characteristic of no familiar animal. The beast's alleged ability to deflect lead balls propelled by musket fire,
for example, was one of the behavioral oddities that pushed Lafont to study
Buffon's representation of the hyena. "It seems quite possible that the length
of its coat may serve as an obstacle to the blows of firearms," Lafont observed
after sharing the details of Buffon's profile, "and that they will penetrate [its
hide] only with difficulty." Other qualities added to the mystery. "Everywhere
they insist that the beast is extremely agile and cunning [rusé]," he wrote in his
long missive to Saint-Priest in late October, "against whom it will be necessary
to utilize traps and the element of surprise." Although the beast was said to be
so timid that "it flees at the first sight of a firearm"—on which news Lafont
ruled out the possibility of a tiger or a leopard, both of whom would surely
display more "boldness"—its stealth allowed it to inflict maximum damage.
"It never strikes except through surprise, when it finds women and young
children in a defenseless position."[70] The Courrier d'Avignon made a similar
point using more colorful language. "It rears up on its hind legs, striking and
felling [its victims] with the other two. It is so avid for human blood that it
eats [its prey] right down to the blood-soaked ground."[71]

Reports of the beast's insatiable appetites also came from other quarters.
Duhamel notified one of his correspondents of a horrific attack near Aumont
in late November, the results of which he had observed firsthand. "On the
23rd, at five o'clock in the evening, this cruel beast throttled a woman in a village two leagues from [Saint-Chély], and after having eaten the neck all the
way down to the shoulders, and having sucked the blood from her body, it

carried away the head."[72] Even before news of this particular atrocity had circulated outside of the Gévaudan, the *Courrier* had provided similarly grisly accents for the beast's portrait. "Of all the cadavers found so far," the paper alleged, "[the beast] has eaten only the liver, heart, intestines, and part of the head; it leaves the rest behind."[73] On the basis of such ghoulish evidence, reported the Parisian observer Magné de Marolles, many peasants of the region "made up their minds that the beast [is] a witch."[74] To them, and to many of the readers now gripped by this story, it must have seemed that reports of a "cunning" animal "avid" for human blood—one able to deflect lead shells!—placed the true identity of the beast beyond the investigative powers of even the best-informed naturalists and huntsmen. The identification and ultimate defeat of "this cruel beast" perhaps required an appeal to a higher power.

God's Monster

The beast's confounding behavior thus stoked the flames of learned (or at least semilearned) theorizing throughout the fall of 1764. Other than the beast itself, the one figure in this drama whose deeds spoke simultaneously to the worlds of the learned and the nonlearned was the septuagenarian bishop of Mende, Gabriel Florent de Choiseul-Beaupré (1685–1767). As the titular comte of the Gévaudan, and as the most powerful seigneur in the region, the bishop of Mende spoke with an authority unrivaled in this remote corner of Languedoc, and on the last day of 1764 he issued an official circular *(mandement)* to all parishes in which he offered his diagnosis of the Gévaudan's trying affliction. The text stands as a masterpiece of provocation, for Choiseul-Beaupré ultimately blamed the "scourge" of the beast on the spiritual failures of the Gévaudanois themselves. The beast, in the bishop's estimation, served as a weapon "drawn from the arsenal of God's anger . . . to execute the death sentences that his justice has pronounced."[75]

Only a generous sampling of the rhetoric of the *mandement* can convey the impact of the bishop's intervention in the affairs of his flock. "A ferocious beast, unknown to our climes, has appeared suddenly, as if by a miracle, no one knowing whence it comes. Wherever it appears, it leaves bloody traces of its cruelty. Fear and consternation spread; the countryside is deserted, the most intrepid men are seized with fear at the sight of this animal, this destroyer of their species, and they do not dare to venture outside unarmed." Against the beast's forces there seemed to be no defense, since "it combines strength with trickery and surprise. It brings down its prey with incredible speed and agility . . . But why rehearse the dreadful qualities of this monster of which your own troubles have informed you only too well?" Rather than tear open "wounds that are still bleeding," the bishop suggested, should he not "wipe your tears and give you the consolation you need?" In fact, the bishop assured his flock, "it is only your well-being that forces me to address this sad subject; if I dredge up the image of your misfortunes, it is only to show you their cause and remedy." As Saint Augustine had explained, divine justice "does not permit innocence to suffer. The punishment it inflicts always presupposes the error that attracted it. From this principle it should be easy for you to see that your misfortunes arise from your own sins. They are the ultimate source of your calamities." Holy Scripture showed—the bishop here quoted both Leviticus and Deuteronomy—that God had always threatened to punish man's sins with agonies "similar to those whose full rigor you are experiencing today." Those who wondered about the origins of the beast of the Gévaudan should therefore "ask no more." The ravages of the beast simply expressed "the immutable order of [God's] eternal justice."

The true targets of this justice were not the young people who suffered from the beast's appetites, but rather the parents who had failed them so miserably. "Fathers and mothers who grieve at the sight of children ripped apart by this monster that God has armed against them, do you not have reason to fear that you yourselves have caused, by your disorderly lives, the terrible scourge that strikes them?" The bishop requested "an accounting of the manner in which you raise them; how negligent have you been in instructing them in the principles of religion and the duties of Christianity? What care have you given their education?" Instead of instructing their children to keep God in their hearts at all times, to be charitable, to care for neighbors weighed down by misfortune, and to avoid pride, the parents of the Gévaudan had allowed their young to be soured by "the contagion of bad examples." Children manifested "malice and corruption" as soon as they became old enough to do so. All exhibited ambition, pride, and indifference to the impoverished. Sexual mores had been degraded. "The sex whose principal ornament has always been decency and modesty seems no longer to know these qualities; [girls] make a spectacle of themselves, displaying their worldliness and glorying in what should cause them shame. They entrap the innocent . . . and seek to attract even in our temples the admiration due only to the Divinity." This specter of general "iniquity" prompted the bishop to offer a harsh judgment of his own. "An idolatrous and criminal flesh that serves as a demon's instrument to seduce and lead to perdition—does it not deserve to be delivered up to the murderous teeth of the ferocious beasts that tear it to pieces?"

The bishop acknowledged that not all who had succumbed to the beast were guilty of the sins he decried, for God sometimes authorizes sad events for reasons that bear on the "eternal happiness" of those affected. But "this does not mean that their fates are not also a punishment for the sins of their elders." The Bible offered proof of God's intent *"to take revenge on the children for the iniquities of the fathers, down to the third or fourth generation."* Thus, only sincere repentance and "tears of remorse" could win relief from the present affliction. "Instead of hoping to push away our fears, let us tremble over our sins . . . Let us follow again the design of God, who strikes us only to cure us."

To help bring about the moral transformation that would visit "holy violence" on the monster at last, the bishop ordered that "public prayers" be observed "in all places that have been infested by this cruel Beast." Specifically, he announced a "forty-hour devotion" to take place in the cathedral of Mende on 6 January 1765, the Sunday of the Epiphany. (Such devotions recalled the forty hours Christ spent in his tomb.) The ceremony would open and close with the performance of a solemn high mass, and it would feature the reciting of versets, songs, and orations selected by the bishop himself. The occasion would be crowned by a public procession of the Holy Sacrament, and the entire ritual would be repeated in all other churches of the diocese for three consecutive Sundays following local reception of the *mandement.* The bishop urged that the terrible suffering of the beast's victims, and not selfish fears for personal safety, be the sole motivation behind these acts of public penance, as well as all private appeals for God's forgiveness. Let all prayers be accompanied "by sentiments of faith and remorse capable of reaching the throne of the Lord and taking from his hands the scourge that afflicts us." In dramatic language, Choiseul-Beaupré had articulated a conviction no doubt shared by many of the peasants who spied sorcery behind the terrible events of the previous months: only through divine intercession could the beast be defeated.

With the notable exception of the abbé Pourcher, whose essential work of 1889 will be discussed in this book's final chapter, historians of the beast of the Gévaudan have generally heaped derision on the *mandement* of the bishop of Mende; at least one has castigated the bishop as "the creator of the myth" of the beast.[76] Modern commentators have seen this document as expressing the superstitions of a bygone era, a cleric's self-serving indulgence of popular fears, or the eccentricities of an aging crank.[77] Contemporary religious skeptics would also have seen the bishop's declaration as symptomatic of the putatively benighted soil from which it sprang. Later evidence suggests that Jean le Rond d'Alembert, for example, probably regarded Choiseul-Beaupré as a "dangerous" fanatic.[78]

What has gone largely unnoticed, however, is the degree to which the substance of the bishop's *mandement* reflected the influence of the most pressing theological issues of the age. Gabriel Florent de Choiseul-Beaupré was neither an isolated rube nor a typical representative of the theologically shallow French episcopacy of the eighteenth century.[79] A member of the influential family of Choiseul, and cousin to the Choiseul who served as minister of war in the 1760s, the bishop was a sober theologian who offered learned commentary on such eminent churchmen as Jacques-Bénigne Bossuet, Roberto Bellarmino, and the church fathers. Born in the same year as Louis XIV's fateful Edict of Fontainebleau (1685), which brought a dramatic end to an official royal policy of toleration toward the Protestant Huguenots, Choiseul-Beaupré had lived long enough to witness the final spasms of Protestant rebellion in the Cévennes mountains, which formed the southeastern border of the Gévaudan.[80] As bishop of Mende since 1723, he had been among the vigilant leaders of the church in Languedoc who expressed alarm at the brazen behavior of Protestant pastors in the mid-1740s.[81] Most important, Choiseul-Beaupré sympathized openly with the influential group of Catholic believers known as Jansenists. By the late 1750s he had become embroiled in the disputes that pitted the Jansenists against the Society of Jesus and the power structures that protected them. Their conflict enlarges the meaning of the bishop's scathing *mandement*.

The conflict's main line of descent takes us back to the mid-seventeenth century. By that time the Jesuit order had become, across Europe and beyond, the very face of the Catholic response to the Protestant Reformation. As militant agents of Catholic reform, the Jesuits insisted on the unitary authority of the pope in Rome. They also promoted respect for the liturgical practices of the church, and they urged intellectual humility in the face of canon law and the church's traditional teachings. From their privileged position at Europe's royal courts, where they served as confessors to kings, and as leaders of hundreds of secondary schools founded to train the minds of Christian youth, the Jesuits' influence over the theory and practice of Catholicism was unsurpassed in the two centuries that followed the Reformation.[82]

Jansenists, named for the Flemish bishop Cornelius Jansenius whose *Augustinus* of 1640 served as the movement's founding document, held to the essentially Augustinian tenets that God's will is inscrutable, that fallen man can behave righteously only with the assistance of grace, and that the church must nurture a Scripture-based spirituality.[83] From an orthodox point of view such beliefs bordered on the heretical, and the Jansenists' apparent affinities with Huguenots made them a persecuted minority in France for much of the eighteenth century.[84] In 1713 the papal bull (or decree) *Unigenitus* condemned more than a hundred Jansenist propositions as unorthodox, and the bull provided the grounds for discriminatory treatment of Jansenists for decades to come. The bishop of Mende, for one, insisted that emphasis on Augustinian precepts implied no association with Calvinists or any other heretical sect, but royal administrators committed to confessional uniformity remained unconvinced.[85]

Adding to suspicions was the Jansenists' uncompromising assault on superstitions, spurious legends, and textual inaccuracies that affected traditional Catholic worship. Jansenist scholars translated the books of the Bible into the vernacular. They drew from Greek and Hebrew versions of Scripture as well as the authorized Latin Vulgate. They discouraged the celebration of apocryphal saints and other observances that encouraged superstitious thinking. They sought to promote a "Christo-centric piety" that would make the Mass more meaningful for the majority of parishioners who understood no Latin. This reformist impulse eventually produced revised missals (which prescribed the form of the Mass) and breviaries (texts used in conjunction with the Mass) that also removed accretions in the liturgy.[86]

The dissemination of the Jansenist-inspired breviary of Paris, revised in 1736, had drawn the bishop of Mende into public debate only months before the beast's rampage began. Composed by several Jansenist clerics on the orders of the orthodox but chronically inattentive archbishop of Paris, the breviary built on Jansenist liturgical reforms implemented in other dioceses over previous decades. The breviary excised many references to canon law, incorporated hymns to "sustain attention," reduced the number of feast days devoted to the saints, and highlighted biblical verses at the expense of other authorities. Jansenism would fall under new suspicions in the 1730s because of the distinctive emotional "enthusiasm" of some of its devotees, but the Paris breviary nevertheless met with unqualified success. Slowly but surely, the Jansenist model outstripped that of Rome, and by 1770 roughly half of all French dioceses had adopted a version of the Paris breviary.[87] Among the clerics who boldly rode this wave of reform was Choiseul-Beaupré, who adopted a version of the Paris breviary for his diocese of Mende in December of 1763.

The rhetoric of the 1764 *mandement* on the beast struck several chords at once and it undoubtedly transmitted multiple meanings to its audience. Natural "prodigies" had been interpreted as signs of divine wrath since the Middle Ages.[88] Without meaning to do so, the bishop may have even reinforced suspicions among the local populace that the beast was a werewolf. After all, earlier Christian critics of "demonological" thinking had refuted the alleged satanic sources of lycanthropy by explaining werewolves' depredations as a form of divine punishment.[89] Whatever interpretations others might have placed upon his *mandement,* however, the text clearly reflected the bishop's advocacy for the Jansenist cause. The emergency in the Gévaudan provided the occasion to implement a public form of "continual prayer" called for in the Jansenist breviary of 1763.[90] When he wrote that "charity for our brothers" must be the sole motivation guiding the prayers of the frightened populace, he echoed the Jansenist precept—condemned in *Unigenitus*—that only those works proceeding from charity and love of God earned divine approval.[91] When he used the opportunity of the beast's violence to warn the young against sexual temptation, he launched an Augustinian attack on the dreaded "concupiscence" that signaled an absence of grace and charity.[92] The bishop also overtly joined the Jansenist assault on superstition. He condemned the "abuse of sacraments" (the wanton deployment of holy water) to which some parishes apparently resorted in their efforts to ward off the seemingly magical beast, and he scoffed at the "fabulous stories" that the beast was invulnerable to "fire and lead." Most important, when the bishop represented the depredations of the beast as the execution of a "death sentence" handed down by God, and when he urged his flock to seek God's mercy through heartfelt contrition, he showed his Jansenist understanding of the operations of grace.[93]

The timing of the crisis in the Gévaudan would only have reinforced the bishop's disposition toward providential interpretation, for the previous months had witnessed the crescendo of the decades-long contest between Jansenists and the Jesuit order. Tensions had been rising since the 1730s, and the conflict escalated in the 1750s when orthodox clergy led by the archbishop of Paris worked to deny the last rites to good Catholics who could not prove their repudiation of Jansenist "heresies." Jansenist sympathizers reacted to this new assault by mounting a propaganda campaign against the alleged political meddling of the Jesuit order. From their powerful bastion within the *parlement* of Paris, Jansenists deployed the tried and true tactic of judicial obstructionism, and they managed to secure a toehold at the royal court. There the defenders of Jansenism exerted their full persuasive powers over ministers on the royal council (including the bishop's cousin, Choiseul). Following the lead of propagandists, some argued that the frightening attempt on the king's life by the regicide Robert-François Damiens in 1757 could be traced to devious Jesuits serving their true master in Rome.[94] With the help of their supporters in the French magistracy, whose Gallican patriotism had long encouraged opposition to the "Romanist" Jesuits, the Jansenists ultimately convinced a reluctant Louis XV to expel the Jesuit order by royal edict. This climactic event in the long and smoldering conflict occurred in November 1764—just one month before Choiseul-Beaupré's momentous *mandement*.

In the conduct of his pastoral duties at the end of the year, the bishop would hardly have been able to pull his mind away from the great quarrel that had occupied the entire Catholic community for decades. Just days before Choiseul-Beaupré published his *mandement,* Jesuit supporters in nearby Alais had rioted and attempted to set fire to a convent, crying "long live the Jesuits and take the Jansenists to the devil."[95] By coincidence, only one week after publication of the *mandement,* the pope issued a new bull defending the "pious and holy" Society of Jesus against attacks leveled at it by the monarchs of Europe. The counter-attacking leaders of the Jesuits, meanwhile, were said to be pressing the pope to render the bull *Unigenitus* a binding "rule of faith."[96]

With emotions at fever pitch, the opportunity to articulate a robust Jansenist explanation for the coming of the beast, which struck the land "as if by a miracle," would have been difficult to resist. Just as heightened scientific attention to the character of the "monstrous" had elicited abundant commentary on species and the nature of God's creation, so heated disputes over the mysteries of grace invited a distinctly Jansenist reflection on the limits of human autonomy and the nature of divine influence in worldly affairs. The wider context in which the bishop deployed his Jansenist reasoning in the Gévaudan surely explains why the editors of the prominent Jansenist publication *Nouvelles Ecclésiastiques* suddenly gave critical attention, in March of

1765, to Choiseul-Beaupré's "excellent" 1761 treatise on the dogma of grace, as well as his earlier *mandement* of 1763.[97]

The pitched battle between Jansenists and Jesuits provides the essential ideological framing for the *mandement* of 31 December 1764, but the bishop's readiness to see the hand of God behind the Gévaudan's unfolding tragedy may also have reflected other religious circumstances specific to his region. For many years Languedoc had been a site of particularly intense religious conflict, its territory thick with zealotry. The Gévaudan was widely known as a "land of priests," and the life of the whole province of Languedoc had been shaped since the previous century by the presence of a large Protestant minority.[98] The Camisards of the Cévennes, moved by their own brand of prophetic spirituality intensified through the experience of persecution under Louis XIV in the 1680s and 1690s, had offered stern military resistance to the crown in the first decade of the eighteenth century. Using to their advantage the inaccessibility of the landscape, they harassed and defeated royal troops regularly between 1702 and 1704 and intermittently thereafter until the final years of Louis XIV's life. Through their intractable rebelliousness and their success in eluding the determined forces of the crown, they raised the specter of a hidden and untameable enemy, of which the beast of the Gévaudan would later provide unwelcome reminders. The closing of the Seven Years' War happened to bring to a head the animosities that had roiled relations between Catholics and Huguenots ever since the Camisard revolt, and the bishop of Mende would have been sensitized to the new spiritual uncertainties released by the events of the early 1760s.

"Spasmodic hostility" had marked private relations between Catholics and Protestants since the 1680s, but in the eighteenth century Protestants endured systematic discrimination, especially at the hands of government officials connected to Versailles.[99] Evidence of tension abounds. By order of the intendant of Languedoc, after 1729 all town and village consuls had been required to send to Montpellier in April of each year a list of the newborn Protestant children of their localities to better enforce their required attendance at Mass and Sunday instructions. Saint-Priest continued to apply this rule rigorously through the middle 1760s.[100] In the early 1750s, troops had been used to "rehabilitate" Protestants in and around Nîmes, after Calvinist pastors there provoked Catholic bishops by presiding openly over baptisms and marriages.[101] The minister Saint-Florentin, whose duties as secretary of state included the policing of all French Protestants, communicated regularly with the intendant of Languedoc about suspicious assemblies and illegal proselytizing, as when he urgently instructed Saint-Priest in early 1764 to "publicly burn" the furnishings of a barn used as a Protestant meeting house near Puylaurens.[102] A year later Saint-Priest expressed his own concern that Protestant assemblies were becoming "more frequent and numerous by the day," including one gathering at Chambon that had attracted "more than six thousand persons."[103]

In the early fall of 1765 this longstanding distrust led to the surprising arrest of an obscure Protestant cloth dyer named Bossignac. The man came under suspicion in October when he ordered the forging of three hundred lances at a smithy in Castres, to the west of the Gévaudan. The blacksmith, aware of Bossignac's reputation as a "zealous Protestant," promptly reported him to the local police. A panel of judges soon interrogated the suspect to find if he acted in league with "Protestant rebels" determined to "defend their liberty."[104] After the dust had settled and Saint-Priest had heard all relevant evidence, he was able to report to Saint-Florentin that, contrary to the blacksmith's fears, Bossignac had ordered his lances not as part of some dark conspiracy to launch a new Protestant rebellion, but only to lay an elaborate trap for "the wild beast that has ravaged the Gévaudan." (Bossignac had heard the troubling news, as he noted in a letter to Lafont in March, that "guns cannot harm it.")[105]

Bossignac's misadventure notwithstanding, official attitudes toward Protestants gradually loosened in the first part of the 1760s, and developments in the south forced the change. During the Seven Years' War royal administrators had feared that French Calvinists might work in league with the English navy to facilitate an invasion of the French southwest.[106] The grand failure of William Pitt's "secret expedition" of 1757 and the patriotism displayed during the assault by Protestants on the Atlantic coast softened government attitudes. Many became persuaded that it made good strategic sense to extend toleration toward moderate Huguenots while easing the state's most repressive measures against its religious dissidents. The military commandant of Languedoc, for example, discontinued the policy of using troops to break up gatherings of Huguenots.[107] Saint-Priest dismissed the case against Bossignac in part because he had learned that the Protestants of his community had planned nothing more dangerous than to "assemble to pray and hear sermons."[108] Meanwhile, the aftermath of the famous Calas affair (1761–1765), in which Jean Calas, a Protestant merchant of Toulouse, had been wrongly and notoriously convicted and executed for the murder of his allegedly Catholic-leaning son, encouraged officials to adopt a more tolerant posture toward Protestants throughout the French realm.[109]

It seems likely that the move to ease restrictions on Protestant assembly and worship after 1763 would have increased the sense of apocalyptic expectancy with which the bishop of Mende greeted the phenomenon of the beast. His reminder of God's willingness *"to take revenge on the children for the iniquities of the fathers, down to the third or fourth generation"* may even have reflected the long shadow cast by the troubles in the Cévennes earlier in the century.[110] Although the Protestant population in the areas most affected by the beast's ravages remained small, one can assume that the bishop worried about the influence of dissenters.[111] The suspicion that Protestants worked secretly toward nefarious ends in the region remained powerful enough in the summer of 1765 that Saint-Priest thought it necessary to investigate a strange allegation sent in from the curé of Vialas, to the southeast of Mende near the mountains of the Cévennes. The curé claimed that Protestants were burying unbaptized babies and desecrating the sacrament of baptism by substituting white wine for holy water.[112]

Choiseul-Beaupré was a Jansenist and Gallicanist whose breviary stressed the health and integrity of the church universal, and who counseled habitual prayer for the monarch. As such he almost surely shared the conservative political outlook of the Jansenist-leaning magistrates of the *parlement* of Toulouse who had first convicted Calas.[113] The Protestants of La Rochelle may have demonstrated their loyalty to the crown during the war, but the restive dissidents of Languedoc had a history that was hard to forget. For the bishop, the potential relaxation of Catholic vigilance would have represented yet another ill-timed threat to the moral stability of the community. Although no one in France could take seriously the *London Chronicle*'s report that the beast was an allegorical fiction invented by a "malignant Jesuit" to provide a pretext for renewed persecution of Protestants, Choiseul-Beaupré almost certainly hoped that the beast's defeat would trigger the return of the proper Catholic spirituality he craved for his suffering diocese.[114]

How the residents of the Gévaudan interpreted the stark language and censorious tone of the bishop's *mandement* is difficult if not impossible to gauge, given the low level of literacy in the region and the fact that the message from Mende would have been mediated by the local curés who spoke the patois of the peasantry. The document's printing and distribution throughout the diocese insured that it became a central point of reference, however, and we know that in and around the capital of the Gévaudan the bishop's declaration met with great acclaim. The *Courrier d'Avignon* shared with its readers a report sent from a local correspondent on 9 January: "Our bishop, vividly and pastorally sensitive to the evils that this terrible animal has visited on his flock, has released a *mandement* ordering public prayers, and last Sunday, on the sixth of this month, the Holy Sacrament was displayed in the Cathedral Church. The people, matching the zeal of their pastor, came to the Church in great numbers: all day the Church remained full, and when [he] gave the benediction the Church, vast as it is, did not come close to containing the many faithful who had flocked there. A large crowd, nearly the greatest number, was forced to remain outdoors."[115] Desperate for relief from their plight, the people of the Gévaudan seem to have been moved by their bishop's forceful call for charity and repentance. Not for the last time, they sought divine assistance in their fight against a mysterious enemy.

Belief in witches, werewolves, and enchanted creatures filled the eighteenth-century French countryside, and popular superstitions contributed to the aura of fear and fascination that surrounded the exploits of the beast of the Gévaudan. Review of the cultural, intellectual, and religious milieu prevailing in France at mid-century shows, however, that the various myths of the beast that blossomed in late 1764 took root in exceptionally fertile soil. The questions that preoccupied scientists and informed the tastes of a growing audience of educated readers after about 1750 could be profitably directed toward the wilds of the Gévaudan. Rumors about the beast and its habits also helped satiate a national appetite for the exotic. And the religious atmosphere of the early 1760s transformed the beast's violent disruption of daily life into a spiritually charged and possibly providential event. In an age defined by the proliferation of adventurous and boundary-testing ideas, readers and observers from all walks of life showed a willingness to contemplate a "beast of the Gévaudan" that transcended the familiar forms of nature. The beast aroused sustained fascination because its actions seemed to signal the presence of a mysterious being: a witch, an agent of divine justice, an unknown hybrid, a werewolf, a creature from Africa, a wolf of extraordinary type. In the Gévaudan, tragic events provided sufficient fodder for continuing speculation about strange monsters through the end of December 1764. By the time of the feast of the Epiphany on 6 January 1765 many thousands, both in the afflicted region and beyond, looked with dread upon the untold horrors the new year might bring.

Having examined the rich and expectant context in which the beast announced its presence, I turn in Chapter 3 to the motives and intentions of several key players whose actions did much to generate the imaginative groundswell of interest in the monsters of the Gévaudan. The beast's victims, pitiful as they were, would not by themselves have attracted the intense interest devoted to this story over the course of many months. Other human factors stoked the flames of public curiosity and bolstered belief in the extraordinary qualities of the terrible animal that prowled the southern hills. Chief among these factors were the subtle imperatives of noble honor and the opportunism displayed by hungry journalists.

3

Digesting Defeat

France's doomed imperial conflict with Britain and Prussia in the late 1750s and early 1760s, long known to Americans as the French and Indian War, made a greater impact on French society than any other event of the middle decades of the eighteenth century. No corner of French territory and no aspect of French life went untouched in the aftermath of the Seven Years' War, and its effects were visible even in the faraway Gévaudan. The European theater of war between 1756 and 1763 never widened to include the remote Massif Central, but the war cast its shadow on the story of the beast in ways large and small.

By the end of the war France lost most of its overseas empire in its settlement with the British, joined Austria in accepting Prussia's control over Silesia, and emerged from the conflict with a national debt nearly doubled in size. The country's rapidly declining fortunes created a "crisis of confidence" that lingered for years.[1] Resentment over the costs of the war complicated the monarchy's own efforts at reform, and the crown's relations with the magistrates of the *parlements,* who repeatedly contested fiscal innovations, became tense and embittered. In the military arena, the war minister Etienne-François, duc de Choiseul initiated a new era of reform aimed at reducing costs, thinning the officer ranks, and increasing discipline. At court, Louis

XV, who had already endured an assassination attempt, conspiracy, and the prospect of rebellion in the late 1750s, found that his military misadventure had failed to endear him to a weary populace. The grand fireworks staged in celebration of the Treaty of Paris in June of 1763 belied the popular mood of dissatisfaction with king and crown. Already in February of that year, the perversely timed erection of a new equestrian statue of Louis XV opposite the Tuileries palace (in the future Place de la Concorde) provided the occasion for "scandalous speech" that mocked the failures of the king. Several malcontents, overheard by royal spies, paid for their impudence with time in the Bastille.[2]

In this atmosphere of national embarrassment, popular resentment, and

"Equestrian Statue of Louis the well Beloved." The erection of this new equestrian statue opposite the Tuileries gardens on 14 February 1763 failed to distract Parisians from the monarchy's embarrassing failure in the Seven Years' War. *Bibliothèque Nationale de France, Qb 301–309, collection Hennin*

rising political tension, it was perhaps inevitable that interested observers would forge associations between the phenomenon of the beast of the Gévaudan and the recent trauma of war. The Parisian Magné de Marolles, whose records mapping his own fascination with the beast constitute our single best source for gauging the impact of news coming from the Gévaudan, wondered if the appearance of man-eating wolves in southern France might be attributable to the cadaver-producing clashes of the late war. Having acquired the taste for human flesh on deserted battlefields, wolves would have been compelled to go off in search of new prey. With the war ended and dead bodies less abundant, he speculated, perhaps the wolves themselves had "declared war on the human species."[3] Other observers also used the vocabulary of armed conflict. The *Courrier d'Avignon* referred to the Gévaudan as a singular "theater of war" in February of 1765 (though it reported a welcome "suspension of hostilities" between man and beast in March).[4] After one victim had successfully fended off an attack by the beast in December of 1764, the dragoon captain Duhamel reported to the military commandant Moncan that he had carefully surveyed the "field of battle" to examine clues of the enemy's presence.[5]

Memories of the Seven Years' War pervaded the atmosphere of anxiety in which the assaults of the beast and hunters' inability to halt the animal's attacks were perceived, interpreted, and reported. The experience of the Seven Years' War figured in the phenomenon of the beast as more than mere backdrop, however. The war, or to be more precise, the sense of loss that took hold of those engaged by the war, proved instrumental in the making of the beast of the Gévaudan in the critical early months of the story. The beast's presence responded to cravings otherwise sated only by war itself.

By late 1764 journalists seized the opportunity to sensationalize the events in the Gévaudan in order to compensate for the disappointing absence of war-related drama, news of which had filled their pages for years. To fix readers' attention, editors (especially at the *Courrier d'Avignon*) highlighted the most spectacular accounts of the beast's activities, thus promoting and continually embellishing an entertaining myth while also creating a gripping news story with international appeal. Journalists were not the only ones who used the story of the beast to support their own ends. Actual veterans of the Seven Years' War—most notably, the huntsmen Duhamel and Morangiès—tried to seize opportunities of their own. Consistent with their status as noble officers, they viewed the protracted hunt for the beast, at least in part, as a test of their own mettle and as an opportunity to assert their honor. The humiliations of the recent war had increased their sensitivity to matters of reputation and made them eager to defeat a newly anointed enemy. Particularly in the case of Duhamel, however, a driving desire for conquest and renown brought exaggerated imaginings (and reports) of the enemy's prowess.

These two powerful forces—journalistic opportunism and injured aristocratic pride—converged notably in early February of 1765, when Duhamel staged a massive hunt of unprecedented scale. The event would mark the beast's most stunning success to date and it proved to be Duhamel's most dramatic setback. Thanks to rapidly spreading news reports and Duhamel's profuse regret over his unfulfilled quest, the hunts of early February also secured the beast's status as an enemy worthy of monstrous legend.

Making News

In his "Recapitulation of the Principal Events of the Year 1764," an expansive summary of recent events with which he opened the year 1765, the editor of the *Courrier d'Avignon,* François Morénas, openly lamented the relative "calm" that had marked the previous two years.[6] "Peace, which is so productive of lasting benefits, is hardly productive of notable occurrences. The years that unfurl in the midst [of peace] are like those peaceful rivers that flow over undisturbed terrain and produce only uniform effects." Lacking the experience of those "extraordinary happenings" that "strike the mind and the senses," the passing of tranquil time turns up only "monotonous objects" that share nothing in common with the "picturesque."

Morénas proceeded to contrast the peaceful but uninteresting conditions of 1764 with those prevailing in times of war. "Pernicious as it is," he acknowledged, war offered "spectacles that arouse and attach [one's] curiosity." Readers struggled to tear their eyes away, for "the bloodier and more tragic" the events, the more "interesting" they proved to be. "[The] counting of the dead, wounded, and imprisoned, . . . the calamities at a besieged garrison town, the dreadful effects produced by the artillery, . . . [These] catastrophes, so terrible for those who witness them, and even more so for the victims, when reported by a gazette, attract many more readers and inspire much more vivid attention" than do dry accounts of government regulations or plans for reform.

Wars were good for the news business. "The popularity enjoyed by gazettes, so long as [wars] last, and the disregard into which they fall, when they end, provide sure proof of this."

These candid remarks, and the conversational essay from which they emerged, provide important clues to the journalistic environment that greeted news of the beast of the Gévaudan in late 1764. They also reflect the engaging and ingratiating style that allowed François Morénas to become one of the most successful editors working in French-language journalism in the middle of the eighteenth century. A brief look back at his career before the mid-1760s suggests that Morénas was just the person—and that the beast's ravages constituted the ideal story of the moment—to create a sudden media sensation that quickly radiated northward from Avignon and the anxious communities of the remote Gévaudan.

Morénas, in partnership first with François Girard and then with the well-heeled publisher Charles Giroud, had founded the *Courrier* in 1733, and from the beginning the paper's success had been a function of historical circumstance. Apprenticed as a notary in Avignon, the young Morénas had also studied law, joined the army, and even entered a monastic community before discovering his talents as a writer and publicist. A restless energy and his instinct to sample widely from life's offerings had also conditioned his various romantic entanglements, which in turn affected the trajectory of his professional life. Married twice within a span of seven months in 1727, he later became embroiled in a sex scandal that prompted his flight from the authorities of Avignon in late 1742. He returned to the city the following spring on hearing of the death of his aggrieved wife. Within four months of that pivotal event, Morénas married his pregnant mistress. The suspiciously convenient timing of his wife's passing meant that he had to endure a canonical inquest before his name, and career, could be rehabilitated.[7]

As this domestic crisis resolved itself, Morénas also found that his erstwhile partner Giroud had sued for breach of contract and successfully expropriated Morénas's ownership interest in the *Courrier*. With mouths to feed, Morénas subsequently fell back on his talents as a writer, his wide network of personal contacts, and his seemingly intuitive understanding of the burgeoning reading market for news and information, a market whose most explosive period of growth paralleled his own passage into mature adulthood.[8] From 1744 to 1749, Morénas wrote and co-published several short-lived periodicals devoted to politics and diplomatic news. Although these texts had limited distribution because of Giroud's legal monopoly on publishing in Avignon, with their production Morénas resuscitated his reputation as an inventive writer and thus set the stage for a return to his true publishing home.

Upon his death in 1746, Charles Giroud was succeeded at the helm of the *Courrier* by his half-brother and longtime collaborator, Alexandre. This event removed one important obstacle to a happy reconciliation with Morénas, but economic necessity played the larger role in bringing the estranged partner back to the site of his most valuable creation. With the *Courrier* facing declining revenues in the wake of another war (the War of the Austrian Succession, 1740–1748), and with the talented Morénas still struggling to make ends meet in a tightly controlled market, the former collaborators saw mutual benefit in burying the hatchet. The terms of the partnership changed; Morénas became a salaried employee of Alexandre Giroud, charged with managing day-to-day operations and providing copy for the paper. But the new partnership, formalized in early 1750, proved fruitful. The next decade saw steadily rising subscription numbers and a more prominent profile for Avignon's only homegrown news journal.

Throughout these tumultuous first decades of Morénas's publishing career, he absorbed two vital lessons about the market in news and information: first, war sells, and second, readers are entertained by vivid and unexpected detail. The timing of the *Courrier's* founding had proven quite fortuitous. Just one month after the first issue rolled off the presses in January 1733, Europe plunged into the War of the Polish Succession (1733–1738). Largely due to the drama of the war, the *Courrier* enjoyed immediate success. Records from the period are ambiguous, but it would seem that the *Courrier's* French sales fell somewhere between 1,000 and 2,000 copies per issue at the height of the war, placing it well ahead of other popular "foreign" gazettes such as the *Gazette d'Amsterdam,* which never topped 1,000 in sales until the late 1750s. Robust sales convinced Charles Giroud to become the *Courrier's* permanent publisher, while surging demand also prompted Morénas to switch from a weekly to a twice-weekly format by November 1733.[9]

What war giveth, peace taketh away, and the *Courrier's* fortunes over the next thirty years followed the unpredictable rhythms of European armed conflict. In 1740, between wars, the *Courrier's* circulation dropped to 500 or fewer copies per issue. By 1747, when hostilities raged in Italy, the Netherlands, and elsewhere, the figures had climbed dramatically higher, with nearly 3,000 copies sold. (France's officially sanctioned *Gazette,* by contrast, sold between

7,000 and 8,000 copies in 1749.) The pattern repeated itself in the next decade. In 1750, two years after the conclusion of the War of the Austrian Succession, the *Courrier* struggled to boost its circulation out of the hundreds. Then the greatest of all eighteenth-century wars before 1792, the Seven Years' War, pushed the *Courrier*'s circulation figures to an all-time high at the end of the 1750s. By 1758 the *Courrier* may have had as many as 9,000 subscribers, which would have placed it second only to the *Gazette de France* among French-language journals trafficking in general news.[10]

When the sixty-two-year-old Morénas discussed in his "Recapitulation" of 1 January 1765 the rising and falling fashion for gazettes and the welcome stimulant that war provided, he obviously spoke from long personal experience. Experience had also taught him, however, that editors and publicists could compensate for the absence of war news by providing the details of strange events and unusual occurrences from everyday life, especially if they were described with color and a gripping style that invited readers' reflection. News of this sort had once been communicated on broadsheets sold in the streets and throughout the countryside by itinerant peddlers. The *colporteur,* named for the bag of goods that hung from the seller's neck, distributed pamphlets, songbooks, engravings, and other cheaply produced ephemeral literature, some of which recycled well-known folk tales with broad popular appeal, and some of which relayed news of strange phenomena from the contemporary world.[11]

Newspaper editors devoted most of their precious type-space to updates from the capitals and courts of Europe. News relating the negotiation of treaties, visits by foreign dignitaries, as well as the movements of kings, ministers, and prominent aristocrats dominated. These accounts were presented as a series of dry first-person reports ostensibly conveyed from contacts on the scene, and they offered no commentary worthy of the name. As the format of the general news weekly matured over time, however, the editors of the most sought-after journals also found ways to mix in reports of compelling events that took place outside the rarefied atmosphere of governments and social elites. By the middle of the eighteenth century it was common to find on the pages of gazettes news about terrible floods, centennial birthdays, crimes or suicides, and the birth of the odd two-headed calf. These items were sparse—some issues featured none at all—and their presentation also usually lacked context and analysis. The very singularity of the events meant that editors struggled to find a strategy for making good use of them. At first unsure of their place and importance, they inserted them willy-nilly in between the dispatches sent from Vienna, London, and Berlin. The *Gazette d'Amsterdam* seems to have been the first paper, in 1734, to create a distinct rubric for these news items. The editors grouped them together at the end of each issue, thus segregating them from political and diplomatic news while also giving formal expression to their growing profile as a news commodity of interest.[12]

In the nineteenth century the French would come to refer to this form of news item as a *fait divers,* that is, the relation of a bizarre episode from everyday life that elicited wonder, fear, or curiosity on the part of the appreciative reader.[13] In eighteenth-century France, however, the precursors of the *fait divers* had a poorly defined status in the hierarchy of journalistic coverage. Throughout much of its publication history, for example, the *Gazette de France,* a semi-official organ of the French government that had a monopoly on news reporting within French borders, tended to ignore *faits divers* altogether. The hints of disruption arising from unexpected incidents may have posed too great a threat to the orderly narratives favored by authorities whose power theoretically lay beyond the vagaries of contingency.[14] The *Gazette's* wary conservatism meant that, for French readers, the human interest news brief came to be associated with the "foreign" press located on the periphery of France—the *Gazette de Leyde,* the *Gazette d'Amsterdam,* the *Courrier d'Avignon,* and a few others. François Morénas had a special talent for the emerging genre.

Morénas's jack-of-all-trades background and sensibility had been evident at the founding of the *Courrier* in 1733, for he resisted the existing typology that classified periodicals either as "political" newssheets or as publications devoted to a single subject, like literature or law. The subtitle of the *Courrier's* inaugural issue announced the editor's intention to provide commentary on all manner of news—political, literary, historical, philosophical.[15] As war increased readers' demand for political news, Morénas happily adjusted to the market and acknowledged the journal's change of direction in 1734, but he also restated his intention to enliven the journal when necessary. He pledged to offer "whatever I can [find] to compensate for the sterility of the news" in tedious times.[16] (Decades later he would use startlingly similar language to explain readers' fascination for the beast of the Gévaudan.)[17]

Morénas would demonstrate this instinct to entice and entertain time and again in his career, but particularly after his return to the management of the *Courrier* in 1750. Throughout the decade of the 1750s Morénas actually supplemented his income from the *Courrier* by supplying material to *colporteurs*. He composed "news" items in the form of broadsheets that detailed shocking murders, sensational trials, and colorful anecdotes concerning the lofty and powerful.[18] Morénas's attraction to gripping detail and his strong will to entertain also informed the content of the *Courrier* itself. After the Lisbon earthquake struck in 1755, the *Courrier* devoted at least fifty stories to the tragedy over the course of a year. Rather than rest content with the unadorned recitations that characterized most coverage of the event, Morénas drew readers into the experience with vivid narrative and emotive language designed to elicit sympathy for the victims of the "horrifying spectacle." Some of these unfortunates, on seeing the river Tagus overspill its banks on either side, "feared that they might be swallowed at any moment by a sudden opening in the earth." The *Courrier* also sought out an array of eyewitness accounts of the devastation.[19] Throughout the 1750s, Morénas's distinctive journalism, characterized by his use of animated language, a willingness to integrate accounts of the unusual to spice up the proceedings, and a narrative style that allowed him to insinuate himself into the reader's confidence, enabled the *Courrier* to compensate for the absence of war-related news.

Even amid the great prosperity brought by the windfall of the Seven Years' War, however, the directors of the *Courrier* could feel the economic ground shifting beneath their feet as the 1750s gave way to the 1760s. Until 1759, the *Courrier* had enjoyed an enviable set of competitive advantages in addition to the singular talents of Morénas. Like all "foreign" newspapers in France, the *Courrier* benefited from the perception that it operated in relative freedom from state censorship. All readers understood that the *Gazette de France*, though valuable in providing a representation of the official perspective on political events, contained silences and rhetorical sleights of hand that made its accounts partly suspect. Foreign papers could report on French domestic politics more freely, since French kings had no power to revoke their right to publish. The expectation of imported candor explains much of the papers' appeal to readers inside French borders. In truth, the *Courrier* exploited its legal freedoms less aggressively than its counterparts in Germany and the Netherlands, but it nevertheless benefited from the special cachet enjoyed by all newspapers produced outside of France. François Dominique de Reynaud, comte de Montlosier, found the *Gazette de France* stultifying, but in his memoirs he wistfully recalled the time "when we began to receive in our province

[Auvergne] a rather more interesting journal called the *Courrier d'Avignon*."
He greeted the arrival of this new publication "as a blessing."[20]

The *Courrier*'s more meaningful competitive advantages derived from the
ad hoc nature of legal privilege under the *ancien régime*. In 1740, with circulation in the doldrums, the Girouds had had the foresight to negotiate a lucra-
tive deal with the tax farmers of the so-called General Farm *(Ferme Générale)*,
who subcontracted from the crown the right to handle postal traffic in French
territory. In exchange for a lump sum paid up front each year, Morénas and
the Girouds gained the right to deliver the *Courrier* to subscribers in southern
France essentially free of postage costs. The benefits were felt immediately.
Whereas an annual French subscription to the *Gazette d'Amsterdam* ran to 104
livres, partly because of the expenses of postage, a subscription to the *Courrier*
sold for 24 livres in the 1740s (and its price would soon move lower). The
Courrier was the first European newspaper to strike such a deal with agents of
the French government, and in 1750 it saw its privilege extended from the
southern provinces to the entirety of the French realm.[21] Complaints from
provincial publishers who were authorized to sell reprints of the *Gazette de
France* suggest that, after 1750, the French journal and its circuits of distribution felt the pinch of competition from the rising star of the papal domin-
ions.[22]

In 1759, however, everything changed. After being prompted by an enter-
prising publisher, Choiseul, who then headed the ministry of foreign affairs,
decided to loosen the tight controls restricting access to most foreign journals
in France. Formerly prohibited journals such as the *Gazette de Leyde* and the
Gazette de Cologne suddenly found the doors to the French market thrown
open to them. Moreover, all publishers of foreign journals (and their readers) could now take advantage of a newly designed relay network that had
multiple provincial cities joining Paris as points of distribution for the newspapers. Best of all, according to terms agreed upon in 1760, the papers would
now benefit from the precedent established by the *Courrier d'Avignon* in 1740.
They, too, would be delivered to their subscribers free of postage.[23]

Choiseul had his own reasons for implementing these reforms. In the late
1750s, as French armies floundered badly in the field and the Jansenist-Jesuit
conflict continued on its tortuous path, he must have hoped that the seductive power of the profitable French market would serve to restrain the editorial liberties for which the newspapers on France's northern periphery were

known. (Choiseul's desire to control press coverage would lead him, in 1761, to bring the *Gazette de France* under his ministry's watchful eye.) Whatever his motives, in one bold stroke Choiseul had transformed the market for news and information in Louis XV's France. Subscription costs plummeted (down to 36 livres for the *Gazette d'Amsterdam*), and readers across the country had new riches to choose from. As a leading historian of French journalism in the eighteenth century has put it, the "great postal reform" of the 1750s proved to be a "decisive turn" in the history of newspaper publishing. The entire French realm now comprised a "media-saturated" space in which it became possible to imagine the formation, and shaping, of "national opinion."[24] Publishers, meanwhile, found themselves navigating an extremely crowded newspaper market. The *Courrier,* though it still enjoyed relatively generous postal rates because of its ongoing contract with the General Farm, had lost its peculiarly advantaged position as a privileged outsider looking in. As the Seven Years' War drew to a close in 1762 and 1763, Giroud and Morénas knew that they faced a potentially turbulent period of transition.

Even before the story of the beast of the Gévaudan emerged to become the unquestioned focus of its nonpolitical news coverage, the content of the *Courrier* in the immediate postwar months reflected Morénas's guiding strategy of engaging his readers by entertaining and diverting as well as informing. Consider the kinds of reports that appeared in the weeks before the beast showed up in print in late fall of 1764. In September readers heard news of a storm in Rouen so terrible that "even the aged, with memories stretching far back into olden times, were astonished" by the experience of it. Windows had been ripped from their frames and vegetable gardens pounded by hail, some of it "the size of a pigeon egg." In Saint-Germain-en-Laye, an octogenarian couple renewed their wedding vows on their fiftieth anniversary, hosting "a magnificent meal with forty-five place settings." In stark contrast to that heartwarming scene of plenty, Caen had apparently been beset by a wave of violent popular riots, occasioned by the controversial "exportation of grain."

Those drawn to the revelations of natural history also found items of interest in the pages of the *Courrier.* In addition to telling of the "great advantages" expected to result from the South American voyages of the famed former soldier and navigator Louis Antoine de Bougainville, the *Courrier* reported on the dubious alchemical experiments of an anonymous "young Gentleman" of London who claimed to have turned copper into gold. The paper also relayed news of a notable public lecture that took place at the French

Academy of Sciences in Paris. The lecture, on the subject of "the philosophical and anatomical history of dwarfs," had been capped off by a presentation of a startling wax likeness of the dwarf Bébé, replete with the deceased's costume and "his own hair." (This was the same diminutive curiosity whose remains would later be collected by the minister Saint-Florentin.)[25]

None of these events figured in Morénas's "Recapitulation" of the year 1764, however. At the dawn of the new year, and even before hearing word of the bishop of Mende's just-issued *mandement,* the director of the *Courrier* recognized that one domestic French story invited the kind of attention devoted to the political vicissitudes of the major European states.

> Finally, in a clime far removed from Africa, and all other countries known for producing terrible animals, as well as the menageries that contain them, in a canton of Languedoc, a ferocious beast of unknown type, coming from who knows where, . . . attacks the human species, killing individuals, drinking their blood, feasting on their flesh, and multiplying its carnage from day to day . . . [The] hunters who are in pursuit have neither been able to stop it, because it is more agile than they, nor lure it into their traps, because it surpasses them in cunning, nor engage in combat when it presents itself to them, because its terrifying appearance weakens their courage, disturbs their vision, sets their hands shaking, and neutralizes their skill. They fire badly, missing because of their fear of missing and of the punishment that may ensue.[26]

For a journalist confronting a barren postwar landscape, and scrambling to secure his paper's share of a national but increasingly volatile market, the ongoing mystery in the Gévaudan must have appeared as a godsend. Not only could the drama be portrayed as a form of "combat," but the carnage was also conveniently "bloodier and more tragic" (and therefore more "interesting") than egg-sized hail, riots, dwarfs, or even the most upsetting political news. The *Courrier d'Avignon* of course had no proprietary control over the story of the beast of the Gévaudan; other papers, including even the *Gazette de France,* would pick up the trail and help draw attention to the beast's exploits. But the *Courrier* can be credited with both the first and last journalistic entries on the events, and in the thirteen months that ended in December of 1765, Morénas devoted no fewer than ninety-eight articles to the phenomenon—nearly two times the number written about the great Lisbon earthquake.[27] No other newspaper came close.

In its dedication to pathos, too, the *Courrier* had few rivals. Morénas collected his news from a wide network of contacts and informants. Some of them lived in the affected region, and others, particularly in Paris, drew on their own sources in Montpellier, Mende, Versailles, and elsewhere. Whatever the original source, Morénas asserted his right to modify or embellish the account he received, since he sometimes purchased the information he relayed and the local informant remained unidentified. The editor rarely missed an opportunity to personalize events that might otherwise seem pedestrian. A prime example appeared early in 1765, when a report from Mende depicted in suspenseful terms an attempted rescue of a child in distress. In the last week of December, in the woods by the village of Saint-Martin, the beast had "spied a young girl of twelve years, and prepared to throw itself on her. The poor child, having noticed [the attacker], ran toward her father who was nearby, crying 'Help me father, the Beast is here. Protect me.' The terrified father, having no weapon other than a large staff, ran to his daughter and picked her up by one arm while, with the other, he fended off the beast for at least a quarter of an hour." As fatigue set in and the beast failed to relent, however, it seemed that the father's efforts would be to "no avail." The beast "would have taken her away, if a group of horned cattle *(bêtes à cornes),* who had been grazing near the same woods, had not come to her aid." Confronting the one enemy that always gave it pause—horned livestock—the beast finally fled the scene. The father had relayed the details of this story to one M. de Courbières, a knight of the Order of Saint Louis and "first magistrate of our city."[28]

Seeing an opportunity in the stunned disbelief aroused by a gruesome horror story that would not end, Morénas published at least one or two articles per week from the vicinity of the Gévaudan throughout the month of January. More than any of the other editors who eventually picked up the story, moreover, Morénas freely tested the limits of credulity. When compelling personal narratives or news of combat were in short supply, he simply filled space with new descriptions of the creature's habits and characteristics, as relayed through alleged firsthand experiences with the beast. In a story from Marvejols that seemed to confirm the beast's ability to deflect lead shells, Morénas alluded once again to a feature that suggested the influence of the diabolical. "Yesterday, someone fired on it with his musket, but the shell only grazed the surface, leaving behind a tuft of fur that was striking for its great stench."[29] The overpowering odor of the beast would receive confirmation from multiple sources throughout the winter, including an additional *Cour-*

rier report about a dog that failed to attack the monster because of the "sensation" created by the "bad odor that the [beast] emits."[30]

In a story on the amazing rapidity with which the beast struck and made its escape, a correspondent from Mende noted that "the agility of the nefarious beast matches its cruelty. It covers approximately eight leagues [about twenty miles] in an hour, which is proven by the uproar it has caused in different places on the same day." The "cunning" animal showed as much talent in "avoiding those who search for it" as in "surprising those who hope to elude it."[31] This seemingly magical ability to vanish into thin air, only to reappear suddenly beside its next startled victim, also conjured thoughts of the supernatural. In the same article that introduced the detail about the beast's terrible odor, and in which the animal acquired at least one new likeness—"its cry is precisely that of a braying ass"—Morénas shared the outlook of some of the spooked locals around the town of Marvejols. "Many of our brave men have asserted that its gaze is more than one can bear; one of them, widely recognized for his valor, and who has seen [the beast] up close, says that if there were devils on the earth, he firmly believes that this ferocious animal would qualify as one."[32]

Evidence of uncommon qualities also filled a report filed from Mende on 18 January. "Three men who encountered [the beast] within the past few days at the Darissatis bridge in the parish of Laubies, . . . finding themselves unarmed except for the staff with bayonet that each of them carried, had to struggle at length before they could finally repel [the beast]." But though they felt fortunate to have escaped with their lives, the impression they carried away from the encounter only made them more frightened, for "they were never able to touch it." The animal's "agility and flexibility were so great that it avoided each blow they tried to land. From whichever direction the staff came, it reacted with perfect timing, leaping in the air, dropping to the ground, turning this way and that, now right, now left, all of this accomplished with such self-possession, they said, that it actually seemed to be *thinking*. The most robust, wily, and skilled Gladiator could not have performed any better, nor any more impressively."[33] Even in its failures, the beast had the capacity to terrorize.

Whether he believed any of these stories himself or simply saw profit in having others believe, Morénas turned them into evidence that the fabulous had invaded the quotidian realm. In the fall of 1764, in its first articles covering the events in the Gévaudan, the *Courrier* had already invoked the African hyena and the serpent from the Bagrada river that Regulus had defeated in the first Punic War. Morénas soon came to rely on phantasmagorical language to convey the terrifying mysteries surrounding the foul being. "The terrible Lion from the forest of Nemea, the Giant Antaeus, the Lernean Hydra, and all the other monsters said to have perished at the hand of Hercules enjoyed no higher standing in the writings of the ancients than that held in our modern accounts by the ferocious Beast that ravages so many regions of this province."[34] Morénas here showed no awareness of his own role in securing the beast's "high standing" in modern accounts, but clues to his gratitude for these journalistic riches are abundant in subsequent issues of the *Courrier*. He casually referred to the Gévaudan in February as "a theater of war as deplorable as it is unique." A correspondent from Paris would later note that the beast had become the subject of daily conversations, "just as war does." An account of any new exploit "will enjoy the same fashion as that of a battle."[35] Morénas had found the "interesting" and "tragic" story that could make up for the inconvenient reality of a lasting peace.

By aggressively capitalizing on the news potential of the beast's story, François Morénas, along with the other journalists who followed his example and recirculated many of the same news items, helped to create the larger-than-life image that fueled popular frenzy over the beast. Morénas and his journalistic brethren had many collaborators, however, in the south of France and elsewhere. The key contributions made by the scientifically curious, the religiously motivated, and the consumers of the exotic have been discussed. Other individuals, closer to the action, require special attention. Influential hunters in Languedoc and Auvergne also helped to sensationalize the beast of the Gévaudan, though for a variety of reasons their role has been insufficiently appreciated and understood by previous purveyors of the tale.

To grasp the role that hunters and war veterans played in the evolution of the beast's tale, we need to pick up the story at a point mentioned only in passing in Chapter 1—the decision taken by the authorities, in October of 1764, to deploy troops to the area. Before returning to the scene of that decision with a newly critical eye, however, I will review the essentials of a much larger turning point in French history, namely, the embarrassing military defeat of the Seven Years' War. The war's effects on the servants of the French state, and especially its aristocratic warriors, almost certainly influenced key players' perception and handling of the crisis in the Gévaudan. The pursuit and defense of honor in the killing fields of the Massif Central provided vicarious opportunities to soldiers eager for a chance at redemption. As the new enemy proved itself more than equal to their skill, huntsmen who had served in the late war did their part to make their opponent's image equal to their pronounced and wounded sense of honor. They thus served as critical activating agents in the genesis and early growth of the beast's legend.

Redeeming Honor

On 5 November 1757, the French army suffered the most humiliating defeat in its history near the Saxon village of Rossbach. In the first pivotal engagement of the Seven Years' War to take place on European soil, an advancing army of French and Austrian forces was annihilated by the vastly outnumbered Prussian forces of Frederick the Great, who outmaneuvered the French and Austrian commanders to embarrassing effect. After first feigning retreat behind the crest of a hill, the Prussians fell upon their pursuers with stunning speed, crushing the cavalry line of the Austrians and slicing through the late-arriving French reinforcements. Roused to action, the French infantry attacked the enemy in column formation, presenting easy targets for the well-positioned Prussian artillery. After absorbing heavy losses, the French forces collapsed into disarray and retreated at full speed from a Prussian cavalry assault. An eyewitness described the scene: "Soon the plain of Rossbach was covered with the bodies of runaways cut down by the horsemen of [the Prussian officer] Seydlitz. Panic-stricken men threw down their guns, their hats, their equipment; they thought only of escaping the carnage."[36] The defeat was overwhelming and nearly instantaneous—the first shots rang out at 3:30 and by 4:30 the Prussians had carried the day—and it yielded stunningly lopsided casualty figures. The Prussians had sustained some 500 casualties compared to the allies' 5,000.[37] The French army also lost virtually all the artillery of its right flank, which had buckled under the Prussian barrage.

Rossbach ended in chaos, as French soldiers failed to show the courage and discipline for which they had once been known. "Terror seized the troops at the first sight of the enemy," wrote one disheartened officer. With the battle lost, the soldiers scrambled for their own personal safety, crossing the Unstrut river in such "indescribable disorder" that many drowned.[38] Their commanders also came in for withering criticism. Officers on the scene did not hesitate to point fingers, and a consensus soon emerged that Charles de Rohan, prince de Soubise—a creature of Versailles who owed his rank of general to favor at court—had blundered badly. He had first hesitated to engage the Prussians, despite the allies' vast numerical advantage, and after finally acceding to the Austrian general's request to launch an attack, he allowed his own cavalry regiment to become separated from the main army. Oblivious to Frederick's intention to strike preemptively, he failed to respond quickly when the firing began and withheld promised reinforcements for the allied cavalry until they were too late to make a difference. The prince also had to answer for the dishonorable behavior of the fleeing soldiers, whose lack of discipline seemed to reflect both poor training and a shocking disregard for authority. "The troops," according to the blunt assessment of one experienced officer, "never had the least bit of confidence in [Soubise]."[39] Although he retained his position thanks to protection at court, and even managed to gain a measure of redemption with victories later in the war, Soubise found himself the object of public mockery by 1758.

"The public cannot get over the shame of this battle," wrote François-Joachim, abbé de Bernis at the end of November, and the psychic wounds inflicted at Rossbach unfortunately remained unaddressed for many months.[40] As Soubise's army retreated westward to lick its wounds, and as activity shifted to the Rhineland, French forces led by their supreme commander, the comte de Clermont, found themselves repeatedly harried, harassed, and outsmarted by the forces of Frederick's gifted general Ferdinand of Brunswick. Louis de Bourbon-Condé, comte de Clermont, a prince of the blood and cousin to the king, unfortunately shared many of the leadership qualities of the hapless Soubise. Enjoying royal favor as a courtly insider, he too displayed both timidity and indecisiveness in the field. He arrived to take command of France's exhausted and underequipped army of Westphalia in February of 1758 and promptly took the situation from bad to worse.

Fearing direct engagement with Brunswick, Clermont pulled back toward the Rhine. But the long retreat that took place between the middle of February and early April resulted in one embarrassment after another, as Clermont and his lieutenants fell for Ferdinand's every feint and false maneuver, repeatedly fleeing "an imaginary enemy, [while] delivering up their supplies, baggage, cannons, [and] their sick and wounded."[41] Clermont resolved to make a last stand at the French-occupied town of Minden (near Hannover) in early March, but miscommunications, faulty coordination, and a lack of will led to the quick surrender of the town before Clermont and his troops had even arrived on the scene. English eyewitnesses reported that the French resistance had been exceptionally weak. Brunswick, for example, supervised the laying of siege trenches "with no opposition at all from the French." When word of the loss reached Versailles, the king's mistress Madame de Pompadour accused the French commander of accepting shameful terms of surrender that protected the interests of craven officers and offered up thousands of common soldiers as prisoners of war. Some of those soldiers, evidently unable to withstand the humiliation, snuck through enemy lines to join up with Clermont's army, still camped miles away. They, too, complained of their commander's capitulation.[42]

Clermont limped back across the Rhine and spent much of the next two months focused desperately on recruitment, even forming an entirely new regiment to be funded partly out of his own private coffers.[43] But a final, devastating defeat at Krefeld in June 1758 mercifully ended Clermont's military career. In spite of superior numbers, the French at Krefeld suffered three times as many casualties as the more aggressive Prussians. The chronic hesitancy, the failure to plan ahead, the inability to take advantage of superior numbers, the disorderly retreats: the experiences of 1758 (as well as a second terrible defeat at Minden in 1759) offered painful proof that the debacle in Saxony had been no anomaly. Laden with privileges, shielded from accountability by court protectors, consumed more by careerism and intrigue than by the demands of their profession, French officers had performed miserably, even dishonorably, in the early stages of a war that would decide the fate of empires. Occasional successes on the continent later in the war would be offset by demoralizing losses to the British in North America. By 1762 all could see that the tides of war would not be reversed.[44] The events of 1757–1758 left marks on French military culture, including a new and determined pursuit of professionalism, that would last for a generation.[45]

The dolorous impact of these events on French morale cannot be overstated. Abject despair could be detected at the highest levels. Bernis, who served as minister of foreign affairs during the disasters that stretched from Rossbach to Krefeld, lamented "the ruin of the reputation and spirit of our nation" in the wake of the siege of Minden. On first hearing news of the surrender, Bernis thought he might "die of shame and sadness." After seeing the army "cut to pieces" at Rossbach and reduced to dreadful "disorders" at Minden, he could only conclude that "ours is the most pitiful of all nations, because it possesses no form of honor, and dreams only of money and repose."[46] Meanwhile an active general, writing to the war ministry also in the gloom of

1758, worried that the moral malaise reflected by recent defeats foretold the "the approaching destruction of our monarchy."[47]

The stain of dishonor extended far beyond the halls of Versailles, and it remained visible long after the conclusion of the war. Napoleon would famously say of Soubise that, at Rossbach, he "lost his army and honor," but the long-term impact of the humiliations of the late 1750s reached beyond those individuals held responsible for defeat.[48] The cumulative effects of a badly managed war created the perception that the honor of the nobility, of the military, and of the French nation itself had been compromised. The broadly shared craving for an emotional palliative in the wake of the war helps explain, for example, the spectacular success of Pierre Buirette de Belloy's "excessively admired" play of 1765, *The Siege of Calais,* which generated enthusiasm disproportionate to the quality of its writing.[49] A hit in Paris, the play enjoyed repeat performances at Versailles after its February debut there, and in the coming months it would attract appreciative audiences all across the country.[50] The costs incurred by some of these productions were underwritten by Louis XV, who saw advantages in satisfying the public appetite for heart-warming and patriotic fare. The script resonated so deeply because it directly countered painful memories of the recent humiliation; Buirette de Belloy had even begun work on the play during the war's last months. His play depicted a dramatic siege from the Hundred Years' War, at which the French had proudly displayed selflessness and patriotism even in the face of certain defeat. Audiences could not have mistaken the playwright's effort to inspire. "Cursed are those nations which, pounded by the tempest / Allow the sting of defeat to debase their courage."[51]

That sting of defeat, felt by many throughout the 1760s, would have been particularly acute for two of the principals scouring the fields of the Gévaudan. Jean-Baptiste Duhamel, the dragoon captain who effectively took command of the hunt for the beast in early November 1764, had strong personal and professional connections to the disgraced comte de Clermont. Born in 1732 in Amiens, Duhamel had followed the typically precocious career path of a scion of nobility. Having landed his first commission in the Cambis infantry regiment at the tender age of fifteen, he was later recruited to serve as regimental adjutant in the corps of "foreign volunteers" (so called because many of the recruits came from Flanders and German-speaking territories). This corps had been raised by the desperate Clermont in the spring of 1758. Commissioned in May of that year, five weeks before the battle of Krefeld, Duhamel would have witnessed firsthand the shameful defeat that cost Clermont the general command of the army and his standing at court. Although Duhamel's personnel file from 1763 shows that he "conducted himself well during the war," he certainly owed his retention as captain in December of 1758 to the continued favor and good opinion of the prince himself, who remained in charge of his Volunteers.[52]

After being placed in charge of a company of dragoons, and finding himself stationed in the south of France after the war ended, Duhamel remained solicitous of his commanding officer, whose incomparably high status and connections could prove valuable. "I sincerely hope," he wrote in one letter to the secretary of the prince, "that I will be able to announce in my next letter . . . that the monster is no more, and that it was the dragoon company of His Serene Highness [Clermont] that put it to death."[53] That wistful letter followed a disappointing interim report in February of 1765, in which Duhamel reiterated his desire to retain the "esteem and good will" of the prince and implored Clermont's secretary to "speak in my favor."[54] In a letter addressed to the prince himself, at the end of Duhamel's assignment in the land of the beast, the captain's tone recalled that of a sheepish child seeking the approval of a parent whose expectations have gone unfulfilled. He wished to assure Clermont that he had earned commendations from "all the nobility of the Gévaudan." He included signed certificates attesting the fact, and he asked his patron to "do me the great favor of reading them."[55] Duhamel never forgot his identity as a dragoon of the Volunteers. He would note with proud satisfaction that the dragoons' uniforms, with their golden habits and red vests, "truly astonish the people of this country."[56] When he began his quest, he fully expected that his triumph over the beast would bring reflected glory back to the founder of the corps in which Duhamel had loyally served "since its creation."[57]

One of Duhamel's local informants, and his sometime collaborator, the comte de Morangiès, would have been no less sensitive to the perceptions of compromised honor that haunted the military in the postwar era. For as it happens, the author of the ignominious surrender at Minden had been none other than his father, Pierre Charles de Mollete, marquis de Morangiès. Like his commanding officer Clermont (who had failed to send promised reinforcements to Minden), the marquis de Morangiès had crept away in disgrace after being stripped of his rank in 1758. He soon retreated to a life in exile at his chateau in Saint-Alban, his military career having come to an inglorious end. The marquis's son, the comte de Morangiès, had also served in the war as a field marshal; as such he had acquitted himself admirably, but the shame of the father's professional fate weighed heavily in the local air. The marquis, after all, was the most powerful secular seigneur in the diocese of Mende.[58] Control over two baronies entitled him to a seat in the provincial Estates-General assembly that met each year in Montpellier or Toulouse. For his valor at Fontenoy in 1745 he had been awarded the Cross of Saint Louis. In the Gévaudan he occupied high royal offices as a district judge *(bailli royal)* and—supreme irony—judge of the "tribunal of the point of honor," a special court that adjudicated cases of wounded honor involving nobles and military personnel.[59] The public disgrace of so important a local dignitary cannot have failed to inform the thoughts and motives of a son who looked on helplessly from the sidelines.

For Duhamel and the comte de Morangiès, the desire to restore a tarnished honor—whether of the army in which they had both served, the unjustly violated local *pays,* or, in the case of Morangiès, the family name—would only have been accentuated by the heartrending profiles of the beast's victims. Of the approximately sixty known deaths and eleven suspected deaths attributed to the beast between June 1764 and the end of 1765, not one involved an adult male. Counting all of the deceased in and around the Gévaudan in this period, adult and child, fully two-thirds of the identified victims were female.[60] Indeed, Morangiès first became seriously engaged by the phenomenon of the beast after hearing news of an attack that transpired in late October "near the place in Saint-Alban where the comte de Morangiès resides." The beast's pitiful prey, according to the obviously irritated Lafont, was a "twenty-one-year-old girl who had been forced by her relatives to lead their herd to pasture." In that field near Saint-Alban Marguerite Malige was "devoured." This event prompted Lafont to seek out the assistance of Morangiès. Soon after he dispatched to Saint-Alban a group of hunters led by Mercier, the innkeeper from Mende, he asked Morangiès to oversee the operations. The comte "responded with his ordinary zeal in all matters relating to the public good."[61] Morangiès organized two canvasses, including one in the Rechauve woods on his own estate, but he had to report to Lafont that his efforts had yielded no results.[62]

The age and gender of the beast's victims rarely served as a subject of extended commentary by Morangiès or the other hunters who tracked the beast in the coming months. The newspapers pressed the theme insistently, however, and all recognized the disproportionate price being paid in this tragedy by women and children, including in early January one "eighteen-year-old shepherdess celebrated for her rare beauty." She had been devoured in a field several leagues from Rodez, and her demise was followed in February by that of another young girl known as "the beauty of her canton." Many other notably "beautiful" maidens would eventually meet the same tragic fate.[63]

The spectacle of ravaged innocents inspired pity, a desire for revenge, and a protective instinct characteristic of chivalric assertions of male honor.[64] Morangiès, an esteemed seigneur of the region, took a direct interest in the sufferings of many of the afflicted, and in March of 1765 he paid a personal visit to the village of Bessière in Saint-Alban to console a grief-stricken mother who had valiantly tried but failed to wrest her child from the voracious jaws of the beast.[65] "It is awful to see one's country *(patrie)* laid waste by a cruel animal that will only become more violent as the weather grows harsher," wrote Morangiès in a letter of 28 October 1764. As the seriousness of the situation began to sink in among the notables of the region, Morangiès eagerly offered his services. Writing on the eve of his first organized pursuit of the beast, he told Lafont of his "truly patriotic" desire to take "the head of this ferocious animal" or to assure that "the war we wage against it will chase it from our land."[66]

Significantly, the professional and "patriotic" soldier Morangiès used the term *war* in more than a metaphorical sense. As he explained to Lafont, in his supervision of the activities involving Mercier he had sought to follow "the true principles of war and of the hunt, which are absolutely the same." In a letter to Lafont (26 October 1764), he had begun to lay the groundwork for an argument he would press more urgently after his experiences with Mercier. Morangiès was convinced that the failure to apply "true principles of war" consistently, for lack of equipment, expertise, and manpower, had hobbled previous efforts to eliminate the beast. Morangiès acknowledged that many well-intentioned people turned out for the "tumultuous hunts" that had become part of the local routine, but they had "no firearms or bad ones," which they then fired "clumsily." Lafont would thus be well advised to summon several hundred soldiers to the area, preferably to be funded by the crown or the province. A few days later he reiterated to Lafont his belief that, unless severe weather drove the beast away, "you have no resource other than troops."[67]

In his letter of 28 October, Morangiès left little doubt about who should be placed in command of those troops. "I would very willingly respond [to the call], under any conditions, in order to destroy this monster." He continued, hopefully, that "if I am charged with this commission, with three or four hundred soldiers and the requisite authority over the communities [in the area], you will not believe what a little military discipline will do for an operation like this." The task just might require "a whole regiment," but Morangiès promised results "in less than two weeks."[68] Even after the provincial authorities assigned troops to the area under Duhamel's command, Morangiès continued to harbor hopes that he would be called on to rescue his beleaguered country. Throughout the winter of 1765, as Duhamel's frustrations accumulated, the comte lobbied Choiseul to send a larger detachment of troops to the south (by late February he was asking for 1,200), and he assured Lafont that Choiseul's assistant held the opinion that "there could be no one better" to put in charge of such a corps than someone "as distinguished for his talents as M. le comte de Morangiès." Whether from an innate sense of patriotic duty, a desire for honor and recognition, or a combination of the two, Morangiès clearly aspired to lead a new war—a successful war—against the "cruel animal" of the Gévaudan.[69]

His hopes would not be realized. Even before Morangiès drafted his last letter to Etienne Lafont in late October, the military commandant Moncan had decided to entrust to Duhamel the task of eliminating the beast. Given Duhamel's early and eager engagement in the hunts around Langogne, the availability of troops stationed in that city, and the character of dragoon service—these "light troops," designed for mobility and often used in reconnaissance, were thought to be equally adept on foot or on horse—the captain would have seemed the most likely and convenient choice for Moncan.[70] In any case we know that Duhamel pushed his own candidacy aggressively, nosing out at least one other proud competitor.[71] He expressed his gratitude to Moncan for the "honor" of the appointment when it came, and he later explained to his friend and patron Roussel, in Paris, that his commission had been granted "in response to my request." He gratefully assured Moncan that "I will take every precaution and spare no trouble . . . I will do all that a gallant man can and must do when he is assigned a commission."[72]

The captain informed Lafont of his selection as lead huntsman on 29 October, and the next day the subdelegate sent word to the intendant Saint-Priest that Moncan had authorized Duhamel to "give chase to the beast throughout the Gévaudan."[73] "Overpowering snow" and a "violent wind" impeded Duhamel's westward progress for several days, but he arrived in Mende on 3 November with Moncan's orders in hand. He was accompanied by fifty-

six "well-chosen" dragoons, seventeen on horse and thirty-nine on foot.[74] Duhamel and Lafont exchanged formal pleasantries and the captain asked Lafont
to send word of his arrival to the region's mayors and consuls, whose cooperation he would undoubtedly need. The next morning, after paying his respects
to the bishop of Mende, "who could not have given me a better reception,"
Duhamel headed north to the town of Saint-Chély, which had been close to
the eye of the storm throughout the month of October.[75] Taking up residence
in an inn, the dragoons used Saint-Chély as their base of operations in the
months to come. As Duhamel set out on his quest he brimmed with optimism, as a letter written to Louis-Charles de Bourbon, comte d'Eu (and governor of Languedoc) at this time makes clear. "If the gods grant my wishes,"
he wrote, "I will soon have the pleasure . . . of receiving you and delivering to
you the monster of the Gévaudan; that is my belief."[76]

Duhamel's zestful but naïve eagerness to please in the three months that
followed his arrival in Mende reflected a genuine desire to rid the country of a
terrible menace but also an acute sense of his reputation in the eyes of those
who would judge him. The phrase *galant homme* is laced throughout the correspondence of Duhamel, and those words conveyed a whole constellation of
qualities valued by the honorable. To be *galant* was to be steady, dependable,
competent, and loyal, with integrity beyond reproach.[77] Duhamel applied the
term to others when he wished to signify strong approval, and he consistently
measured himself by the same standard.[78] In his letter of appreciation to Moncan on 1 November 1764 he pledged to do all that a "gallant man" must do,
just as he also assured the bishop of Mende that he would perform all that "a
gallant man can and must do when he is animated by the public good."[79]
Later, as his dreams of glory faded, he insisted in an exchange with Morangiès
that he had done all that could be expected of a "gallant man."[80]

Sensitivity to one's standing was a characteristic widely shared under the
ancien régime, and for a noble army officer harboring memories of a humiliating war, the desire to win renown, or redemption, would have been acute. Duhamel, moreover, had been told pointedly of the potential glory that awaited
him. Moncan had promised that "I will not neglect to inform the [war min-
ister] Choiseul and the comte de Saint-Florentin of your offer to destroy
[this animal], should you succeed in finding it."[81] Duhamel subsequently announced in a letter to M. Roussel that he and his comrades saw the successful
fulfillment of their assignment as a "point of honor," and he acknowledged
that a happy ending would permit him "to draw great advantages" from the

commission he had secured.[82] No wonder Duhamel anticipated that his victory over the beast would constitute "the most thrilling day of my life."[83]

Unfortunately, in the face of difficult circumstances Duhamel allowed his sensitivities and dreams of glory to distort the nature of the task at hand, in his own mind and in the minds of others. As each disappointment in the late fall of 1764 called forth explanations that could adequately account for the failures of capable men, the beast's runaway reputation diminished its pursuers by force of contrast. The changed equilibrium between hunter and hunted, in turn, renewed frustrated desires and elicited desperate new measures whose unsatisfying outcomes added to an increasingly intimidating legend.

Evidence of the burning desire to square off against a singular opponent both worthy and inspiring of the best efforts of the honorable also shows up in the writing of Morangiès. Early in the process, the comte saw in the beast of the Gévaudan not merely a "cruel" and "dangerous" animal, but a "Monster," a "Beast" with a capital B. Morangiès was among the first of the local inhabitants to hypothesize that the beast had African origins, and he signaled to Lafont his readiness to face a "lion" if necessity required. He expressed little wonder that the peasants of the countryside "are afraid when they see this Beast" and were thus rendered incapable of action whenever it appeared.[84] In his mind it was precisely the menacing aspect of the beast's figure that made the presence of experienced and steely riflemen so essential. Already by late October, when no more than ten deaths could be credited to its attacks, and when it had faced only scattered efforts by disorganized and poorly armed locals, the beast's prowess had so fired the imagination of Morangiès that, to his mind, only a small army headed by a decorated field marshal seemed equal to the task of its elimination.

Duhamel, however, played the greater role in promoting the beast's fantastic image. In early October, already fixated on the exotic nature of the creature, he had shared with Moncan his suspicion that a "leopard" prowled the hills around Langogne. By the time he commenced his activities as hunter-in-chief, Duhamel was prepared to bestow on his enemy the honorific title, "monster of the Gévaudan." As a well-read and well-traveled representative of France's urban elites, Duhamel of course would not have been immune to the influence of learned discourses on monsters and hybrids, and his willingness to imagine an exotic presence hardly made him unique in this period. Perhaps he was encouraged by the speculations of naturalists or by local hearsay confirming his suspicions of the extraordinary. By November he had already

noted the great similarities linking descriptions of the beast among the peasantry, where rumors spread fast. Whatever his initial assumptions, he clearly
allowed his imagination to run free in his efforts to fill out the profile of the
monster.[85]

A quick victory over the malefactor would have prevented excessive and
counterproductive mythologizing, but a speedy resolution was not in the
cards. Following a brief lull in the beast's activity in early November, Lafont wondered if the sudden calm, coupled with Duhamel's constant activity,
should be taken as a sign "of our deliverance." Yet misfortune struck again in
the last week of the month, when the beast killed Catherine Valy as she led
cows to water by the village of Buffeirettes, near Aumont.[86] Recounting the
incident in a letter to a superior, Duhamel explained that the beast had "throttled a woman in a village two leagues from [Saint-Chély]," decapitating the
victim and leaving her other remains lying in a field where she would be discovered by her adult children the following day.[87] After being apprised of the
events that afternoon by a consul of the parish, Duhamel raced to the scene
and put into action a new tactic he had decided upon days earlier (and described in a letter to Moncan.)[88]

Accompanied by the troops, "I went to the house of the poor woman,
where her children had taken her. As this wild beast always returns to the
place where it has devoured someone, I explained to the children that, their
mother now being dead, it would make little difference if her burial were delayed for twenty-four hours." He made them see that "it was in their own interest and that of the public good to allow me to watch over their mother's
body [overnight] on the very spot where she had perished." After the an-
guished children consented to the plan, Duhamel placed a ragged skirt over
the body "for decency's sake" and had four of his dragoons move Valy back to
the scene of the assault. There Duhamel and his men "passed the night in the
most profound silence," though unfortunately "the beast did not come." Not
easily deterred, Duhamel left several of his dragoons on patrol near the body
throughout the next day, while their commanding officer scouted the environs. Still frustrated as sunset approached, Duhamel followed impulse and
stationed twelve more dragoons by the side of the deceased Catherine Valy,
where they waited under the stars for an additional night. The next morning
the disappointed dragoons finally surrendered Valy's moldering body to her
grieving children.[89]

The practice of using human remains to lure a predator back within range of its captors was not unknown in French rural life. A month earlier, Morangiès had suggested that the tactic might well be necessary in the Gévaudan.[90] But Duhamel's introduction of the method and his heedless improvisation after Valy's first night in the field was a troubling harbinger of things to come. Repeatedly over the next ten weeks he showed a willingness to use unorthodox tactics that risked alienating the locals and visibly heightened the stakes involved in each attempt to kill or capture the beast. As word of his treatment of cadavers spread through the region, for example, some of the other afflicted families, evidently unable to face the spectacle Duhamel had in store for them, refused to notify the authorities of the deaths of their loved ones. The captain reacted furiously when he learned of one such case in the village of Chavanols (in Auvergne) in late January. The family had interred the body of the victim without informing any authorities other than their complicitous curé. Duhamel learned of the death only when a consul from a neighboring village conveyed news of the victim's burial. Stung by this incident and determined to enforce compliance with his announced procedures, Duhamel later jailed the father of a wounded victim from Javols because he had failed to promptly notify authorities of his daughter's trying ordeal.[91]

The failure of unorthodox tactics only increased the sense of frustration that began to grip Duhamel by the end of November. Signs of that frustration took one of two forms: exasperated expressions of self-pity or lists of the mitigating circumstances of failure. In offering his excuses, Duhamel hewed closely to what today would be called a "single-killer hypothesis," and he did all he could to accentuate the impressive, if not magical, features of the enemy he faced. In the wake of his disappointment in Buffeirettes, for example, he crafted for his superior a vivid account of the discovery of Catherine Valy's missing remains. Her skull had been found by peasants "while beating the bushes" in the large forest near the village. "Her head, both inside and out, [was] clean as if polished with a tool." For Duhamel, the signs of the beast's handiwork conjured images of a "devil," and the decapitated skull provided compelling evidence of the creature's prowess. "Judging by the teeth marks imprinted [on the skull], this animal must have terrifying jaws and a powerful bite, because this woman's head was split in two in the way a man's mouth might crack a nut." To provide the commandant Moncan a talisman representing the mystery of the monster, he enclosed in his letter to the general "a tuft of hair of this beast," recovered on the very spot where Catherine Valy had met her end.[92]

In addition to evidence of the beast's dastardly powers, Duhamel noted the less-than-ideal conditions in which he worked. The weather, and the constant demands placed upon the dragoons, had begun to take a toll. During a particularly dispiriting hunt in the woods of Chazaux just south of Saint-Denis, moisture caused by pelting snow had threatened the dragoons' gun powder and forced their muskets under their cloaks, thus preventing them from getting off a shot during the beast's one brief appearance. After that disappointment Duhamel and his men repaired to Saint-Denis, where they were "obliged to sleep on straw." Three days later the unhappy conclusion of the Catherine Valy episode underlined the need for recuperation. "As my dragoons had been in the field for six days, morning until night, with snow up to their thighs and more falling on them constantly from the sky, I returned [to Saint-Chély] on the 28th, in order to give the troops a rest and to have shoes made for them."[93]

Duhamel's sad litany may have secured the temporary indulgence of Moncan and other superiors, but December unfortunately did not change his fortunes. The month was marked by a series of fruitless expeditions, two more grisly decapitations, more punishing weather, and missed opportunities that left Duhamel with feelings of desperation. In a Christmas Eve letter to the intendant of Auvergne, Duhamel shared news of another horrifying attack before detailing his own most recent disappointment. Writing again from Saint-Chély, Duhamel explained that on 20 December another woman had been attacked by the beast, who "lay in ambush" for her as she passed through the garden adjoining her house. Before she could react, the beast "jumped on top of her and ripped her neck right away from her shoulders, carrying off her head." After a detachment of his dragoons once again spent the night near the dismembered corpse, again with no results, they proceeded to organize a hunt in a forest on the grounds of the nearby chateau of La Baume, where they beat the bushes for hours in hopes of encountering the animal.

As the troops completed a second cycle around the forest, Duhamel, who was positioned in a copse of trees on the perimeter, had the beast square in his sights, and he was set to fire on it at only a few paces' distance. Then disaster struck. Several of his companions, on horseback and unaware of their leader's optimal position, appeared suddenly behind Duhamel and made their own charge at the animal. The beast quickly "changed direction," and in the confusion no one managed to fire a shot. The mounted dragoons gave chase but lost sight of the animal just before nightfall after it passed through a marsh that the horses could not cross. They "slept on straw," again, in hopes of resuming their search at the crack of dawn, but the arrival of a "terrible rain" foiled their plans. Duhamel pronounced himself "inconsolable."[94]

The depths of Duhamel's despair are revealed in a remarkable piece of self-disclosure composed a few days later, as the captain reached out to a confidant whose judgment he had no reason to fear. He wrote his letter from Montpellier, in a coincidence of timing and circumstance that only compounded his distress. "Imagine my sadness," he wrote to his friend Roussel, as he described the beast's startled reaction at La Baume and its fortuitous removal from his line of fire. "I had three [lead] balls in my musket; ask yourself if I could have missed, firing from four paces." Repeating a term used in his correspondence with the intendant Ballainvilliers, he described himself as "inconsolable." The severity of the disappointment was understandable, for he considered this golden opportunity "the most glorious moment of my life." "After having endured so much pain and fatigue, I myself would have had the satisfaction of delivering this country from the scourge that afflicts it." But the

Chateau of La Baume. On the grounds of this chateau Captain Duhamel and his dragoons spent a fruitless day and a half in pursuit of the beast. The disappointment at La Baume would leave Duhamel scarred for the duration of his mission in the Gévaudan. *Author photo*

glorious opportunity had slipped from his grasp. After his footman brought him his horse, "I mounted it straight away and, to save time, I did not reload my musket but took pistol in hand and ran into the woods as fast as the horse would carry me. As fate would have it, no one was present at the edge of the wood to tell me which way the beast had gone. Instead of going right, I went left." The animal had naturally gone the other way. The coming rains would merely complete the captain's crushing turn of fortune.

Duhamel addressed his friend from quarters in Montpellier because he had been summoned there for discussions with the provincial governor, who attended the annual meeting of the Estates-General then in session. "What satisfaction I would have felt if I had been able to respond to the prince's letter with the announcement of my arrival in Montpellier at the first of the year, [accompanied by] the monster that I myself had destroyed." With days remaining before the closure of the Estates meeting, there would have been ample time for public celebrations honoring the liberator of the Gévaudan. "If I live for a thousand years, I will never recover from this cruel stroke of fate."[95]

There is no way to know, of course, whether the beast at La Baume was really *the* beast, or whether its death would have brought an end to the terror that had stalked the Gévaudan for nearly six months. The animal that eluded Duhamel may have been merely one among many wolves that prowled the territory. We do know, however, that Duhamel's interest in placing himself in an exculpatory light and in portraying the beast as an outsized instrument of evil would have grown markedly by Christmas of 1764, for in the weeks after mid-December he began to feel disapproving pressure from several fronts. Most significantly, Versailles had begun to take serious notice of the protracted crisis in the Gévaudan. On 16 December the minister Saint-Florentin expressed surprise that the situation had still not been resolved. In an impatient letter written to the intendant Saint-Priest, he declared, "I have a hard time understanding how all of the hunts organized up to this point have turned up such poor results." Saint-Florentin would express further skepticism about Duhamel's prospects two weeks later, and by January some officials in Auvergne clearly had the impression that the minister had already ordered the dragoons' return to their winter quarters.[96] In light of the minister's obvious displeasure, news of which would have circulated quickly through Languedoc's administrative circles, the comte d'Eu also considered pulling Duhamel from the field. Already on 24 December—the day after the events at La

Baume—Duhamel was pleading for more time, announcing to the governor in melodramatic terms that "my soul is paralyzed" at the thought of discontinuing the search before achieving success.[97] Upon Duhamel's arrival in Montpellier, the frustrated governor informed him that the deputies attending the Estates-General meeting had expressed doubts about the wisdom of subsidizing his efforts.[98]

More broadly, the people of the Gévaudan began to murmur their frustrations. In the *Courrier d'Avignon,* a dispatch from Marvejols on the second day of the new year bluntly stated that the beast's continuing carnage "does not promote a very high opinion of the courage or skill of those who have been charged to deliver us from the [ferocious beast]; hardly a day passes without someone being devoured." Another dispatch from 12 January avoided similar exaggeration, but its author suggested that the "detachment of dragoons" had "wasted its troubles." This writer implored "some Hercules" to come to the rescue of the devastated land.[99]

By the end of 1764, Duhamel had become aware of his deteriorating status in the eyes of both public opinion and the officials he served. (Later, after his dismissal, he would express regret for not having allowed the "public papers" to write in greater detail about the "daily itineraries and the exhaustions that my detachment endured." He disingenuously suggested that instead of working to manage his image, he had steadfastly followed the principles of his métier—"to obey and be silent.")[100] As pressure grew, Duhamel reacted by becoming even more creative with his tactics and by embracing what seems to have been a deliberate strategy to salvage his reputation. The story of the big one that got away at La Baume, details of which would soon show up in a Parisian broadsheet, constituted only one aspect of his plan.[101] With his reputation as a *galant homme* at stake, Duhamel aggressively promoted a terrifying image of the elusive monster. In the last week to ten days of December, the legend of the beast burst out of its still-embryonic form, and the broadcasting of Duhamel's tales provided critical momentum for the explosion that would arrive in January. All of the key developments in the weeks to come— the bishop's composition of his urgent *mandement,* the *Courrier's* decision to make the beast a centerpiece of its news coverage, the wide circulation of fantastic images of the creature—owed a great deal to Duhamel's strategic effort to protect his honor, defend his actions, and retain his position.

The latest rash of attacks had begun on 15 December, with a killing and decapitation in Auvergne near the northern limits of the affected area in Védrines-Saint-Loup. The terror continued in concentrated form through the 27th, during which time the beast claimed the lives of four victims and made attempts on at least two others. After an unsuccessful attack on a woman from the village of Civergot on 18 December, Duhamel, in nearby Saint-Chély, made the short trek to "the home of the heroine" to gather eyewitness evidence about the assailant. On his frantically busy day of 24 December, Duhamel wrote one more letter, this one directed to Moncan. In it Duhamel provided a gripping account of the woman's struggle with her attacker (she struck it with her hatchet, "splitting the muzzle" of the beast) and relayed the following:

> She drew for me the following portrait—this animal is about the size of a year-old bull, its neck and belly are white, the fur of its body is red and the length of that of a wolf; it has a black stripe running down its back, with very long fur [longer than the rest of the coat], the tail resembles that of a horse, red and bushy, with touches of black. The paws are very powerful, with six talons, each the length of a finger. The head is black, with a wide forehead, the eyes are large and sparkling, and its muzzle is the length of that of a pig, with the difference that the muzzle points down instead of up. Its mouth is extraordinarily broad (measuring at least a foot according to the portrait provided by this woman.) The teeth are wide and pointy at the end, with a half-inch gap separating one from the other. The ears are straight and roughly the length of those of a wolf.[102]

Whether the woman responded to leading questions or channeled local hearsay, her description definitely shared features with other descriptions current in the fall of 1764. The black stripe and the sparkling eyes, for example, had already become standard. More striking than the details she related, however, is Duhamel's uncritical acceptance of the report. Eager to secure confirmation of the beast's singularity, he absorbed seemingly unfiltered testimony by someone scarred by the intensity of a life-threatening encounter. Highly attracted to the idea of the "six talons"—perhaps because it ruled out the theory of the hyena, which Buffon had described as having four toes on its front paws—Duhamel would return to this testimony weeks later, insisting that the woman had done battle with the beast "for a quarter of an hour" and therefore had had "plenty of time to count its talons." He added, without irony, that at the time of her deposition "the woman assured me" that she had even taken note of the talons' length, "each time [the beast] reared up on its hind legs to throw itself on her."[103]

Curiously, these striking physical features of the beast had apparently gone unnoticed, or at least unremarked upon, by Duhamel during his encounter at La Baume a few days later. Before December had passed, however, the image inspired by the woman's description had taken shape in his mind's eye, and Duhamel put it to effective use during his visit to Montpellier. He must have impressed the comte d'Eu with tales of his adventures, because the governor relented and authorized Duhamel to continue hunting the beast "until I finally have it in my hands."[104] Before he left the capital city he also paid a visit to an artist whose work would make a lasting impact on public perception. Duhamel himself had produced a rough sketch of the creature, and he presented his original to the artist, who "did me the favor of painting it." A publisher in Montpellier then produced a print of that image, one that "exactly reproduced" the beast's likeness.[105] Over the next several weeks, Duhamel sent or delivered copies of the print to a range of interested observers, including the bishop of Mende, his friend François, comte de Lastic, his patron Roussel, and the two intendants, who then put the images into wider circulation. Duhamel also hinted strongly to Roussel that Clermont should be provided a copy of the likeness—since the captain "did not dare take the liberty" to send one to the prince directly.[106]

The governor of Languedoc, after receiving in the mail his own copy of the print from the intendant Saint-Priest, expressed skepticism about the image that had grown from Duhamel's loose recollections. "I would like to believe that it resembles [the beast]," he wrote from his chateau of Anet in Normandy, "but I suspect there is more imagination than reality in it, because I doubt that the beast was willing to pose for the artist for such a long time."[107] Anne Claude, comte de Caylus, writing to a friend from Paris in early March, expressed similar misgivings. A famed collector of classical antiquities who was also a skilled artist and printmaker, Caylus confessed that "the portrait of this hyena, or this animal, that has committed so many ravages," left him with the same questions suggested by "all these sorts of pictures." Surely "anyone who has the time to draw such an animal must also have the time to shoot and kill it."[108]

Despite the skepticism it may have generated in some quarters, Duhamel's image soon reached its public, quickly becoming a paradigmatic representation of the beast of the Gévaudan for other engravers and printmakers throughout 1765. Printshops marketed the image with the caption "Portrait of the Hyena . . . as seen by M. Duhamel, Officer of the Volunteer Dragoons of Clermont." Duhamel himself achieved a certain national notoriety, and his descriptive language—the "year-old bull," the "sparkling" eyes, the "extraordinarily broad mouth"—created topoi for use and adaptation by journalists and others.

The words and picture produced by Duhamel even contributed to a certain stabilization of the beast's image in the first months of the year. Lions,

"Portrait of the Hyena, a ferocious Beast that desolates the Gévaudan, as seen by M. Duhamel, Officer of the Volunteer Dragoons of Clermont." One of many images that appeared between late January and the middle of April, 1765, this March print may have been modeled on the original Duhamel representation from January (impossible to identify), or it may have been one of the many counterfeit images that so troubled him. *Bibliothèque Nationale de France, Rés. 4-LK2-786, fol. 99*

panthers, bears, and demons appeared with much less frequency in public representations of the beast after January, and speculation began to focus on a narrower range of characteristics and images. Indeed, the accompanying letter that Duhamel sent to the intendant Ballainvilliers in January, when he began distributing his print, contained a description of the beast strikingly similar to the one he had written for Moncan immediately after the woman's seminal encounter. Imaginative hybridity was more pronounced in this second letter. In it the beast acquired the length of a leopard, the eyes of a calf, the feet of a bear, the chest of a horse, and perhaps the parentage of a lion, but the physical characteristics of the teeth, claws, coat, tail, ears, and forehead showed an admirable consistency with the earlier report.[109] The *Courrier d'Avignon* included in its description of the beast in mid-January several of the features emphasized in Duhamel's letters to Moncan and Ballainvilliers—the chest as broad as a horse, the wide forehead "a foot across"—and the *Gazette de Leyde* soon followed suit.[110] The suddenly possessive Duhamel even expressed displeasure when he noticed, in February, that a variation on his image produced by a painter in Mende deviated from the original in important ways. Other misleading variations on the Duhamel beast had also entered into circulation, and the captain felt compelled to reassure the comte de Lastic that "the one I sent to you perfectly resembles" the animal. The artist in Mende "did not consult me" on his engraving, and neither his nor other counterfeits should be trusted.[111]

By working to reinforce the perception that his enemy posed challenges that could be overcome only with patience, Duhamel won some limited breathing space. But he understood the need to produce results, and over the course of the next month Duhamel and his men used every arrow in their quiver. In January Duhamel sought to enforce with strictest severity the requirement that he be informed immediately of all sightings and incidents involving the beast. He also informed Moncan of his intention to lay traps for the beast, acknowledging the generosity of the comtesse de Fournels, who had offered him the use of traps owned by her brother Jean-Joseph, the marquis d'Apcher.[112] Meanwhile, he seems to have avoided further contact with the comte d'Eu, not wanting to risk revocation of his commission before he had big news to share.[113]

Soon after returning to Saint-Chély from Montpellier, on 10 January, the captain hatched his most original plan. He now prepared to capitalize on the beast's repugnant but clearly insatiable appetite for women and children. "As it is impossible to employ too many measures to achieve the destruction of such a cruel animal," he explained to Saint-Priest, "we have devised [a measure] that would seem certain to succeed, and which the comte de Moncan has already authorized." The consuls of various villages scattered throughout the land would be called on to furnish one or two dragoons with "some old skirts and women's wigs, so that the dragoons, disguised as women, can escort and accompany children who go to the fields to guard their herds." Disguised as frail targets, they would lie in wait for their cunning predator, ready to deploy their concealed weapons at the first opportunity.[114] Duhamel insisted, in his letter to Moncan announcing the initiation of the mission, that "all the inhabitants of the country expect great success from this ruse." It seems likely, however, that the use of children as live bait and the heavy-handedness that accompanied the logistical preparations almost certainly contributed to the local resentments that began to flare up in early February.[115]

In spite of the high hopes and the sheer audacity of his plan, which drew appreciative coverage from both the *Gazette de France* and the *Gazette de Leyde,* in a letter to Lastic written weeks later Duhamel ruefully explained that his plans had come to naught.[116] He had stationed two camouflaged dragoons in each of eight villages widely dispersed throughout the region, in both Auvergne and Languedoc. Accompanied by small patrols that proceeded to scour the woods in the vicinity, the disguised dragoons went out into the fields with children, cows, and sheep for twelve consecutive days. Each day proved as fruitless as the last. Following his pattern, Duhamel suggested that the beast's uncanny abilities explained the dragoons' failure. On the very day that "I called in my men," he announced incredulously, the beast attacked a child near one of the villages that had been under patrol. The attack did not lead to a fatality, and it has left no traces in local archives, but Duhamel must have seen the alleged incident as sufficiently mysterious, and sufficiently serious, to offer new hope for exoneration. To hear Duhamel tell it, the beast had slyly waited out the dragoons, striking only when the coast was clear. He swore to Lastic that there was nothing more he could have done.[117]

This latest disappointment inspired feelings of desperation in Duhamel, and when the deadly month of January ended with news that the beast had claimed another victim, an unsuspecting woman who had been "cleaning her laundry in the stream at Montchamps" near Saint-Flour, the captain settled on a new plan of attack.[118] With the help of provincial administrators and many local notables of the region, Duhamel scheduled a "general hunt" *(chasse générale)* for 7 February, a hunt so large, thorough, and painstaking that magic alone would be able to account for the beast's surviving it. At the end of the great spectacle, the beast crossed a new threshold of celebrity, and Duhamel faced the depressing nadir of his career.

Duhamel's Coup de Grâce

The general hunt of 7 February, together with a second general hunt planned for 11 February in case of need, hardly marked Duhamel's first attempt at large-scale coordination. From the beginning the captain had sought the co-operation of many seigneurs, notables, and local consuls of the region. In November and early December there had been numerous hunts involving residents across multiple parishes, many of them taking place on Sundays and feast days, when the availability of male labor made "beating the bushes" less of a hardship for the affected communities.[119] But the hunt organized for 7 February was unprecedented in scope. Coordinating especially with Ballainvilliers, Duhamel had subdelegates issue specific instructions to the designated leader (usually the local seigneur) of each locality. Firearms were not to be given to inexperienced hunters; rather, they would be armed with sabers, pickaxes, and pitchforks, and no one was to be permitted to participate in the hunt unless his reputation placed him "beyond suspicion" of mischief. Peasants were warned against firing at game (always reserved for the pleasures of the nobility) and they were urged to stay focused on their "principal object," though the killing of wolves and "harmful animals" would be permitted.[120]

According to multiple contemporary estimates, on the morning of the 7th, a Thursday, approximately 20,000 people from about one hundred parishes gathered across a vast expanse of territory to systematically scour the woods, hills, caves, and outcroppings of the Gévaudan and its environs.[121] The sheer scale of the mobilization and the inspiring presence of so many experienced hunters must have leavened the winter chill with a hopeful air of expectancy. Morangiès, Lafont, the comte d'Apcher (father of the marquis), and other notables were among those charged with supervising local communities. The people who gathered in each locality were divided into small hunting parties, with some assigned flushing duty and others stationed nearby in strategic locations, ready to fire should the opportunity arise. Copies of an engraving of the beast—almost certainly modeled on Duhamel's original—were distributed to the parties to help with the identification of the monster.

All the communities would comb through the lands in their own parishes, and Duhamel had coordinated the efforts in such a way that, if all went according to plan, the beast would ultimately find itself encircled and trapped by hunters converging somewhere west of Malzieu on the Gévaudan's border with Auvergne.[122]

Not everything went according to plan.[123] Six inches of snow and dense fog slowed the movement of the parties, and a spectacular breakdown in discipline occurred late in the morning of 7 February. The most valuable opportunity of the day came when a hunting party from the parish of Prunières gave chase to the beast, or a prime suspect, near the Truyère river. In a fit of heroism that would attract admiring attention from the gazettes and the Parisian chronicler Magné de Marolles, the vicar of Prunières and several of his parishioners plunged straight into the river in feverish pursuit of the fleeing animal, "despite the rigors of the season."[124] Half walking, half swimming, they fitfully progressed toward the other side of the river, but the beast arrived on the opposite bank well ahead of its pursuers.

The river snaked along the perimeter of the town of Malzieu, and inhabitants of that city had been given the assignment of patrolling its banks. They would have been in an ideal position to take advantage of the exertions of the determined vicar—if only they had not decided to stay home instead. A monsieur Brun, "one of the principal bourgeois of the city," had long bristled at Duhamel's fondness for issuing commands, and he had earlier let the captain know that any cooperation he might receive from the parish of Malzieu would result from "our good will and not your orders." On the morning of the general hunt, Brun apparently encouraged his fellow citizens to stay home and keep their feet dry and warm, and many had followed his obstinate example, even including "several of the common people."[125] Thus facing no opposition when it reached the far side of the Truyère, the beast easily made its getaway. After emerging from the icy water, the vicar of Prunières and his parishioners followed the beast's tracks to the edge of a densely packed wood, at which point they lost all trace of the animal.

The disheartening, and infuriating, mishap at the river Truyère opened a demoralizing four-day period, one that perfectly encapsulated Duhamel's long experience as hunter-in-chief. The captain at least had the satisfaction of commiserating in good company. At his chateau in Saint-Alban, Morangiès invited both Duhamel and Lafont to join him Friday morning for a review of the results of their long labors of the previous day. At the chateau they were greeted by a hunting party, also from Malzieu, that shared details of its own frustrating encounter with the putative beast the day before. Early in the afternoon on Thursday, as they told the story, four peasants and a *valet de ville* (a low-level functionary of the city government) spotted the beast and reacted excitedly. The valet's musket misfired, but one of the peasants managed to get off a shot with a pistol, hitting his target. The beast fell forward and "let out a great cry, which the five hunters all heard." Unfortunately, the stage had merely been set for another wondrous escape. The animal "recovered promptly" and slipped away. The party claimed to have followed it until nightfall, but never "got close enough to fire again." While in pursuit, they also came across droplets of blood on the snow-covered ground, though they could not agree whether the blood came from the beast or from one of the peasants, whose heel had evidently blistered after the long day in the field.

In spite of the discreditable behavior of their fellow residents of Malzieu —Saint-Florentin himself called the town's collective failure on 7 February "reprehensible"—Morangiès found the hunters' testimony compelling.[126]

The city of Malzieu, with the belfry of the sixteenth-century collegial church of Saint Hippolyte in the left background, looks out over the banks of the Truyère River. The residents of Malzieu famously neglected to guard the banks of this river on 7 February 1765. *Author photo*

With the beast evidently still in the immediate vicinity and suffering from a wound that could be serious, Morangiès convinced Duhamel and Lafont that they should not wait until Monday the 11th to give chase. Duhamel thus sent his dragoons to announce and make preparations for a more focused hunt involving seventeen parishes, on Sunday, 10 February. He returned to Saint-Chély to retrieve the rest of his company, planning to return for an early start on Sunday morning.

The events of the weekend ranked among the most horrible and deflating in all of the Gévaudan's long experience with its affliction. On Saturday afternoon near the village of Mialanette, within the parish of Malzieu and only about half a league from the Morangiès chateau in Saint-Alban, the beast struck again. A "young and pretty girl of fourteen or fifteen years" was killed and decapitated, probably as she led livestock to or from a nearby pasture. A peasant in the village noticed the beast carrying away what looked like a human head as it made its way toward the woods. He and several companions set off after the beast, which fled on their arrival. A ghastly sight greeted the villagers. The girl's head had been gnawed almost beyond recognition, though her eyes, seemingly "untouched," stared out in blank horror.[127]

Morangiès and Duhamel both came running when they heard the news, no doubt stunned that the violence had occurred directly under the nose of a mobilized populace. The shaken Morangiès delivered a sympathetic but bracing speech to the grieving peasants who had assembled in a great crowd over the body of the victim. "My children," he is reported to have said, "today you are spectators; on another day you yourself may serve as the spectacle. Join me tomorrow so that we may prevent that misfortune."[128] The captain, meanwhile, reacted by employing his full hunting repertoire, hoping that the beast's stable location, combined with the concentrated activity of energized hunters, would finally bring an end to the reign of terror. Duhamel laid traps in the area, probably those borrowed from the comtesse de Fournels, and he left the body exposed near the spot where the unfortunate girl had fallen, leaving a detachment of dragoons to stand guard "with weapons ready." While the detachment waited through the cold February night, Duhamel and Morangiès went to prepare for the coming day's hunt.

At least two thousand people showed up for the hunt on Sunday morning, and their activity naturally centered around the stricken village of Mialanette. Small groups traipsed through the woods all day, but perhaps because the countryside was "covered with snow," Lafont suggested, "no one found a trace of [the beast] anywhere." Duhamel surely braced himself to receive the news he half-expected to hear from his dragoons at the end of the day. As Lafont remembered it in his typically laconic style, "the comte de Morangiès, M. Du-hamel and I passed by the village of Mialanette on our way back. The dra-goons told us that the Beast had not reappeared." Duhamel returned the girl's body to her parents (this time after just one night) and pinned his remaining hopes on the general hunt scheduled for the next day.

Bad luck continued on Monday. The weather again refused to cooperate, and at this point Duhamel could almost be forgiven for blaming the fates for his lack of success. Lafont characterized the weather as "cruel," citing a heavy snowfall and the arrival of a "most violent wind." The cold and miserable vil-lagers, again numbering in the thousands, plodded through the fields "from morning until night" to no effect whatever, for "the Beast was nowhere to be seen." At the end of the day Duhamel and Lafont took their leave of Morangiès and headed back to Saint-Chély, where the harsh weather forced Lafont to seek shelter against the elements before continuing to Mende on Thursday.[129] For Lafont and Duhamel, whose affinity for one another had grown strong through the shared burdens of a trying winter, the long trip back from Mialanette could not have been a happy one.

The four-day span from 7 to 11 February offered a condensed version of the whole sorry history of Duhamel and his dragoons in the Gévaudan. The hunts featured carnage grisly enough to shock the conscience, admirable courage, difficult weather, unforgiving terrain, a misfiring gun, exposed hu-man remains, feckless locals, great escapes, an exasperating close call, and, adding insult to injury, a signal failure on the part of the male hierarchy to protect a vulnerable female in distress. The general hunts of February exem-plify the fall and winter phase of the story of the beast, for in their aftermath was crystallized the symbiotic relationship so essential to the beast's "making." In the glare of accountability that he found both attractive and inescapable, Duhamel, man of honor and witness to slaughter, put the finishing touches on the image of the "monster of the Gévaudan," the product of a series of failures and repeated excuses.

Immediately upon his return to Saint-Chély, Duhamel sprang to action in an effort to control the damage to his reputation and prospects. He has-tened to send a series of letters to people whose support he wanted to main-tain and whose word could possibly help him in high places. Relating the de-tails of the general hunts to the secretary of the comte de Clermont, Duhamel admitted his great disappointment at their lack of success, though he called attention to the "good order" he had imposed on the operations, as well as the "zeal" shown during the hunts by all individuals "of highest standing." But he also used the opportunity of the failure to offer yet another theory about the beast's identity, even as he ostensibly discounted it. "I would be tempted to imagine that we are dealing with a witch, or the devil in person, if only I could believe it."[130] This rhetorical strategy—combining a defense of his own honor and skill with a terrifying depiction of the mysterious opponent who had denied him victory—marked all of Duhamel's correspondence during these dark days.

The comte de Lastic, a native of Auvergne, evidently spent the winter in Paris or somewhere near the halls of power, because Duhamel now pleaded with him to "talk to those who cannot understand why I have been unable to destroy the monster that ravages this country." None of them, he remarked indignantly, had accompanied him on "the hunts I perform daily." After experiencing seven or eight such hunts, "they would judge a little more soundly the obstacles to [my] success." Countering those who remained unconvinced about the existence of a monster, and who wondered how a mere wolf could cause such trouble, Duhamel rehearsed the physical exaggerations for which he had distinguished himself since late December. Saying "I know without a doubt" that the beast possesses "six talons" on each paw—he cited several respectable witnesses who would vouch for unusual tracks—he noted that the beast had scalped a child in the village of Pouget "with one swipe of the paw," also leaving a wound on the chest "as deep as a saber thrust." Another woman had half her scalp ripped away and left hanging about her shoulders. Duhamel could not understand why some would "wish to contradict such incontestable facts."

In this same letter Duhamel assured Lastic that the picture he had sent to him captured the true character and dimensions of the monster, so much so that all who had done battle with the beast "recognize the original" in his copy. How could one be faulted for struggling to kill or capture such a creature, one of the most cunning animals ever seen? Duhamel reported to Lastic that he had already sought out Lafont's sympathy and support, and the subdelegate had promised to inform the bishop of "all who have spoken in [my] favor." Lafont, evidently consoling Duhamel during the long ride back from Mialanette, had helpfully added that he would even try to persuade the bishop "to write on my behalf to [war minister] Choiseul, his relative." Now

Duhamel also implored Lastic, a man who "know[s] the locale," to help him
halt the spreading word that the "failure to destroy this animal" reflected the
captain's incompetence.[131]

The drumbeat continued in a letter written to Morangiès on 13 February.
Duhamel wrote in part so that he could commit to paper his many frustrations with the town council of Malzieu, whose insolent resentment toward
Duhamel was responsible for the missed chance at the river Truyère. But there
was a larger purpose behind the letter. "As you are in regular communication
with various people at court," he wrote to his esteemed hunting partner, "I
would be deeply obliged if you would take the trouble to defend me in that
land." An informant "who takes an interest in my affairs [possibly Lastic] and
who knows beyond any doubt the trouble I have taken to deliver this country
from the monster that ravages it," had recently written Duhamel from Versailles. There the currents of opinion had clearly shifted against him. At court
people seemed "very surprised that I have not yet destroyed this animal," and
the halls hummed with "murmuring about negligence on my part." This turn
of events Duhamel could not accept. "[Because] I have done and will continue to do all that a gallant man can and must do when animated by the
public good, I reject that criticism, as well as the contemptible individuals
who give voice to it." As "no one knows better than you" the difficulties presented by the challenge in the Gévaudan, Duhamel hoped that the comte de
Morangiès would tell the authorities at Versailles that "all honorable people"
of the region agreed that Duhamel himself could not be blamed. After all, a
well-organized general hunt involving "30,000" men in the field (this would
not be the last exaggeration of the figures for February) had just failed to eliminate the beast. Did Duhamel's critics really imagine that they could do any
better against such a formidable enemy? Duhamel closed by expressing a fantasy of avenged honor. "I would love to bring along with me—if only for a
few days, and especially in this weather—all these dandies who, lounging in
their parquet apartments, think that nothing could be easier than to find and
destroy this animal."[132]

In his pleas for understanding, Duhamel emphasized that the beast and
its environment presented so powerful a challenge that no man could be
faulted for failing to overcome it. In the months of February and March the
Courrier d'Avignon and other papers reinforced this message, as the failed general hunts became one of two genuinely sensational stories that propelled
news coverage throughout late winter. (The other story, involving a band of

courageous children, figures in Chapter 6.) From the perspective of François Morénas, the events of early February had turned the beast into a perverse antihero, one whose exploits had earned—in contradistinction to Duhamel— a form of honor, "if animals can have honor, and are sensitive to it."[133] Morénas devoted seven articles to the general hunts in issues of February and early March, with news of the hunts taking more than two full columns—that is, more than one quarter of the entire issue—on 26 February. The beast had become "more remarkable by the day," clearly "emboldened by the impunity it enjoys."[134]

The *Courrier* partnered with Duhamel in portraying "the beast" as one extraordinary actor whose feats inspired awe. "A single ferocious animal coming from who knows where and of a species still unknown, spreads terror [in the Gévaudan], delighting in slaughter. A large group of men, armed against this single animal, and animated by the most ardent desire to destroy it, labors in vain." All the lowlights from the general hunt received their due attention —the lost opportunity at Truyère, the musket that failed to fire, the tracks lost in the snow. The *Courrier* revealed in graphic detail the attack at Mialanette. There, "the Monster that they could not destroy" had pounced on the young girl, decapitating her and "eating all of her upper body down to the clavicle, but leaving the rest untouched, including the clothes." (The clever Morénas surely knew that this last observation spoke in code about a werewolf, for it had long been thought that werewolves, "like men[,] know how to undress the girls they wish to ravage.")[135] In view of the beast's "appetite for such tender flesh," the dragoons had hoped that "it would come back for a second meal after digesting the first," and had left the girl exposed for the night, with the usual results. In Malzieu, the horrors of Saturday prompted the clergy to schedule a Mass on Sunday "to ask the Lord for the success" of the operations planned for that day. The Mass proved fruitless, and the beast taunted its enemies by howling within earshot long into the night.[136]

The exploits of the beast provided grist for the journalistic mill, but they also underlined the ineffectiveness of the animal's pursuers, and this became another theme of the coverage in February and March. "[It] is astonishing that so many men armed against the Beast have been unable to bring about its destruction, especially since, they say, it is not nearly as courageous as it is cruel." People who had encountered it and offered resistance had managed to survive, after all. The *Courrier* noted the case of a servant girl who had struck the beast on the nose with her baton and threw stones at the beast while it retreated. (The girl believed the beast's nose to be made of wood.)[137] A story written on the eve of the general hunt of 11 February predicted failure and asserted that the frustrations would continue "until they learn how to handle [the animal]; it makes no sense to run after so agile a Beast, it will have to be surrounded."[138] A report from Paris, written in the wake of the two general hunts, sounded a deeply pessimistic note. After fantasizing about seeing the beast transported to Paris "in an iron cage," the writer confronted reality. "By what ruse, through what stratagem, with what trap could [the beast] ever be taken alive, since long-range firearms carried by thousands of hunters hot on its heels have been unable to touch it, or have only lightly wounded it?" After all, on 7 February "nearly 40,000 men" [sic] had taken the field, and only "one peasant" managed to get off a shot.[139]

This attitude of frustrated disbelief had spread widely since the first of the year. In fact, the court, apparently unknown to Duhamel, had already made the decision in late January to dispatch to the Gévaudan a reputed hunter from Normandy, Jean-Charles-Marc-Antoine de Vaumesle d'Enneval, whose arrival in the area near the end of February would open a new chapter in the ongoing saga of the beast. The authorities allowed Duhamel to stay on for a time, but the long list of disappointments, near-misses, and horrific fatalities associated with Duhamel's stint as lead huntsman, along with the signal failures of the general hunts, probably made it inevitable that he would be reassigned soon after the arrival of the renowned expert form the north. The captain's campaign to save his reputation had little effect in the short term, although Morangiès would write a letter to Morénas at the *Courrier* vouching for the captain's good efforts.[140] Duhamel's campaign to make "the beast" into a fantastic enemy with otherworldly abilities, a campaign assisted by if not exactly coordinated with the *Courrier d'Avignon,* would be sustained and emulated.

When the reality of his fate dawned on him over the course of late February and March, Duhamel reacted dutifully, offering to help his compatriots in any way he could. But his private correspondence seethed with anger and self-pity. He continued to share his fascination with the "singular traits" of the beast. He relayed to Lastic an anecdote about the beast's concealing itself from a victim while crouching behind a rock, in the way "a cat prepares to pounce on a mouse," and he sent the secretary of Clermont a new engraving that showed a "collection of tragic adventures" so compelling that "everyone wants a copy."[141] Between the lines, however, he expressed resentment toward those who had failed to recognize his labors and dedication. Duhamel's commander Clermont of course understood well the bitter experience of premature dismissal brought about by intrigue at court. Perhaps mindful of that common bond, the captain took the liberty of opening up to Clermont in one of his last letters from the region. Duhamel shared his disgust at being replaced just at the moment when the promise of better weather created glimmers of optimism. "My hope, after braving the horrors of winter for six months and pursuing this ferocious animal every day during that time, was that the court would allow me to finish the job. I never expected to see myself recalled at the outset of a season that positively invites continuation of this important task."[142] (In an earlier letter to Lastic Duhamel had cited his "nineteen years of service" and "the zeal I have brought to the commission with which I am charged." After trudging through "snow up to my knees" for months on end, he would write to Moncan, he felt entitled to carry his task to completion.)[143] By the middle of March, despite his pleas, Duhamel had been displaced as hunter-in-chief. At that point the beast was well on its way to becoming the legendary fiend that, according to Horace Walpole, "the French seem as much afraid of as if the soul of Mr. Pitt had transmigrated into a hyena."[144]

Walpole surely exaggerated, for not all of the French would have been inclined to see the beast as a stand-in for France's mortal enemy from the Seven Years' War. For Duhamel, however, a veteran of that conflict who had witnessed the painful humiliation of his commander and patron, the pursuit of the beast had indeed functioned as a kind of proxy war, one that was supposed to lead to happier endings. Like François Morénas, the journalist for whom the story of the beast offered compensating riches that helped to make up for the dearth of war-related violence, Duhamel (preceded by his sometime collaborator Morangiès) saw the beast's presence in the Gévaudan as a precious opportunity "advantageous to my glory."[145]

The beast's conquest was supposed to bring a measure of redemption for the nation, for the army, for Clermont, and for an otherwise idle dragoon company stationed in a forgotten corner of the country. Duhamel also expected that the defeat of this enemy—was it a foreign invader, or some malign force within?—would greatly enhance the reputation and prospects of the gallant officer who had managed to secure the assignment to eliminate the creature. For all of these reasons, Duhamel experienced the beast's continuing success as a piercing personal defeat. The certificates of good conduct that the captain felt compelled to include in his final letter to Clermont, signed by "all the nobility of the Gévaudan" (another of his exaggerations), simply underlined for one last time the self-conscious sensitivity that had been the defining characteristic of Duhamel's performance throughout his mission.

Like Morangiès, who assured readers in his published letter to the *Courrier* that he had "aspired only to the glory of making myself useful" for "the common cause," Duhamel could at least take satisfaction in his unflagging dedication to the defense of the beleaguered people of the Gévaudan.[146] Many of the locals, led by Lafont, expressed sincere appreciation for his efforts there.[147] For the epitaph of his trials in the region, he undoubtedly would have chosen his proud declaration to the comte de Lastic, made in February in the humiliating wake of what must have felt like another crushing loss in another pivotal battle: "I was guided by honor alone."[148] Neither in his extreme sensitivity to personal honor, nor in his odd relationship of mutual dependence with the beast, would Duhamel prove unique among the noble huntsmen who worked for the Gévaudan's deliverance.

4

A Star Is Born

The denouement of Duhamel's February hunts coincided with an explosion of interest in the exploits of the beast of the Gévaudan. The growing fascination with the story cannot be credited solely to the effects of Duhamel's work, however. Other circumstances specific to the time and place also helped to make the beast's arena of combat irresistibly interesting by early 1765: the monarchy's investment in the story's outcome, the existence of a reading audience capable of sustained attention, widespread identification with the victims of the afflicted region, the lure of cash rewards.

The presence and power of these conditions signal the growing size and cultural unity of the "imagined community" of the French nation in the eighteenth century.[1] The story of the beast resonated in a "media-saturated" space where the performance of all concerned—the monster, its opponents, and those forced to officiate the contest—commanded critical attention across the realm (and beyond). Those who publicized the events in the Gévaudan, including many who helped to generate new attention only unwittingly or unwillingly, shaped the experience at the time and ultimately determined how the rampage of the beast would be thought about and remembered.

The next three chapters explore the different ways in which the publicity surrounding the event defined its essence. Chapter 6 will examine the process through which the most sympathetic heroes of the tale came to be identified and defined. Chapters 4 and 5, focused especially on the events of late winter and spring of 1765, explore the double-sided nature of public attention, its power as both boon and bane for those caught in its web. As the eyes and feet of people from across France and beyond raced toward the Gévaudan like moths to a flame, the clash of different worlds and different interests produced unpleasant results for many of those involved in the story. The realignment of perspectives that occurred within a cauldron of publicity in 1765 had profound consequences—both for the theater of operations in the Gévaudan and for later French memories of what happened there.

The nation's engagement with the Gévaudan in the middle of the eighteenth century illuminates some of the emerging features of French public life recognizable to us today. The word *celebrity (célébrité),* for example, had only begun to acquire its modern connotations of fame and wide reputation in the first half of the eighteenth century. Before that time, as shown in the 1694 edition of the *Dictionary of the French Academy,* the term had been synonymous with "solemnity." The word applied almost exclusively to official events that had been staged to have the proper effect on an audience ("the ceremony was performed with great celebrity"). As the French monarchy gradually lost control over the definition of public space and the parameters of public engagement, however, the meaning of the term expanded, and the change was reflected in lagging lexicographical indicators over the course of the next century and more. The word's meaning as "great reputation" had already crept into the *Dictionary* of 1762 as a secondary definition of the term, and by the end of the eighteenth century, in the edition of 1798, the status of the two definitions had been reversed. *Celebrity* now chiefly meant "great reputation, [as in] celebrity of a name, person, work, or event." In 1832, "solemnity" continued to be included in the French Academy's definition of the word, but it appeared there only as an archaism. Whereas *celebrity* had connoted ritualized gravity in the seventeenth century, the nineteenth century would know *celebrity* only as a "reputation that extends far."[2]

The phenomenon of the beast of the Gévaudan allows us to grasp this eighteenth-century transformation as a visible social reality. The beast itself was not a celebrity, since that connotation, applying to a person (or performer) who enjoys fame, would not arrive before the twentieth century. But the beast was certainly celebrated, and celebrated not because of any form of monarchical affirmation but because of insatiable public curiosity. Indeed, the wide curiosity generated by the beast that stalked the Gévaudan indicates the development of an early celebrity culture, one marked by all the accoutrements of celebrity production: a genuine media "star," spectators in large numbers, an acute awareness of public perception on the part of all actors in the drama, the elevation of obscure or otherwise unremarkable individuals to the status of national hero, and the conversion of popular experience into an item for mass consumption by literate elites. These features of a celebrity culture were partly symptomatic of France's mid-century creation of what the German sociologist Jürgen Habermas has famously described as a "rational public sphere." This active form of public space, partly aroused in opposition to the secretive operations of a theoretically "absolute" monarchy, was animated by readers' voracious appetite for information and their critical processing of news relating to public affairs. The appearance of this latent but powerful public force in the eighteenth century foreshadowed the role played by publicity and transparency in the liberal democracies that rose to power after the American and French revolutions.[3]

The story of the beast attests to the power and accelerating speed of all these cultural changes. At the same time, however, the nation's experience in the Gévaudan also affords a glimpse at the mechanisms through which traces of the traditional could be concealed within or imperfectly repressed by the rational forms of publicity seemingly favored by modernity. The public sphere as described by Habermas was defined by its permeable and egalitarian character, its sober practicality, and its role in facilitating informed critique of public issues. But in the time of the beast, public discourse was only beginning to take on these features; even a generation later the "rational" ideal remained largely unfulfilled. Superstition, consciousness of status hierarchies, suspicion of official narratives, and suspension of disbelief all survived the crucible of 1765 to condition later consumption of the beast's tale by publics of the nineteenth century and beyond. Important clues to the nature of the beast's two-sided public legacy in the modern world (embraced as folklore, neglected as history) can be found in the mutations to the story that were caused or provoked by the unrelenting glare of public attention in 1765.

This chapter begins with an overview of the vectors of news that carried information about the beast and its enemies. As word spread, an ever-expanding network of interested consumers began to receive and respond to the news from the Gévaudan. The analysis then focuses on two sets of responses elicited by the story—the forms of assistance that emanated from the

Bourbon monarchy, on the one hand, and the problem-solving initiative brought to bear by individuals from across the realm, on the other.

Spreading the Word

Subscription figures do not begin to convey the impact of the reporting of the *Courrier d'Avignon* and other papers like it. A single issue of any major newspaper reached many readers in the 1760s, and not only because of sharing among family and friends. The sudden increase in book and newspaper publishing in the middle decades of the eighteenth century brought with it an expanding infrastructure that assured wide dissemination of the printed word. Some booksellers lent newssheets on site for a small fee; others sold outdated issues at a discounted rate. In Paris, peddlers of news *(nouvellistes)* who sold their wares at the Palais Royal, the quai des Augustins, the Hôtel Soubise, and other well-known gathering places allowed readers to peruse the latest newspapers for the widely affordable price of one *sou.* For readers who could not afford the cost of a newspaper subscription, or who wished to combine reading with socializing, reading rooms *(cabinets de lecture)* offered another attractive venue for news consumption. The new and rising importance of these institutions, which would grow rapidly in the two decades before the French Revolution, coincided roughly with the arrival of the Seven Years' War. A notably welcoming and comfortable reading room was established in Nantes in 1759. The first reading room in Paris appeared in 1761, and Lyons had at least two such *cabinets* by 1764. Eventually they functioned as fee-collecting libraries, providing paying clients full access to recently published materials. Groups of like-minded readers also gathered in small and informal societies where they pooled their resources to purchase subscriptions to all of their favorite newspapers; particularly avid readers ran public advertisements in search of such partners.[4]

Physical contact with the printed word represented only one avenue for the communication of journalistic reporting, however. In Paris, according to one observer in the late 1750s, the *Gazette de France* and the popular foreign papers were read aloud free of charge "in the most renowned and heavily frequented cafés."[5] Parks and street corners also hosted public readings of gazettes on a routine basis. Popular almanachs and other products of *colportage,* which overlapped and borrowed from the more sensational items from the newspapers, also had their contents transmitted orally, which made it possible even for the unlettered to keep up with appealing news stories.[6] At the highest end of the social spectrum, manuscript newssheets *(nouvelles à la main)* composed for a select clientele of aristocrats, political elites, and the wealthy were also informed by newspaper coverage and relied on many of the same sources that fueled the reports published in gazettes.[7] For example, Frederick II of Prussia, who became so immersed in the story that he could teasingly claim to know the beast's "true" identity (he blamed his friend and noted freethinker, Jean-Baptiste de Boyer, marquis d'Argens), would have read of the monster in F.-M. Grimm's *Correspondance Littéraire,* a refined manuscript newssheet sent to the courts of northern Europe.[8] Grimm focused on cultural developments in Paris, but he remained alert to current news and the latest fashions, especially if Parisian elites showed an interest in them.

The wide reverberations of the accounts reported in gazettes confirm the predominant role of the *Courrier d'Avignon* in propagating the story of the beast. Although journalists of the eighteenth century were not yet regarded as the composers of the "first draft of history," there is little doubt that the *Courrier* wrote the first draft of the Gévaudan's experience with its beast, even in spite of Morénas's reputation for truth-stretching.[9] In an era that had not yet enshrined the principle of copyright, newspapers routinely borrowed from other periodicals, and the *Courrier,* by virtue of its steady attention to the story and its fondness for the spectacular, became a favorite target for such borrowings, either directly or through third parties. Morénas's early January rendition of a father's panicked rescue of his young daughter (assisted by helpful bovines) landed in the *Gazette d'Amsterdam* two weeks later, establishing a borrowing schedule that the Dutch newssheet would follow throughout 1765.[10] The startling agility displayed by the beast on the Darissatis bridge, reported first by the *Courrier* in late January, appeared in both the *Gazette de Leyde* and London's *St. James's Chronicle.* The details in the London account were lifted, in turn, from the *Gazette de Bruxelles,* whose editor, the notorious "lying Maubert," must have appreciated Morénas's compulsion to entertain.[11] When the *Gazette de France* placed its imprimatur on the story with regular reports beginning in February, the beast's orbit undoubtedly expanded; notwithstanding the *Gazette's* status as the French news source of record, however, the *Courrier* served as the primary supplier of raw material throughout the beast's rampage.

The central role of the gazettes also underlines the disproportionate influence wielded by individuals reporting from or near the scene. The personal letter, after all, remained the indispensable source of both information and "narrative unity" in the journalistic world of the *ancien régime*.[12] For the story of the beast, this meant that the notables of the Gévaudan, such as Morangiès, Lafont, the bishop of Mende and others, had an enormous capacity to shape public perception. Preeminent among these players, especially from November through February, were Duhamel and his dragoon company. In that period, when Duhamel remained in constant contact with all of the principals

"Figure of the ferocious Beast that has been called a Hyena." The events depicted in this print place its publication sometime before mid-March, when more specific occurrences came to dominate artwork on the beast. Given the expanding orbit of rumors about La Baume, which had entered into wide circulation by the end of January, and the presence here of a large wall that the beast approaches with evident intent to leap, this print may have appeared even before the general hunts of February. In any case, the image was familiar enough by late March for the Marvejols native Tardieu de La Barthe to discuss the engraving and make light of its implausibility in a letter to Elie Fréron of the *Année Littéraire.* La Barthe's letter is discussed in Chapter 6. *Bibliothèque Nationale de France, Rés. 4-LK2-786, fol. 104*

and spoke with countless local inhabitants of the affected areas, the captain's authoritative word had great credit among local notables from Marvejols to Mende to Montpellier. These well-connected citizens, who served as informers for their own contacts in Paris and other cities, were often as anxious to perpetuate intriguing rumors as Duhamel would have been to create and lend credence to them.

By far the best example of the generative power of the captain's words and deeds is found in the evolving narrative of the great missed opportunity at La Baume. In each of his own detailed accounts of the episode, Duhamel explained that his comrades had been forced to give up the chase for the beast when their horses encountered a "cursed impassable marsh."[13] By the time the anecdote made its way to the public some weeks later, however, it had acquired a detail that added new mystique to the captain's enemy.

One of Duhamel's men, who evidently took great relish in relating the tale to locals in Saint-Chély, claimed that he had been so hot on the heels of the beast that he "would have split it with his saber" if not for the sudden ap-

"A general but detailed accounting of all the disorders committed by the beast that ravages the Gévaudan and surrounding territories." The most distinctive feature of this lizardlike creature, a detail from an image produced for an April broadsheet, is the presence of six talons—one of the few depictions of the beast that included that feature so dear to Duhamel. *Archives Départementales de l'Hérault, C 44, 1764, no. 10.*

pearance of an unfortunate wall that disrupted the dragoons' progress.[14] As this version of events began to be fixed in print, more than a month after the incident, the alleged wall became nearly as extraordinary as the beast that used the structure to its advantage. In the pages of the *Gazette d'Amsterdam,* the beast countered "the speed of its pursuers" by "leaping a rather high wall that it found in its path." The *London Chronicle* said of the wall that it was "a great deal too much for the horses." A March broadsheet that related the "Disorders caused by a ferocious Beast that ravages the Gévaudan" explained that the dragoons at La Baume had nearly caught up to the animal when "they confronted a very high wall which the Monster cleared in a single bound, but which stopped the dragoons."[15] Just a few weeks later, another broadsheet amplified the message with a detailed text that was accompanied by a terrifying illustration—one that depicted a beast with six talons, as the captain had famously specified. The author of this newssheet excitedly reported that the beast had "escaped death" only because it "found an extremely elevated wall" that it used to evade its pursuers. As a matter of routine, the beast's "astonishing light-footedness" evidently enabled it to "clear the highest walls in a single bound [*franchit d'un seul saut les murs les plus élévés*]."[16] References to the beast's remarkable leaping talents would become standard fare in papers and newssheets after the first of February, and visual evidence reinforced the theme. (Frederick II would comment on the beast's "great nimbleness in leaping from branch to branch" in a March letter.) Thanks in no small part to Duhamel and the memory of La Baume, the ability to jump over imposing structures with a "surprising lightness of touch" became another distinctive characteristic of the beast of the Gévaudan.[17]

The tale of La Baume and the terrifying image Duhamel later fabricated in Montpellier made long-lasting impressions, but the captain's most important contribution to the beast's celebrity was his series of attention-getting failures. The tragic grandiosity of his winter efforts, from the masquerades of late January to the mobilization of thousands for the snowy general hunts of February, impressed even the most jaded readers of news and the most circumspect inhabitants of the Gévaudan. Reports of the beast's extraordinary characteristics now increased in both quantity and quality, fueling the animal's rise to national and international prominence.

The inability of well-equipped forces to find and kill the beast naturally spurred rumor in the Gévaudan. One subdelegate would note in mid-February that "a large number of fables are making the rounds," and a few weeks later a parish priest communicated a sense of the heightened fears by reporting on the killing of another young girl "by a man-eater or ferocious beast whose name and species we do not know to this day."[18] But reports of the beast's prowess also stimulated the imaginations of urban dwellers and the journalists who served them, making them more receptive to wild theories and more prone to fantasies of their own. The *Journal Encyclopédique*, a journal of the sciences, arts, and literature that had given scant attention to the story of the beast before hearing word of the general hunts, reported on Duhamel's great disappointments in a March issue and referred casually to an earlier beast that had allegedly "devoured 240 persons in the forest of Fontainebleau" before meeting its demise.[19] The general hunts inspired an exceptionally long story in the *Gazette d'Amsterdam*—by far the paper's longest to date on the phenomenon of the beast. In it readers learned that a dog in the parish of Aumont had eerily "refused to give chase" to the beast after its initial encounter with the creature at a village well, despite the exhortations of the frustrated villagers.[20]

Many other unsettling incidents occurred in the two months following the failed general hunts, and the cryptic reporting on these events often suggested, without quite claiming, that the beast's unusual physical appearance masked a rational, and perhaps human, actor. According to the *Journal Encyclopédique*, in early April the beast spied a man and a girl guarding sheep by the village of Mazel, near Montchauvet. Training its appetites on the girl, but seeing its passage blocked by the interfering presence of the flock, the beast simply "opened a path through the sheep by throwing aside all those standing in its way." The calculating beast had the strength to throw the sheep "five or six feet" to either side, and it did so deliberately and single-mindedly, "without causing them any other harm." The girl would surely have died if she had not been rescued by villagers who rushed to the scene.[21]

Both the *Année Littéraire* and the *St. James's Chronicle* reported that on 8 February the beast had escaped a mob of angry villagers in Grandvals by jumping into the Bes, a "rather significant river," which it then "passed erect on its hind paws."[22] The beast's bipedal dexterity also figured prominently in a story from the *St. James's Chronicle* that relayed the curious adventure of an English gentleman, "heir to a title," who had gone to the south of France to recuperate from poor health. Traveling through the Gévaudan in February with a small party of servants and companions, the group allegedly had an encounter with a most unwelcome stranger that observed their progress from a distance. Seeing the footman's horse take an inopportune tumble, throwing its rider in the process, the beast suddenly launched an attack on the prostrate horse. "[On] the footman's erecting his right hand to draw a cutlass, and strike the beast, it pricked up his ears, stood on its hind feet, and shewing its teeth full of froth, turned round and gave the fellow a most violent blow with the swing of his tail." With his face bloodied, the servant failed to prevent the beast from making its escape, which it did by bursting into the gentleman's carriage, re-emerging through a window on the opposite side, and running "at a great rate to the adjoining wood."[23]

Such bold behavior (or reports thereof) expressed a brazen confidence uncharacteristic of any familiar animal. It is not entirely surprising, then, that Fréron's *Année Littéraire* published in February an anonymous letter from Marvejols that brought into question the beast's status as an animal. Fréron's letter shared eyewitness accounts of beastly cunning and agility "outside the rules of nature," including one encounter at which the beast had once again shown quick feet and impressive jumping ability. According to the story, the peasant who witnessed the beast's performance experienced the shock of a lifetime when the animal concluded by addressing him in an audible voice: "Admit it, my friend, for an old man of eighty years, that's pretty good jumping."[24] No further conversation was reported.

One journalistic flight of imagination inspired by the beast in the winter of 1765 captures particularly well the creative partnership that connected events to their fascinated audience in the media-saturated space of the eighteenth-century public sphere. The obviously fictionalized account, published in the *London Chronicle,* is revealing precisely because it did not trace its origins to the ground of the Gévaudan, where the supposedly benighted locals steeped in their distorting superstitions. Rather, it sprang from the mind of an urban wit whose imagination had been activated by the stunning reports that had become part of the journalistic landscape. The account represents well the fascination that the beast inspired among consumers of news in 1765, even as it also signals the enduring resonance of the Seven Years' War on both sides of the English Channel.

In the wake of Duhamel's general hunts and the reports alleging some 20,000 to 40,000 people in attendance there, the *Chronicle* published a satire that added new dimensions to the terrible beast while it simultaneously mocked French futility. In a featured front-page story on 27 March, the paper reported that the beast "that makes such a noise all over Europe" had apparently descended from the "famous dragon of Wantley," whom English readers would have recognized as the central character of a popular medieval romance. The *Chronicle*'s beast evidently lacked the capacity for speech, but it possessed other impressive powers. With "a wag of his tail he throws down a church," and he eats houses "as an Alderman eats a custard." The animal had inadvertently destroyed a convent when, while pausing to smell grapes in a vineyard, it "unfortunately broke wind," leaving 144 souls to die in the ruins of the collapsed building. Recently attacked in his den "by a detachment of 14,000 men," the beast had emerged unscathed, giving "a flash of his tail, by which we lost 7,000." Showing off its talent for leaping, the beast then made "a jump over the heads of the left wing, [and] made his escape. He unfortunately made water as he passed, by which means 500 grenadiers were drowned in the puddle."

Amazingly, this rout was only a prelude to the epic confrontation that followed. Just days after its great escape, the beast found itself under attack "by the whole French army, consisting of 120,000 effective men." The beast administered a beating "in the twinkling of an eye," swallowing the entire train of French artillery "and devouring 25,000 men." The animal was later determined to have swallowed, in addition to countless flags and banners, five mortars, twenty-two brass cannon, and at least one hundred small arms, "beside which he voided a great quantity as he went along." In a great show of irony, the beast followed up its smashing victory over the French army by provoking its true nemesis. Walking through a small village the next day, "he devoured a little kitten that lay at a door; which so enraged the old cat mother, that she flew at him, and killed him on the spot." An announcement soon followed that "the cat, that killed the beast, that beat the army, is to make a triumphant entry into Paris the first of April," where it would be made a "Peeress" of the realm.[25]

The *Chronicle*'s satire seems to have been intended in good fun. There are reasons to suppose that the sardonic Francophile Horace Walpole, in France at the time, may even have been responsible for the piece.[26] But this rendition of the beast "that beat the army" could not have failed to touch a nerve among any French readers who learned of its publication. Government officials surely numbered among them, since the ministry of foreign affairs regarded the *London Chronicle* as a paper of record, and throughout 1763 the ministry had commissioned translations of *Chronicle* articles dedicated to France or to English perceptions of the French.[27] In 1765, the *Chronicle*'s allusions to crushed artillery and battles lost to vastly outnumbered forces evoked all too vividly the military embarrassments of recent times. After all, the piece asserted that the "whole French army" had been outdone by an angry cat.

One Parisian *nouvelliste,* writing a manuscript newssheet for a provincial magistrate in Dijon, dismissed what he called (inaccurately) the "dull and leaden" prose of the *Chronicle* essay, which "does no honor to the wit who dreamed it up."[28] The Parisian contact for the *Courrier d'Avignon* found the imagery equally unamusing. Noting that some "English journalists have fun at our expense, in the English way," the writer confessed to being unable to "see the point of this sarcasm."[29] The abbé Coyer would later ask why "London did not want to believe in our beast of the Gévaudan," even though English naturalists credited the existence of giants from the New World.[30] The French would eventually have their revenge, as François Morénas impishly pointed out in January of 1766. Although the English had taken pleasure in ridiculing France's "strange war" against its beast, he wrote, recent developments in America, where colonists spoke of breaking their "ties of dependence," had turned out to be "no laughing matter" for France's former tormenter, Mr. Pitt.[31]

Thanks in part to the proliferation of stories featuring froth-mouthed assailants, sorcerers who walked and talked, leaping acrobats, and flatulent dragons, popular excitement over the strange news from the Gévaudan grew markedly as the winter of 1765 progressed. In its 12 February issue, the *Courrier d'Avignon* published a dispatch from Mende in which the writer lamented the status of his poor country, which had acquired an unwanted "celebrity founded only on disasters." The correspondent probably had no idea just how celebrated his *pays* had become. A week later, the paper reported that Parisian readers could not get their fill of news from the land of the beast. Savage animals were so much "in vogue" that some readers, desperate for "something to talk about," happily circulated stories about murderous fiends of yore—big bad wolves from Limousin, Normandy, and elsewhere—while awaiting impatiently the latest news from the Gévaudan. The *nouvellistes* in the streets now seemed to make their living relaying news of the monster. The beast, "which is the daily subject of their reports[,] is the item most talked about here; anything that has, or appears to have, some connection to it piques the curiosity of the public." From the vantage point of Paris, "there is no event in France, or indeed all the universe, that our audience is more keen to learn about than the goings on in the Gévaudan." As long as the "cruel beast" drew breath, it would be "the subject of our daily conversations." An engraving had recently hit the streets—as useless as the "confused ideas" upon which it was based— yet "everyone rushes to buy it." The press, though diligent in trying to meet the demands of its readers, had not even come close to producing as many images "as the public desires." By the end of March, the level of curiosity in Paris grew "from day to day." The *nouvellistes* could be heard at all hours, "either asking what others have heard or telling others what they themselves have learned."[32]

The newshounds' incessant chatter made a lasting impact on the inhabitants of the city. Magné de Marolles, an ardent hunter and former infantry officer who now resided in Paris, became such a devoted follower of the news by early 1765 that he began collecting and copying newspaper accounts by hand—sixty-two folio pages' worth—in part with the intention of providing the government a complete record of "one of the most singular public events of this century." (He hinted with evident pride that he had used one of his contacts at court to secure some of the private correspondence of the hunter d'Enneval.) In June of 1782 he donated to the Bibliothèque du Roi his laboriously copied extracts, and his letters, newspaper accounts, and engravings now form the core of the most comprehensive collection of beast-related documents found outside French archives.[33]

Few went to the obsessive lengths of Magné de Marolles, but in Paris and other cities there were many signs of the public's absorption in the events of the Gévaudan. Not only did engravings proliferate beginning in January, but poems and popular songs (called *complaintes*) on the subject of the beast also began to circulate.[34] One of these would ultimately be converted into a nursery rhyme involving the loving repetition of a single melodic phrase, *Elle a tant mangé de monde, la Bête du Gévaudan.* (In translation the meter loses both its rhyme and its charm: "It has eaten so many, the beast of the Gévaudan"). In the 1790s the marquise de Créquy remembered this song being sung over the cradle of her grandson, Tancrède, after his birth in 1769.[35] A poem "On the Cruel and Monstrous Beast of the Gévaudan," clearly inspired by the warnings of the bishop of Mende ("Has God, in his fury against a certain people, dispatched a Monster to inspire horror?"), gave voice to the most hysterical fears:

Could it be that from the bowels of hell has come
This Monster, abominable, execrable, inhuman!

Is not some Demon on earth incarnate
Making war against the human race
One that, even before the Antichrist begins to reign,
Exerts its will here on the earthly plain?

The poet elsewhere speculated that the creature might be a monster "sent by famous sorcerers," the product of a "malign influence" of an evil star, or even a werewolf, a "singular animal that M. Buffon unfortunately forgot to include in his *Natural History*."[36]

Despite the many apparent mysteries of its identity, Parisian polite society found frames of reference with which to make sense of the beast. In the fashionable salons of Madame Marie Thérèse Rodet Geoffrin and Marie Anne de Vichy, marquise du Deffand, "the beast" seems to have become a jocular metaphor used to describe the ferocious Russian czarina, Catherine II.[37] Walpole repeatedly compared the beast to the English foreign minister, William Pitt. The renowned actress Mademoiselle Clairon, central attraction of the *Comédie Française* and Voltaire's favorite performer, appears to have taken Elie Fréron's February description of the fearsome beast in the *Année Littéraire* as a veiled attack on her voice and appearance. Fréron had earlier provided commentary on a published ode to the "irreproachable" Mademoiselle Olligny, a rival actress. In it, he had contrasted Olligny's virtues to the "dissolute life" led by many other actresses, and it seems likely that his perceived allusion to the most famous actress of the day was responsible for igniting Fréron's heated dispute with Clairon, who may have seen his February description of the beast as a snide escalation of tensions.[38] Because the acting troupe enjoyed the patronage of the king, the controversy might well have landed Fréron in prison had he not persuaded the minister Saint-Florentin in March that Clairon's hurt feelings resulted from a terrible misunderstanding.

Saint-Florentin's intervention in the dispute between Fréron and the actress certainly would not have been the first time that the bothersome animal in the Gévaudan had caused agitation at Versailles. The minister himself had been following events since December, and in late January the controller-general L'Averdy began the discussions that would launch the southward trek of the renowned wolf-killer, d'Enneval. Nevertheless, the agents of the French crown could not have failed to notice, and to have been touched by, the swirl of publicity that grew in intensity after the first of the year. By becoming more active in late January and thereafter in the unfolding story of the beast, the monarchy magnified, responded to, and participated in the enthusiastic publicity surrounding the strange monster of the Gévaudan.

One Crisis among Many

For personal and official reasons, the minister Saint-Florentin took an acute interest in the Gévaudan story. Scion of the powerful Phélypeaux dynasty that had served French kings since the seventeenth century, Saint-Florentin had frequented the court since his youth. As secretary of state for the "king's household" *(Maison du roi)* since 1749, he embraced the courtly and aristocratic pastime of the hunt with enthusiasm. Saint-Florentin's passion for the chase even led to what is arguably the greatest irony in the irony-filled history of the beast of the Gévaudan. The minister was prevented from rejoicing in the story's apparent climax in the autumn of 1765 because in early September, just two weeks before François Antoine killed his large wolf in southern Auvergne, Saint-Florentin accidentally shot himself while participating in a leisurely hunt near Versailles. His mangled left hand had to be amputated at the chateau, where he was also "bled two times." The event caused widespread concern for the minister's well-being. ("Between you and me," noted Buffon in a letter to a friend, the comte "is the only one of our ministers that everyone wants to keep around.")[39] But the minister fortunately proved resilient. Having survived not only the accident but also his medical care, Saint-Florentin was soon fitted with an "artificial hand" that allowed him "to fasten buttons," "pick up tobacco," and return to work within three weeks, before the wound had fully healed. At a public audience where he greeted wellwishers, Saint-Florentin joked, with his "ordinary gaiety," that he found some consolation in having blown off his least useful hand.[40]

Pressing professional duty also compelled Saint-Florentin to take an interest in the story of the beast. The secretary in charge of the king's household had a wide array of responsibilities, including the planning of court spectacles, management of the royal library, supervision of the opera, the policing of Protestants, and seeing to the appropriate splendor of the royal botanical garden and its natural history displays. In that last capacity, Saint-Florentin sought to enhance the king's collections by pursuing exceptional specimens of flora and fauna—deceased dwarfs (as we have seen), dragon's blood from Sumatra, zebras and other animals from exotic places near and far.[41] By virtue of its strangeness alone, then, the alleged monster of the Gévaudan would

Louis Phelypeaux   *Comte de Saint Florentin*

Commandeur des Ordres du Roy,   Secretaire d'Etat &

des Commandements de sa Majesté,   Chancelier de la Reine.

Massilia Civitas beneficiorum memor   offerebat Anno M.DCC.LI.

have attracted the attention of the court. Both Saint-Florentin and controller-general Charles-François L'Averdy repeatedly reminded officials in Languedoc and Auvergne that the king himself intended to personally inspect the beast after its death. L'Averdy alluded to "the curiosity of the king" in an April letter instructing Saint-Priest to take great care in preserving the beast's remains in the event of success. (He suggested that it be "stuffed with straw" to prevent the carcass from rotting while in transit.) In late January the court had issued specific instructions to insure that "the hide and skeleton" of the beast would be promptly "sent here to be placed in the king's garden," where "free and open" anatomical lectures were regularly given for the benefit of both medical students and the general public.[42]

A hunter by avocation, collector of curiosities by vocation, and secretary of state with a portfolio that included the provinces of Languedoc and Auvergne, Saint-Florentin naturally followed with great interest the ongoing developments in the south. He and L'Averdy had other reasons to stay alert to the public commotion caused by the beast, however. Although local frustrations over the continuing carnage in the Gévaudan never threatened to mutate into wide popular anger, and any recriminations remained personal and specific to the issues at hand, agents of the crown guarded the reputation of Louis XV and the monarchy with special care in the immediate postwar era. Consequently, in the crown's approach to the crisis in the Gévaudan we glimpse the effects of the badly strained public relations that had hampered royal governance since at least the middle 1750s.

The congenitally taciturn Louis XV had never enjoyed easy relations with the constituent members of the body politic, but the fog of war had introduced higher levels of rancor to political discussion and a fresh assertiveness on the part of those who opposed royal policies. The changing tone was most evident in the king's relationship with his twelve *parlements,* the august law courts whose noble magistrates needed to ratify royal legislation before it could officially become the law of the land. Fiscal policy lay at the root of

opposite page: Louis Phélypeaux, comte de Saint-Florentin (1705–1777). Secretary of state for the king's household and minister with a jurisdiction that included the provinces of Languedoc and Auvergne, Saint-Florentin necessarily paid close attention to the ravages of the beast. This portrait, produced fourteen years before the accident that would cost him the use of his left hand, portrays the minister at work. *Bibliothèque Nationale de France, N3, Saint-Florentin*

most conflicts. Because French kings for centuries had stifled the creation of a parliament in the English style (which would have been able to negotiate and approve new taxes at the request of the executive power), and because the rate of France's basic land tax (the *taille*) had reached its permissible limits in the late seventeenth century, the monarchy had to resort to various short-term expedients to raise money. In 1749, the crown had responded to the debts imposed by the War of the Austrian Succession by creating a temporary twentieth tax (the *vingtième*) levied on all incomes, regardless of the taxpayer's social status. This measure had generated dissent, especially from the tax-exempt clergy, but the *parlements* accepted the edict on grounds that exceptional circumstances justified exceptional short-term measures.

The coming of the Seven Years' War tested the limits of parlementary compliance.[43] In 1756, after the June declaration of war, the crown unexpectedly extended the duration of the 1749 *vingtième* even while creating a second *vingtième* that it pledged to abolish at the end of the new conflict. These measures won approval only after protracted argument and the king's eventual performance of a little-used legal ceremony—the "bed of justice" *(lit de justice)*—that asserted the principle of royal supremacy in terms the judges could not resist. In 1759 the crown came back for more. The controller-general Etienne de Silhouette invented a 10 percent tax on property and rushed its approval by staging a preemptive *lit de justice* in September. So loud was the uproar that Louis XV was forced to dismiss Silhouette in December and suspend implementation of the new tax.

In early 1760 the new controller-general, Henri-Léonard Bertin, proposed an edict that created a third *vingtième* in addition to sales taxes and new levies on the privileged. The outcry lasted for years, as the *parlement* of Paris and its sister courts in the provinces mobilized to oppose taxes that looked not only burdensome but alarmingly corrosive of the traditional prerogatives of the privileged. The many twists and turns in the long dispute that followed need not be detailed, but magistrates in courts all across the country offered spirited resistance to the king's fiscal plans. Over the next three years they provoked many forced registrations and two more *lits de justice*. When the crown reneged on more promises by seeking to extend taxes in the spring of 1763 even after the war had ended, the magistrates of the *parlement* of Rouen actually resigned *en masse*.

While butting heads with Versailles, parlementary magistrates often employed a provocative political rhetoric that Louis XV and his agents found insulting and dangerous. The judges accused the crown of "despotism," claimed to defend "liberty" and property against arbitrary force, and spoke in behalf of the interests of the "nation" and its "citizens." Such rhetoric would be used to devastating effect in 1788–1789, but already in the 1760s jurists created the impression that France stood "ready for a revolution."[44] Bertin worried openly that the magistrates' recent practice of publishing its objections to royal legislation would elicit a harmful "fermentation in people's minds." One magistrate sympathetic to the cause of the king went further and claimed that some of his colleagues evidently hoped to "indispose the people against the crown" and even bring "a change in the form of government."[45]

In an effort to assuage dangerously elevated tensions in December of 1763, the monarchy replaced the hard-nosed Bertin with a magistrate from the *parlement* of Paris, one who had helped to engineer the campaign against the Jesuits: L'Averdy.[46] The new controller-general was known for his cooperative style, and at the outset of his ministry he ingratiated himself with the *parlements* by humbly admitting his lack of expertise in financial matters and signaling his willingness to learn from others.[47] Worried that the publicity of parlementary complaints had served to weaken "the ties that attach the peoples to [the] king," the crown sought to soften judicial rhetoric by creating at least the appearance of the king's thoughtful weighing of the judges' grievances.[48]

Unfortunately for the defenders of the crown, Louis XV himself did little to bolster his image. The debates over Jansenism, the friction resulting from the 1756 "reversal of alliances" that fatefully linked France's destiny to that of Austria, the assassination attempt of 1757, the disasters of the war—all of these crises had left the king exhausted and demoralized. In late 1757, rumors circulated that the king was actually contemplating abdication.[49] Although that unlikely prospect had passed by the mid-1760s, he remained dour and withdrawn. Well regarded in his earliest youth, Louis XV had long since acquired the reputation for being weak-willed, dominated by his lusts for women and the hunt, and insufficiently attentive to the needs of the state.[50] Decades before the appearance of the beast, spies had overheard a critic referring to Louis XV as "a do-nothing king, of whom history will not say that he had defeated all the nations of Europe as had his great-grandfather, but that he made war only on deer." The rampage in the Gévaudan could not have reflected well on the dejected hunter-king.[51]

Instead of working to repair his poor reputation, the king seemed intent on justifying it. He whiled away the hours on the royal hunting grounds, and he continued his debauched ways by consorting with the many available young women with which his official mistress, Madame de Pompadour, kept him supplied.[52] When the *parlement* of Rouen resisted imposition of the third *vingtième* in 1760, the king's ally Armand Thomas Hue de Miromesnil had to coax him to address in person a delegation of dissenting magistrates. Louis XV must "show himself," Miromesnil tried to explain, to counteract "the belief shared by everyone that the king does not want to take the trouble to govern."[53]

The king's personal habits and temperament thus aggravated the government's relations with its increasingly critical public. While officials at Versailles worked to improve the monarchy's image by launching a propaganda campaign designed to inspire patriotic affection for king and crown, the police remained alert to shows of disrespect for the monarch.[54] Virulent rumors about the king's alleged involvement in the abduction of working-class children in Paris had already led to popular riots in 1750, and in the tense environment of the early 1760s the monarchy's servants left nothing to chance.[55] Like a dangerous contagion, they thought, ugly sentiments had to be rooted out and eliminated before they could do widespread damage.

In 1762, a down-on-his-luck nobleman was executed for having intentionally raised a false alarm about the king's safety at Versailles. (He had posed as a heroic defender of the king in hopes of earning a much-needed pension.) Saint-Florentin pressed to make an example of the culprit on grounds that the merest suggestion of ill-will toward Louis XV was "capable of alarming the king" about the true depths of his subjects' "love and fidelity" for him.[56] Others paid for ill-considered words. In Amiens in February of 1765, François Routtier, a master cloth maker, found himself in trouble for allegedly declaring at a contentious guild meeting that he would do to his opponents what Frederick II had done to his enemies in the recent war. He apparently meant this as a threat, since "the king of Prussia had roundly fucked the king of France" and forced him into submission. Two fellow guild members, scandalized by words "injurious to the majesty of the king," denounced their colleague to a municipal official in the city. Once informed of the incident, Saint-Florentin decided "to employ the king's authority rather than the courts," and he ordered the provincial intendant to throw the offender in prison without further ado. There he remained for six weeks, until a thorough investigation showed that Routtier had been falsely accused.[57]

The fact that Routtier's enemies would have chosen the humiliating war as a plausible pretext for "injurious" conversation about the king underscores the fragility of the king's reputation in the aftermath of the Treaty of Paris. The hasty decision to imprison the accused—the vice-chancellor René-Charles de Maupeou commended the "very wise" decision of officials in Amiens to contact Saint-Florentin immediately—also points to the government's sensitivity to public perceptions.[58] Officials had every reason to suspect that 1765 might see a repeat of the turbulence of 1763. L'Averdy had liberalized the grain trade in the summer of 1764, authorizing general exportation of grain for the first time in France's history, and this bold experiment with the physiocrats' *laissez-faire* theory faced a hostile reception.[59] Normandy saw unrest almost immediately, and Languedoc dealt with grain riots in Montpellier, Narbonne, and at least ten other cities between the summers of 1764 and 1766.[60] In Brittany, meanwhile, the *parlement* and other notables had begun to mount a resistance to crown authority that would prove to be the most violent spasm in the antitax protest that had roiled French politics since 1760. Vile insults leveled against the king and Saint-Florentin, allegedly written by a ringleader of the Breton protest, proved to be the pivot point in the whole drama. News of this developing "Brittany affair" would run alongside the dispatches from the Gévaudan throughout 1765.[61]

In this unsettled atmosphere, in which the king faced waning public confidence and emboldened critics, the ravages of the beast inspired carefully calibrated responses from the authorities at Versailles. Needless to say, the tragedy unfolding in the faraway Gévaudan could never register as more than a minor distraction at a royal palace confronting broad economic uncertainties, constitutional debates, scattered uprisings, and troublesome elites. The long arc of the monarchy's involvement in the story of the beast nevertheless reveals that the crown's engagement helped to secure the beast's status as a subject worthy of public curiosity and attention. By the end of the episode, if not always at the beginning, agents of the crown were well aware of the double-edged qualities of their entanglement in the narrative of the beast.

Hoping for and expecting a quick resolution to the drama, at the outset the crown allowed provincial officials to handle the crisis. Saint-Florentin's reluctance to intervene reflected his own belief that local hunters with knowledge of the Gévaudan's terrain had the best chance to capture or kill the creature. The minister had also been genuinely ambivalent about offering serious reward money for the hide of the beast; he suspected that this could encourage disruptive mercenaries.[62] As Duhamel floundered and public amazement grew, however, Saint-Florentin and L'Averdy felt compelled, or enticed, to change strategies. With the king's consent, they decided to announce a royal commitment of funds guaranteed to attract attention. Already in the fall of 1764, the municipalities of Mende and Viviers (200 livres each), the bishop of Mende (1,000 livres), the Estates-General of Languedoc (2,000 livres), and the intendant of Auvergne (600 livres) had offered rewards to the hunter or hunters who would rid the region of its infamous monster. On 27 January, L'Averdy informed the intendant Ballainvilliers that the king was now prepared to raise the ante substantially. Within a week, in the first days of February, the intendants of Languedoc and Auvergne announced publicly that the king, "understandably touched by the fate of his subjects," and wishing to end the suffering of all those "exposed to the carnage of the wild beast," offered an astounding 6,000 livres in recompense to the person or persons "who will finally destroy this cruel animal."[63] With reward money in excess of 10,000 livres placed on the table, the suffering inhabitants of the Gévaudan could at least take pride in having generated the greatest reward ever offered in France—before or since—for the destruction of a single *bête féroce*.[64]

Beyond the coveted carcass of the beast itself, the "touched" king could rightfully expect to derive some benefit from this conspicuous show of compassion. Out of gratitude for the king's role in resolving the crisis, long-suffering communities would surely reciprocate with affection for their monarch. Saint-Priest assured L'Averdy that the public would rejoice at this latest "mark of the king's paternal kindness, and of the attentions of his minister."[65] Moreover, the publicized efforts of the beast's pursuers, even if motivated partly by the desire for gain, would inspire patriotic solidarity in a time of nagging tensions. Within days after the intendants' announcement of the royal bounty, the *Courrier d'Avignon* could already report that in Languedoc "several Gentlemen, accompanied by many skilled hunters," were making their way toward the Gévaudan, having been roused to action by the placards that the intendant had posted "in all the towns and burgs of this province." The "love of glory and of gold" had evidently "excited their courage."[66]

As Saint-Florentin seems to have recognized, however, the monarchy's new strategy carried its own risks. The offering of prize money might spark an impressive "vertigo of chivalry," as one consul of Nîmes expected, but no one could be sure where vertigo might lead.[67] By appealing to the self-interest of hunters from across the kingdom and beyond, the crown complicated the task of local authorities, who could not be sure that the beast remained within their effective jurisdiction. The appeal to the public also bolstered or introduced to the Gévaudan the presence of myriad unwelcome forces: tellers of tall tales, horses trampling tilled fields, a prize-seeking mentality that discouraged teamwork, and outsiders oblivious to the needs of rural laborers. The crown's more public involvement in the hunt for the beast thus had the potential to backfire with unpleasant results. A letter published in the *Année Littéraire* captured the level of excitement, and the slightly troublesome motivations, that characterized the adventuresome travelers of early 1765. Writing from Montpellier in March, the writer recalled many overheard conversations, some involving "boastful inhabitants of this province," others involving English, German, and Polish visitors, all sure of their ability to take down this so-called monster within "two days."[68] The mix of optimism and consternation with which officials confronted the forces unleashed in late winter reflected the heightened stakes generated by the hunt for the beast after January of 1765.

Dreams of Conquest

Not all of the difficulties created by the lure of rewards could be attributed to the greed of outsiders, to be sure. As early as mid-January, two weeks after Ballainvilliers had announced his province's 600-livre prize, he disciplined a habitual "drunkard" from the town of Mauriac who tried to take advantage of official generosity by claiming he had suffered an attack from a "wild animal." On "close inspection," the victim's wounds were found to have been caused by a nasty tumble on a rocky path after a night of drinking "too much wine." The intendant threw him in prison for several days, an action that won the approval of the like-minded Saint-Florentin.[69]

Unscrupulous natives were in plentiful supply, but the concerns of the locals focused chiefly on *étrangers*—literally, those "foreign" to the affected communities (most of them French). The officials of the Gévaudan had good reasons to be concerned. The area from the Cévennes to the Margeride had long constituted a kind of lawless frontier, its low population density and often impenetrable terrain offering criminals the prospect of lasting impunity. The famed brigand and smuggler Louis Mandrin, based in Savoy, occasionally skirted the edges of the Cévennes in the 1750s and once came as far west as Mende, which he and his outlaw band captured and governed for a memorable day in 1754.[70] Much more common, however, were the crimes committed by small groups of nameless thieves and extortionists who took advantage of the overwhelmed system of local justice. The artisan Jacques-Louis Ménétra, stopped and interrogated by agents of the local *maréchaussée* while traveling through the region in 1761, was warned that "the woods were full of robbers and smugglers."[71] Almost four years later, in January of 1765, Duhamel expressed concern about a rumor that outlaws in the area planned to emulate his plan to dress men in women's clothing—so as to seek cover for their petty crimes.[72] Administrative correspondence unrelated to the hunt for the beast reveals the solid grounds for Duhamel's fears.

The years 1764–1767 witnessed a veritable crime wave in the lower Vivarais, just to the east of the Gévaudan. The conscientious subdelegate Laforest warned Saint-Priest repeatedly and insistently that the "contagion" of lawlessness was spreading out from the mountains to infect the rest of the region.[73] In January of 1765 Laforest reported that roads were no longer safe for travelers, commerce had been disrupted, witnesses had become too intimidated to report crimes, and frightened judicial officers refused to execute the duties of their offices. By the end of the year, well-armed "assassins and bandits" operated so brazenly that they "violated and abducted from their own homes" private residents whose families had to pay ransom for their freedom. Alarmed by Laforest's increasingly panicked reports, Saint-Priest began to discuss with vice-chancellor Maupeou a "disarmament" strategy for the more intractable areas of his province. The intendant's concern for the dire situation in the lower Vivarais helps explain his tepid response, written at almost the same moment, to Lafont's suggestion that the peasantry be equipped with firearms in their struggle against the beast.[74]

Although the notoriously untamed Cévennes belonged in a category all its own, the Gévaudan's northern precincts also faced rampant criminality that presented difficult challenges to local officials, whose battles against lawlessness followed a steady rhythm. In 1739 the Estates of the Gévaudan had been compelled to allocate money to several municipalities—including Saint-Chély, Marvejols, and Malzieu—that had commissioned royal troops to "give chase to thieves" in the vicinity. Twenty years later, in 1759, Etienne Lafont reported to the Estates on a rash of crimes committed by a thieving band "alarming as much by the number as by the status of the persons involved." For a time this band occupied a large swath of territory that stretched from Saint-Flour to the Cévennes.[75] Other "troops of brigands" within the "confines of the Gévaudan and the Vivarais" would become sufficiently trouble-some to attract attention from Versailles in the early 1780s.[76]

Criminal proceedings occurred infrequently in the Gévaudan. The sparsely populated region had to await annual visitations by deputies from the présidial court residing at Nîmes, and visiting judges generally confronted a full, often overcrowded, docket. Laforest complained in the spring of 1764 that the tardy prosecution of a renegade soldier in the Vivarais stemmed from the extended stay of judicial officers in the Gévaudan, where "a great number of rogues" had faced prosecution months earlier. In November of 1764, as Duhamel began his hunting operations, Lafont had to return from Saint-Chély to Mende in order to assist the visiting judges in their prosecution of "diverse miscreants."[77] Criminality seemed so endemic that officials gave serious thought in 1768 to expanding the size and functions of the court in Le Puy—just to accommodate the heavy criminal traffic generated in the Gévaudan.[78]

By injecting into this disorderly landscape the promise of riches to be won, the monarchy further stretched a social fabric already strained by chronic illegality. The intendants' announcements of the royal bounty effectively opened the region to an influx of bandits and mercenaries in addition to the many hunters who came with honorable motives. Despite the *Courrier d'Avignon*'s half-serious remark that the presence of the beast had at least cut down on the theft of firewood—thieves had evidently decided to "prudently abstain from approaching" the woods at night—locals remained concerned by the prospect of armed strangers roaming the land with an inclination to shoot first and ask questions later.[79] Lafont and Saint-Priest agreed on a procedure that placed some restraints on visitors to the area. Upon arrival, foreign hunters had to proceed to Mende where Lafont issued certificates authorizing their presence and activities. Any hunters caught without such certificates were to be escorted from the region by Duhamel's men. Without adequate controls, Lafont contended, "there would be reason to fear that, under pretext of these hunts, some ill-intentioned foreigners, or even some locals, would spread out in bands and commit crimes."[80] The threat of disorder remained serious enough that Lafont soon asked Saint-Priest for several brigades of police then stationed in the Vivarais.[81]

Even relatively well-intentioned "foreigners" could be disruptive and annoying, as Duhamel learned in his last months in the region. In one of his more embittered letters, written just weeks before his departure, the captain complained of the fortune-hunters who arrived each day "with the most con-

fident air," but who had "no knowledge of the locale or of the difficulties involved in finding this animal." Within a week or two, he wrote, most of these
"Don Quixotes," put off by the rough terrain and the expenses they incurred,
resolved to "slink away in shame, promising never to return."[82] The determined hunters who stayed beyond this probationary period found other ways
to rankle. They ignored official instructions about organized hunts, effectively
discouraging the beast's capture by others, and they irritated farmers by allowing their horses to trample freshly sown fields—just as Duhamel's men had
once run afoul of several villages near Marvejols.[83] Not surprisingly the locals
quickly became skeptical of "the assistance that we can expect to derive from
foreigners."[84]

The foreigners nevertheless found the Gévaudan hard to resist. The se-
ductions of the hunt were many: the prospect of riches, the promise of glory,
the air of mystery enveloping the beast and its predation, the temptation to
tame a region—widely seen as a primitive backwater—whose problems would
either yield to worldly expertise or prove a worthy challenge to the curious
adventurer. Even people who lived a great distance from the area, or who
were too old or too feeble to travel there, found their minds gravitating toward the Gévaudan. Hoping to influence events with their new strategies,
these armchair warriors responded to the clamor of publicity by mailing to
the authorities their own detailed plans for capturing or eliminating the voracious creature they had read or heard so much about. Like the Protestant
dyer Bossignac, whose good intentions would eventually get him into trouble,
these outsiders felt invited and compelled to concoct plans that might prove
effective against a terrible public threat. Their projects point to the eighteenth-
century existence of a phenomenon seemingly inherent in the modern condition: the private citizen moved to engage public concerns through the mediated prompting of print journalism (or other media). The plans also reveal,
for the case of the Gévaudan, the other risks entailed in the monarchy's new
investments of attention and reward money. By effectively nationalizing the
hunt for the beast, the crown inadvertently solicited the submission of proposals frequently compromised by shameless profit-seeking.[85] Worse, the often frivolous or outlandish ideas given shape in these projects consumed the
energies of officials whose time could have been used more productively.

Some proponents of schemes to ensnare the beast entered directly into
dialogue with the newspaper editors who had introduced them to the object
of their fascination. An anonymous female wrote to the *Année Littéraire* call-

ing for a new strategy to take advantage of the beast's proclivity for the weaker sex. In this "Letter from Mad*** to M. Fréron," she averred that it was long past time to "furnish these women [of the Gévaudan] with firearms, powder, and lead." Unleash these armed women into the woods and hillsides of the region, the writer predicted, and "one of them, before the end of the month, will have brought down her aggressor, made her reputation, and avenged my sex."[86] More often, spellbound observers from points distant addressed their ideas to government agents—subdelegates, intendants, ministers—even as they acknowledged that their perspective on the events in the Gévaudan derived wholly from their reading of published accounts. "Reading all the news, all the gazettes," wrote a M. Hébert on the outskirts of Paris, "[I note that] there are few over the past three months that have not mentioned the numerous misdeeds performed by the hyena in your province." "I desire with all my heart, and as a good citizen," he wrote to the subdelegate Jean-François Tassy de Montluc, "to see my plan succeed, and [I hope] that you will do me the favor of letting me know how it all turns out."

Hébert's impractical plan, however much it might have resonated with the inventive Duhamel, would seem to have had little chance of success. He suggested that lambs be dressed in women's clothing, "topped with a girl's bonnet," and dispersed in "different places throughout your department," where armed men could lie in ambush waiting for the beast to appear. He further specified that "it would be best to arrange the lamb in a standing position," attach it to a "good post," and be sure that "it approximates the size of a child." To complete the ruse, villagers would probably need to place around each lamb "two or three straw children, dressed in ordinary country garb." Hébert assured Montluc that this same stratagem had worked like a charm "forty years ago, or thereabouts," when a large lynx had terrorized Bonnières.[87]

Montluc's response to Hébert appears not to have survived, though he referred briefly to the project before concurring with the disapproving Ballainvilliers that "it is awfully difficult to surprise this beast."[88] Another local dignitary with whom Hébert appears to have corresponded, and who may have steered him in the direction of the usually sympathetic Montluc, at least took the proposal seriously enough to write to Fréron about it. In the pages of the *Année Littéraire* the comte de Brioude praised the plan for adding "trickery" to force, a step he considered long overdue.[89]

We know that other projects received close attention from officials and generated interested discussion among them. A curé from Champagne, moved by "patriotic zeal," addressed to L'Averdy an intriguing plan reflecting his evidently deep knowledge of foreign lands. The curé of Boucainville opened his letter by stating the novel hypothesis that lay beneath his proposed plan of pursuit. The beast described "in the journals and gazettes" was almost certainly a "tiger-cat," a "singular animal" the likes of which could rarely be found outside "the Yucatan peninsula of Mexico, where there are a great many." Boucainville had deduced the beast's identity from his close reading of natural history.[90] The tiger-cat's taste for diminutive calves paralleled the beast's inclination to attack children and helpless women, and many reports had remarked on the beast's fear of livestock and "even large dogs." Besides, one could easily imagine a tiger-cat being carried on board a merchant vessel and smuggled into France through a Mediterranean or Atlantic port. Consequently, calves ranging in age from six weeks to two months should be exposed in the countryside, or next to woods, and placed "amid several traps." The traps might vary in kind—poison smeared on the animals' hides, a contraption from which the beast could not escape, even a battery of muskets rigged to fire when tripped—but only by coaxing the beast with its "favorite nourishment" could the authorities succeed in leading it to its destruction.[91]

L'Averdy listened to the curé. He quickly sent a copy of the letter to Saint-Priest in Montpellier. The intendant promptly fed details of the plan to the hunter d'Enneval, who had begun work in the area at about the same time that Boucainville submitted his letter. D'Enneval impatiently dismissed the curé's ideas, noting that "the poison would soon lose its quality in the water, rain, and bad weather." Boucainville's ability to secure the attention of ministers and intendants nevertheless highlights the power and reach of the cycle of publicity that had now seized the beast's story.[92] This particular cycle of imaginative speculation—running from Paris to Versailles (via Mexico) to Montpellier and back to the Gévaudan—completed itself within about three weeks' time.

The likelihood of the region's assimilation to other exotic locations only increased when the content of the news seemed to reinforce personal experience. In an April letter to Saint-Priest, a retired lieutenant-colonel named Duparquet proposed to activate in the Gévaudan his own knowledge of primitive lands. The officer had always sought to make his zeal "useful" to the king by supplementing it with enlightening knowledge of all kinds, and he now yearned to put to use insights gained "while making war with the cunning savages of Canada." Duparquet's proposal called for weapons that could pierce the seemingly impenetrable hide of the monster in the Gévaudan. "If this animal is really as depicted, its back covered with scales," steel shells will be "absolutely indispensable," as the more common lead shells were destined to flatten on contact with the hard surface of the beast's hide. More important, Duparquet offered to lead a troop of twelve skilled and intrepid hunters, each of whom would be equipped with extremely sharp lances modeled on those used by the "savages" of Canada. A drawing of a prototype designed by Duparquet himself accompanied the letter. His time in the Canadian wild had taught him that "these lances are much more reliable than a musket armed with a bayonet, which snaps at the butt from the shock of the first impact." Only "hunters who can understand this kind of hunt"—Duparquet cited his experience navigating marshes, for which the Gévaudan was famous—had any hope of destroying the monster. Provided Languedoc would pay to produce the necessary lances and steel balls, and small subsidies could be provided to his men, Duparquet would gladly perform the duty of "a good fellow citizen and faithful subject of the king." He regarded his plan as a "can't miss."[93]

Saint-Priest put off the lieutenant-colonel by politely suggesting that he share his ideas with "the minister" (meaning either Saint-Florentin or, perhaps more likely, L'Averdy, controller of the purse strings.)[94] Many more such proposals made their way to officials' desks, however, and all of them required the same delicate combination of appreciative encouragement and defensive evasion. A Lespinasse de Mongibaud, inventor of "an infallible wooden machine" with which the beast could be taken alive, insistently peddled his ideas at Versailles. He eventually caught the ear of the wife of Charles-Gratien, marquis de Bonneguise, who was known to be close to the governor of Languedoc, and he also waylaid the king's surgeon, Germain Pichault de Lamartinière. Both referred the inventor to the intendant Saint-Priest. Even though a smaller model of Lespinasse's machine had already been tested with neighborhood dogs "near my village, where every morning I found one or two large mastiffs trapped inside," Saint-Priest appears not to have pursued this new marvel of engineering.[95] Meanwhile, a plan submitted by a M. Rodier was circulated among various officials in Auvergne, including Montluc, Ballainvilliers, and Duhamel.[96] Despite his rousing introduction ("A cruel and anonymous animal continues to shock humanity; an entire society desires its extirpation"), Rodier's plan to supply all peasants with spears, so that they could defeat their own tormentor, was bound to die a quiet death once it fell into the hands of these proud but humbled elites.[97]

The most bizarre, and probably the least heeded, of the projects that crossed the desk of Saint-Priest in these months came from nearby Nîmes. There an obscure but educated citizen named Joas de Papoux, resident of the rue des Marchands, developed a project "inspired by God" but clearly informed by a familiarity with witchcraft. Without announcing it directly, Papoux proposed to fight sorcery with sorcery. The plan called for hunters to disguise themselves and lie in ambush, hardly a unique idea. What set the plan apart was the set of tools devised for use in the ambush. Papoux proposed a combination of potions and totems designed to counter the magical aura that surrounded the beast. He imagined a team of twenty-five men, a dozen of whom would serve as decoys, draping themselves in an assortment of animal skins. Papoux did not explain his method of selection, but he specified that the disguises should include, "if possible, the skin of a lion, a bear, a leopard, a stag, a doe, a calf, a goat, a boar, a male and a female wolf, and two sheep." The other men would don waistcoats and long pants "garnished with feathers of different colors." They would also need to wear cardboard hats resembling helmets "also adorned with feathers, but interspersed with several knife-blades." The hunters, armed with pistols, would "slowly patrol the woods . . . three by three," keeping at least thirty paces between them and maintaining "complete silence." Their costumes would need to be smeared with honey and sprayed with musk. Everyone would need to be equipped with a small container holding a substance consisting of "the fat of a Christian man or woman and, if possible, the blood of a viper." The shells destined for each man's pistol would need to bear the teeth marks of a woman or girl. (The essence of the beast's favored victims would presumably counteract the magical powers deployed against them.) Only then could they be coated with the admixture of blood and Christian fat that the men carried with them in their special containers. These instructions having been followed carefully, one of the hunters would surely vanquish the "foul monster." Papoux expressed confidence that "God will bless this enterprise," but he also offered to come and execute the project himself "if you judge me capable of commanding this brigade." He would do anything required of "a faithful subject of His Majesty."[98]

Papoux's project, which skirted the margins of the culturally permissible, expresses well the double-edged quality of the publicity attending the beast's exploits in the first half of 1765. In this period the land of the beast attracted attention, offers of aid, and generous gestures of concern that could not have been wholly unwelcome. Papoux's offer to serve the king faithfully by marching off to the Gévaudan, like Boucainville's patriotic zeal and Duparquet's celebration of good citizenship, was representative of the enormous surge of (sometimes patronizing) sympathy that flowed toward the region in the late winter and spring of 1765. But publicity also brought with it a host of new complications. Publicity, like a magnetic force, drew to the area people whose presence obstructed progress and even threatened the safety and well being of the locals. Publicity stimulated and gave voice to imaginative fancies that clouded people's vision and delayed identification of the true problem afflicting the region. For officials, including the mightiest at Versailles, publicity increased the pressure to act but simultaneously magnified a continuing and incriminating failure. The yeast of publicity interacted with the reality of fear to produce a self-perpetuating dynamic akin to a speculative bubble—one fated to end either in a rapid deflation or a spectacular climax.

No event from the entire episode better captures the full range of publicity's impact on the story than d'Enneval's ill-fated excursion to the south. Jean-Charles d'Enneval's mission to the Gévaudan can be seen as a direct product of the beast's elevation to the status of media star. The hunter had become fascinated by stories of the creature, and he was more than ready to believe in the spectacular. Almost immediately after arriving on the scene in late February he provided to a fellow hunter in Normandy an excited description of the beast based on accounts by local peasants. He studied the tracks of the creature, which supposedly revealed evidence that the beast had leapt "twenty-eight feet from one spot to another on flat ground."[99] Like so many others, the Norman obviously allowed his thoughts and expectations to be shaped by intriguing public reports of beastly behavior. He would soon be introduced to the boomerang effects of uncontrolled publicity, however, as he saw his own image remade by the power of unremitting public attention.

5

The Perils of Publicity

Jean-Charles d'Enneval's recruitment to the Gévaudan was itself a symptom of the increased public attention that the beast attracted by late January 1765. His assignment resulted from the crown's second direct intervention in the Gévaudan's problems at the end of that trying month, following the decision to offer the large royal bounty. The famed wolf-hunter would have been well known both to the governor of Languedoc, a Norman native, and to J.-D. Cromot du Bourg, who hailed from d'Enneval's home of Argentan and now served as one of the trusted "head commissioners" who assisted L'Averdy's day-to-day supervision of finances. Through one or both of these intermediaries, the controller-general sought out d'Enneval in an attempt to find an antidote to Duhamel's continuing troubles.[1] D'Enneval would have required little persuading, but he wished to be accompanied on the mission by his thirty-two-year-old son, Jean-François, who needed to be released from his service as a captain in the Bresse regiment. L'Averdy applied the requisite pressure in the first week of February, and the d'Ennevals, *père et fils,* were soon making their way south, no doubt impelled by "the hope of acquiring a sort of celebrity by defeating this public enemy already known practically all across Europe."[2]

Large reputations preceded the Normans, for word of the elder d'Enneval's exploits soon entered into the maw of publicity that propelled interest in the story of the beast. Magné de Marolles, that practiced distiller of newspaper coverage, reflected the prevailing wisdom about the Norman's extraordinary prowess. D'Enneval, wrote Magné de Marolles, was a wizened veteran of wolf-hunting, a noble exercise "that he has practiced continually since his youth." Normandy would forever be in his debt, for he had eliminated "more than 1,200 wolves" in his long career. Even now, in his sixties, this hardy nobleman "still retains the energy of his youth and sturdy health that can withstand anything, an advantage that he owes as much to his hard and rigorous life as to the strength of his constitution. At his age one still sees him leading his hounds, with reins in hand, through the woods day after day. Those who know hunting understand how fatiguing that is." Only "the most robust" men could hold up under the strain.[3]

The press reinforced this image, and d'Enneval did nothing to discourage it. By the time of his arrival in the south in late February, residents of the Gévaudan and its environs were prepared to bestow laurel wreaths. "M. d'Enneval is very celebrated" for his services to the country, reported the comte de Brioude, in a 1 March letter to the *Année Littéraire.* The level of detail in his assessment suggests that his information came straight from the ultimate source. "No wolf escapes him. He will often travel fifty or sixty leagues rather than give up on an animal he is pursuing." To judge from Brioude, Magné de Marolles' estimate of d'Enneval's wolf-killing prowess might have been insultingly low. "I have been assured that he has purged from the realm more than 3,000 wolves; in the Heroic Age, there would have been altars [in his honor], as with Hercules and Theseus."[4] The *Courrier d'Avignon* concurred, calling d'Enneval "the greatest hunter of wolves in his province." Since late February, there had been reports of a dangerous wolf prowling the northern province of the Soissonnais. "If they attributed to the ferocious beast that desolates the Gévaudan as much intelligence as agility, one might suppose that, having been alerted to the coming of the Grand Wolfhunter of Normandy," the beast had decamped for the Soissonnais in an effort to evade its pursuer. But given the near simultaneity of the troubles in the two areas, this would not be possible "unless they also suspect that [the beast] has wings."[5]

In addition to long experience, the d'Ennevals would bring other advantages to the fight. They would be accompanied by "monstrous dogs of a singular type," animals so skilled that "they say these dogs can pick up the scent of their prey even twenty-four hours after its passing." These bloodhounds had helped d'Enneval exterminate in his province "all the wolves within a twenty-league radius." Best of all, d'Enneval and his son had killed in the Soissonnais some years earlier another wild beast that, "according to the description they have provided, closely resembled ours." The hunters therefore had every confidence that they would quickly dispatch the monster of the Gévaudan, which they would do only out of "zeal for the public good."[6]

Great expectations thus awaited "this great hunter that the court has sent us to purge the province of this monster."[7] Saint-Priest viewed the impending arrival of the Norman hunters as a sign that "the court is seriously occupied" by the south's problems. In happy anticipation of the coming kill, the intendant again reminded Lafont of the need to find a surgeon quickly after the beast's death, so as to insure the proper care of the skeleton, "which must be placed in the king's garden."[8] But like Duhamel before them, the d'Ennevals arrived to take on a task for which past experience had not prepared them. Before his final departure from the area, the unsuccessful father would be reduced to tears of shame. Long before that cathartic moment, the people of the region had come to recognize that the d'Ennevals were both out of their depth and glaringly out of place.

Familiarity Breeds Contempt

The d'Ennevals made an inauspicious debut in the Midi. Before embarking on their journey, d'Enneval *père* had asked L'Averdy to supply them a covered carriage for the transport of their dogs, and the controller-general's refusal ("he will have to find some other means if he cannot take them directly") meant that they had to make their own arrangements to have the dogs delivered to the south.[9] The dogs, whose reputed prowess would become an object of mockery, trailed their masters by weeks. The d'Ennevals and their two assistants left Alençon on 12 February, and they reached southern Auvergne one week later, on Shrove Tuesday. On 9 March, however, the senior d'Enneval was still complaining to Ballainvilliers: "I await my dogs impatiently."[10] Although the d'Ennevals were "well received everywhere," and even had dinner with the bishop of Mende at the end of February, they killed time not by joining Duhamel on his own daily hunts, according to the original plan, or by working to gain the trust of the locals.[11] Instead they talked. They talked mostly about themselves, their tales of conquest, and the ease with which they expected to conquer their new enemy. With their haughty style and their polished French—the d'Ennevals stand out from the other participants in the drama for their almost slavish devotion to a rather sophisticated French grammatical form, the *passé simple*—they alienated virtually every local resident with whom they came into contact.[12]

The hostility generated by the d'Ennevals needs to be placed in context, of course. Two of their most heated and outspoken opponents, Duhamel and Morangiès, had reasons to take pleasure in the Normans' difficulties and may have worked to establish their unpopularity. Nevertheless, the evidence shows that the d'Ennevals got off to a terrible start and never quite recovered. Early hints of friction came from their very first encounter with Duhamel, who met them on 28 February while dining at the home of a gendarme named Vedrine near the village of Chabrier, on the border between Auvergne and the Gévaudan. (For jurisdictional reasons, the d'Ennevals generally preferred the Auvergne side of the border until Duhamel's final departure in early April.)[13] In a letter to the comte de Lastic, Duhamel noted having made the acquaintance of "Messrs. d'Enneval, father and son, who come from Normandy, with six dogs from whom they expect much." The d'Ennevals made a troubling first impression, and not only because of their startling claim that "they would have this beast within two weeks." When the frazzled consul of Chabrier unexpectedly arrived to inform the captain of an attack on a child "stolen from the door of his home," the d'Ennevals oddly requested that Duhamel stay put and not give chase to the assailant. Their prized dogs had not yet arrived, and they said that a premature pursuit might only send the beast into hiding. More curious still, the younger d'Enneval claimed to possess orders from Versailles that gave the Normans ultimate authority over hunting operations in the region. After making this assertion, however, d'Enneval *fils* would not "do me the honor" of producing the all-important document. "As this lack of courtesy was a discredit to no one but himself, I thought it best to rise above this formality, which I nevertheless would have had every right to insist upon, according to my own orders from the comte d'Eu."[14] The rivals finished their dinner, and the next morning the nonplussed Duhamel sent off several of his dragoons to pick up the beast's trail.

Subsequent events would explain the d'Ennevals' puzzling behavior. Practically from the moment of their arrival, they had decided to press the authorities for exclusive control over the search for the beast. Duhamel would later complain that the younger d'Enneval, in particular, "likes to play the bigwig."[15] But the d'Ennevals' behavior toward the locals, including provin-

cial officials, reflected a deliberate strategy of intimidation designed to force
the capitulation of those who had been in control of the hunts. On 4 March
the elder d'Enneval pleaded his case with Ballainvilliers. He grumbled, "it will
not be possible for us to hunt in this country as long as M. Duhamel and his
dragoons remain. Each day they beat the area, and this startles the animal
to the point where no one will be able to approach it." Had four months of
failure not been enough to discredit the dragoon? "I ask you to please give
the orders" for Duhamel's dismissal from the province.[16] A few days later
d'Enneval continued. Feigning powerlessness in the field, he alluded to a
number of recent attacks by the beast, the details of which he could not provide, since "it is to Monsieur Duhamel that they report these incidents." So
much remained beyond the man's control. "Many men with guns have arrived
from the Gévaudan and other places in Languedoc, and they beat the woods
every day with dragoons at their side. This will only cause more trouble, since
we have no command over them." D'Enneval found it difficult to work under
such conditions, but "I will do what I can."[17]

The d'Ennevals' desire to have final authority over the hunts is not hard
to understand. In contrast to Duhamel's habit of staging multiple, often large
and noisy, hunts at the same time, the Normans proposed to use a very different strategy requiring targeted searches in circumscribed areas where hard evidence indicated the beast's presence. As they sought to secure and wield authority, however, the d'Ennevals made one unfortunate misstep after another.
Thinking they would promptly master circumstances whose complexity they
had underestimated, they soon found themselves overwhelmed by them.

The refusal to collaborate with Duhamel constituted the d'Ennevals'
original sin. This first public act sounded a false note in the region, where
Duhamel had, after all, earned wide if sometimes grudging respect, and it
provided the template through which the locals would interpret all of the
d'Ennevals' later failings. The many offenses for which they would eventually stand accused or suspected—disdain for provincials, excessive self-regard,
greed, laziness, dishonesty, brute inadequacy—all stemmed in one way or another from their self-centered maneuvering in late February and early March.
They communicated their desire for Duhamel's removal with such distaste-
ful egotism that even the unflappable Lafont could not refrain from lodging
complaints against them.

Lafont reported in a lengthy letter to Saint-Priest that his first meeting
with the d'Ennevals had been dominated by their obsession with securing ex-

clusive jurisdiction over the hunts. As Lafont saw it, these misplaced priorities reflected the Normans' overriding concern to earn prize money and due credit for their efforts. They had told Lafont "that they absolutely could not hunt with the dragoons because of the disorders that would result." And what was the nature of the disorders they dreaded? They said "there is reason to fear that if one of their men managed to kill the beast, the dragoons could shoot at it even after its death, and they could claim to have killed it themselves and thus take possession of it." The indignant Lafont responded that competing claims for credit might occur in any event, but that it was nonetheless "important to the common cause to act in concert." Lafont showed the Normans the placard that had been posted in all corners of the province, the one inviting all interested parties to give chase to the animal and to seek royal recompense. The d'Ennevals uncomfortably acknowledged the presence of these competitors in the area, but they insisted that there was "no way" to reconcile with Duhamel. They warned that if the commandant Moncan did not intervene to control the captain, "they would write to the court" to seek clarification of their jurisdiction.[18]

Before March was out, Lafont had concluded that the new "Hercules" and his son were untrustworthy frauds foisted on the region by misguided men at Versailles. Their first few conversations had been enough to show Lafont that the illustrious visitors had given no forethought to the nature of their mission. When they set out on their journey they obviously had "a different idea of this country," one that scarcely matched reality. "They were not expecting to find so many mountains, forests, marshes, and snow, nor did they realize that the beast covered so much ground." (Duhamel sniped that the younger d'Enneval, "who has no doubts about anything, tells us that he knows the terrain as well as the natives.")[19] When Lafont and other locals shared with their guests their various descriptions of the shape and manners of the beast, and offered their own thoughts about "what it might be," d'Enneval *père* "soaked it all in and took on a look of concern. He mumbled something about not being able to guarantee that his dogs would dive right into the chase, but he said that if they did, he was sure he could destroy [the beast] or chase it away."[20]

More troubling than the d'Ennevals' overweening confidence and lack of preparation was their naked dishonesty. On 9 March Lafont shared a meal with d'Enneval *fils* in Saint-Chély, and the aristocrat wasted no time before trying to bluff the subdelegate into accepting the Normans' superior standing.

"He talked at length about the orders he had from the king, and he told me that he would show them to me—and to me alone. He repeated this several times." Lafont signaled that he would respect the younger d'Enneval's mystifying wish for confidentiality. "After dining I accompanied him to his quarters where he was supposed to show me the orders." Jean-François unveiled a letter from L'Averdy to Lallement de Lévignen, the intendant of Alençon, as well as other letters from L'Averdy and Ballainvilliers that authorized reimbursements for the d'Ennevals' expenses, but none of these documents referred to the scope of the hunters' authority. Then, pointing to a place "in the middle of some other papers" in his satchel, d'Enneval claimed to produce "an order from the king, which seemed to be signed by the king as far as I could judge. Just when I expected that he was about to have me read it," Lafont added incredulously, "he closed his case. When I said that he had made me believe that I would have the opportunity to see what was in the order, he responded that what he had let me see would suffice for now." This sudden misdirection "left me surprised, though I said nothing."

Only a few hours after this disturbing encounter, Lafont observed strange behavior in the elder d'Enneval. Word had finally arrived in Saint-Chély at five o'clock on 9 March that the d'Ennevals' dogs had reached their destination in nearby La Garde. Suspicion about the actual whereabouts and even the existence of these mystery hounds had been percolating through the area for some time. Rumor held that the dogs had reached Clermont, Auvergne's administrative capital, around the first of the month. No one could account for the long interval between their initial arrival in the south and the launch of their pursuit of the beast. Lafont asserted matter-of-factly that the public widely believed "the dogs had been held in some secret depôt for days" preceding the announcement of their arrival. In any case, the prospect of the dogs' long-awaited reunion with their masters seemed like cause for celebration, and Lafont rushed to Jean-Charles to tell him the news. The deflated subdelegate expressed his surprise on learning that the elder d'Enneval already knew about the dogs' whereabouts. He announced his plans to collect the hounds at La Garde the next day. "We were supposed to see each other on Sunday morning [the 10th]," Lafont added accusingly, "but he left without saying a word," thereby adding to a troubling pattern of duplicity.

Lafont apologized to Saint-Priest for providing such lurid detail, but the intendant needed to see the full "state of things" so that he could judge for himself "what we can expect from those who are representing themselves as our liberators." Lafont mentioned in passing that he had warned Duhamel to keep his distance from the visitors from Normandy. They were obviously "quick with the quill," and he impressed upon Duhamel how painful it would be "to have to answer for his behavior if some complaint were addressed to the minister."[21] But Duhamel's caution, and Lafont's attempt to cultivate on his behalf the still open-minded Saint-Priest, amounted to wasted effort. One week after Lafont drafted his imploring letter, L'Averdy answered the d'Ennevals' prayers by ordering the relocation of Duhamel and his men to the safely distant town of Pont-Saint-Esprit—despite the reservations that both Saint-Priest and Moncan still harbored with respect to the would-be "liberators."[22]

The plot thickened in the days and weeks after Lafont's seminal encounter with the d'Ennevals, for the Normans hesitated before deploying their dogs. (The outgoing Duhamel joked with Lafont that "you have entrusted your country to the safe-keeping of dogs, who, like their masters, have barely made themselves known.")[23] The level of local exasperation increased in the second half of March, but as long as the stand-off with Duhamel remained unresolved, personal frictions provided a handy explanation for the d'Ennevals' inaction. The subdelegate Montluc reported that "public rumor" blamed "the slowness of the operations" on the irreconcilability of the two strategies pursued by d'Enneval and the long-suffering captain. If only for change's sake, Montluc hoped to see the struggle resolved in favor of the Norman, from whom "the public expects rapid relief."[24]

But the d'Ennevals' dilatory manner soon required other explanations. A month after he had written sympathetically of the d'Ennevals, Montluc complained that the ever-secretive northerners still lacked the appropriate vigor, even weeks after the departure of their hated rival. Montluc saw reasons to have confidence in the celebrated dogs, he wrote to Ballainvilliers, if only their masters would "set them loose."[25] Others, too, took note of the d'Ennevals' lack of urgency. The deputies at the Estates of the Gévaudan, meeting in late March, instructed Lafont to urge d'Enneval "to bring the greatest possible energy to his operations."[26] A letter from Saugues in the first week of April, later published in the *Gazette de Leyde,* noted that "in our cantons we await the famous hunters from Normandy with ever more impatience, in view of the frequent sightings of the ferocious beast."[27]

The d'Ennevals' inactive schedule in late March and early April surely reflected their growing doubts about the wisdom and likely outcome of their

mission. Deep snow impeded their movement, as it had often done for Duhamel, and the beast's ability to disappear into a maze of dense woods and
impenetrable patches of marshy ground and craggy slopes left the d'Ennevals
struggling for answers. They may have already begun to wonder what they
had gotten themselves into at the time of their first meeting with Duhamel at
the end of February, when they had been reluctant to venture outside. Or
perhaps the disillusionment had begun with their extended conversations
with Lafont on 8–9 March, when the elder d'Enneval had been sobered by
anecdotes about the beast and Lafont detected their first concerns about the
nature and expanse of the terrain. However they came upon the realization,
the d'Ennevals recognized that they faced an imposing task, and their confidence wobbled. The subdelegate Montluc, whose brother had accompanied
the d'Ennevals on several hunts in April, told Ballainvilliers that they had
expressed their "despair" of ever destroying the beast. Lafont's brother Trophime, who had also assisted the d'Ennevals on some of their hunts in March,
used the same word to report the same news. He even claimed that the
Normans had signaled to him "that after this month they would be departing
the area."[28]

Trophime's prophecy proved false. A somewhat chastened father and son
would stick with it until July. Nevertheless, the d'Ennevals' frustrations deeply
affected their relationship to the Gévaudan, making their presence there a
painful experience for all concerned. Some sense of their feelings for the land
can be gleaned from a letter written by one of their assistants, a pikeman borrowed from the comte de Montesson in Normandy, to his patron who eagerly awaited news from the front. After admitting that the hunting party had
"great need of someone who truly knows the country," the d'Ennevals' trusted
lieutenant made sure that the comte de Montesson resisted any sudden temp-
tations to jump into the fray. "Snow, hail, thunderstorms, wind, wet feet, and
reduced to sleeping on straw—I beg you, sir, if you have not already left for
the Gévaudan yourself, forget about it. This is an abominable country, with
terrible food; they tide us over with a broth made from bad butter. You don't
see beef in this country."[29]

Unsated appetites may help to explain why the d'Ennevals and their team
so often blamed the local peasantry for their failures. The pikeman, for example, complained of a hunt that took place in the woods of the comte de
Morangiès on 4 April. "If all gunmen had shown up at the rendezvous," he
insisted, "the outcome would have been a happy one." He had spotted the

creature once, but lack of support meant that his efforts had been wasted. According to d'Enneval's own account of the same event, the locals had disappointed in other ways. The hounds had caught up to the beast in the forests of the Margeride after a two-hour pursuit. "Peasants came after hearing the noise," but they squandered their great opportunity. "[They] would have destroyed it if they had stayed with it and surrounded it; the beast shook free from the distracted dogs and made off into the woods." This failure echoed an event from two weeks earlier near Albaret. "[We] had our dogs," d'Enneval wrote to the intendant of Alençon, "and they chased hard for half an hour. . . [The beast] would have been fired on by a peasant, who should have killed it, but he was afraid and allowed it to get too far away before firing."[30]

The d'Ennevals' contempt for the local inhabitants is perhaps best shown by their reaction to news of the killing of a wolf by bayonet on 23 April near the woods of La Panouse, an event dramatic enough to arouse short-lived hope that the beast itself, or one of its consorts, had been conquered. (An ill-informed and overexcited *nouvelliste* would report, in a manuscript news journal, that d'Enneval himself, "a man of almost sixty years," had killed the animal with his bare hands—in a village just outside of Montpellier!)[31] Lafont commissioned a local doctor in Mende to cut open and examine the specimen, whose innards contained fragments of cloth and bone. Since the bones appeared to be those of a rabbit, the evidence for a man-eating predator seemed less than compelling, but d'Enneval preemptively pierced through the excitement in any case. The animal "weighed only forty pounds," and d'Enneval asserted that the peasants, "avid for a better reward [than the standard six livres for a dead wolf]," had probably used a stick to force the incriminating items down the throat and into the stomach of the inert wolf.[32]

The d'Ennevals found plenty of reasons to fault the peasantry, but impatient officials began to point the finger of blame in a different direction. Lafont wrote to Saint-Priest on 2 April to inform him of the "low expectations, perhaps not well founded but widespread, of the degree of success likely to come from the operations of Messrs. d'Enneval." One could only hope, Lafont added sarcastically, that the long-desired removal of Duhamel's troops "will give [d'Enneval] new opportunities to manifest his talents." Nor was Lafont, an established skeptic, the only pessimist. The curé of Langogne predicted that d'Enneval would be "less successful here than in Normandy." A monsieur Dulignon *fils,* petitioning the intendant about the *vingtième* tax, volunteered that the terrain of the Gévaudan posed too many difficulties "even for d'Enneval's dogs," whose early performance "does not augur well." A syndic of Languedoc told Lafont that "I have spoken to no one who expects much to come from these hunts they're planning."[33]

The d'Ennevals' lack of urgency strained the patience of local officials because, as the *Gazette de France* announced on the first of April, the beast "continues with its project and has not stopped spreading alarm and consternation" in the region.[34] Nightmarish assaults occurred in rapid succession. March and April together saw fourteen deaths, second in volume only to the fifteen of January and February, which outpaced any other two-month span during the beast's rampage. Lafont reported on an eight-year-old girl from Arzenc d'Apcher who had been attacked in her village. The beast carried her off to a field where later "they found nothing but leftover bones."[35] Duhamel,

The beast's ravages were especially heartrending because the animal targeted children. The identity of the victim depicted in this untitled print from June, 1765 is ambiguous, perhaps intentionally so. The attack resembles in its details the case of François Fontugne, a nine-year-old from the parish of Javols, but the child's state of undress and physical features that look at least vaguely feminine also recall the ability of werewolves "to undress the girls they wish to ravage." In color, this image shows an attacker with a dark brown coat, a detail that would later resurface in musings about the beast's possible Dauphiné roots. *Archives Départementales du Puy-de-Dôme, 1 C 1731*

in one of his last letters to the bishop of Mende, wrote of a pitiful five-year-old from Malaviellette (between Saint-Alban and Serverette) who had been practically ripped "from the door of her home." The "cruel beast" had dragged her to a nearby wood where it ate "her chest, entrails, bottom, and a leg," though "contrary to habit, it scarcely touched her head, which was damaged only by teeth marks, the beast having carried her off with her head in its mouth."[36] In Ruines on 14 March, the lawyer Bès de la Bessière was summoned to a heart-wrenching scene after the beast had attacked a thirty-year-old woman, ripping open the victim's jugular in three places. The lawyer arrived to find the woman's father clutching her "still quivering" body; witnesses struggled to lead him away from his daughter's remains.[37]

Perhaps the most gruesome event of March came at the end of the month. A nine-year-old boy from the parish of Javols was walking with his teenaged sister to a nearby village, where they were to pick up some woolen fabric. François Fontugne was attacked so suddenly that his sister, paralyzed with fear, could do nothing to assist him. By the time villagers came running, they found the boy "lying on his back, with his entrails spilled out on one side and his liver on the other, his chest and lungs were eaten without a trace of blood left behind; the interior of the chest up to the neck was ravaged, with the skin left hanging. The rest of the body was covered with wounds."[38] In the face of such unspeakable violence, terror gripped the countryside. "The fairs and markets are practically deserted. No one goes there alone. The few who venture out go in groups."[39] In light of "all these horrors"—which Lafont and others feared would only worsen in warm weather, when the growing crops in the fields would provide new cover for the predator—the d'Ennevals' strange ways became ever harder to tolerate.[40]

Lost Illusions

Popular discontent over the pace and results of their activities eventually forced the d'Ennevals to change their strategy. After holding out for weeks, they finally acquiesced in the wishes of Lafont and the local seigneurs and resorted to the very technique they had initially disdained: the large and multiparish "general" hunt.[41] They had already shown a willingness to work with other noble gentlemen from the Gévaudan and beyond—their enmity for Duhamel appears to have been unique in its intensity—and by mid-April they began to plan for larger operations, usually carried out with the assistance of "three gentlemen, good marksmen, named Lafayette," who had been sent from Auvergne.[42] Although certainly smaller than the massive mobilizations of early February, the d'Ennevals' general hunts reflected Duhamel's basic strategy of sweeping across large areas with groups of small but interconnected bands of hunters. A correspondent from Marvejols expressed relief on hearing of this new approach, since d'Enneval's many targeted searches had met with "no success."[43]

The first general hunt of 21 April, involving twenty parishes, unfortunately continued a familiar pattern. The only sighting of the animal on that day provided yet another opportunity for the d'Ennevals to wash their hands of responsibility for a failure. A fearful peasant, an eighteen-year-old armed only with "an old saber," had become so frightened when he stumbled upon the beast resting under a large rock that "he screamed out for help when it growled and showed its teeth." As the elder d'Enneval told the story, the beast then promptly fled the scene. The disgusted Lafont cited this unlucky occurrence as the image "to which all the events of this hunt can be reduced."[44] Between 30 April and 23 May, however, the d'Ennevals led a series of general hunts that, though equally lacking in concrete results, proved decisive in other ways. Late April and early May provided the d'Ennevals their last best chance either to kill the monster or to inspire confidence in their ability to do so. Instead, conspicuous displays of arrogance, indolence, and ineffectiveness brought local resentments to a crescendo and also tipped the scales for anxious authorities watching from afar.

The tide turned decisively against the d'Ennevals in the days that followed the general hunt of 30 April. They botched the pursuit of an animal widely believed to be the beast and then compounded their error with new insensitivities that the locals found intolerable. Snow and rain had ruined the large forty-parish general hunt carried out on the day before, but at dusk on the first of May the beast made an appearance on a noble estate situated to the south of the Morangiès residence. Jean-François Marlet de La Chaumette peered out of his bedroom window and spied a large animal sitting patiently on its haunches at the edge of a wood. The seigneur alerted his two brothers, who came running with their firearms. The three separated so as to approach their prey from several directions, but the beast detected them and began to move into the woods. Before it disappeared, two of the brothers managed to fire, inflicting serious wounds on the retreating beast, which bled profusely. The brothers followed the animal into the woods, anticipating that they would soon stumble upon a dead carcass, but by nightfall they still had not located the beast and their hopes dimmed. They sent an urgent dispatch to the d'Ennevals in Saint-Alban, evidently expecting the Normans to come quickly.[45]

The dilatory d'Ennevals decided to wait until the next morning to investigate, and their dallying proved to be the straw that broke the camel's back in the realm of local opinion. These days were marked by poor weather—the younger d'Enneval complained of "snow up to the knees in the mountains of the Margeride" on 30 April, the day of the unsuccessful general hunt—and the d'Ennevals allowed the unpleasantness of the elements to restrict their movement in the days after. On 1 May it had been the d'Ennevals' "men," not the d'Ennevals themselves, who had beaten "the woods of Saint-Alban and the rocks of Prunières" in the hours before the La Chaumettes contended with their surprise visitor. The younger d'Enneval explained that they had been unable to join the La Chaumettes before the morning of the next day because "rain was falling very hard" when they received news of the sighting. When they arrived the next morning—to find the La Chaumettes "with many peasants" and herd dogs already scouring the woods—the elder d'Enneval proceeded to investigate, finding many branches stained with blood. Led by one of the hounds, the d'Ennevals then tried to follow the animal's trail, going as far as the woods of Apcher, across the Truyère to the northwest, but they had no luck.

Even on this day of heightened tensions, and for the next twenty-four hours, the d'Ennevals continued to find reasons to call in the dogs and wait for better times. Jean-François insisted, in a letter to Lallemant de Lévignen, that on 2 May father and son had "worked on foot, from the break of day until six o'clock in the evening, without eating or drinking." But the credibility of that claim was undermined not only by his overcompensating effort to draw attention to the alleged hard labor but also by his own repeated references to the difficult weather conditions. He complained that "the hail and snow would not cease" on 2 May, thus forcing them "to return empty handed" to Saint-Alban. Worse, their behavior on hearing news of other sightings of the beast in the twelve hours after they repaired to Saint-Alban confirmed suspicions about their inclination to indolence. The beast had attempted to attack a shepherd in the tiny village of Pouges, near Fontans, "not an hour before" the d'Ennevals had called it a day, but in Jean-François's own words, the hunters resolved to go to the site not the moment they received the news but only "the next morning." They woke to find even those plans ruined by "hail and rain." Then, topping off a memorable three days' work, the d'Ennevals received urgent news of a deadly attack in the village of Pépinet, to the northeast of Saint-Alban, on that same morning of 3 May. They reacted not by speeding to the scene but by sending their pikeman to place poison on the corpse. The comte de Morangiès, by coincidence, arrived at his chateau later that day after completing a trip to Saugues. His sisters, who had dined with the d'Ennevals earlier in the day, briefed the comte on recent developments. When he heard that the Normans had sent a subaltern to place poison

"More on the frightful ravages caused by the cruel Beast of the Gévaudan." This print depicts the killing of a forty-year-old woman at Pépinet on 2 May, an event that raised "public consternation" to a peak. The grisly remains of the male victim at the rear of the beast are those of a "young boy from the village of Prunières" killed on 22 April. The beast continued to strike unexpectedly, as the caption notes, despite "the continual pursuit of Mssrs. Denneval and other famous hunters." *Bibliothèque Nationale de France, Rés. 4-LK2-786, fol. 102*

on the body in Pépinet but intended "to do nothing else" in the face of this new disaster, he could no longer contain his fury and contempt.

The angry letter that Morangiès fired off to the subdelegate Lafont on the afternoon of 3 May set the tone of local discourse for weeks to come. The comte felt compelled to share details about the recent events, which he regarded as a final indictment of the Normans' performance. Following their lackadaisical pattern, wrote Morangiès, the d'Ennevals eventually showed up at the La Chaumettes on the morning of 2 May only to provide fresh examples of "their customary insufferability and sad uselessness." This latest provocation now drove him "to speak the truth about the conduct of Messrs. d'Enneval." It should be enough to know, he informed Lafont, that "all of the parishes on this side of Saugues as well as in that canton are so indignant over the incompetence of these hunters that I greatly fear that when they are convoked again, the inhabitants will refuse to march." People who work for their living had made painful sacrifices to participate in hunts that proved "always fruitless" because of the standard "absurdity" of the d'Ennevals' projects. Making matters worse, the locals had to be subordinated to men indecent enough to place their own comforts and the pursuit of "sordid gain" above "the success of their mission." Noting the hunters' incriminating liking for the city of Malzieu, whose officials had made such trouble for Duhamel, Morangiès characterized the d'Ennevals' presence in the region as a slap in the face. "The fate of our unhappy country is being decided, in Malzieu, by these adventurers[,] surrounded by clinking glasses as they connive with the schemers of that foolish city." In the eyes of this honor-bound nobleman, the situation "calls out for vengeance." Lafont had an obligation to "lift the veil from the eyes of the powers that be" so that they, too, could finally see that the Normans—"human in appearance only"—had to go.[46]

The rage of Morangiès, news of which Lafont dutifully pushed up the chain of command, began a surge of anti-Norman sentiment that gathered force over the next month. Saint-Priest informed L'Averdy and Saint-Florentin about the events at the woods of La Chaumette, and the locals continued to pressure the intendant for relief. Morangiès wasted little time before launching new broadsides (he called d'Enneval an "impostor," reported his use of intimidation tactics, and accused him of sympathies inimical to "love of the *patrie*"), but it was Lafont himself who wrote the most effective summation of the locals' many arguments against the d'Ennevals' continued presence.[47] On 23 May he calmly composed a thorough list of failings about which the residents of the Gévaudan had been complaining for three months, and though he asked for Saint-Priest's discretion, he knew that the intendant was prepared to listen. Like the practicing lawyer he had once been, Lafont approached Saint-Priest as a sympathetic juror who nevertheless needed convincing, and he presented as compelling a case as he could manage.

More than anything, the d'Ennevals stood accused of bad manners and the bad character that poor manners reflected. From the moment they arrived in the country, they "made an unfavorable impression by their manner of living." They distrusted everyone, and created "an air of mystery over the delays to their first hunts." They kept their own counsel and avoided having anyone from the region placed in a position to observe their activities. The bad management they eventually displayed in the field "set the public against them," and yet they continued to make unreasonable demands on the peasantry, taking them far from their fields and staging frequent hunts that disrupted their work. They certainly knew the basic rules of politeness, and Lafont had no personal complaints of bad treatment at their hands, but the father always behaved with a certain "finesse" that bespoke hidden agendas. They kept even the most well-intentioned people at arm's length (including Trophime Lafont, who had been told in coded language that his assistance was no longer desired). "The gentlemen and principal inhabitants of the region, who evinced so much good will" at the beginning of the Gévaudan's tragedy, "no longer show it," and the blame for this development lay squarely with the d'Ennevals. The son had "adopted a tone of superiority that shocks many," and esteemed seigneurs had been treated rudely at general hunts. The notables who continued to cooperate with the d'Ennevals did so mainly because they wanted no trouble from Versailles, and everyone knew that "these men, who always search for pretexts to excuse their own bad results," would shift blame to others at the drop of a hat.

The d'Ennevals had a great need for scapegoats, since their indolence often kept them immobilized. The father actually stayed home during one of the major hunts, and he rarely ventured more than two leagues beyond Malzieu. The son went "a little farther," but Lafont openly questioned whether the d'Ennevals—and their dogs—were physically tough enough to stand up to the rigors of such a harsh country. "Everyone here is surprised that a person who, according to reports, has destroyed so many wolves in Normandy and elsewhere has nonetheless failed to kill a single one in three months in the Gévaudan, which is well stocked with them." All the evidence pointed to an inescapable conclusion: the region would not be delivered from the calamity that afflicted it unless the authorities implemented a "change of methods."[48]

At Versailles, the wheels had already begun to turn in this direction. Eye-opening complaints had reached the court by late May, and the resulting chatter undoubtedly explains why Jean comte de Scordeck, an experienced soldier who "has lived in countries where there are monsters as formidable as the hyena desolating the Gévaudan," began to pressure his friend Saint-Priest to have Saint-Florentin give him the commission to destroy the beast.[49] Instead the minister turned to François Antoine, a lieutenant of the hunt at the chateau of Saint-Germain-en-Laye and occupant of the honorific position of royal gun-bearer. In light of the "very urgent" need for Antoine to embark on his trip, Saint-Florentin instructed L'Averdy to advance the gun-bearer 3,000 livres to defray immediate expenses. By the middle of the month Antoine, joined by his young son Robert-François Antoine de Beauterne, had set out for the south.[50] Like Duhamel before them, the d'Ennevals were fated to spend the final weeks of their sojourn in the Gévaudan playing second fiddle to a newly appointed lead huntsman, who arrived in Malzieu on 22 June.

The d'Ennevals had almost certainly seen the writing on the wall after the failure at La Chaumette. For a brief two-week period between 6 and 19 May, when the beast drew no attention to itself, the elder d'Enneval allowed himself to hope that the monster had been eliminated after all—perhaps at the general hunt of 6 May, when one of the Lafayettes had wounded a wolf after firing from fifteen paces. When the inevitable next casualty came on 19 May, Lafont reported that d'Enneval appeared to have been "greatly affected" by the news. A few weeks later the Norman asked for Ballainvilliers' "protection" with the higher powers at Versailles, assuring him in a desperate tone that "we have done all that we can do." But d'Enneval would not feel the full weight of his "disgrace," as Antoine would call it, until July, when he was finally ordered to leave the area.[51] At a final debriefing with Antoine at the village of Sauzet, the proud nobleman "dissolved into tears" when asked for an explanation for the souring of his relationships in the region. Antoine assured his counterpart that he had left Versailles with the intention of reconciling the warring parties and helping to restore d'Enneval's good name, but he had quickly recognized that "the bomb went off too early" to attempt such repairs. D'Enneval conceded that he had "behaved badly toward several individuals," and he expressed regret. As he took his leave, after embracing Antoine, he seemed "overcome with sadness," and the gun-bearer reported that the sight "left me extremely touched."[52] In a final attempt to save face, d'Enneval *fils* asked Lafont to complete a certificate attesting to the labors they had expended and acknowledging that their hunts had been carried out in "rugged weather and difficult terrain." Lafont obliged ("I could not refuse him without exposing myself to recriminations"), and at long last the d'Ennevals exited the stage.[53]

In hindsight, the painful episode of the d'Ennevals in the Gévaudan comes across as an amusing and all-too-common accident involving the clash of incompatible personalities and egregious displays of uncomprehending arrogance. The poor fit between the self-consciously aristocratic d'Ennevals and their relatively humble southern hosts rings familiar to anyone who has been the victim of rude condescension or has otherwise experienced the distinctions of class. Still, the superficial familiarity of the encounter should not obscure its highly specific historical roots.

The unpleasantness that resulted from the Norman hunters' unsuccessful mission in the Gévaudan was a product of forces unleashed as the beast was transformed into a publicity phenomenon. From commentary buried inside their copious correspondence and even the occasional letter to the editor, we know that the principals from the drama in the Gévaudan consumed journalistic coverage of the story along with everyone else. (Lafont had complained in late 1764 that the *Courrier d'Avignon* was "very badly informed" about the number of the beast's casualties, and both Duhamel and Morangiès had kept one eye on the coverage provided in the *Courrier*.)[54] D'Enneval had been intrigued by the strangeness of the creature described in the journals, and he continued to believe in its extraordinary qualities to the bitter end.[55] He and his son found themselves initially attracted to the region also because of the high stakes attached to the pursuit of the beast, rewards whose value, in both prize money and reputation, rose in direct proportion to the level of attention accorded the Gévaudan's monster. When L'Averdy anointed d'Enneval as the court's hunter of choice in the struggle against the beast, he consummated a partnership of convenience forged within and through the glare of publicity.

As he became enmeshed in the novel machinery of publicity—not exactly against his will but also not entirely of his own accord—d'Enneval also slowly awakened to the many obstacles that had been placed in his path by the light that shone so intently on the Gévaudan. First, he arrived on the scene equipped with an outsized reputation as the "great" hunter, the new "Hercules" sent by the court, assisted by super dogs that never failed to bring down their prey. D'Enneval showed a brash willingness to exploit that reputation at first, but the image also proved impossible to live up to, as he must have realized almost from his first moments in the area. Fear of being exposed as a fraud, as much as stubborn pride, explains both the habitual excuse-making and the teary confession to Antoine, before whom d'Enneval finally allowed himself an emotional release after months of mounting pressure.

Second, the duration of the beast's rampage insured that d'Enneval arrived just in time to contend with other long-suffering individuals whose own sense of honor had become entangled in the public spectacle of the beast's impunity. Duhamel, who acknowledged in his last letter to Lafont that he had craved success in his mission because it was "advantageous to my glory," resented d'Enneval from the outset.[56] His aversion to the Normans reflected more than his frustration over assorted discourtesies and insensitive displays. Duhamel saw in their very presence an affront to his honor, an official rebuke that would forever tarnish his reputation—both in the eyes of his own men, who now lost their chance at collecting a portion of prize money, and in the eyes of his superiors. In late March he openly relished the d'Ennevals' lack of progress.[57] Morangiès, too, reacted to the d'Ennevals' haplessness with a vehemence that betrayed aggrieved sentiments. His attempts to undermine the d'Ennevals in May evinced a pettiness fully worthy of d'Enneval *fils,* and his threats to contact the court with his own complaints suggested nagging insecurities about his standing in the eyes of the government, which had failed to take advantage of his generous offer to lead a small army against the monster.[58] The brusque d'Ennevals faced long odds once they wound up on the wrong side of noble hunters, respected in the locale, who nursed their own wounded reputations.

Finally, the evolving attitudes of the afflicted population deserve emphasis. In the wake of the January announcement of the royal bounty, in the vacuum of authority created by Duhamel's disastrous February, and with "everything conspiring to bring celebrity to the ferocious beast" and its victims, the hunters from Normandy inevitably ranged over a territory rubbed raw by the presence of foreigners.[59] Anxious because of the increased risks of crime, resentful of the "Don Quixotes" searching for reward money, persuaded that they could do the job better themselves, the proud inhabitants of the Gévaudan had little patience for what Morangiès called "impostors." The d'Ennevals represented themselves "as our liberators," and a desperate local population was initially inclined to expect wonders from the awesome talents they had heard described. But when the d'Ennevals showed up and impressed mainly by their rudeness, their insufferable air of superiority, and their alien speech and manners, disillusionment came fast. The hunters became the hunted, and their every false move was magnified in the public eye. The suspicions about their motives and abilities in turn reinforced the d'Ennevals' secretive nature and made them fatally mistrustful.

The failure to defeat the beast owed something to the Normans' personal flaws and their surprising limitations as hunters. But the larger resonance of their sojourn—their reception in the region, the chronic dysfunctionality of their activities, their eventual retreat into disgrace—resulted from the intense and distorting expectations created by the phenomenon of publicity. In the end both the Gévaudan and the d'Ennevals turned out to be victims of false advertising. The hunters excitedly jumped into an oversold adventure in a rugged land they had never visited and did not understand. The locals found themselves rejecting false heroes puffed up by official promises and their own need for deliverance. An increasingly cynical Duhamel probably got it right when he used the d'Ennevals to exemplify the unfortunate turn taken in the hunt for the beast after the first of February. The d'Ennevals were mere *"étrangers,"* he wrote in one of his candid letters to Lafont. The unsuspecting Normans were "already beaten" before April dawned.[60]

6

Heroes and Skeptics

In the middle of February 1765, readers of newspapers and listeners in public squares began to absorb details of a recent clash in the Gévaudan that carried an "air of the fabulous" and the feel of a "novel."[1] A group of young children guarding cattle in the parish of Chanaleilles had been attacked by the beast in the usual way. The animal emerged suddenly from its hiding place and quickly selected as easy prey one of the youngest in the crowd, a boy of about eight years of age. This time, however, the beast failed to get its expected results. At the urging of the eldest among them, Jacques Portefaix, the remaining children (the whole group consisted of five boys and two girls) fought back against the attacker and gave chase until the beast mired itself in one of the Gévaudan's famously treacherous bogs. With their makeshift bayonets, the children pummeled the frustrated animal until it finally released its prey. An adult villager soon arrived to lend assistance, but the culprit made its way into the woods while Portefaix and his comrades turned to care for their injured friend, who survived a truly harrowing experience.

The stories of Portefaix were told alongside those of one other notable hero, Jeanne Varlet, a modest but formidable mother of six who had her own dramatic encounter with the beast two months later.[2] Portefaix and Varlet, whose inspiring actions attracted close attention throughout the spring of

1765, gave the story of the beast a strong contrapuntal harmony to accompany the prominent failures of Duhamel and d'Enneval. Together, the tribulations of the bumbling hunters and the examples of unflinching bravery provided by rustic heroes propelled the Gévaudan to new heights of celebrity and supplied a compelling "air of the fabulous" to the beast's exploits.

The tales of heroism that emerged from the hills of the Gévaudan provide another telling sign of the extent to which the entire phenomenon of the beast was embedded in the cultural currents of the age. The stories of Portefaix and Varlet had great appeal because their trials showed the extraordinary lengths to which ordinary people could go when moved by primal feelings of empathy and loyalty. Their feats were folded into a potent cultural initiative evident in many corners of French public life in the 1760s. In the wake of a disheartening war, many writers—government propagandists, historians, educators, moralists, journalists, novelists, and pamphleteers—worked to boost national morale and encourage new sentiments of national pride. Their project grew out of the hardening conviction that even "subaltern heroes," or persons of inferior status, could rise to the level of patriotic paragon, and it reflected the belief that a French identity based on proud sentiments of honor should inspire "patriotic enthusiasm" throughout the "mass of the nation."[3]

Patriotic sentiment bubbled to the surface often in the course of the emergency in the Gévaudan. Morangiès referred frequently to his own patriotic motivations while questioning the patriotism of others. The authors of projects submitted to newspapers and royal officials likewise cited good citizenship and patriotic ardor as explanations for their helpfulness. The hunter Antoine would eventually link the success of his mission to the interests of "the entire nation."[4] But the loving bonds of family had recently emerged as a powerful new model for patriotic fellowship, and the feats of Portefaix and Varlet therefore carried special resonance.[5]

The stories of the humble heroes also bring to light a change in how the phenomenon of the beast was perceived and a growing tension in public attitudes toward events in the Gévaudan over the course of 1765. A desire and willingness to accept accounts of the fantastic contended increasingly with a creeping skepticism, with both dispositions sometimes joined uneasily in the same mind. Public awareness of careless hyperbole increased suspicions in late winter and spring. Already in February one compiler of a manuscript newssheet reported to a Burgundian magistrate that "there are reasons to presume that reports [of the beast's] shape and exploits are exaggerated."[6] By late June the speculative bubble that had long enveloped the beast had begun to deflate. As the slow progress of deductive reasoning prompted officials to reflect on the destructive history of wolves, details of new atrocities continued to pour in. Public ambivalence to the story of the beast, though nothing new, grew. Even as heroes like Portefaix elicited new psychic investments in the image of an extraordinary monster, the contrary idea began to spread, in the Gévaudan and beyond, that the phenomenon of the beast might be indistinguishable from other afflictions involving predatory wolves. The publicity surrounding the beast continued to raise expectations for a grand climax, but the lure of the supernatural had to contend with public exhaustion and the pull of common sense.

The slow and steady demystification of the beast of the Gévaudan nevertheless took place in the shadows of an emotionally gripping development: the construction of new and inspirational public heroes. In the spring of 1765, word and image combined to create exemplars of common strength and virtue whose qualities stood in stark contrast to an ever-menacing fiend. Appreciative of the patriotic services and examples of these new heroes, both monarchy and public were engrossed in the process of mythologizing them. Thanks in part to the mutual necessity that connected the images of the beast and its heroic opponents, the myth of the heroes' great villain acquired a self-sustaining dynamic. That cultural dynamic proved powerful enough to weather the considerable winds of doubt that gathered as summer approached.

Fighting Back

Jacques Portefaix's elevation to the status of national icon can be attributed to a snap decision made under duress. Instead of running away from the beast, he resolved to stand and fight. Unfortunately the facts of the case are hopelessly tangled with the purposeful embellishments that accompanied its communication to the public. No adults were present to witness the confrontation, at least until the very end of the ordeal, and hearsay and exaggeration often passed unfiltered to authorities even when children were not involved in such events. From the very first account of the incident in the 12 February issue of the *Courrier d'Avignon*, however, all agreed that Portefaix had shown singular courage. After the beast dragged away the smallest and most vulnerable child in the crowd, "most of the others wanted to flee, for fear that the beast might next come after them." The twelve-year-old Portefaix disagreed, and "he told them that they must pursue the beast, kill it if possible, or at least force it to let go of its prey."[7] Lifting his bayonet, "he put himself at the head of his comrades" and they gave chase, eventually catching up to the beast after it happened upon a bog that slowed its progress. "The little hero laid siege" to the animal, landing so many blows on the beast's hindquarters that it finally released its prey and fled. The child who had been carried away "has been wounded only on the face, and they say that the wounds are not mortal; he will thus have time to contemplate what he owes to the courageous friendship of his comrade."[8]

The dramatic encounter in the village of Villeret occurred on 12 January. Notables in the immediate vicinity had heard of the incident by the end of the month, and they began to spread the news. All could instantly appreciate the affecting image of a small band of poorly armed children fending for themselves against a vicious predator, and the humble status of the "little hero" and his friends even found reinforcement in the leader's name, Portefaix, meaning "porter" or "carter"—the most menial occupation of the common day laborer. The intendant Saint-Priest was so moved by the story when he heard word of it that he interrupted a draft letter he was composing for L'Averdy and Saint-Florentin and squeezed into the margins the details of the children's exploits.[9] The admiring governor, the comte d'Eu, expressed mock disappointment that their strength had not matched their bravery. If it had, he mused, the hardy band would now be reaping the glory due to the eventual conqueror of the monster.[10]

The raw details of the story resonated far and wide, but this did not prevent publicists from adding or inventing others. In the weeks after the story broke, Portefaix's actions became even more impressive, as newspapers collectively made the encounter at Villeret into one of the defining moments of the ongoing tragedy in the Gévaudan. The Courrier's first story had been brief and to the point, a twenty-line summation that took up half a paragraph. Portefaix and his adventure reappeared in the paper at regular intervals, however, and the boy's words and actions soon took on a more compelling tone, one better suited to a hero. Whereas the first story merely stated that Portefaix had exhorted his companions to pursue the beast "and kill it if possible," by 22 February the little shepherd's rhetoric had become redolent of the ancients. Portefaix declared "that they had to save their comrade or perish," and this selfless "speech" had encouraged the others to follow their leader in pursuit.[11]

Portefaix had also been perceptive enough to notice, according to a report in the 19 February issue, that the children's blades "could not pierce the animal's skin." After having formed them "into a kind of battalion" to do battle, he therefore instructed them to aim their blows at the beast's eyes (a contradiction of the original report of 12 February, which had Portefaix striking the beast from behind). The fortunate turn that saved a life—the beast's fall into the marsh—now became a product of the children's indomitable will, as they cleverly "pushed" the beast there by design.

The wonder surrounding the feats of Portefaix made the events in Villeret an irresistible story. As Magné de Marolles put it, Portefaix and his stout battalion were "celebrated over and over again in the gazettes." The excitement even reached as far as Boston.[12] Most telling, however, was the reaction of the *Gazette de France.* The French *Gazette,* as noted earlier, traditionally avoided reporting on unusual items from the world of the everyday, and between its first notice in November and the middle of February the *Gazette* had published only one story on the beast of the Gévaudan. Portefaix's entrance into the narrative inaugurated a new and more aggressive phase in the *Gazette*'s coverage. The *Gazette* devoted a long piece to the inspiring exploits of "the little troupe," one so evocative and rich with detail that it became the target of plagiarizing editors everywhere. Subsequently, between 18 February and 10 June, the *Gazette* ran seven more stories on the crisis in the Midi—still far behind the pace of the *Courrier d'Avignon,* but comparable to that of the attentive *Gazette de Leyde* and ahead of the *Gazette d'Amsterdam* in the same months.[13]

The *Gazette*'s investment in the Portefaix story surprised some of the newspaper's more skeptical readers. In April the compilers of the popular newssheets *Mémoires Secrets* and *Correspondance Littéraire* mocked the credulity of the *Gazette*'s editors, Jean-Baptiste-Antoine Suard and the abbé François Arnaud. The impatient F.-M. Grimm threw his darts at a new target. "On the basis of whose word do they report these marvels?" If they added to the five eyewitnesses from Villeret "the children who run the *Gazette* and the children who credit these flimsy accounts, you'll have a lot of children."[14] But the *Gazette*'s coverage of the Portefaix story was no momentary aberration. Ever since Choiseul had subsumed the *Gazette*'s publishing privilege under the aegis of the Ministry of Foreign Affairs in 1761, the government and its appointed journalists had struggled to find a winning strategy to "satisfy and attract public curiosity."[15]

Between 1762 and 1763 the managers of the paper changed the title of the journal from *Gazette* to *Gazette de France,* as well as its appearance and publication schedule. At the same time, they began to see the advantage of including news of inventions, experiments, and notable accomplishments from the wider realm of French civil society. They also discovered the value of the *fait divers.* Throughout the 1760s and until at least 1771, the editors, and Choiseul himself, repeatedly enjoined intendants, ambassadors, and other officials to send to the *Gazette* news of curious events they had witnessed or heard about. "Singular facts of natural history" and "remarkable expressions of patriotism" were among the items specifically solicited.[16] Although the seriously divided attention of busy local officials made lay reporting a losing proposition in the long run, many royal servants tried to comply with the ministry's directives. The *Gazette*'s long entry of 18 February, in which Portefaix played the featured role, can be traced directly to a letter written by the obliging Saint-Priest.[17]

The *Gazette*'s discernible shift in direction in February of 1765 may have reflected a tactical concern for marketing, but the paper's attention to Portefaix was also an expression of the king's own interest in the story. Louis XV was drawn more to the combat in Villeret than to any other event from the whole spellbinding history of the beast. He "wants to know to whom this child belongs," L'Averdy would write.[18] On the day following the appearance of the *Gazette*'s story on Portefaix—the timing could not have been coincidental—the controller-general sent a letter to Saint-Priest informing him of the king's intention to grant Portefaix a reward of 300 livres in recognition of the "firm courage and intelligence" he had shown in his battle against the beast. (The king surely did not want to be outdone by the bishop of Mende, who had instantly offered the children small monetary rewards, as reported in the *Courrier d'Avignon.*) The king awarded the same amount of 300 livres to "the little troupe of children that [Portefaix] commanded," to be divided evenly among them.[19]

As shown in previous chapters, the month between late January and late February was the period in which the monarchy's involvement in the phenomenon of the beast became pronounced, public, and deliberate. Versailles's embrace of the Portefaix story, which had broken fortuitously in early February, provided another expression of this new sensitivity. At the same time, the king's solicitousness can be read as a sign of royal opportunism. The sympathetic image of a brave child in need of support offered the king an ideal opportunity to affirm his abiding "paternal kindness" while also associating himself with a young boy whose boldness could provide a useful boost to French morale.[20] After all, the baron Montperoux, French envoy to Geneva, reported to Saint-Priest at the end of February that "I have not encountered a Frenchman who is not moved by [Portefaix's] actions." The precocious hero was reminiscent of "Hercules in his cradle"—the baron excitedly quoted the boy's intention to free his friend or perish—and his future would surely reflect well "the honor and glory of his *patrie*." Perhaps he could even be schooled at the Ecole Militaire (a military academy for young noblemen), given that "the nobility of his soul is superior to that of his birth."[21]

Louis XV evidently shared these sentiments, and he resolved to place the boy on a course toward a different future. Again the king seems to have been spurred by the alacrity of the bishop of Mende, who had begun to inquire "if this determined little boy, who had emboldened others by his words and example, is susceptible to [receive] an education." Having learned that "other good qualities" complemented the boy's bravery, the bishop, according to the *Courrier d'Avignon,* began in mid-February to develop "plans to provide for his education."[22] Before the month was out, the bishop found himself out-flanked by the king himself. Portefaix would receive not only an education but "a suitable education, and be usefully instructed in the military art," where he could perform patriotic services for the monarchy.[23]

For the young hero from Villeret, the attention that came from on high must have been exhilarating, though perhaps a little exhausting. By mid-March Lafont had gone to see "the little Portefaix and his comrades" in their home village, and he predictably paraded the boy before the bishop of Mende. By the end of March "an epic poem in two cantos" was circulating in Paris, where Grimm scoffed at the boy's growing legend.[24] Broadsheets and engravings depicting Portefaix's heroic struggle soon followed. Lafont even had the entire troop of children travel to Serverette, a bustling weaving center in the Gévaudan, where, "in the presence of a number of people," they reenacted the "same maneuvers they had performed on the mountain." All were impressed by the "simplicity and truthfulness" of Portefaix's speech and manners.[25]

All of these events would have been exciting, but the most dizzying consequence of Portefaix's notable confrontation with the beast had to be his trip to Montpellier in April, a trip that would prove life-changing. Having made the decision to prepare Portefaix for military service, the crown had first to provide him a basic education. (Lafont had investigated and found that the boy, though not from the basest poverty, "does not even know how to read.")[26] After exploring the educational facilities available in Mende, Saint-Priest quickly decided that Portefaix would need to be relocated to Languedoc's administrative center. With the approval of the royal ministers, the intendant arranged for Portefaix's placement at a Montpellier *collège* run by Jean-Baptiste de LaSalle's *Frères des écoles chrétiennes.*[27]

Portefaix lived in Villeret with seven siblings and a set of overburdened parents, so his closest male relative of adequate means and occasional free time, an uncle who served as the curé of Bagnol les Bains, just east of Mende, soon received word that he would need to deliver his young charge to the capital city at his earliest convenience. Probably through the helpful mediation of either Lafont or Morangiès, who also became involved in the affair in late March, the curé rented two horses and hired a servant who came along for the adventurous three-day descent into Montpellier.[28] On arriving in the capital, the boy and his uncle were hosted by Saint-Priest, who received visitors eager to catch a glimpse of the common hero who had stared down the beast.[29] The uncle and the servant would soon depart on their return journey to the Gévaudan, while Portefaix stayed behind to embark on a path that would soon lead him to the king's artillery school at Douai. There he made "good progress in mathematics and drafting" while showing a "natural inclination" for hard work. For his efforts he earned a trip to Fontainebleau for an audience with the king in 1770. Before Portefaix began his successful career in the Auxonne regiment of the royal artillery, the court erased the stigma of low status attached to his name by reanointing him (in the manner of a legal ennoblement) Portefaix de Villeret, after the village where he had performed his memorable heroics. His career in the army was cut short by a tragically premature death in 1785, but not before he had risen to the rank of lieutenant, thereby justifying all the effort and attention lavished on him in the twenty years that followed his notorious battle with the beast on that pivotal January day.[30]

Despite the king's steady attention, public curiosity about the Portefaix story seems to have crested by mid-April of 1765. Surprisingly, none of the newspapers that had followed the events in the south wrote an account of the boy's trek to Montpellier. Portefaix's fading star had less to do with the public's loss of interest in everyday heroism, however, than with an abrupt shift of attention precipitated by news of another remarkable encounter that had recently occurred about ten miles to the southwest of Villeret, in the comte de Morangiès' parish of Saint-Alban. There, in the tiny village of Bessière, the beast had launched another brazen attack on 13 March, this one affecting not a band of young friends but "an entire family."[31] The courageous resistance put on display in this instance struck the *Gazette de France*'s informant as even more "marvelous" than the bravery shown by Portefaix and company. The fortitude shown by the stricken mother of Bessière, wrote Magné de Marolles, inspired sentiments "more vivid and touching than those that come from simple admiration." For Tardieu de Labarthe (or Labarthe *fils*), a perceptive correspondent from Marvejols, the clash at Bessière counted as "perhaps the most astonishing of all the [stories] that have come to us."[32]

The *Courrier d'Avignon,* the *Gazette de Leyde,* and the *Gazette de France* differed over some details of the event—the sequence of the attacks, the extent of the injuries, even the name of the heroine's home village—but they and the purveyors of their stories concurred in praising the uncommon courage of a mother who rushed to her children's defense when they found themselves in harm's way.[33] The setting for the attacks, at least, was beyond dispute. The mother, Jeanne Varlet—more consistently called Mrs. Jouve (the *femme* Jouve)—had entered the enclosed garden adjoining her humble home in Bessière. She simultaneously watched over three of her children, aged ten years, six years, and approximately eighteen months (the latter "not yet weaned" in the words of the *Gazette de France*). According to the *Gazette*'s story, evidently informed by an account of the action written by the curé of Saint-Alban, the ten-year-old girl was carrying the baby in her arms when the beast suddenly fell on both of them.[34] In the account provided by the *Courrier,* by contrast, Varlet herself carried the youngest as she turned to see the beast wrap its jaws around the head of the six-year-old, a boy. What is clear is that Varlet immediately lunged at the predator and grabbed hold of the legs of the beast's first victim, refusing to surrender the child to its attacker.

Although a slender woman, and said to be pregnant with her seventh child, Varlet fought bravely through this first stage of the encounter.[35] The *Gazette* explained: "The terrified mother went to the aid of her two children, removing them one by one from the mouth of the beast which, no sooner than one had been rescued, moved on to the other." (In the *Courrier,* instead of juggling between two stricken children, Varlet had to engage in an awful game of tug-of-war in an effort to save the six-year-old; the beast had taken hold of the head, and "the mother seized the [child's] feet, and each pulled on one side.")[36] During this first struggle, which lasted for several minutes, both mother and children were struck several times by the animal's head, and they also had their clothing "torn to shreds." All accounts reported a brief break in the action as the beast paused to reconsider its tactics in the face of the mother's brave resistance. Eventually, the beast turned with new fury on the wounded six-year-old and sought to escape the garden with its prey.

It was at this juncture, after several death-defying minutes already spent in combat, that Jeanne Varlet performed an extraordinary feat that marked her, in some eyes, as superhuman. After her child's head had disappeared into the gaping mouth of the beast, and after she had tried without success to wrest the child free of the attacker, she impulsively climbed up onto the beast's back as one would mount a horse, hoping to distract the monster from its deadly mission. Unable to remain atop the beast for long, Varlet then tried "as a last resort" to grab the beast "at one of the most sensitive parts of its body." The *Gazette de France* neglected to specify the body part on which Varlet had fixed her attention, but the *Courrier* discreetly noted that the desperate mother grabbed the beast by one of its rear legs as it tried to escape through a hole in the enclosure around the garden. With her strength at last failing her, she was forced to release the beast's limb and leave her pitiful child "at the mercy of the monster."

Even in her state of exhaustion, however, Varlet would not allow herself to give up. The beast, up to its familiar tricks, jumped over both a wall and a hedge "at least ten feet high, all the while holding the child in its mouth." But Varlet managed to collect her wits and give chase. (The *Courrier* asserted that she, too, cleared the wall, though in these pages the obstruction stood at a relatively modest four feet.) Fortunately, by this time Varlet's adolescent son, having heard the commotion in the garden, had also come running to help with lance in hand and followed by a large sheepdog. Catching up to the beast just as it prepared to devour the six-year-old, the boy and the dog—one thrusting with his lance, the other boldly jumping on top of the monster— presented enough of an irritant to keep the predator from eating its prey. The beast finally became fatigued and released the mangled child, who clung to life despite lacking his upper lip, most of his nose, and "most dangerously, all the skin from his head." The languishing mother had given chase, "beseeching the heavens" for assistance according to the curé, but she arrived too late to rejoin the battle. When she saw the "horrible spectacle" of her son's condition, her face was "bathed in tears, tenderness, and sorrow," her heart "divided between the joy of having saved two of her children and the despair from seeing her third [child] mauled so cruelly." Despite efforts to repair the damage—the *Courrier* reported that much of the scalp was reattached with thread, as was part of the nose—the traumatized child did not survive the attack.

Public reaction came swiftly. The comte de Morangiès immediately went to Bessière to pay his respects to the agonized survivors, generously bestowing "largesse on all these unfortunates." Newspapers, engravings, and broadsheets covered the story within weeks of the event, their fast-moving producers having been primed by the earlier excitement over Portefaix.[37] And government officials responded with interest and compassion. Lafont praised Varlet's "heroic tenderness," while Saint-Priest noted the woman's "supernatural" courage in the face of a "barrage" of attacks. The king, at the urging of Morangiès and Saint-Priest, wasted no time before signaling his intent to award the woman a gift of 300 livres in consolation for her loss and in recognition of her bravery. The king's generosity was quickly publicized, appearing in the *Gazette*'s story about *femme* Jouve on 1 April, less than three weeks after the event. Before the end of the month a royal notary had met with Varlet and her husband, Pierre Jouve, to authorize the transfer of royal funds; Lafont's ever-dependable brother Trophime stood by as witness.[38]

The monarchy had good reasons to associate itself with the beast's latest victim. The feats of *femme* Jouve quickly aroused "the curiosity of the public," as Morénas observed.[39] For many, the heroine of "the combats in the Garden" would have called to mind Jean-Jacques Rousseau's adored protagonist from his bestselling epistolary novel *Julie* (1761), who gives her life in a valiant effort to save her own drowning son. Julie's heroic fate (she experiences her final "transports of joy" on seeing that her son has indeed been saved) and her impressive moral fortitude in the face of temptation and loss had inspired an unprecedented emotional outpouring among readers.[40] Demand for the book was so great that owners of *cabinets de lecture* cut the novel into pieces so that copies could be read by more than one reader at a time.[41] Some of these readers identified so firmly with this virtuous wife and mother living "at the foot of the Alps" that they refused to accept that she was "only a clever fabrication." Jeanne Varlet had avoided Julie's fate, of course, but like her fictional predecessor she exemplified rural simplicity, and the resounding purity of her love presented an aching contrast with the corrupt mores of the city. By reenacting Julie's spirit of virtuous self-sacrifice, the *femme* Jouve had provided a real-life expression of maternal tenderness that would have struck a chord for all readers touched by a character whose example, according to one of Julie's admirers, "made me weep such sweet tears."[42]

As François Morénas and other journalists would have recognized, the exemplary power of familial love had assumed a new importance in the political and cultural environment of the age. Two years after Rousseau's celebration of the domestic virtues in *Julie,* the historian and moralist Gabriel-Bonnot de Mably published a popular and influential paean to patriotic virtues that drew heavily from ancient examples of private integrity. Morénas evoked the arguments of the abbé Mably when he used Jeanne Varlet's devotion to her children as a model for the citizen's desirable attachments to community, religion, and nation. Even before her bravery in the garden, the *Courrier* emphasized, Varlet had already enjoyed "public esteem" for her "wisdom and good morals." Her signal courage had come as no surprise to those already familiar with the example of her daily life. "A good mother is ordinarily a good wife, a good citizen, an honest woman, and a good Christian."[43] It was in light of this fact, Morénas suggested, that the king had been moved to grant the heroine a royal recompense—a form of public recognition that would merely supplement the already great satisfaction she could take in knowing that her love and bravery had been placed in the service of her own children.

Others also viewed the events in Bessière through the filter of civic life and its demands. Magné de Marolles declared the mother's feats a "rare example of the power of maternal love within a virtuous heart."[44] The author of a "heroic poem" dedicated to *femme* Jouve saw Varlet's actions as worthy of attention precisely because they revived ancient examples.[45] Her character seemed to offer the modern world a perfect illustration of Mably's dictum that "domestic morals determine political morals." The author of "The Triumph of Maternal Love" specifically invoked "two magnanimous mothers" who had given the ancient Greeks powerful examples of maternal virtue and the spirit of self-sacrifice. Andromache, widow of Hector, had generously "offered herself to her son's executioner" and married king Pyrrhus against her wishes. Clytemnestra witnessed the selfless devotion of her own daughter Iphigenia, who, because of overpowering duty to father and country, had offered her own life in sacrifice to the gods; only divine intervention finally saved her from the executioner's blade. These examples of selfless duty and compassion, performed by mythic royalty, had now been followed in modern times by a humble woman ensconced in a world of "rural huts."

> Such then is virtue, by the brilliance of its luster
> It lifts from obscurity the least illustrious name

I have pity for those hearts that have never known
How through this brilliance a name can be ennobled![46]

The poem drew its details directly from the *Gazette de France,* and the quality of the verse was far from inspiring. Grimm, noting that "each century has its heroes" and that not every century could be blessed with heroes like Turenne, dismissively observed: "heroes get the poets they deserve."[47]

"Triumph" is notable less for its literary value, however, than for the themes that structure its presentation. Since the 1750s French proponents of so-called "bourgeois drama" had been clamoring for staged depictions of moving moral lessons accessible to all classes. "[We] would weep with the same pleasure over the sad fate of a bourgeois Iphigenia, or the cruel anxieties of a common Andromache," wrote one such champion in 1752.[48] Denis Diderot, Michel Sedaine, and other early developers of the genre in the late 1750s and 1760s created middle-class settings in which the sturdy domestic virtues of merchants or other urban professionals ultimately saved the day and overcame family divisions. In the late 1760s and 1770s Sedaine and Louis-Sebastien Mercier would further widen the circle of virtue in plays that featured peasants, artisans, and common soldiers behaving selflessly and wisely.[49]

The theatrical but authentic exploits of Jeanne Varlet, who had "consult[ed] only her desperate heart" to determine her course of action, helped to underscore the natural and potentially universal moral resources that made possible all extraordinary acts. These moral resources could "ennoble" even those of peasant status, and they were as vital to the polity as to families, a point not lost on the author of "Triumph." The final verses of the poem focused on the action of the king/father whose paternal affections and tangible signs of appreciation had placed an official seal of approval on Varlet's impressive moral victory.

To the gifts that Heaven bestowed on [your] heart
Has been added one last triumph
A King who is himself the model of all the virtues
Has given yours a new glory
Father of a contented people, his beneficent gaze
Sees in the least of his subjects his own children.[50]

The most "subaltern" of heroes felt the paternal embrace of the most exalted of rulers.

The courage and selflessness shown by Portefaix and *femme* Jouve projected patriotic ideals that more and more French readers found desirable, and all found ubiquitous, in this time of ebbing national fortunes. In April of 1765, only weeks after *femme* Jouve's display of maternal heroism, one representative admirer of Buirette de Belloy's patriotic *Siege of Calais* would assert that "love of the *patrie*" had the capacity to elicit from every French citizen "a hero's tears."[51] (The playwright himself exhorted readers in a preface to his published play: "Let us imitate the ancients!")[52] The glorious actions of the Gévaudan's humble heroes expressed the admirable instincts buried in the hearts of all French subjects. The king himself, meanwhile, whose propagandists busily reminded readers in these years that "the patriotism of the French [is] founded principally on their love for their kings," offered generous rewards to the rustic heroes and regarded them as "his own children," reinforcing the familial character of French patriotic affections.[53] For governors and governed alike, the stories of Portefaix and Varlet helped to satisfy a strong craving for civic bonding.

Depicting the Enemy

However impressive the moral reserves of the protagonists, the noteworthy highlights of the stories of Portefaix and Varlet emerged through confrontation with the extraordinary features of their foe, which found new confirmation even in the circumstances of its retreat. To accent the drama of the experiences, public renderings of the encounters in Villeret and Bessière invariably depicted the animal as both sinister and exotic. The "Triumph of Maternal Love" spoke of "this strange monster" and "this formidable Hyena," just as the same author's poem about Portefaix had described the enemy as an "escaped monster . . . from the shores of Africa," one that sported a "sparkling gaze."[54]

Even the *Gazette de France* indulged suspicions about the extraordinary nature of the killer at large. The *Gazette*'s story on *femme* Jouve became the template for most others—the *Année Littéraire* and the *Mercure de France,* for example, simply copied the *Gazette*'s account word for word—and it contained generous amounts of hyperbole. The shepherd who came to Varlet's assistance rained blows on the beast, but "without being able to do it any harm." The report that the beast had jumped a ten-foot hedge "with the child still in its mouth" appeared not in the willfully entertaining *Courrier* but in the typically restrained *Gazette.* And the *Gazette*'s description of the beast's final act on the battlefield had an air of strangeness sufficient to produce chills.

The beast "released its prey" after tiring of the fight. Then, "turning toward the dog, it lifted it off the ground with one swipe of its head and, without biting it, threw it twenty feet from the spot. Afterwards, it took flight." In response to this fantastical story, one *nouvelliste* in Paris expressed disbelief that the *Gazette*'s editors would publish such fictions.[55]

After its uncharacteristically slow start on the story from Bessière, the *Courrier d'Avignon* made up for earlier generalizations with typically piquant details. As the beast made its escape from the garden, for example, Morénas had the beast doing to its six-year-old victim what the *Gazette* saw happening only to the dog. "Seeing that force was not succeeding, the beast employed cunning. With one strike of its nose, it heaved its first victim [the six-year-old] over a wall and a hedge that reached three or four feet on the inside of the garden and about seven feet on the outside." Only after first securing the optimal position of its prey did the beast then "pass through a small hole at the bottom of the wall." At the final showdown in the clearing, the *Courrier* also

"An actual representation of the wild hyena, which has been appearing since September, 1764 in the Gévaudan in the French province of Languedoc." This German print attests to the wide notoriety of Portefaix's combat with the beast in January, 1765. The background scenes, helpfully numbered to ease the narrative flow, show the stages of the contest between the "hyena" and the children led by Portefaix. In number 10, right of center, the beast rears up on its hind legs to make its escape, and in number 13, just above and to the left of number 10, it rolls in the grass to dry itself. *Bibliothèque Nationale de France, Qb 1764, collection Hennin*

had the beast tossing the dog aside with surprising ease. "All of these details, however fabulous they may appear, are incontestably true."[56]

The fabulous details only increased wonder at the peasants' heroism. In Villeret, the beast had thrown itself upon the children "without having been noticed." Before the dramatic rescue at the bog, the beast had actually initiated the fight by attacking one of the larger children, which it held in place on the ground with one paw "while, with the other, it parried the blows of the little troupe." The beast resolved to back away and take a chance at seizing another of the children, but before the monster released its first victim it tore away "with one swipe of the paw" a morsel of flesh from the child's cheek, which it savored in front of the other children, as if "toying" with his oppo-

Portefaix and company attack the beast around the eyes and head to force it to release its prey. Conflating the two dangerous encounters that defined the contest between the beast and the children of Villeret, the printmaker shows a rescued boy clutching his cheek in the foreground—a reference to the beast's first unsuccessful attack. *Bibliothèque Nationale de France, Qb1 1764–1788*

nents before launching its next attack. After seizing the smallest of the group and finding itself pursued to the fateful bog, the beast continued to parry the blows directed at it—the animal sustained blows on the mouth but the children "never managed to touch the eyes"—and when it finally tired of the fight it simply "reared up on its hind legs" and fled. Perhaps strangest of all, while making its retreat the beast dallied in a stream, as if taking a refreshing swim, and the villagers who had pursued it saw the beast rolling in the grass to dry itself after its dip. Evidently feeling renewed, the beast headed north to Mazel, in the neighboring parish of Grezes, where it "devoured a fifteen-year-old boy" later that same day.[57]

Producers of visual images also accented the unusual. An elegantly produced German engraving displayed the entire Portefaix episode in a series of scenes that progressed from left to right—up to and including a depiction of the beast's peculiar roll in the grass. A menacing animal with bared fangs and sharp talons exults in the foreground, looming over the story that unfolds behind it. Another image of Portefaix and his friends shows the bogged-down beast surrounded by a band of boys, arms raised and preparing to attack. (Perhaps to simplify this martial scene, the artist has removed all trace of the girls.) Only the beast's head, chest, and forelegs are visible, but here, too, the beast's features compose a frightening image. The animal's left foreleg, partly concealed, vaguely resembles a dragon's claw, and its taut and wavy coat resembles chain mail, feathers, or scaly reptilian skin more than a mammal's fur. The head is unnaturally rectangular, and the eyes glisten menacingly—in fact, the beast's are the only clearly defined eyes in the entire portrait. The animal's gaping mouth, meanwhile, is easily large enough to swallow up the head of a twelve-year-old, and its terrible effects are on display in the foreground, where the rescued victim lies prostrate as he clutches his left cheek, a portion of which has been removed by the beast.

Other representations of the Portefaix episode derived their power from the striking visual context. In two multi-image prints that functioned as what might be called "greatest hits" collections of the beast's escapades, Portefaix is shown assailing the beast while it casually holds its victim securely in place on the ground. The *femme* Jouve is shown straddling the beast in both prints, and in one the beast holds the mother's unfortunate six-year-old in the way a dog might wield a bone. Adding decisively to the terror is the oversized monster that dominates the center panel. In the first published image, evidently produced in April, Varlet and Portefaix are depicted in the background, along with capsule summaries of their adventures, while in the center of the composition the beast attacks a woman from behind, enclosing her bloodied head between its vise-like jaws. Mauled bodies are strewn across the foreground, and the beast exhibits the physical characteristics for which it had become famous. The tail is unusually long (d'Enneval and others had described its playful and feline twitching), the teeth are sharp and spaced widely apart, its talons are long and piercing, and the beast walks upright like a human.[58]

In a second multipaneled print, apparently created by the same artist in May, the central figure is set to devour a bare-breasted woman while surrounded by scenes of its earlier devastation and trickery.[59] In addition to Portefaix and *femme* Jouve, the image depicts the luckless boy from Mazel on

"Furious beast thought to be a Hyena." This dramatic print, one of the first that followed the "forever memorable" events at Villeret and Bessière, represents an outsized beast as large as a pony. The enormous size would help to explain why the *femme* Jouve instinctively mounted its back, as depicted in the background at far left. *Bibliothèque Nationale de France, Rés. 4-LK2-786, fol. 101*

whom the beast vented its frustrations after its flight from Villeret, the wall that famously halted the progress of Duhamel's dragoons at La Baume, an against-all-odds escape that also refers to the captain's great missed opportunity, and the attack alleged to be the first notice of the beast's presence in the Gévaudan.[60] These representations of serial atrocity left no doubt that the same beast was to be blamed for all the unpleasantness. The long tail and a

"Representation of the ferocious beast called a hyena." This print seems to date from May, given that the scenes of the beast's ravages come from the winter and the caption beneath the engraving updates readers on events through late April. *Femme* Jouve rides the beast in the second panel from the top right. Portefaix and friends do battle with the beast in the third panel from the top left. The escape at La Baume is represented in two panels up from the right bottom. The similar features of the beast in the prints of April and May point to the standardization, or transportability, of the beast's image in late winter and spring, at least for some artists. *Bibliothèque Nationale de France, Rés. 4-LK2-786, fol. 103*

protruding tongue serve as useful identifying marks in most of the miniature images, and all of the animal's terrible features were highlighted in the center panel, where the monster towered over its next victim.

The feats of Portefaix and Varlet were hardly the only stories of interest in the spring and summer months. "Many believe there are exaggerations in what is published on the subject of the Beast," wrote the defiant Morénas in the middle of April. (Expressions of skepticism were indeed beginning to mount, and early April seems to have been a turning point).[61] He nevertheless guaranteed his readers that "far from attributing to this Beast actions for which it is not responsible, we have allowed to go unmentioned other events" that, for all their intrinsic interest, had not been marked by some "singular circumstance."[62]

Morénas's exacting standards still permitted the *Courrier* to provide touching details about a fatal attack in the parish of Saint-Denis, carried out in the shadows of the Margeride mountains. There an "extremely beautiful girl of sixteen years," one whose "lovely face could tame a Rhinoceros," had been unfortunate enough to be taken from behind by the beast—it probably never glimpsed her bewitching face—as the maiden walked unawares with her sister. The survivor had been the first to detect the danger, and she had cried out to the victim, "Look out, there's a large wolf behind you," before she sprinted in the direction of a nearby village. The "alleged wolf" grabbed her sister before the words of warning had even left her mouth. Sensing her sister's dreadful fate, the breathless escapee stopped to turn and see what had become of her sibling. "And what did she see? The head of her dear sister falling to the ground while the body remained upright." On witnessing the beast's savagery, the surviving sibling promptly "took leave of her senses." When men from the village came running to help, she even accused them of murderous intent. "Why are you trying to kill me?" she cried. "It is unclear if she has since returned to her senses or whether her derangement continues."[63] Temporary insanity and loss of the senses became recurring themes in the pages of the *Courrier* during the summer months, as in the case of the young shepherd who "wandered like a blind man" after surviving a July attack in Ventuejols, near Saugues.[64]

The pivotal engagement at the woods of La Chaumette, discussed in Chapter 5, had also added important new evidence of the exotic. The particulars of the brothers' ill-fated pursuit during the first two days of May had appeared in all of the newspapers covering the story of the beast. Just as important as the details of the near-miss, however, was the brothers' description of the animal. The *Gazette de France* emphasized that the brothers La Chaumette had assured all who would listen that the beast "bears only a slight resemblance" to the lupine form. In fact, with its "elongated muzzle," a "black stripe down the length of its back," an "enormous, gaping mouth," a broad chest, and small and pointed ears, the portrait they had provided greatly resembled "that already given by M. Duhamel."[65] The unsettling news that this bizarre animal had lived to strike again helped to raise "public consternation to its peak" in early May, as Lafont explained in a letter to Saint-Priest.[66] On cue, an engraving that appeared in June portrayed a wounded beast "called a hyena," sporting a face more ghoulish than that of any other contemporary image of the monster. That the bloodied creature had escaped the clutches of the La Chaumettes as they closed in around it would have only added to the horror.

"Representation of the ferocious beast called a hyena." The image depicts the shooting of the beast by the brothers La Chaumette on 1 May. The animal was said to have left large patches of blood on the ground, leading to the false belief that it had been mortally wounded. Together with another evasion on 6 May, the event at La Chaumette caused wide consternation. This identical image would be resuscitated, with a new caption and labels that changed the identity of the principals, for the celebration of François Antoine's September shooting at Les Chazes. *Bibliothèque Nationale de France, Rés. 4-LK2-786, fol. 105*

What were the effects of this steady diet of troubling but sensational news? From February through June, the public experience of the beast of the Gévaudan had offered inspiring combats, spine-tingling descriptions of the beast's behavior, and fearsome images of human carnage and of the monster believed to be responsible for it. Did these compelling words and images resonate only within a distinct realm of entertaining fantasy, one that rational actors held at arm's length? Grimm, we have seen, thought the tales of the beast suitable only for children. Bachaumont, in his *Mémoires Secrets,* criticized the accounts in the *Gazette* for "lacking in verisimilitude." Walpole saw in the beast "the enchanted monster of old romances," and he regretted not having discovered it in time to include it in his pathbreaking gothic novel of 1764, *The Castle of Otranto.*[67] Did the wry mockery exhibited by these urban literati stand in for enlightened opinion everywhere? Or did the tales and images continue to inform, and perhaps reflect, the opinions of discerning hunters, administrators, and other educated actors who sought the beast's elimination?

Clues to contemporary thinking can be found in the half-conscious methods and assumptions that guided those who sorted through the maze of conflicting evidence about the beast. Beyond the public glare, thoughtful speculations about the monster's origins, movements, and behavior, formulated by well-positioned observers, suggest that the most "rational" actors on the stage continued to contemplate the existence of an extraordinary creature even as they pondered the mounting evidence of the ordinary. The will to believe in a great monster worthy of devilish crimes and the heroic deeds of its enemies remained so powerful through early summer of 1765 that it delayed full realization of the Gévaudan's struggle with a dangerously dense wolf infestation. By the time this relatively mundane reality had dawned on those responsible for stopping the carnage, the time for public candor had passed, and officials found themselves facing two equally unpleasant alternatives. Increasingly doubtful that they would be able to herald the conquest of a monstrous specimen fascinating to naturalists everywhere, they were also loath to dismiss as wasteful and inefficient a year's worth of effort, attention, and expertise expended in the mountains and marshes of the Gévaudan. The resolution they would ultimately provide for this remarkable episode would create the conditions for two sets of memories about the Gévaudan's rampaging monster, neither of which would do full justice to the history of the beast and of the many people it had touched.

Thinking with Monsters

The events at La Chaumette provide an ideal point of entry into the befuddled thinking of contemporaries, because they reveal the distorting impact of pre-existing expectations on the forensic sensibilities of the locals. Lafont explained in his report to Saint-Priest that one of the most dispiriting aspects of the events in the first days of May had been the successive attacks in Pouges and Pépinet that followed the initial encounter on the La Chaumettes' estate. The attacks had occurred within twenty-four hours of the beast's being wounded. The animal's speed and agility had been much remarked upon ever since the fall of 1764, but this latest manifestation of supernatural ability proved particularly hard to accept. The animal had lost copious amounts of blood, and on the morning of 2 May the La Chaumettes had expected to find the beast dead or dying in a forest where the wounded creature had taken cover. Yet new additions to the casualty list continued to appear in the hours after the shooting.

Many found it hard to escape the conclusion that the beast had accomplices. "More than ever we believe that there are several ferocious beasts in the country," wrote Lafont to the intendant. The subdelegate noted that there had been general fear "for a long time" that dangerous beasts were reproducing in the area, and the bishop and commissioners of the diocese of Mende had therefore instructed the syndic to double the reward money for all who destroyed "wolf litters." In the wake of the encounter at La Chaumette, Lafont wrote letters to all consuls of the diocese urging them to publicize the augmentation of the reward money now offered to successful wolf hunters.[68] The ever-industrious Lafont even began to scour the archives of the diocese and parish burial records to compare the experience of 1765 with earlier episodes of wolf infestation in the Gévaudan's history. He found evidence from the 1630s of a "calamity that parallels that of today," with "strange" ravages committed sometimes by one and sometimes by several voracious wolves.[69]

Vague and intermittent doubts about the solitary character of the beast of the Gévaudan had arisen long before the events at La Chaumette, Pouges, and Pépinet. Duhamel himself, in his first, unvexed days in Saint-Chély, had expressed confidence that "there are two animals."[70] The *Courrier,* noting how difficult it was to believe that a single animal could cover "eight leagues in one hour," reported in January of 1765 that there seemed to be two beasts at work, and that a local peasant had seen them together on at least one occasion. A consul in Auvergne observed, also in January, "we have good reasons to believe that there are several animals of this type, in view of the dates of [the] different events." The *Courrier* reported that "there [was] no longer any doubt" of the plural menace in June.[71]

Nor were local sightings of multiple animals the only evidence that might have pointed the finger of suspicion at wolf packs. In the winter of 1765, wolf scares in the Soissonnais and the nearby Limousin had caused consternation sufficient to garner international news attention. The killer of the rampaging wolf of the Soissonnais had even received the royal treatment accorded to Portefaix and *femme* Jouve. In late March he, too, was awarded a royal gratuity of 300 livres.[72] In one of its accounts of the Soissons story, the *Gazette de Leyde* reported that voracious beasts, including a "monstrous wolf" killed in the Limousin in early February, seemed determined to "make war on the realm."[73] Whether because the surfeit of unlikely heroes had grown tiresome or because the widespread occurrence of lupine violence undermined the unique appeal of the Gévaudan story, the *Gazette de Cologne* virtually abandoned coverage of the beast of the Gévaudan after reporting on the news from the Soissonnais in late March.

In spite of strong evidence suggesting the conventional character of their experience, however, most residents of the Gévaudan, as well as many outsiders, generally continued to read new evidence in a way that magnified the singularity of the phenomenon they endured. The events of early May provide a prime example of the tendency. By their own reckoning and according to multiple newspaper accounts, the La Chaumettes had seen their beast only at a distance. Jean-François Marlet de La Chaumette had glimpsed the creature through his window as it sat at the edge of a wood 250 paces from his house. When his brothers got into position to fire on the animal, they, too, acted at a considerable distance. Their two shots were delivered at sixty-seven and fifty-two paces, respectively, after which the beast disappeared behind a rock, which prevented Jean-François from getting off a shot of his own.

Yet despite the less than optimal conditions and poor weather, the La Chaumettes had apparently seen enough to know that the beast "exactly" resembled the creature shown in Duhamel's famous portrait. They shared the news with Trophime Lafont. "Larger than a year-old calf," the animal had a gaping mouth of "prodigious" size. Broad in the chest and thin in the rear, the animal's black stripe ended precisely where the tail began, and it seemed "proud" in its gait, "just as it has so often been depicted."[74] Even as the events of early May pointed to the presence of multiple *bêtes féroces* in the region, the feature of the story that made its way into the newspapers, and inspired a new engraving, was the apparent confirmation of the beast's unwolflike singularity.[75] The testimony of the La Chaumettes, considered to be "among the most renowned hunters in the country" according to Lafont, was widely credited.

Early doubts about the beast's species had never been dispelled, and it was through that prism of uncertainty that all new evidence had to pass. When the *Courrier* first noted the possibility of a second beast in January, for example, it made no reference to wolves' penchant for traveling in groups. Instead the news came packaged in a story that also described one of the two animals—the beast's companion—as "much smaller than the other." (A March report would share eyewitness accounts that identified this second animal, implausibly enough, as a deer.) The leading partner, meanwhile, had a devilish appearance and a terrifying gaze that even brave hunters could not withstand. Furthermore, evidence that the beast liked to keep company with other creatures seemed to account for, and thus minimized the importance of, the conflicting descriptions produced by eyewitnesses. "There is no longer any reason to be astonished at the differences between the descriptions that have been provided," Morénas helpfully pointed out.[76]

The uncertainty that persisted in the minds of those engaged by the story of the beast in no way reflected willing abandonment of the critical faculties. The opportunistic Morénas and a handful of other publicists knowingly fanned the flames of doubt, but few people close to the action were inclined to indulge in raw fantasy or foolishness. They continued to winnow out the least credible claims and to discount theories that could not be reconciled with the evidence as they knew it. (Hypotheses involving witches or werewolves, for example, were never seriously entertained, or at least not publicly discussed, by officials working on the problem in 1765.) Despite this salutary habit of skepticism, the mental environment simply did not permit the preemptive dismissal of strange possibilities. On the contrary, the climate in which the beast of the Gévaudan had forced itself into public consciousness strongly encouraged an inclination toward "thinking with monsters."[77] Contemporary fascination for hybrid animals, abnormal or monstrous births, and other exotic forms had prepared many to expect the presence of extraordinary creatures. Other forces, more specific to the time and place, worked to insure widespread belief in the monster of the Gévaudan.

Many months of sensational journalism had certainly done little to counteract readers' tendencies to fixate on evidence of the marvelous, and on the local level the bishop of Mende's evocation of the specter of divine magic had had lingering effects. Beginning in late 1764, Duhamel's self-interested but at least partly sincere promotion of the myth of a virtually insurmountable monster—replete with illustrations distributed to the localities and committed to memory by the likes of the La Chaumettes—also had an immeasurable impact on both local and national opinion. Then, far from bringing rampant speculation to an end, the failure of the d'Ennevals created new reasons to imagine the beast as a wondrous if not magical creature. One of the *Courrier's* informants confidently declared at the end of April that the "vain" and "useless" efforts of the great wolf-hunter from the north had offered "decisive" proof that the beast could not possibly be a wolf.[78] D'Enneval himself found the idea comforting, and he continued to flog the story of the extraordinary monster long after his departure from the Gévaudan.[79] Meanwhile, the widely renowned heroism of Portefaix and *femme* Jouve had compounded the mystery by seeming to confirm rumors about the beast's hide, its dexterity, its strength, and its cunning. Even the actions of the monarchy could be taken as proof of the extraordinary character of what the French widely regarded—in Magné de Marolles's assessment—as "a public enemy."[80]

Facing a welter of baffling and inconsistent evidence, officials and concerned locals made only slow but steady progress in solving the puzzle of the beast's identity. Already in March Lafont had moved toward the wolf hypothesis. He reported to the Estates of the Gévaudan that the wolf stood out as "the animal to which [the beast] now seems, judging all the evidence, to have the closest resemblance." (He was shaken two weeks later, however, when the beast managed to kill four people within five days. "This monster," he added in a sad note to Saint-Priest, "had not yet shown such fury."[81]) Other officials also began to separate the plausible from the fabulous. The subdelegate Montluc, who employed distinctly Duhamelian language in an official circular of 1 February ("large head," "pointed muzzle," "elongated body," "believed to be a leopard"), had settled on the wolf as the likeliest species for the animal just two weeks later. He admitted that he continued to harbor some doubts. "Although I do not think that this is anything other than a wolf," he wrote in the wake of Duhamel's general hunts, a local peasant's testimony that the beast sported a bristly patch of fur between its ears continued to trouble Montluc's thoughts.[82]

The best example of the searching ruminations that the beast inspired in the first half of 1765 came from Marvejols, where Labarthe *fils* offered a lengthy distillation of all relevant evidence on the first of April. Versions of the letter he composed would be published in the *Année Littéraire* and the *Courrier d'Avignon,* and his thoughts reflect the potent mixture of skepticism and wonder with which locals greeted news of the beast.[83] Labarthe sorted through all the public reports, noting the contradictions and dismissing the unfounded assertions that "belong in the land of fables." He had spoken with no one, for example, who had actually seen the beast leaping over walls and gullies, and he scoffed at the idea of the beast's deadly talons. He assured his readers that calm investigation would cause the dissipation of "many miracles."

Yet the "Voltairean" Labarthe was also intrigued by much of the anecdotal evidence. Earlier, he himself had been an active rumormonger.[84] He chided readers who doubted the feats of Portefaix, which he believed were attested by "exact information" collected by the authorities. He accepted the story of the beast's crossing of the river Bes, which it did while standing upright on its hind legs—perhaps "because the volume of the water was too great for it to be able to walk [on all fours]." He saw no reason to doubt that the beast could cover great distances in a day's time, and he regarded the beast's preference for women and children as a puzzling mystery, since the most "terrible" animals made no distinction between genders. Only gentle creatures, such as dogs, donkeys, and monkeys, had displayed that talent.

When he weighed the evidence for the beast's identity, then, Labarthe brought to the task the dispositions of a skeptic and the openmindedness of an intrigued bystander. He wanted only to "hazard some reasonable conjectures about an animal that we may never know." Its finesse, agility, and strength had "astonished everyone," he noted, but did this mean that its identity must be equally astonishing? "Should we place [the beast] in the class of monsters, or that of wolves, hyenas, or lynxes? Most of the partisans of these various persuasions are in no position to clarify matters for one who seeks the truth." To provide a trustworthy account of the creature's appearance, one would have to be close enough to get a good look, maintain one's attention long enough to study all the relevant features, and possess admirable *sang-froid* in the presence of danger. Labarthe doubted that all three of these conditions had been satisfied by even one eyewitness. Ever since the first description had been published in the *Gazette de France* in 1764, "the parts of the body have changed configuration with each successive account; the color of the fur, tending toward the tawny, has become more yellow; the body has shrunk and expanded with different renditions; the legs and tail have grown beyond measure; the head has become enlarged and has grown prodigiously in length, its ears and its back have undergone changes. If this continues, one will have to conclude that the beast was placed here only to cause arguments among us." Labarthe singled out for its unreliability "one engraving drawn in the Gévaudan" that represented the beast "with an enormous body" but with the legs of a "basset," marked also by "an excessively long and tufted tail, a terrifying tongue, and talons capable of cutting an elephant to pieces in the blink of an eye." Such images surely reflected human imagination more than reality.

Labarthe carefully sifted through the leading theories concerning the beast's identity. Monsters, "if they emerge from the coupling of different species," must be exceedingly rare, and he therefore decided that the beast of the Gévaudan could be classed in that category only on the basis of "certain" evidence, which was lacking. The lynx seemed unlikely because its bushy ears and brown stripes made its appearance unmistakable, and these features had not been widely remarked. Because of the beast's sudden appearance in the region, he also remained skeptical of claims that the beast could be a hyena. Would any hyena travel "twenty degrees of latitude" in order to prove that "it is in the Gévaudan alone that it finds human flesh so appetizing?" If a specimen had escaped from a keeper of exotic animals, would no one have brought this news to the attention of the public? And would the beast have kept perfectly quiet until it reached the Gévaudan? Labarthe settled on the wolf as the likeliest culprit, and he took note of the recent events in the Limousin and the Soissonnais, as well the experience of the Lyonnais in the 1750s, all of which had been linked specifically to the ravages of wolves. While Labarthe awaited the destruction of the beast—which still had the potential to be an "epochal" event in natural history—he resolved to allow his own assumptions about the creature's identity to be overturned only by "very exact observations."

For all of Labarthe's professed skepticism, he, too, continued to imagine the beast as a single "animal that we may never know." Even those who became aware of the historical precedents of wolf infestation and noted the geographic dispersion of beastlike attacks on French territory continued to seek answers for the behavior of what they took to be a singularly destructive specimen of *bête féroce.* One of Ballainvilliers' subdelegates, writing in late January, reported hearing of destructive wolves in the Limousin. But according to rumor "several" of these were of a "singular species," barely larger than a fox and with an extremely elongated body. Another subdelegate suggested that the beast of the Gévaudan "is of the same species" as another animal that had wreaked havoc in Auvergne a generation earlier before it mysteriously disappeared without having been identified.[85] Ballainvilliers, who saw himself as a man of the Enlightenment, insisted in an August letter to Versailles that he "cannot believe" that wolves alone were responsible for the ravages of the previous year.[86]

Perhaps the most striking manifestation of this receptivity to ideas of the extraordinary—striking because of the status of those caught up in the speculation and because of the timing of the search for new evidence—involved the high-level effort to link the Gévaudan's beast to the southeastern province of Dauphiné. A detailed and heavily annotated report composed in July of 1765, perhaps solicited by Saint-Priest, was consulted by members of Antoine's hunting party, and eventually made its way to ministers at Versailles. This report maintained that the beast of the Gévaudan had come down from the hills of Dauphiné after laying waste to that province in 1762 and 1763.[87] The document dismissed as pure speculation the theory of the escaped hyena from Africa "transported [here] by sea as an object of curiosity." Instead the report rested largely on the testimony of one Raphael, curé of Laval, who claimed to have been close enough to the Dauphiné creature to render an exact account of its figure. More to the point, the curé had depicted the beast of the Dauphiné "in the same manner as Mssrs. Duhamel and La Chaumette."

Here the connection between the investigative processes followed by educated and enlightened officials, on the one hand, and their suspension of disbelief in the face of bold claims of the extraordinary, on the other hand, becomes indisputable. After reading this report Saint-Priest would say, with regard to his own province's troubling beast, that "it seems rather likely today that it came from the mountains of Dauphiné." The hard-to-impress Saint-Florentin, in responding to the report, conceded to Saint-Priest that "it does seem plausible" that the two beasts were one and the same. One of Antoine's deputies used this report as the basis for a wider investigation into the various types of wolves known in the Mediterranean world. The Dauphiné *mémoire*, in sum, received serious and sustained attention at the highest levels, and for a short time it seemed to hold the key to the mystery of the beast's origins.

The report nevertheless contained details that could be believed only by readers harboring dark suspicions about nature's secrets. The description provided by the curé actually seems to have been modeled on one or several of the images of the beast of the Gévaudan produced earlier in 1765. The beast was said to be about the size of a large wolf, with the color of "roasted coffee" (an element of the symbolic repertoire that seems to have been added by an artist in June). The curé's account of other features hewed closely to the standard script. The Dauphiné beast sported a "nearly black" stripe on its back, and its head, unusually wide, featured an elongated muzzle. Although neither Duhamel nor La Chaumette had specifically mentioned the "raised tuft of hair on top of the head and between the ears," several published reports about the Gévaudan's beast had noted catlike features and claimed that the animal's fur stood on end when it prepared to attack.[88] In January or February the "Figure

"Figure of the Monster that desolates the Gévaudan." This representation of the beast, the text of which dates it no later than the first of February, would be borrowed for use in other prints. The picture suggests the long and twitching tail frequently attributed to the beast, and it depicts a pronounced mane that could account for the repeated sightings of a distinctive black stripe on the animal's back. *Bibliothèque Nationale de France, Qb 1764, collection Hennin*

of the Monster that desolates the Gévaudan," an image widely disseminated and widely imitated, had shown raised and bristly fur from head to tail along the distinctive black stripe. That same print also captured well the final physical feature noted by Raphael—a tail that ran "a little longer" than that of a wolf, "sticking up at the end."

The similarities did not end there. As the curé and others recalled, the Dauphiné animal's tastes and habits had struck the locals as strange if not inexplicable. On 18 September 1762 a young shepherd boy had been fooled by the animal's cunning. At first the beast had seemed nonthreatening; in fact, it "seemed to want to play with [the shepherd]," who therefore took no precautions. (The curé did not specify how he had come by this knowledge.) The boy's mistake proved fatal, and the curé buried the young shepherd's remains the next day. In October of 1763 the beast had calmly navigated its way through a flock of sheep, who remained oddly unafraid, in order to reach its desired prey—a fourteen-year-old shepherd who escaped only because of the quick attention of friends. According to a local seigneur, the fleeing animal showed "surprising agility" in bounding across a river that flowed near the field. With remarkable speed, it then fled up into the mountains toward its next victim.

Rather than arousing any suspicions about long-distance powers of suggestion or the presence of overactive imaginations in Dauphiné, this *mémoire* moved Saint-Priest to seek independent confirmation of the geography of wolf variation. Hoping to solve the riddle of the beast by linking it to an unusual kind of wolf specific to the Alpine region that stretched from eastern France down into northern Italy, he consulted M. Reinchard, a native of Switzerland and a widely traveled hunter who had journeyed south from Versailles with François Antoine in June. Reinchard, an officer of the hunt in the household of the Duc d'Orléans, would play a critical role in the events at Les Chazes in September. While awaiting his time in the sun in early August, he obliged the intendant by composing a response to the Dauphiné report, one based on his own informed opinion and answers to queries sent to friends in distant lands.

Reinchard had to report to Saint-Priest that his contacts had "never seen any species of this animal that had fur of the color of roasted coffee, nor any which had a black line running along its back from the ears to the tail, nor one with a patch of fur forming a tuft between the ears." The wolves of the Piedmont instead tended to the silvery side of grey, with those in the mountains of Savoy substantially the same color, only a somewhat darker shade. A friend in Nice had assured him that the wolves between the western slopes of the Alps and the plateaus of Provence resembled those in Dauphiné. Reinchard therefore found it hard to imagine that an unusual wolf had wandered into or out of Dauphiné. He preferred a more conventional explanation for the appearance of the beast of the Gévaudan. He thought it safe to assume, in general, that "as soon as wolves have tasted human flesh and blood, they become more dangerous and want no other nourishment."[89]

But Reinchard, too, remained on the lookout for a single foul creature. He informed Saint-Priest that he had heard reliable reports about a "unique" animal in the Clusone valley of Lombardy that had spread terror in the 1730s. This wolf had committed the same sorts of ravages as those committed today by "the hyena, or so-called hyena, in the environs of Mende." Another dangerous animal, "the wolf of Prajelas" (in the Piedmont), had shown itself to be "so avid for human flesh" that it risked detection in daylight in both summer and winter for a period of years. The beast proved elusive, even though parishioners gathered to give chase to the creature whenever the tocsin sounded. The reassuring news was that the elimination of these "unique" creatures had brought an end to the terror in both places.

The reflections of Labarthe *fils,* Saint-Priest, Reinchard, Lafont, Montluc, and other thoughtful subdelegates provide important clues to the state of mind of the beast's enemies as spring gave way to summer in 1765. Their references to the "so-called hyena," "wolf litters," "singular species," and "strange" ravages suggest that their thoughts were linked by two powerful common threads. Inescapably affected by the craze that had lasted for a year, none discounted the possibility that in the end the beast would indeed prove to be a ferocious specimen hitherto unknown. Yet all focused increasingly on the wolf as their prime suspect.

By early August, officials at Versailles had come down even more solidly on the side of the wolf. They had become noticeably less open to the possibility that the animal in the Gévaudan would prove to be a hybrid or some other extraordinary form. Perhaps the coincidental timing of the heroic events in the Soissonnais and the Gévaudan—in March the king had granted 300-livre gifts to unlikely champions at opposite ends of the realm—had created a frisson of insight among key officials. L'Averdy, in mid-June, asked Saint-Priest to "let me know what you learn about the means taken in 1637 to destroy several animals that similarly ravaged the Gévaudan in the last century."[90] Meanwhile,

Ballainvilliers received from Orléans a letter from a Polluche Lumina whose recollection of earlier experiences made him presume that "these are wolves and nothing more."[91] Hydrophobia, the latter stages of a rabies infection, was now rampant in the Soissonnais, and the area around Verdun had emerged as a new trouble spot for wolf attacks in 1765. Increased attacks across the realm may have cast the experiences of the Gévaudan in a new and less distinctive light.[92] Whatever the cause, the skepticism voiced faintly by Saint-Florentin in December, when he wondered what was taking so long, had become general by August of 1765.

The convergence of key players at the royal chateau of Compiègne offered a chance to gauge the mindset of the king and his ministers. Antoine's oldest son Jean-François, a cavalry captain, had stepped in to fill the gun-bearer's shoes in his father's absence, and in early August he accompanied the king and his entourage to Compiègne, just north of Paris, where the company planned to hunt deer on the richly stocked royal grounds. By coincidence, d'Enneval *père,* recently departed from the Gévaudan, had also arrived on the scene; he eagerly joined in some of the king's hunts. "They tell me that he talked a lot," Jean-François reported to his father, and the Norman evidently spent much of his time regaling his hosts with tales about his quest for the beast of the Gévaudan. The king awarded the hunter a pension, but d'Enneval's stories at Compiègne seem not to have had quite the impact he intended.[93] Perhaps prolonged exposure to an obvious braggart brought sudden illumination; the links between willful storytelling and the beast's frightful image became clearer. Antoine's son gathered from his own conversations at the royal chateau that "they no longer believe in [d'Enneval's] Beast, at least no more than they believe in the beasts now in Champagne, which are causing the same disorders as in the Gévaudan." Royal policy had already begun to reflect the change in thinking. "They tell me that M. de Saint-Florentin has just given the order to pay thirty livres per head to anyone who kills a wolf anywhere in the realm."[94] The crown now signaled its awareness of a wolf problem that transcended the troubles specific to the Gévaudan.

The *Gazette de France* had suddenly ceased all reporting on the beast of the Gévaudan in the middle of June. Three and a half months would pass before the newspaper published another word about hunters or hunted, until Antoine's kill at Les Chazes revived the story long enough for the paper to provide a perfunctory review of the events of late September. Given Choiseul's close attention to the content and management of the *Gazette,* and the newspaper's deliberate gravitation toward the story earlier in the year, there can be little doubt that the *Gazette*'s silence from June until October reflected a considered decision on the part of the monarchy to scale back the publicity accorded the developments in the Gévaudan. In light of the skepticism present even in the Gévaudan itself, it seems fair to ask: Did the decision to suspend coverage reflect the crown's belated realization that news of the great beast amounted to much ado about nothing?

The grinding gears of administrative rationalism fail to tell the whole story behind officials' change in attitude. Saint-Florentin, after all, still appeared willing to consider the hypothesis of the oddly tufted and unique wolf of Dauphiné as late as July. The best explanation for the *Gazette*'s disinvestment of time and attention in the beast is found in the chronology that brackets the *Gazette*'s greatest degree of interest in the story. Throughout the period 1764–1765, the *Gazette* published fifteen pieces touching on the beast or those who hunted for it. Of the twelve stories actually published before the satisfying climax of late September, ten had appeared in the four months between 8 February and 10 June. Those two dates corresponded almost precisely to two royal interventions in the trials of the Gévaudan—the public announcement of the king's bounty and the assignment of Antoine to the south.

Those four months had seen a series of false hopes dashed by new killings. For several brief periods between early February and the middle of May, the wounding or elimination of various troublesome beasts had raised hopes that the monster's ravages had at last come to an end. Each time the violence resumed it confounded hunters, dazzled those predisposed to imagine the workings of a supernatural beast, and provided telling evidence for those who began to suspect that "the beast" designated merely one among many animals spreading destruction in the region. For frustrated royal officials, the beast's alleged rise from the ashes after the Lafayettes' point-blank shooting on 6 May—just days after the heartbreak at La Chaumette—may well have brought to mind the proverbial wild goose chase.

The period of the *Gazette*'s heightened attention to the story, from February to June, also corresponded to the tenure of the d'Ennevals, and the humiliation suffered by "this great hunter that the court has sent us" inevitably extended to the court itself. Perhaps this served to dampen court enthusiasm for official coverage of the beast in the *Gazette*. Officials at court were known to have had "the most perfect confidence in [d'Enneval's] experience," as Saint-Priest had once explained to a frustrated Lafont.[95] In that same letter Saint-

Priest reported that L'Averdy had also defended the d'Ennevals' early refusal to engage in general hunts. The controller-general had literally parroted the Normans' concern that noisy and massive hunts would "startle the animal to the point where no one will be able to approach it."[96] Saint-Priest, acting on L'Averdy's wishes, had even published an ordinance on 5 April declaring that d'Enneval had come to the Gévaudan "on behalf of the court." It specified that all consuls, mayors, and other officials of the region must respect subdelegates' instructions and "obey all that [the d'Ennevals] command." The message could not have been clearer: the court stood behind d'Enneval and had little patience for complaints about his behavior. Days later the *Gazette* even offered excuses for the Norman, noting that poor weather and barely navigable roads "make the hunt difficult."[97] When d'Enneval finally confronted his failure, with tears in his downcast eyes, he could at least take satisfaction in knowing that all who had backed his mission shared in his shame. His patrons, by contrast, would have had strong motives to avoid any risk of a repeat.

By discontinuing coverage of the beast of the Gévaudan in June, just as Antoine was dispatched to the scene, the *Gazette* reflected a new wait-and-see circumspection on the part of the king and his ministers. After all, everyone accepted that the *Gazette* spoke tacitly for the monarchy, and that its coverage provided an indicator of what mattered to the crown. Even in distant Massachusetts, the *Gazette*'s attention to the story of the beast after the first of February had been taken as a sign of the gravity, and reality, of the terrible events in the Gévaudan.[98] Now, having learned a difficult lesson through their visible support for d'Enneval, having done their part to glorify the heroes of the hallowed sites at Villeret and Bessière, and having moved gradually toward the conclusion that the beast might be a wolf and nothing more, officials at court hedged their bets and had the *Gazette*'s coverage suspended. Tellingly, other publications that took their cue from the *Gazette,* or remained dependent on information provided in its pages or leaked by its editors, also turned abruptly quiet in the summer months.[99]

François Antoine thus went to work in an environment very different from that prevailing at the time of d'Enneval's ballyhooed arrival in Auvergne in February. A transfixed nation was now having second thoughts. By the first of July, journalistic attention had begun to wane (or had been forcibly restrained), and the king and his ministers seem to have resigned themselves to the prospect of an anticlimactic finale. Antoine himself, finding traces of "the claws of a large wolf" near the body of a victim in Lorcières on 4 July, quickly concluded that the beast of the Gévaudan would most likely turn out to be a wolf or wolves.[100] The thinking of many local officials had begun to turn in the same direction. Even taking into account the forces working to sustain a popular sensation—the public's sympathy for Portefaix and *femme* Jouve, the dissemination of impressive new images of the beast, and the *Courrier d'Avignon*'s still-breathless reporting—the stage seems to have been set in the summer of 1765 for an honest reckoning with an unspectacular reality.

But the honest reckoning never came. Even discreet modulation of tone is nowhere evident in the public record. The beast and its fascinating story worked new forms of magic over the course of the summer, reaching once again into the dark corners of the eighteenth-century imagination. By October the image of a spectacular creature had gathered sufficient new strength to survive the onset of winter and the passing of many seasons to come.

7

Exaggerated Expectations and Extraordinary Endings

Whereas Jacques Portefaix and *femme* Jouve drove the story of the beast to ever-greater popularity through their signal efforts to save sympathetic victims, François Antoine can be said to have saved "the beast" itself. He did so not literally but figuratively. His efforts ultimately rescued a construct of the popular imagination that had begun to falter under the terrific weight of its own celebrity. Antoine arrived on the scene in late June sharing some of the skepticism associated with no less a luminary than Voltaire, whom he would cite in his correspondence. He wasted little time before conveying to Etienne Lafont that "he believes strongly that a wolf, or perhaps several, is the author of our troubles." He would repeat the sentiment two weeks later.[1]

Yet Antoine's language shows that he never ruled out more fantastic possibilities, and as the summer wore on he continued to find new reasons to sustain belief in the extraordinary. The accumulating weight of great expectations, combined with his own growing sense that he had become mired in a potentially thankless effort, led him to reinflate a legend whose complete demise he was unwilling to face. The gun-bearer's inclinations were encouraged by a variety of people and forces, including a powerful and affecting story that had acquired a life of its own, but by the end of the summer Antoine had clearly decided that his long efforts and his climactic kill at the abbey of Les

Chazes could not be allowed to appear as routine. *La Bête* had to live so that a long-awaited Hercules could be credited with its death. The dimensions of Antoine's victory would remain open to debate long after the event, fueling speculation that would provide the beast's story an immortality few could have foreseen in the first light of 1766.

Entering the Bog

Like those who had preceded him in the unofficial role of hunter-in-chief, François Antoine arrived in the Gévaudan to find that the local terrain was more unforgiving than he had imagined and that the skies could always find new ways to disrupt and discourage the most determined parties. Snow had bothered d'Enneval until the first of May; incessant rain frustrated Antoine through the month of July. "Since 24 June, when we began reconnoitering in the region," he informed Saint-Priest on 18 July, "we have had fifteen days of rain and thick fog which has lasted for days at a time." The conditions rendered movement nearly impossible and prevented him from compiling a full list of his expected needs during his stay in the south.[2]

In spite of the miserable weather, Antoine had seen enough to know that in order to comb through the uneven and treacherous lands of the Gévaudan he would need more dogs and additional well-trained men. The gun-bearer and his son Robert-François had been accompanied by an impressive team of fourteen hunting officers from the households of the king's cousins (the duc de Penthièvre, the duc d'Orléans, and the prince de Condé), and he had had the foresight to bring with him several dogs from the stables at Saint-Germain-en-Laye, where he served as a lieutenant of the hunt. Antoine still felt underequipped, however, because after fifty years' experience as a hunter, which included excursions to the Pyrenees, the Piedmont, Germany, and all corners of France, he could confidently declare, "I have never seen a country like this one."

In a thoughtful report drafted during the weather-impaired days of July and hand-delivered to Saint-Florentin at Compiègne, Antoine offered a blunt (if slightly exaggerated) assessment of the challenge he faced. The entire afflicted region, he reported, consisted of high mountains separated "by gorges or deep valleys," most of which contained "small rivers and streams." The sides of the mountains were "steep and untamed, cut by ravines, topped with rocks, or covered with thick and rock-filled woods concealing deep and inaccessible caverns that serve as dens for wolves and other wild animals." Hunters could traverse this hazardous land only by treading lightly, for most of the existing paths proved "impractical for man and beast, due to the precipices one encounters." Perhaps worst of all, an "infinity" of natural springs played havoc with the ground beneath one's feet, creating plentiful but well-disguised marshes that trapped horses and men and imperiled anyone hardy enough to brave the area's rugged hillsides.[3] Antoine himself, while on horseback, later suffered an injury to his left hand while avoiding a fall into one of these marshes. The event prompted the good-natured Lafont to express concern about the gun-bearer's apparent contempt for his own safety.[4]

Even on horseback, men could not fully penetrate such forbidding terrain, and Antoine therefore requested that more dogs be sent from the various facilities under the control of the royal family. Of the four hounds the gun-bearer had brought along for the journey, one had fallen sick en route and had not even completed the trip.[5] With the imminent departure of d'Enneval and his prized canines, Antoine's contingent would surely prove inadequate to the task at hand, even accounting for the local dogs that would be added to the team. Antoine hoped that the marquis de Champigny would be willing to lend several of his hounds, known to be "good for chasing wolves," and that the female hound Dorade, an outstanding specimen at the chateau of Fontainebleau, would also be available. He asked that the gamekeeper (garde-chasse) of Louis Jean-Marie de Bourbon, duc de Penthièvre, bring seven other dogs of various breeds, combining a mixture of different specialties—keen sense of smell, sharp eyesight, the ability to flush and chase. Three long-haired greyhounds would fill out the complement, and Antoine also requested the services of two additional dog-keepers (valets de limiers) whose talents he knew firsthand. Finally, to help the untrained local peasants carry out hunts under the gun-bearer's supervision, Antoine asked the king to send a contingent of thirteen soldiers who could enforce discipline and maintain order in the field.[6] (Others concurred. Labarthe fils joked that both Antoines would "die of old age" in the Gévaudan unless the court dispatched enough troops to "occupy a hundred villages.")[7]

Antoine knew that at this late hour, with the king's patience wearing thin, his petition would face an uncomfortable reception at court. He therefore left little to chance. He wrote to Ballainvilliers and confessed that "I need your insights and the honor of your counsel" in determining how to make the best case for additional assistance. Because he initially planned to dispatch his son

Robert-François to court, he indicated to the intendant that he would have his son stop at Clermont for a consultation on his way north. Antoine also actively sought the help of Saint-Priest and the military commandant, Moncan. "Only by your recommendations at court can this [request] succeed," he wrote.[8] Antoine ultimately decided to send on the mission one of the trusted hunting officers who had accompanied him to the south. M. Regnault, from the stables at Saint-German-en-Laye, had the experience and standing needed to make an informed argument to the ministers about Antoine's need for special dogs and personnel.

Antoine's strategy worked, though the scale of his victory would diminish in hindsight. Jean-François Antoine wrote to inform his father on 5 August that he had given the report to Saint-Florentin "as soon as Regnault arrived" with document in hand, and the minister, after discussing the proposal behind closed doors in the royal council, emerged to say that the king had every intention of granting Antoine's request. The level and timing of the assistance offered by the court nevertheless fell short of Antoine's aspirations. "As for the men-at-arms that you request, M. de Saint-Florentin believes that they would do more harm than good."[9] Antoine had requested a total of fifteen dogs. In the end he would receive twelve, including several substitutes and none at all from the estate of the marquis de Champigny. Worst of all, the court acted without urgency. Antoine had stressed that the issues were "pressing," but help did not arrive in the south for a full six weeks after Jean-François first conveyed the minister's encouraging news.[10] In the interim, Antoine was forced to rely on the generosity of the comte de Tournon, a seigneur from the Vivarais who came to the Gévaudan in the first week of August to lend a hand. He brought with him several domestic servants and a pack of about twenty hunting dogs that entered the fray immediately. Along with the brothers Lafont, the comte de Tournon proved to be Antoine's most reliable partner through August and early September.[11]

King and court still wanted Antoine to succeed, of course. The *Gazette*'s announcement of his mission had noted that the royal gun-bearer's assignment originated in the will of the king.[12] The crown had broadcast the king's desire, on more than one occasion, to place the remains of the famous beast in the botanical gardens in Paris, and Louis XV had recently rewarded the brave sacrifices of the heroes Portefaix and *femme* Jouve, in one stroke acknowledging the extraordinary nature of the Gévaudan's trials and his own responsibility to do everything necessary to bring them to an end.

At the same time, however, the king and his ministers can be excused for questioning the wisdom of investing more resources, and royal credibility, into a problem that had gradually revealed its chronic nature, a problem whose unprecedented notoriety could yet prove unfounded. The people of the Gévaudan had long since developed conflicting attitudes about the presence and purpose of the *étrangers* who had come to the region in search of the beast. By the time Antoine began his work, the denizens of court and capital had likewise developed two minds about the story of the beast and its meaning. Jean-François, in his cheerful 5 August letter to his father, had noted matter-of-factly that "M. de Saint-Florentin . . . is persuaded, like you, that these are wolves." In that closing observation Antoine's son had inadvertently conveyed the court's mixed feelings about the work still going on in the south. If attacks by wolves in the Gévaudan warranted visitations by court officials and the expenditure of thousands of livres, how would the court contend with expectations in Champagne or the Soissonnais when the next emergency arrived? Even assuming that Antoine managed to kill a wolf or wolves responsible for human casualties, what were the chances of his bringing the phenomenon to a definitive end? With other matters much more pressing—the simmering Brittany affair had blown up in June, when Saint-Florentin received threatening letters said to have been written by a leader of the *parlement* at Rennes—the crown understandably downgraded the nagging crisis in the Gévaudan and essentially left Antoine to make the best of his circumstances. But in refusing to call off the hunt for a spectacular beast, the court also left room for Antoine to negotiate the terms of his own relationship with the scourge of the Gévaudan.

No Man's Land

Antoine soldiered on, but by the beginning of his second month in the region he began to show symptoms of what locals then might have recognized as beast-hunting syndrome. In contrast to the preening d'Ennevals, Antoine spent his first weeks in the area winning the respect and admiration of residents and officials of the Gévaudan and Auvergne. In early July Lafont described him as a "gallant man, full of zeal and intelligence and ready to bring all possible energy to the execution of his commission." A month later Saint-Priest sounded unusually solicitous in a letter to the gun-bearer that expressed his "great interest" in his well-being, and exhorted him to take more care for his own safety "than you have thus far."[13] Most would have agreed that Antoine is "generally held in high esteem here," noted a resident of Besset in August.[14]

Antoine won over the locals because of his unfailingly polite manners, his above-board procedures (he recorded depositions after every significant event), and also because he showed genuine compassion for the suffering of the rural population.[15] He promised the intendants early on that he would not drag the peasants away from their fields except on Sundays and feast days, unless necessity required it, and he expressed shock at the pitiful poverty of the peasantry. Most "could not subsist" without the milk and cheese produced by their cows, which only added to the tragic character of the beast's life-or-death contests with area shepherds. In a letter to Ballainvilliers, he noted that the "misery is so great here that almost all of the inhabitants lack bread." Well-intentioned peasants showed up for hunts barely able to follow orders, lacking in stamina, and sometimes even collapsing from exhaustion in their under-nourished state. Desperate families had been forced to grind their grain before it had ripened. He commended Lafont for providing alms for the purchase of bread in every parish of his diocese—and he hinted that Ballainvilliers should do the same in the parishes of southern Auvergne.[16]

Antoine signaled his solidarity with the locals in a variety of ways. On 19 August he attended a religious procession that he had organized in conjunction with the curé Fournier, the parish priest of tiny Bessyre-Saint-Mary. Before celebrating the Mass, Fournier and an assemblage of invited clergy processed through the streets of the village, accompanied by both Antoines, the comte de Tournon, Trophime Lafont, and all of the *gardes-chasse* and other hunting officers, "in uniform and carrying arms." The curé of Ventuejols had arrived at the event followed by an exceptionally large crowd of people from his own parish, and the Mass drew so many clergy and other visitors from neighboring villages that the small church "could not contain" all who had come. Antoine used the occasion of the religious ceremony to distribute alms to the poor of Bessyre-Saint-Mary. Six days later, on the eve of the Feast of Saint Louis—a holy day especially sacred to the French monarchy—Antoine organized and funded a splendid fireworks display in the same vicinity. As described in a lengthy letter written from Malzieu, the show was punctuated by the sound of trumpets and the "salvos of musketeers," and the exploding fireworks had a truly "enchanting effect" over the dark woods, despite the forbidding mysteries contained therein. For the inhabitants of the villages in the Margeride, this collective affirmation of community would have been one of the few occasions for untroubled pleasure in 1765.[17]

The magnanimous Antoine was not immune to frustration and self-doubt, however, and his correspondence reveals that by late July he had begun to have real worries about the outcome of his mission. Earlier in the month, after his reconnaissance had persuaded him that wolves were abundant in the area and that he should focus on their ravages, he had announced a generous reward of twelve livres for the head of any wolf, hoping to encourage the locals to take matters into their own hands whenever possible. After weeks passed without a single soul having shown up to seek recompense, Antoine denounced the peasants as "cowards." They had allowed themselves to become paralyzed by their "mortal fear" of the beast, which, he added contemptuously, "most of them believe is a witch." In this same letter, Antoine grumbled about having been forced to pay out of pocket for the care and feeding of his team's horses when in Auvergne, an expense he had not anticipated and "had no funds for."[18] Elsewhere he urged the intendant and others to keep in mind the mitigating circumstances in which he worked—the poor weather, the need to obey the rhythms of field labor, the lack of dogs, and inevitably, the "sleeping on straw." He would stop at no obstacle in pursuit of the "monsters," he assured his readers, but "consider the fact, if you please, that if one has nothing one can do nothing."[19] The self-pity followed a pattern set first by Duhamel, but Antoine's own sense of desperation may have been aggravated by suspicions that the court had abandoned him.

Antoine's dwindling patience became evident in a mid-August incident that would be long remembered. On a day when residents from several communities—Saugues, Ventuejols, Pébrac, and Bessière—had been called on to beat the woods in the parish of Servières, two of Antoine's comrades found themselves on the receiving end of a prank they considered none too amusing. Louis Pélissier, *garde-chasse* at Saint-Germain-en-Laye, and François La Chesnaye, *garde-chasse* for the duc de Penthièvre, were about to pass through a corner of a forest at Montchauvet when they asked Jean Chastel and his two sons (all natives of Bessyre-Saint-Mary), whether it was safe to assume that no marshes would impede their progress. The Chastels assured them they had no worries, whereupon the two proceeded into the woods and Pélissier became mired in a bog so deep that he sank in up to his waist. His horse escaped only with great difficulty and Pélissier later testified, "I thought I would die." For the Chastels the sight of the sinking Pélissier ignited gales of laughter, which led predictably to an exchange of heated insults. When he extricated himself from the marsh, Pélissier went to grab the youngest Chastel by the collar, which prompted his father and brother to point their guns at the *garde-chasse.* La Chesnaye then accosted Chastel *père,* in turn provoking all three of the Chastels to turn their guns on him.[20] Tempers eventually cooled, but Antoine shared his colleagues' outrage when he learned what had happened. He had the Chastels imprisoned in Saugues, and because he did not want these "malicious" characters to have an opportunity to seek revenge or to set other examples of insubordination for the locals, he asked Saint-Priest to see that they were held in jail until several days after the final departure of Antoine's hunting team.[21]

Pélissier's life was probably never at risk at Montchauvet, but the puckish Chastels had picked a poor time to play a practical joke on the *étrangers.* Antoine himself knew firsthand about the pitfalls in the marshlands. More important, the Chastels' flagrant show of disrespect converged with his own increasing sensitivity to public perceptions. His strong reaction is best understood in the context of that delicate sensitivity. In his letter of complaint to the consuls of Saugues, Antoine explained that he found it hard to believe that "having come here by the king's orders to provide assistance to these provinces, and wanting only to win the esteem of all honorable people," his men had been subjected to death threats from the ungrateful Chastels. He insisted "in the name of His Majesty and of the princes of the blood" that the malefactors be detained until further notice.[22] To Saint-Priest, Antoine pledged that in the meantime he would "redouble my efforts to fulfill the desires of the king, yourself, and of the entire nation." Later, in a September letter, he would remind the intendant that "honor alone" had brought him to this country, where he aspired to live up to the "personal confidence" that the king and M. de Saint-Florentin "have done me the honor of showing."[23]

Antoine possessed the kind of self-confidence that came with secure standing at court, but his privileged status hardly meant that he was prepared to leave his image untended. In his restatement of Duhamel's sentiment that "honor alone" had guided his actions, Antoine revealed a habit of mind developed over the course of a long career dedicated to the cultivation of status and standing. Antoine came from an extended family of servants of the royal household that had risen patiently through the ranks after more than a century of shrewd strategizing. Beginning in the 1630s, this originally common family had developed a tradition of performing ceremonial court functions and filling positions attached to the royal hunting grounds; they exercised offices such as sub-lieutenant of the hunt and guard of the king's powder magazine. But the Antoines also filled military offices (François Antoine, like Duhamel, served for a time as a dragoon officer) and positions involving personal service to the king—usher of the king's bedchamber, keeper of the king's spaniels, royal gun-bearer. The Antoines' strategies of upward mobility even reached across collateral lines.[24] Through careful management of the patrimony, timely patronage, and astute marriage alliances, the Antoines had risen from relative obscurity to positions of prestige by the end of Louis XIV's reign.[25]

Much room for growth remained, however, and François Antoine had used all of his seventy years marking progress in his family's upward path. As a young man Antoine had earned distinction by serving creditably in a number of military positions. After he reached adulthood, the purchase price of the various court offices he occupied was usually provided in whole or in part through his wives' dowries. His second wife, Elisabeth Longy, had helpfully been born to a well-heeled tax collector in Châlons.[26] Antoine reached the holy grail of legal ennoblement only in 1723, when his elderly father received letters of nobility after years of loyal service, and the new nobleman worked hard thereafter to provide appropriate offices for his progeny. His sons Jean-François and Robert-François would continue to receive pensions and appointments from the crown long after their father's effective retirement in 1768; both would serve stints as the royal gun-bearer.[27] An inexhaustible wellspring of ambition thus helps to account for Antoine's willingness, at the advanced age of seventy, to accept Saint-Florentin's request that he take on the unbeatable beast of the Gévaudan.

The particular psychological needs fostered by the pressurized social environment of the royal court explain much about Antoine's behavior in the fields of the Gévaudan. From the beginning Antoine may have "believe[d] strongly that a wolf, or perhaps several" had brought devastation to the Gévaudan. But as shown by his probing and slightly exaggerated description of the treacherous landscape and by his urgent quest to win more support from the crown, Antoine would never be able to see his mission to the Gévaudan as merely ordinary. He hoped and expected to be recognized for accomplishing something important, for defeating a redoubtable enemy.

For that reason, as well as a residual open-mindedness characteristic of many in this era of cultural ferment, Antoine never stopped invoking the presence of "the beast," even as he conveyed his developing belief that wolves would likely emerge as the source of the Gévaudan's problems. As he explained in the report drafted for Saint-Florentin in July, "I say the ferocious Beast or wolves [when referring to the animal] because in the last three depositions that I have drawn up and signed, . . . we have found no difference between the tracks [of the attacker] and those of a large wolf. If there is a ferocious Beast of another species causing these ravages, the guards and I have not yet been able to find it, in spite of our continual searches."[28] In this way Antoine expressed an inclination toward the most conventional explanation for the killings, but he did not simply banish the specter of a strange and monstrous enemy.

In his rhetoric Antoine remained consistent about the dual possibilities he contemplated. Around the first of July Ballainvilliers distributed a placard publicizing Antoine's recent arrival in the region and calling on the cooperation of the local inhabitants. The text of the document had been drafted by Antoine himself, and it announced the gun-bearer's intention "to destroy the Cruel Beast that desolates these provinces, as well as all of the wolves that can be destroyed in the process." Antoine provided specific instructions on how "to fire on the Cruel Beast or wolves." He had already ordered the digging of earthen trenches that would be used as traps for the unsuspecting creature, and he urged those stationed beside these traps to maintain complete silence so as to avoid alerting "the Beast or wolves" to their existence. Anyone who killed or came upon the carcass of "this Cruel Beast or wolves" should bring it to Antoine "without making any mark on the hide." Later in the month, Antoine signaled that he could not know whether the region remained hostage to a single "killer animal" or several.[29]

Not unlike his colleague Reinchard, whose inclination to blame wolves did not prevent him from acknowledging that the "so-called hyena" might be a "unique" creature, Antoine remained open to the possibility that an extraordinary animal was afoot. He could mock the popular belief that witches moved through the fields of the Gévaudan, but he still hoped to conquer a specimen of wolf or a creature of unknown species that would satisfy a nation's curiosity and prove advantageous to his glory. A few weeks after publication of the placard announcing his pursuit of "this Cruel Beast or wolves," Antoine investigated a terrifying attack near Saugues that left a young boy mortally injured. According to the initial report of Etienne Lafont, on a Saturday evening in late July the beast had appeared suddenly to steal the boy away as he stood in a field alongside his father, mother, and sister. Panic-stricken, the family ran after the beast, and they were startled by what they saw. "Before their eyes the beast dragged [the boy] for more than five hundred feet, leaping over three walls that were each about three feet in height." Feeling pressure from its pursuers, the beast finally gave up and left the child behind, but "his life is at risk," and Antoine had failed to locate the beast's tracks.[30] When he informed Ballainvilliers of the attack, Antoine observed that poor Claude Biscarrat had been "killed and carried off by the Beast or by a wolf."[31] Three days after the attack, the parish priest who presided over the burial of the "half-eaten" boy echoed Antoine. He attributed the death either to the "ferocious beast" or to "a man-eating wolf."[32] The agile leaper of uncommon strength, cruel intentions, and miraculous evasiveness had reared its head once again, and Antoine had taken note.

Two weeks later, the gun-bearer's open-ended rhetoric remained unchanged. In the deposition drawn up after an attack on one Marie-Jeanne Valet, Antoine explained that he, the comte de Tournon, and Trophime Lafont had been beating the woods in Servières on 11 August when they heard word that a girl had been assaulted "by the Beast or by wolves" at a river outside of Paulhac. They arrived to investigate the scene and to take the sworn testimony of the twenty-year-old, who had bravely fought back with a bayonet and had even drawn blood from the predator. Antoine concluded after an examination of its tracks that this was "the same animal" that had caused other recent troubles in Auvergne.

But this evidence of the familiar and normal was once again distorted by a whiff of the extraordinary. Marie-Jeanne and her sixteen-year-old sister provided a description of their attacker that recalled the fiend of recent legend. Trophime Lafont, who in May had fallen under the spell of the Duhamel–La Chaumette rendition of the monster, accompanied Antoine to the site and may well have played a role in translating between the peasants' patois and Antoine's standard French; his presence may have had a significant impact on the record that emerged. In any case, the sisters apparently claimed that the creature had a "very large and flat head," "big teeth," a body "much broader in front than in the rear," and a "black back." After the attack, the beast even "rolled around in the river" in an eerie replay of the events at Villeret. (The *Courrier* would assert that the beast "washed its wound" there.) When Antoine examined the bayonet Valet had wielded against her foe, with the animal's blood extending three inches from the tip, he needed no further proof of the girl's bravery. Soon after the deposition he would evoke the heroism of

Joan of Arc when he anointed Valet "a second *Pucelle* of Orléans, or of the Gévaudan" in letters to Saint-Priest and Ballainvilliers. Like the original *Pucelle,* Valet seemed "destined by the heavens to deliver her province from a terrible monster"—in this case an animal made easier to track because of the freshness of its wound. Antoine's request that the maiden be given a royal recompense was met with silence—the crown seems to have lost interest in anointing heroes. But locally, at least, a new heroine had been born, and the beast's legend gained new sustenance. To the *Courrier* Valet appeared as a new "Amazon."[33]

The record of Antoine's sojourn in the Gévaudan and the accumulated lessons of his prior experience help to explain the series of actions and decisions that finally led to his crowning achievement at Les Chazes. Consider a long career spent in pursuit of social standing; grinding frustration over the beast's continued ravages; the court's insufficient appreciation of the enormity of his task; the special challenges of the terrain; a stated desire to win and justify the respect of the king, Saint-Florentin, and all "honorable people." These conditions mingled with conscious or unconscious complicity with the pervasive culture of uncertainty that had complicated the identification of the beast for months. All of these forces predisposed Antoine both to accept the existence of a super wolf and to find ultimate vindication in the woods of the royal abbey.

Crafting a Grand Finale

Antoine's last six weeks in the Gévaudan made his summer difficulties all worthwhile. The great turn in the gun-bearer's fortunes came suddenly with the arrival of the dogs from the king's wolf-hunting stables (the *louveterie*) on 16 September. As Antoine later recalled, the appearance of the dogs coincided with news that "wolves were doing a lot of damage in the woods [controlled by] the Ladies of the royal abbey at Les Chazes." The abbey was situated on the far side of the Allier river and northeast of the area most recently affected by the beast's ravages, but Antoine, now eager to act on all leads, decided to investigate. On 18 September he dispatched several members of his party—including Pélissier and one of the newly arrived *valets de limiers*—to search the grounds of the abbey and report their findings. After hearing news that his men had spotted not only one large wolf but also a female wolf and several wolf cubs nearing maturity, Antoine and the *gardes-chasse* set out for Les

Chazes on 19 September. The next day, forty gunmen recruited from Langeac and surrounding parishes also joined the party that had gathered at the abbey. Notified early in the day that the valets and their dogs had flushed a wolf from the center of the Pommier woods, Antoine and his troops assumed their positions around the perimeter of the forest.

Soon a large wolf—Antoine would later say he mistook it for a donkey—happened upon the path occupied by the gun-bearer.[34] This time there would be no tragic echoes of Duhamel's mishap at La Baume. When the wolf turned its head to regard the man standing fifty paces away in the middle of the path, Antoine fired. The gun-bearer had come to this showdown extraordinarily well equipped. He carried a long-barreled musket (a *canardière*), which he claimed to have loaded with five rounds of powder, one lead ball, and thirty-five smaller pieces of shot. As Antoine told the story, the terrific blast from his overcharged firearm knocked him back several paces, but he looked up to find that his aim had been true. The shell made contact at the right eye socket, and the small shot was sprayed across the upper right side of the wolf's body near the shoulder. The animal dropped to the ground instantly from the force of the impact. But Antoine's enemy, it almost goes without saying, could not tolerate such a sudden termination to the encounter. In typical fashion, the beast picked itself up for one more lunge at its opponent. Just as Antoine yelled out "Hallali"—the celebratory signal for a successful strike—"it got up and came toward me, as I turned and realized I had no time to reload my firearm." Antoine looked for help, and Reinchard, the officer of the duc d'Orléans, who happened to be posted nearby, came quickly to the rescue. With his smaller, short-barreled carbine, Reinchard fired on the wolf as it moved toward the gun-bearer, ending any expectations of another miraculous escape. The animal trudged on for another twenty feet and finally collapsed on the ground "cold dead."[35]

Antoine's beast seems to have been somewhat larger than the typical male wolf.[36] But the animal's dimensions were not sufficiently monstrous, nor its characteristics sufficiently strange, to provide self-evident proof that the legendary beast of the Gévaudan had actually perished. Given Antoine's close call with a surprisingly resilient animal, his own impression that he had just survived a thrilling encounter with the beast itself is understandable. Nevertheless, the management of the event's aftermath also defines the encounter at Les Chazes as a transformative meeting site where great expectations openly collided with reality. The synthesis of hopes and realities that gradually emerged from that climactic scene underscores the capacity of the mind (and of the cultural frameworks it navigates) to shape the meaning of experience.

The discourse that quickly rose up around the monster from Les Chazes led to so many curious inventions and inconsistencies that the evidence of image-making calls attention to itself. Antoine first had the wolf taken to the nearby chateau of Besset, where the gun-bearer had recently been keeping quarters. He summoned a surgeon from Saugues to examine the slain animal. Before the day was out consuls and curés in the parish of Ventuejols had been asked to round up as many surviving victims and eyewitnesses as they could contact. All of the eight witnesses summoned to Besset ultimately confirmed that Antoine had conquered their attacker, but the circumstances of their testimony call into question the reliability of the message they conveyed. Needless to say, all locals would have been elated at the prospect that the beast had expired, and for that reason alone they would have been inclined to give the signal for a celebration. The surroundings in which the peasant witnesses were called on to pronounce victory over their enemy, however, made confirmation of the conquest all but inevitable. After being escorted into a seigneurial residence filled with local notables and courtly officials in princely liveries and interrogated by a personal servant of the king—the man who had personally killed the specimen placed before them—even the most mature and self-possessed inhabitants of the Gévaudan would have had trouble mustering the courage to disappoint or contradict their questioners.

The likelihood of such conflict diminished with the age and competence of the witnesses. One of Antoine's witnesses was an eleven-year-old girl who had seen a dangerous animal only once, on 9 August. Both she and the man who had come running to her rescue nevertheless confirmed that Antoine had found their attacker. For two other witnesses, aged twelve and fifteen, three full months had elapsed since their own frightening encounter, yet they, too, reportedly had no trouble identifying this as "the same beast" that had threatened them. Marie-Jeanne Valet and her sister Thérèse had also come to examine the specimen, and, according to Antoine, "both declared it to be the beast that had attacked them." Buried toward the end of their deposition, however, lay one ambiguous piece of testimony that signaled a degree of uncertainty. The *Pucelle*—whose less-than-definitive testimony prevented Etienne Lafont from getting his hopes up—stated only that she "recognized" a wound on the shoulder of the deceased animal as having come from a bayonet, even though she could not remember exactly where she had struck her beast in August.[37]

This one muted expression of doubt provides the only documentary trace of the imbalance of power that hung over the body of Antoine's wolf. Little other such evidence would have found its way into the record, since all of the local witnesses were illiterate; their testimony had to be attested by the signatures of the twenty dignitaries who surrounded them with quill in hand.[38] There appears to have been no talk at Besset of sparkling eyes, black stripes, bushy tails, smelly tufts of fur, or threatening talons, but the document drafted there affirms the conquest of an awful beast.

Immediately after the killing at Les Chazes, Antoine cautioned the locals and his various collaborators not to jump to conclusions about the consequences of the event. His warning perhaps reflected his own uncertainty; he had neglected to mention in his deposition that the surgeon "saw nothing indicating that this animal had eaten human flesh."[39] Any subsequent attack on a shepherd in the fields could quickly turn hope into despair. "I do not claim to prove that there are not other wolves" on the loose, Antoine admitted in a letter to Saint-Priest.[40] By coincidence, a report submitted to the *Courrier* from "the Gévaudan" on 24 September—Morénas evidently had not heard the news from Les Chazes—asserted matter-of-factly that the region's affliction involved "several monsters scattered [over the territory], sharing a fierce hostility toward the human species." Conventional wisdom held that any fallen wolf would be "only one among many."[41]

But within the space of hours, Antoine had evidently convinced himself that his wolf possessed extraordinary qualities, and he set out to impress upon others the magnitude of his conquest and the literal magnitude of his dead wolf. "None of us had ever seen a [wolf] of similar size," he informed Saint-Priest. The "width and length of its fangs" were a sight to behold, and it had "the largest paws we had ever seen," with its claws sinking "more than an inch into the ground." Antoine drew on circumstantial evidence from other recent events to suggest that the wolf from Les Chazes could be none other than the scourge of the Gévaudan. Using "a supernatural strength," the "so-called Beast" had been known to "drag heavy bodies, both dead and alive, a very considerable distance." Antoine undoubtedly referred to the attacks of 30 July, described by Lafont, and 9 September, when a young girl from La Vachelerie had been dragged to the top of a high mountain before being devoured. In both cases, the animal had carried its victim "a distance of more than five hundred feet."[42] Such feats "could only be done by this animal," Antoine averred, given its own "height, strength, and weight."[43]

In his deposition of 21 September, which would soon find its way into print, Antoine again emphasized the animal's great size. Having examined its length (five feet seven inches), its weight (130 pounds), its height (thirty-two inches), the size of its trunk (three feet), and the great size of its fangs, molars, and paws, all of which appeared to his team "quite extraordinary," all present agreed that no other wolf "compared to this animal."[44] The supposedly giant dimensions of the beast quickly became a principal motif in public discussions and images of Antoine's famous shooting at the abbey.

Although Antoine accented the unusual in his first official reports, the transformation of his dead animal into something bizarrely out of the ordinary accelerated suddenly and in an unpredictable fashion after the specimen arrived at Clermont on 22 September. Reflecting on the results of his kill and the testimony it had generated, by the wee hours of the 21st Antoine

"Representation of the Ferocious Beast that committed so many Cruel Ravages in the Provinces of Auvergne and the Gévaudan." This portrayal of the killing at Les Chazes captures well what Antoine would describe as "a monster in every way, but especially in its size." In the original, the beast was given blazing red eyes that matched the interior of its gaping mouth. *Bibliothèque Nationale de France, Rés. 4-LK2-786, fol. 106*

had decided to have Robert-François take the body of the deceased wolf to Auvergne's capital, an act that would set in motion the delivery of the carcass to Versailles like the honored spoils of war. (Antoine himself would stay at Besset to continue the hunt for the mate and the cubs.) Before Antoine's animal would be delivered to Versailles, however, it would assume an honored place in the public imagination thanks to the concerted efforts of a constellation of people in Clermont who had reasons to bestow grandeur on the events at Les Chazes. Robert-François, the *garde-chasse* La Coste (a longtime acquaintance from Saint-Germain-en-Laye), the intendant Ballainvilliers, and the local surgeon Charles Jaladon (assisted by a small team of master surgeons of the city) combined to forge a consensus around the singular identity of the animal killed in the woods of Pommier. Whether they intended to deceive or bowed unknowingly under the sheer weight of cultural expectation, they seem to have accomplished their feat with at least the implicit approval of Antoine himself.

Ballainvilliers had earlier expressed disbelief that "all this carnage has been done by wolves," and he had questioned Antoine's open articulation of that view.[45] Much affected by the graphic depictions provided by Captain Duhamel, and perhaps in thrall to the spell cast by the beast's legend over the course of 1765, the intendant remained convinced that the monster of the Gévaudan had to be a surprising and unusual creature. Consequently, for the two full days between 22 and 24 September, Ballainvilliers proved highly susceptible to powers of suggestion and the transformative effect of his own prejudices. He deftly blended the errors, exaggerations, and fictions supplied to him by his various associates and stirred this mixture until it hardened into an impressive mold sufficient to satisfy the demands of officialdom and an ever-curious populace.

No evidence records Ballainvilliers' very first impressions of the specimen delivered to him on 22 September, but traces of the early conversations he had with Robert-François, La Coste, and Jaladon survive in his correspondence from these critical days. "The arrival of the dogs that the king was good enough to send for the hunt of the ferocious beast has produced a happy effect," the intendant informed L'Averdy on 22 September, graciously handing credit to the king for the timing of the great event at Les Chazes. "M. Antoine," he announced with obvious relief, "has killed a monstrous beast."[46] In separate letters, Ballainvilliers also relayed the news to the other luminaries who had taken keen interest in the beast's activities—Saint-Florentin; Choiseul; the vice-chancellor Maupeou; Bertin (who had a pronounced interest in veterinary science); and the king himself.[47] Excited to be in a position to declare the case closed, and no doubt eager to please his superiors, Ballainvilliers proceeded to underscore the strangeness of the creature from Les Chazes. His account of the "monstrous beast," assembled from hearsay, secondhand reports, and the testimony of his associates, wove a rich tapestry that connected Les Chazes to other prominent threads in the fabric of the year-long story of the beast of the Gévaudan.

Ballainvilliers began, as Antoine had done in his deposition, by emphasizing the animal's size. Although its height reached an impressive thirty-two inches, the intendant had reason to believe that before its death, and the drying and shrinkage that inevitably followed, the animal stood several inches taller. The beast's most dazzling characteristics, however, had been conveyed by others. "M. Antoine has assured me that this animal had very large and sparkling eyes, almost more than one can believe, and that they were capable of frightening even the least timid of men." Antoine's deposition in fact made no mention of sparkling eyes, and that document had been drafted in the presence of others who had seen the animal immediately after its death. The ultimate source of the intendant's assertion therefore remains a mystery. Did Ballainvilliers here refer to a letter from Antoine that has since disappeared? Robert-François might have sought to embellish the narrative of his father's great confrontation with the terrifying quadruped. Had he or others in the party at Les Chazes wished to see what they could not document? No doubt La Coste, who had been told by Antoine that he would be permitted to host public showings of the beast for the profit of the loyal and hard-working *gardes-chasse,* saw advantages in attributing to the animal features long associated with the wicked beast of the Gévaudan.

Whatever the source of the useful exaggeration about the eyes, Ballainvilliers further specified that Antoine *fils* had also informed him of an "unbearable odor" that emanated from the beast at the moment of its death. The intendant's correspondents were unlikely to see in this observation the suggested presence of a werewolf, but the unusual stench of the Gévaudan's monster had been much remarked upon in previous accounts. By ascribing this feature to Antoine's animal, Ballainvilliers and Robert-François surely piqued the curiosity of those who hoped to engage the exotic. Together with the sparkling eyes, the stench provided a degree of strangeness sufficient to satisfy long-raised expectations about the monster of the Midi. Perhaps overcome by enthusiasm, Ballainvilliers and company even moved to resuscitate the hypothesis of the errant hyena. "Authors who have written on the hyena," the intendant added, "claim that that animal possesses a similarly foul odor."[48]

The level of encouragement for this line of reasoning that may have been provided by Lacoste and the Antoines, father and son, cannot be determined in light of the existing sources, but their contributions would not have been indispensable. Other forces, including most prominently the writing of the absent and unwitting Buffon, reinforced Ballainvilliers' readiness to accept far-fetched ideas. In his speculative letter to the court, the intendant insistently pressed the hypothesis of the beast's African origins.

The influence of Buffon and other naturalists is everywhere evident in the documents of late September. Jaladon, after his initial examination, must have mentioned to Ballainvilliers that the beast seemed to have more than a wolf's usual number of teeth, for in his draft letter to the ministers at court, the intendant made a point of mentioning that the creature has "thirty-four teeth, . . . that is to say, eight more than a wolf." He asserted that this number was "proper only to the hyena, according to M. Buffon."

In making this exotic connection, however, Ballainvilliers mainly showed the effects of a close familiarity with the *Natural History*, which indeed stated that "the hyena has thirty-four teeth."[49] In the margins of his letter, Ballainvilliers later had to amend the record to reflect Jaladon's closer scrutiny of the deceased animal. The jaw, "examined with more attention," contained forty teeth, which seemed to make the anatomical deviation from wolves all the more astonishing. In fact, wolves typically have forty-two teeth, and later investigations would confirm that the Les Chazes animal was normal in every respect—though Walpole would have fun with the dental speculations, noting of the beast's teeth that it apparently had "six less than the czarina."[50]

But there was more. "The muscles of the neck are very large and suggest extraordinary strength. [The vertebrae] are disposed in such a fashion as to give the animal the freedom to bend in half from head to tail, which a wolf cannot do." This detail must have been communicated through conversation with Jaladon, because the doctor's written report made no mention of this wiry flexibility (though Buffon's observation that the hyena's last five vertebrae "resemble those of the leopard more than those of the wolf" may have left room for such suppositions).[51] The tail, added Ballainvilliers, was long and covered with bristly black fur, "resembling that of a hyena, as depicted in Jonston." Here the intendant appears to have drawn on the work of the celebrated English naturalist John Johnstone (known on the continent as Jonsto-nus), a polymath who had written a natural history of quadrupeds in the late seventeenth century. This search for corroborating evidence certainly attests to the flurry of activity that surrounded the examinations in Clermont. It must be said, however, that the intendant's interpretation of Jonstonus's im-age, which showed a spotted animal with a long tail that was bristly enough but not even fully black, seems to have been more faithful to his inventive purposes than to the visual evidence provided in the naturalist's illustration.[52]

Jaladon's report, the essential contents of which had made their way to Ballainvilliers in time for the intendant's letter of 24 September, also added other details that lent support to the theory of the beast-as-hyena. "The mus-cles of the sacral region of the back and of the lower jaw are masses of flesh of a strength well beyond that of ordinary wolves, and [the specimen's] other proportions are more considerable than in that species of animal." Jaladon further signaled his fidelity to the *Natural History* by providing detailed mea-surements of the parts of the body, just as Buffon had done in his treatment of the hyena. Jaladon's "distance from the muzzle to the anterior angle of the eye," for example, exceeded by half an inch the same measurement taken for the specimen of hyena examined by Buffon. Although Jaladon's "length of the ears" came up an inch shorter than those of Buffon, his "length of the longest claw" topped one inch, whereas Buffon's fell just short of that. Jaladon also added his own estimates of the (allegedly superior) size of the body parts at the animal's time of death.[53]

With so many intriguing details to process, Ballainvilliers could highlight with a clear conscience the seemingly exotic features of the animal slain at Les Chazes. "Whatever species it turns out to be," he wrote in his letter to the court, Antoine's son was "extremely happy for the province that it has at last been destroyed." In the meantime, while Antoine *père* dedicated himself to eliminating the beast's offspring, Ballainvilliers would prepare the body of the great beast for presentation to the king. Saint-Florentin, for one, looked for-ward to its delivery with great anticipation. In a draft letter written in response to the intendant's informative missive, the minister wrote that he felt "obliged for the level of detail you provide in your characterization of this animal." Al-though Saint-Florentin had long suspected the beast's ravages to be the work of wolves, he had to admit that the animal described by the intendant "does seem, in fact, to fit with what we know about the hyena." On carefully examining the creature's remains after its arrival, he predicted, "we may be able to determine its true nature."[54]

In light of the modest and level-headed approach that Antoine had brought to his mission in the months leading up to the event at Les Chazes, one might suppose that the runaway speculation that overtook Ballainvilliers and his circle in the last days of September created a measure of uneasiness or embarrassment on the part of the gun-bearer. Claims about the all-important character of the events at Les Chazes diverged significantly, after all, from the conclusion toward which the evidence seemed to be pointing. As recently as late August a correspondent for the *Courrier d'Avignon* had attributed to Antoine himself the "less than consoling" thought that "instead of having one animal to destroy, there may be over thirty of them."[55] In the immediate wake of the killing at the royal abbey, Etienne Lafont even reported to Saint-Priest that Antoine had definitively concluded that the animal, though "prodigious" in size, was "nothing other than a wolf."[56]

How consciously he exploited the uncertainties that had been exaggerated or introduced by Ballainvilliers can never be known, but Antoine quickly reconciled himself to the change in atmosphere that attended the beast's noisy arrival in Clermont. His writings show him basking in the glow of his role in the hunt at the abbey, and he showed a willingness to play along with speculations voiced by others. In a letter of 23 September, Ballainvilliers had notified Antoine of the arrival of "the enormous wolf you have killed," but the intendant with the active imagination immediately rushed into a discussion of Buffon, the thirty-four teeth, and the "characteristics that are proper only to a hyena, according to ancient and modern authors."[57] Rather than seek to disabuse the intendant of such notions, Antoine lent credence to the idea. In a letter to his friend Tournon that would soon be published—a letter in which the gun-bearer described his conquest as "a monster in every way, but especially in its size"—he brought his comrade up to date on the opinions of Ballainvilliers, Jaladon, and his assistants. "Following an observation by M. de Buffon," he wrote, the men in Clermont had evidently detected in the Les Chazes creature a strong resemblance to a hyena, "by virtue of the number and position of its teeth, as well as a number of other circumstances." For that reason, Antoine reported, the intendant thought it imperative that Robert-François embark immediately for Versailles.[58]

The speculations from Clermont soon made their imprint on public discussions about Antoine's feat. Engraved images of the beast appearing in early October purported to represent the "hyena" of the Gévaudan (as depicted in Chapter 2). The *Mercure de France,* citing the authority of Buffon and relaying the assessments from Clermont, characterized several of the animal's qualities as hyenalike. The journal pointed especially to the animal's strange ability to bend from head to tail, something it said "a wolf could not do."[59] (This direct echo of Ballainvilliers identifies the *Mercure*'s source as one of the intendant's august correspondents at Versailles.) Antoine issued no public denials of these various reports. On the contrary, when he received word from friends and family that Ballainvilliers' letters had created a sensation at court that redounded to the gun-bearer's benefit, he wrote a gushing letter of appreciation to the intendant. He assured him that "I am devoted to you for life."[60]

Antoine had written an earlier letter to the intendant on 23 September, even before he had heard Ballainvilliers' excited speculations (relayed in a letter of the same day) about the beast's resemblance to a hyena. In this letter he specified what was required for the beast's presentation at court and for its representation in the wider public sphere. From the start, Antoine was anxious to insure that the beast would be represented in the most impressive and terrifying guise possible, and that it would still retain its full stature when its preserved carcass arrived at Versailles. Because the hunter had been "so rushed" to send the animal off to Clermont two days earlier, he had forgotten to ask the intendant to commission a painter to compose a portrait of the beast "in its natural state." The artist specifically needed to capture "its large and flat head, narrowing toward the end of the muzzle." Its mouth should be depicted wide open, exposing its "huge fangs, its tongue, and all sides of its dual teeth." (Antoine may have mistaken the wide rear molars of the wolf for twin teeth existing side by side, though, conversely, his detection of "dual" teeth may point to a miscount by Jaladon.) The artist must also be sure to get the white coloring under the throat, the reddish coat on the sides of the wolf, and "the black portion that runs down to the end of the tail."[61] "Not having had time to mention this [presence of black coloring] in the deposition,"—how could he have overlooked this crucial detail?—"I ask you to please send me a signed certificate attesting this observation." The certificate should be accompanied by a depiction also showing "the right eye and side of [the animal], representing the wound that it received from my shell, as well as the pieces of shot." (Antoine seems to have been less concerned to insure that the effects of Reinchard's blow found proper pictorial expression). Antoine promised Ballainvilliers a personal copy of the artist's rendering.[62]

The gun-bearer had further instructions. He specified that a sculptor would need to produce a wooden effigy of the beast, over which the beast's skin would eventually be stretched and mounted. Antoine's attention to this project reflected a remarkable degree of planning and forethought. He informed Ballainvilliers that the sculptor would need to make the contours of the carved figure "larger than it now is" in reality, since—given the effects of desiccation—it would be better to run the risk of over-estimating the animal's size than to reduce the scale of the model needlessly. When the time came to mount the hide on the effigy, "there will be plenty of time to remove any excess wood that the skin will not be able to contain." The wooden model, once "well covered with [the animal's] skin," would then be ready for the final preparations. Made steadily "upright on its four feet," the effigy could "be taken to Versailles to be seen by the king, by the princes, and by the ministers."

In the thick of the hunt for the beast's offspring on the grounds of Les Chazes, Antoine did all that he could to insure and augment public appreciation for the scale of his achievement. The gun-bearer nevertheless had his detractors in the aftermath of the killing of 20 September. Some wondered why Antoine seemed poised to reap the rewards when Reinchard had actually inflicted the fatal blow.[63] Horace Walpole waggishly reported the talk at court, with assistance from the book of Mark: "The critics deny it to be the true beast; and I find most people think the beast's name is *legion,* for there are *many.*"[64] To account for the presence of doubters, Magné de Marolles, in his own retrospective narrative of the beast's ravages, pointed to Antoine's own publicly expressed suspicions that multiple predators prowled the Gévaudan. In light of the emerging consensus about the multiplicity of the threat, some naturally questioned how the one wolf at Les Chazes could now be represented as the sole offender. Magné de Marolles even wondered about Antoine's account of his preparations for the hunt at the royal abbey. "Anyone who knows about arms and the effects of powder, especially royal powder . . . would not be easily persuaded that a man could withstand the kick from five charges of powder, or even four."[65]

In many quarters suspicions would grow after word spread that the beast made little impact during its highly anticipated showing at Versailles. Antoine *fils,* La Coste, and their prized cargo had traveled by postal carriage—making the trek to the capital via Lyons and the country's most well-traveled highways—and their trip went smoothly. After a brief stop at the residence of Saint-Florentin, where the convalescent minister was treated to his own private viewing, Robert-François delivered the specimen to Versailles on the first of October.[66] The animal assumed a prominent position in the antechamber of the queen, Marie Leczinska, where it remained for several days to entertain courtiers, ambassadors, and other visiting dignitaries invited to marvel at the sight of the legendary animal, now frozen in time. The effigy was covered with a sheet, the better to emphasize the drama of the unveiling, which Lacoste and Antoine *fils* performed each time a new party was escorted into the chamber.[67] The mere strangeness of the spectacle must have made the event memorable, but the recorded reactions to the show suggest that the beast fell short of expectations. Its appearance failed to dazzle.

One of the more poignant, and revealing, signs of the psychic deflation caused by the actual delivery of the intriguing beast of the Gévaudan is found in Saint-Florentin's draft letter to Ballainvilliers. After laying eyes on the animal and perhaps gathering assessments from others (though not from Buffon, who had retreated to his Burgundian estate of Montbard), Saint-Florentin returned to his letter to make changes.[68] Specifically, he struck through the lines expressing gratitude to the intendant for his detailed description and for the identification of physical marks consistent with "what we know about the hyena." The letter that the minister ultimately sent to the intendant on 4 October, thanking him "for the two letters you took the trouble of writing me on the 21st and 24th of this month [sic]," contained not a word about the species of the *bête féroce* from which Auvergne had evidently been liberated. Nor did it refer to any examinations carried out to determine the "true nature" of the creature. The letter merely reiterated the importance of having Antoine eliminate the animal's spawn.[69]

Others also noted discrepancies between reality and its representations. A *nouvelliste* reported that the animal had been "displayed before the eyes of the entire court," but that onlookers had seen "only a voracious wolf armed with defenses slightly more extraordinary than those to which we are accustomed."[70] The English traveler William Cole, after attending a public showing, described the beast as "not bigger than a large Mastiff Dog." He complained that he had purchased two prints representing the animal, including one that captured the recent spectacle at court, and "neither were like the creature in shape or color."[71] The ever-present Walpole earned a personal invitation to visit the queen's antechamber, "where [the beast] was exhibited to us with as much parade as if it was Mr. Pitt." His disappointment on seeing the famed animal did nothing to dilute his natural cynicism. "It is a thought less than a leviathan and the beast in the Revelations, and has not half so many wings and eyes and talons as I believe they have . . . a wolf it certainly was, and not more above the common size than Mrs [Cavendish] is." This comparison to a famously portly woman of English society seems apt, since Walpole hap-

Représentation de la Bête du Gévaudan qui a fait tant de ravage dans ce Pays et dans l'Auver[gne] la qu'elle a été tuée le 20° septembre dernier par Mr Antoine chevalier de St Louis, seul Porte Arquebuse de sa Majesté, et présentée le 1er Octobre au Roy et a la Famille Royale par Mr Antoine de Beauterne Fils.
Pour que cet Animal se conservât, dans son naturel, on l'a dissequé, embaumé et attaché sur une planche tel qu'il est ici representé. A Paris chez Mondhare rue St Jacques a l'Hotel S[t]

"Representation of the Beast of the Gévaudan that committed so many ravages." The presentation at court on 1 October. The hatted figure to the left is King Louis XV, gesturing to the animal with a nonchalance that shows his control over the scene. One of the queen's attendants lays her hand on the beast at center while the ill-fated dauphin looks on from her immediate right (and the queen's left). The dauphin wears a boutonniere to match the king. In addition to the beast's almost reptilian jaws and teeth, which had become a standard topos, note the "six talons," a fiction that here made its final impact on the visual record. *Bibliothèque Nationale de France, Rés. 4-LK2-786, fol. 112*

pily conceded elsewhere that the beast was "a very large wolf to be sure," one with an "expression of agony . . . strongly imprinted on its dead jaws."[72]

Even the *Gazette de France,* in a notice that broke its long silence on the story and announced the news of the happy event at Les Chazes, ended its piece with an understated declaration made no less devastating by its appearance at the very conclusion of the story. "The most experienced hunters have concluded that [the beast] was a true wolf that boasted nothing extraordinary, neither in its size nor in its composition." This deflating and oddly ambiguous news was repeated in other publications that tended to borrow from or plagiarize the *Gazette.*[73] The *Gazette*'s story expresses well the curious bind in which king and ministers now found themselves. Lacking evidence of the extraordinary, how could the court declare victory? The king clearly reveled in the staging of a celebration that concluded a tragic and very public story. The only engraving depicting the unveiling of the creature would show a large but thoroughly emasculated beast, finally tamed by the forces of royalty—safe enough even for the king, the queen, and her attendants to touch. But the *Gazette*'s restrained rhetoric also provided a sign of royal recognition that, in fact, there was not much to see here. That surprising reality proved valuable in its own way. As he provided closure for a dramatic story, the satisfied king could strategically signal that there had been "nothing extraordinary" about the source of the nation's anxiety. Here the circumstances justified marking the occasion with flourish (only barely), but there was no reason to expect similar celebrations, or similar hunts, in the future.

The beast's less-than-extraordinary dimensions would raise eyebrows, but in late September Paris waited impatiently for the beast's delivery—perhaps this provincial product would portend an abundant fall harvest—and the corridors of Versailles echoed with jubilation. According to Antoine's elated wife, Louis XV "would not stop talking about it" for a whole day after receiving the news of the successful hunt at Les Chazes. When he subsequently received his copy of Antoine's deposition of 21 September, "he wanted to read it aloud himself to the entire court." (Antoine thought he would "die of joy" on hearing this news, which created a most "happy moment for a sensitive heart.")[74] His wife expressed disappointment that Antoine himself could not be present to witness "the satisfaction this [event] has given to the court and the city." Jean-François Antoine, who had served in his father's stead at court, had been invited to a personal audience with the king, at which Louis XV held forth "for an hour." "All the lords of the court" had embraced and congratulated

Jean-François, and a steady stream of visitors had come to the family home to pay compliments to the wife. The recuperating Saint-Florentin, still getting used to life without his left hand, had sent such "gracious" greetings to *femme* Antoine that she had planned to render a visit to show the minister her appreciation. "Having learned that his condition did not permit him to receive visitors, I did not dare insist."

Neither the minister's recent misfortune nor his failure to be awed by the sight of the monster when it arrived could dampen the festive mood at court or in the heart of the Antoine home. The fact that "you yourself killed this furious animal" made the gun-bearer "the hero of your entire family, which you have covered with glory." But many others, too, owed a debt of gratitude to the hero, as Antoine's daughter stressed in her personal note to "my dear papa." Remarking the qualities of his "sensitive soul" and his concern for the "unfortunates" of the Gévaudan, she called attention to his service to the nation. "Not only do you deserve to be loved as a good father, but as a good citizen, zealous and active for the public welfare."[75]

The visual record of Antoine's accomplishment reinforced the civic character of his feat. A "Representation of the ferocious Beast killed on 20 September" shows Antoine and Reinchard closing in on horseback—a wholly invented detail—to exterminate a threat to civil society. The order finally restored by the mounted warriors is captured visually by the cultivated garden that stretches into the background and frames the scene of extermination. The helpful hounds of the royal *louveterie* fiercely police the perimeter. In the next two scenes of the shooting, the confrontation between the powers of civilization and the disruptive potential of the untamed is shown in the contrast between the outsized beast of the foreground and the undisturbed royal abbey nestled in the background. In these and other contemporary scenes, the suggestively positioned equipment of the victorious huntsmen expressed the reassertion of patriarchal authority over a particularly resistant force of nature.

Some wished to denigrate Antoine's achievement, but he had provided a finale that reflected well on king and court. Feelings of relief and gratitude thus insured that the finale would be remembered officially as a victorious moment. In a published letter written from Fontainebleau, to which the court relocated only days after the beast's presentation at Versailles, one well-placed defender of "the liberator of two provinces" attacked Antoine's critics as jealous and jaded. Those who had expressed their contempt for Antoine's accomplishment by saying of the creature that "it's only a wolf" had merely shown their own stubborn attachment to a discredited notion. "As if the idea that it was a hyena causing the terror should trump the consistent reporting of the hunter himself," who had always said that the so-called hyena was nothing but a wolf. Others would deny Antoine the glory of having inflicted the mortal blow, "since there was a second shot." But all the caviling was refuted by the corroborated facts and the candor of Antoine's deposition. Antoine's unassailable "honor and merit" had been further demonstrated by his conduct after the killing. Although he himself could have travelled to Versailles to "present to his Master the fruit of his labors," he had delegated that honorable task to his son so that he could "fulfill the last obligations of his mission." The in-

"Representation of the ferocious Beast killed on 20 September." Antoine, on the left, and Reinchard, on the right, are shown simultaneously eliminating the terrible creature that has emerged from the depths of the forest. The equestrian theme and the orderly path that opens behind the expiring animal underscore the hunters' role in reasserting civilized order at the royal abbey. *Bibliothèque Nationale de France, Rés. 4-LK2-786, fol. III*

habitants of the region "will always cherish the moment when he was called to their aid."[76]

The beast's presentation at Versailles and in the capital satisfied needs both psychological and material. As king and court prepared to decamp for Fontainebleau, Lacoste arranged for the temporary installation of the specimen in a private residence in Paris on the Quai de la Ferraille, where "a vast collection of prints" always filled bustling bookstalls.[77] On 7 October and for several days thereafter, the citizens of Paris could peruse advertisements and broadsheets depicting the beast and its conqueror and, in exchange for a small admission fee, step up to view the famous beast from the forests of Auvergne.[78] The proceeds from these showings were used, as Antoine had promised, to compensate the hard-working *gardes-chasse* and *valets,* many of whom had stayed behind to assist him in the elimination of the beast's progeny.[79] As "the beast of the Gévaudan" put in its final public performance, Lacoste and the

"This ferocious Beast which has committed so many ravages . . . was killed on 20 September." The suggestively positioned saber of Reinchard, on the left, reminds the viewer of the monarchy's male virtues. *Bibliothèque Nationale de France, Rés. 4-LK2-786, fol. 108*

other officers of the hunt could take satisfaction in a job well done and well recognized.

Others, too, could take pleasure in long-deferred feelings of closure. The grand finale had probably surpassed the expectations that the gun-bearer himself had taken to the Gévaudan in late June. He had brought to this wolf hunt great confidence in his own expertise and methods, and he had certainly not anticipated so many frustrating twists and turns during an exhausting three-month sojourn in a rugged country. Like others who had been drawn into the operations of the seemingly endless pursuit of the beast, however, Antoine ultimately found that his own perspective, and the very meaning of his actions, had been transformed by the irresistible momentum of a monstrous story. At

"True figure of the ferocious Beast." This depiction of the shooting at the abbey seems to capture most of what Antoine specified in his request to Ballainvilliers concerning the artistic rendering of his feat. The animal shows a large head, giant fangs, a protruding tongue, and the bleeding wounds—both at the eye and on the side—inflicted by Antoine (and not Reinchard). Reinchard, to the left, supplies another protuberance that, joined with other evidence from multiple images that commemorated this event, seems intended to signal masculine power over nature. *Bibliothèque Nationale de France, Rés. 4-LK2-786, fol. 107*

first perhaps unsuspecting of his own absorption in its long-developing script, he eventually became a full and conscious participant in it. In the woods of Pommier, Antoine's hopes and frustrations converged with public expectations and the unspoken requirements of heroic narrative—as embodied in ancient myths, medieval legends, and eighteenth-century fairy tales.[80] Antoine and his many collaborators may have bypassed the honest reckoning whose likelihood had seemed to grow in the two months between mid-June and mid-August of 1765. But they provided a fitting end, and an air of finality, to a vexing episode that the *Courrier d'Avignon* had compared to both ancient epics and modern novels. A terrible monster had been defeated, yielding credit great enough to be shared widely among the animal's conqueror and all who had enabled the hero's quest.

L'Averdy was still cautioning Saint-Priest on 10 October that, "much as we hope that this animal is the same that has caused so many ravages, only time will tell."[81] At first Antoine himself had expressed similarly cautious feelings. But within a few short weeks, sufficient time had passed to begin the process of disengagement from the Gévaudan. This was true not only for Antoine but for the nation at large. In the course of the summer many forces had converged to prepare the public for an end to the intrigue emanating from the south. Perhaps sensing their readers' exhaustion, or seeing an important signal in the sudden reticence of the *Gazette de France,* news journals generally stopped feeding their readers updates on the beast and its activities after early July. With only the *Courrier d'Avignon* still engaged, interest began to wane. No famed naturalist had come forward to offer unusual hypotheses about the identity of the beast. The detached Buffon, "who does not have as much taste for the marvelous as the authors of the *Gazette de France,*" according to the cynical Grimm, was reported in April to have credited the beast's predation to "several large wolves."[82] No other religious figures had espoused the providential interpretation of the bishop of Mende, and no traveler had confessed to smuggling an exotic import onto French territory. In the absence of hard evidence confirming the unusual, after months of implicit promises of forthcoming proof, readers, like officials at court, gradually recognized the appeal of more conventional interpretations of rural terror. By September, Antoine's victory over an animal that could be construed as extraordinary came as both a pleasant surprise and a welcome excuse to drop the curtain on a long-running drama.

After the gun-bearer had eliminated the last of the wolf's family on the grounds of Les Chazes on 17 October, and after six weeks had passed "without anyone being devoured or even attacked," the court, the capital, and their denizens were prepared to close the book on the intriguing history of the beast. Antoine traveled to Mende to take formal leave of the bishop and to say goodbye to "my dear friends" the Lafonts in the last week of October. On 3 November—precisely one year to the day after the dragoon captain Duhamel had arrived in Mende filled with optimism and energy—Antoine at last embarked on the long road home to Paris.[83] Before the end of the year, his renown had spread as far as the British colonies: in New Hampshire, a gazette announced Antoine's conquest of the beast "which hath made such shocking ravages."[84]

Antoine would soon begin the long process required to secure the one reward he truly coveted, the kind of reward cherished by status-conscious nobles who saw themselves observing the principles of "honor alone."[85] After collecting several official letters attesting to the quality and importance of his work in the south, and after petitioning Saint-Florentin for the privilege, Antoine eventually received royal permission to modify his family's coat of arms. (When he asked Ballainvilliers on 23 September for a certificate attesting his assertion of black coloring in the beast, Antoine's head may already have been filled with such dreams.) Displayed at the center of his family escutcheon now lay the figure of a dying wolf, an iconic image that would "perpetuate for his posterity the memory of his tireless efforts and of the bravery with which in 1765 he delivered the provinces of Auvergne and the Gévaudan of a monstrous wolf that ravaged them."[86] This royal gesture of appreciation, formalized in November of 1766, sounded a distinct but faint echo for a story that had achieved its official climax some thirteen months earlier in a crowded antechamber at Versailles.

8

Narrative Echoes Past and Present

By all appearances the crown disposed of its notorious beast in short order. In the middle of the eighteenth century, taxidermical arts were still in their infancy, and even if trained naturalists had treated the wolf from Les Chazes immediately with state of the art techniques, its carcass would likely have deteriorated sooner rather than later.[1] The odds against success in this particular case increased in the hours and days after the shooting at the abbey. Despite the fast thinking of Antoine, who immediately urged Ballainvilliers to have the animal skinned because its odor suggested the onset of decomposition, his wolf received less than optimal treatment.[2] The day after the animal's arrival in Clermont, Ballainvilliers reported that instead of skinning the specimen and draping its remains over a wooden model as Antoine wished, he had decided to have it "embalmed and injected so that it can be sent [to court] in its natural state." In Paris there would be "more skilled men" to do the work of preserving the body, and there should be adequate time there "to prepare the animal as they see fit."[3]

In the meantime, Jaladon and his assistants did all that they could. Jaladon would proudly write in his report of 27 September that "I dried the fleshy parts with the fluid recommended by M. Buffon." But the raw material he worked with evidently left much to be desired. By the time the carcass had been transported to the surgeon's quarters, he reported, it had already "fallen into a state of putrefaction," as indicated by its strong odor and by the sagging of its coat and epidermis.[4] In addition to injecting it with fluids, the doctors must have settled on a means for providing structural support for the animal's public display, but the specimen that arrived at Versailles on 1 October was in decay and beyond hope of long-term preservation. Surely the less-than-stunning visual impact it made at court (and its status as a specimen not much above a run-of-the-mill wolf) persuaded Saint-Florentin that further efforts were not worth the trouble. The evidence is less than conclusive, but it seems highly unlikely that the Les Chazes beast ever assumed a place of honor in the king's botanical gardens.[5]

The state of the beast's body and its rather ordinary appearance may have disappointed the king and others who had anticipated the display of an exotic trophy, but officials at Versailles were more than ready to move past the story of the beast of the Gévaudan. The autumn of 1765 offered up so many other festering problems that the king and his ministers would have been happy indeed to see at least one chronic distraction finally eliminated. The celebration of a triumph, however fleeting, provided a sharp contrast to the time of troubles that followed Antoine's apotheosis.

In the countryside, the fall harvest disappointed expectations in 1765; a prolonged subsistence crisis thus took hold of the country at a delicate juncture in the crown's evolving relationship to public opinion.[6] For decades rumors had swirled, in times of dearth and misery, that the king of France and other wealthy landlords conspired to hoard grain in order to boost prices and line their pockets at the expense of the hungry masses. The destabilizing potential of such rumormongering, the force of which would help to precipitate the fall of L'Averdy's ministry in 1768, had increased exponentially after the freeing of the grain trade in 1764. The unfortunate intersection of a controversial economic policy and dire shortages of bread made the crown and its agents targets of popular anger throughout the mid-1760s. As news of poor harvests and rising prices set nerves on edge, Louis XV's image continued its steady deterioration in late 1765. For the next three years, writes the preeminent historian of the subject, the specter of a "famine pact" thought to lie behind fluctuating bread prices "prowled the streets, demoralized merchants, haunted the *parlements,* unnerved [the economists], and embarrassed and worried the government."[7]

Popular discontent grew, moreover, at a moment when the king's ability to quash the resistance of its independent-minded *parlements* faced another crucial test. In early November the king arrested several magistrates from the *parlement* of Brittany, including the obstreperous lawyer L.-R. de Caradeuc de La Chalotais (alleged author of the inflammatory letters sent to Saint-Florentin in June). Their opposition to new taxes had gradually escalated into a heated confrontation over the limits of royal authority. La Chalotais' arrest and trial ignited a firestorm of protest that widened and worsened for more than a year.[8] Coming on top of an unexpected personal tragedy—Louis XV's only son, the thirty-six-year-old dauphin Louis de France, died at Fontainebleau in December after a long illness—the institutional crisis of the "Brittany affair" would have left the monarchy little time or energy for continuing worries about a rampaging monster in the rural south. From the vantage point of late 1765, Antoine's conquest at Les Chazes, and the subsequent celebration at Versailles, could not have been better timed.

And yet the beast lived. Officials at court were soon forced to confront this unwelcome complication. As had happened at several earlier points in the drama of the Gévaudan, a period of deceptive hibernation—this one lasting for more than two months—was followed by new ravages and new reasons for locals to feel disheartened and discouraged. There had been unsubstantiated reports of beast sightings in late October, but the region's "most perfect tranquility" came crashing down around Etienne Lafont and his compatriots on 2 December. On that day, not far from Antoine's former headquarters at Besset, two boys guarding cattle that grazed in the heather of the Margeride found themselves under attack by the beast "not seen around here in some time," as the curé of Bessyre-Saint-Mary put it.[9] The boys survived, but on 21 December an eleven-year-old girl from Lorcières met "the ferocious Beast that roams the country," and her encounter with the predator led to the customary tragic results. By the first of January, the subdelegate Montluc would say of the beast that "there is no more doubting its existence." The disconcerting testimony from the incident at Bessyre-Saint-Mary—"flat head," "much larger than a wolf," "black stripe from its shoulders to the end of its tail," moves "by leaps and bounds"—convinced many locals that the magical beast had returned, and that they would now be forced to reap the consequences of Antoine's premature declaration of victory.[10]

The reactions to the renascent panic in the Gévaudan and Auvergne, on the part of both officials at Versailles and people close to the action, reveal much about the different lessons learned between 1764 and 1765. The vary-

ing responses to the renewal of violence also point helpfully toward the competing interpretations of the beast of the Gévaudan that developed in the contemporary era—that is, after the revival of wide interest in the story in the late
nineteenth century. The first seeds of modern memory were sown in the six
months that elapsed between the beast's reappearance and the fixing of the
government's new strategy for addressing the threat.

After some deliberation, Versailles dispensed with all talk of "the beast,"
and opted to treat the phenomenon of animal attacks on the peasantry as an
ordinary and generalized problem requiring serious but not frenzied attention. In the Gévaudan and Auvergne, by contrast, many continued to regard
the affliction of the beast as a mysteriously intractable problem, one that faraway officials had conspicuously failed to understand and master. In the development of these two very different perspectives on the meaning of the
Gévaudan's experience, one finds the template for later interpretive stances.

From Crisis to Annoyance?

The showing of the beast of the Gévaudan at Versailles on 1 October served as
a watershed event in more ways than one. Paradoxically, the celebration of
Antoine and his accomplishment enabled the ministers to embrace a position
that belied the great attention bestowed on the gun-bearer's feat. Until that
moment, they had entertained this position only tentatively. By closing the
door on the publicity-fueled story of the terrible monster from the Gévaudan,
and thereby tacitly acknowledging the existence (and destruction) of a unique
creature, the ministers gave themselves the freedom to characterize all other
predatory animals—in the Gévaudan and elsewhere—as ordinary *bêtes féroces*.
They could now attack the problem of the wide presence of these *bêtes* with
the tools of bureaucratic routine rather than with the personalized tool of
the heroic huntsman-on-a-mission. The spectacle in the queen's antechamber
thus marked not only the ending of a dramatic story but also the beginning of
contemporary efforts to interpret that story and fix its meaning. In some ways
closure brought with it superior wisdom, but as with all history that carries
implications for the present, the story fell victim to the distortions and forgetfulness of those with the power to shape collective understandings.

The signs of the monarchy's changed attitude toward wolves and their
sometimes monstrous behavior began to appear in December of 1765 and accumulated steadily throughout the winter and spring. In a December letter

written just days after the new attacks near Bessyre-Saint-Mary (the timing is at least slightly suspicious), L'Averdy signaled to Saint-Priest that the crown would now be taking a new approach to the problem of predators in the countryside.[11] "The ravages that voracious wolves have visited upon *several provinces of the realm for some time* have become so considerable that it seems necessary to focus attention on the destruction of these animals" [italics added]. Consequently, he continued, "we have assembled in a memoir the recipe and the instructions for different methods and weapons that have been used with success against these animals"—particularly around Verdun, where another royal hunting officer named Nicolas Delisle de Moncel had met with great success fighting a thick wolf infestation.[12] The memoir, versions of which were distributed over the next six months, specifically described a poison with the active ingredient of strychnine extracted from an evergreen known as *nux vomica*. The tried and true methods called for the poison's placement in a slaughtered dog ("in several openings of the flesh, like the rear, the shanks, and the shoulders"), which should be left to marinate in horse dung for one day or several, depending on climatic conditions. The bait fully prepared, it should then be transported to areas frequented by wolves ("along rivers and streams, ponds, woods, mountains") and staked to the ground so that the wolf would be forced to eat the flesh on site. Over time this method would "infallibly destroy all the wolves in the region."[13] L'Averdy included forty copies of his memoir with his letter, and he instructed Saint-Priest to provide them to "gentlemen who engage in the hunt" and others who would take the precautions necessary to prevent "mishaps" with the poison.

Concerned provincial officials obediently took their cue from Versailles.[14] Officials embraced L'Averdy's methods even though the accounts of the new attacks could have been borrowed from an earlier time. Saint-Priest informed the court of a frightening assault on a female miller in the parish of Lorcières, in Auvergne, in the middle of February. Using a pick-axe to break up ice in the canal that brought water to her mill, Jeanne Delmas experienced a surprise attack similar even in its particulars to the horrors laced throughout the winter of 1765. As the intendant explained it, the animal—repeatedly labeled "the monster" in the deposition drawn up after the fact—seized the woman "by the neck and face," and she had been able to escape only because she used the pick-axe to fend off the attacker. "She continued to defend herself with her weapon, and the beast followed her all the way to the door of her home, which was not far away." Although she received several serious wounds—her right cheek had been nearly split in two—Delmas was expected to survive. For the drafters of the deposition, however, the most unsettling evidence from the attack pointed to a chilling close call. "All along the base of her neck ran a red scratch, as if the said monster wanted to cut off her head according to its ordinary procedures." Saint-Priest nonetheless assured L'Averdy that, in the Gévaudan, Lafont now planned "to make use of the recipe for poison recommended by the court."[15]

For a brief period, officials at court appear to have deliberated over the level of response appropriate to the new problems in the Massif Central. Some who had the ministers' ear still theorized about the existence of a single, devilishly effective creature. In January the financial officer Henri-François de Paule Lefèvre d'Ormesson expressed sympathy to Ballainvilliers when he heard the rumors that the beast had reappeared, adding that "if it is real, you undoubtedly know whom to address in order to secure new orders, if necessary, to pursue its destruction."[16] The governor of Languedoc, writing from Versailles in March, thanked Saint-Priest for bringing him up to date on the actions of "the ferocious beast." The recent killing of an eight-year-old girl "leaves no further doubt about the existence of this terrible animal, from which we have everything to fear."[17] Judging from the *Courrier d'Avignon,* word had begun to circulate that Antoine himself might be planning a return engagement. In an article heralding the reappearance of the beast, the *Courrier* looked forward to the resumption of the chase. The paper assumed that if the very same beast had not resumed its "cruel war," the culprit had been replaced by "another so similar to it in cunning and nastiness that it must be not only of the same species but of the same blood, nourished by its milk, formed at the same school." Fortunately, "M. de Lafont is ready to go, and it seems that M. Antoine is set to return."[18]

Antoine of course would have had no desire to return to the region, and to reopen for discussion the meaning of his recently completed mission. Like L'Averdy's announcement of new "methods and weapons" on 10 December, Antoine's request for signed certificates attesting his valuable service, written at the end of that month, looks suspiciously like an effort to lock in perceptions that the real beast had already fallen. But the prospect that the court might dispatch some new expert to the region would have seemed at least plausible, especially early in the year. Saint-Florentin encouraged Ballainvilliers to find "the best marksmen from Lorcières and neighboring parishes and

put them in pursuit of these animals," but he also continued to receive detailed projects for government action in the Gévaudan.[19]

These plans came not from impulsive eccentrics but from hunting officers who had known and worked with Antoine. M. Regnault, who had been
instrumental in securing the additional hounds for the gun-bearer in August
of 1765, proposed a new strategy focused on the use of traps. Teams of dogs
had proved to be both ineffective and expensive, he argued, and the locals
preferred trapping to hunting, since they had little experience in the methods
favored by expert hunters. Besides, "the prejudices of some of these unfortunates, who believe that it is an Evil Spirit that ravages them, robs them of their
courage and makes them negligent" when engaged in hunts. He therefore
proposed gathering five experienced fox-hunters from Saint-Germain, one
with a great "knowledge of the region and of the language spoken there," and
heading out for Saugues with twenty-four traps in tow. By spending enough
time in the south to train the locals in the setting and maintenance of the
traps, Regnault would inspire "emulation" in the local population and thus
finally relieve the court of any responsibility for eliminating troublesome
wolves there.[20]

Whereas Regnault targeted wolves, another detailed plan submitted to
the minister expressed new certainty that the beast of the Gévaudan could not
be a wolf. This report, too, was apparently written or inspired by an experienced hunter who knew the Gévaudan.[21] "Despite all that has been said on
the subject of the ferocious beast, the author of this plan, relying on the many
reports he has received and his knowledge of different kinds of wolves, main-
tains that this animal is not a true wolf. It may be part wolf, on either the male
or the female side, but it is the product of two different species." The peti-
tioner's detailed scheme called for a single, sustained hunt that would encircle
the western Margeride and eventually close in on the "cruel animal," eliminating wolves and other "ferocious beasts" along the way. In the proposed encir-
clement locals from forty-six parishes would be called on to participate. The
hunter estimated that he would need 150 good marksmen and 4,500 people
arrayed along the perimeter.

These combined efforts nevertheless represented the last gasp of courtly
interest in the proceedings in the Gévaudan, as well as the last recorded speculation about the beast's species and identity. After learning from Saint-Priest
about a string of killings in February and early March, L'Averdy responded

with language that emphasized the general over the particular. The news, he said, "establishes all too well the truth of the rumors that have been spreading about voracious animals *(animaux carnassiers)* that have reappeared in that part of Languedoc and in Auvergne. Final deliverance from this scourge is most desirable."[22] Saint-Florentin, who had also used the plural term *animaux carnassiers* in a January message to Ballainvilliers, was similarly noncommital in March.[23] Responding in June to the intendant's news of recent ravages in Saint-Flour and Langeac, he tersely conveyed the rationale behind the crown's hands-off policy. "This canton is unfortunately not the only one afflicted with such a scourge; I have received very similar reports from a number of other places. I will be obliged if you keep me informed of whatever you learn about it." L'Averdy wrote to Ballainvilliers that "I believe, like you, that this is only a voracious wolf, similar to those often seen in those cantons."[24]

Ballainvilliers, who had played the vital role in establishing the extraordinary character of the animal from Les Chazes, would have had his own reasons for maintaining that the new troubles were caused by ordinary wolves.[25] But what about Saint-Florentin and L'Averdy? What explains their determination to pursue a strategy that contrasted so dramatically with the approach taken in 1765?

Their innermost reflections are beyond recovery, but at least two distinct factors seem to have shaped their thoughts. First, the timing of the reappearance of these *bêtes féroces* made it highly unlikely that the crown could regard the problem as a pressing priority. Expressions of southern concern rose in volume at the very moment when the Brittany affair approached its dramatic climax. On 3 March, the day that Saint-Priest apprised L'Averdy of the frightening attack on Jeanne Delmas, Louis XV delivered an unusually harsh rebuke to the *parlement* of Paris in what quickly came to be known as the "session of the scourging." In the course of February the judges had provocatively explained their solidarity with the Breton magistrates by asserting that all the *parlements* of the realm formed a union that had its basis in the (unwritten) constitution, a union that empowered them to speak on behalf of the nation's liberties. On the morning of 3 March, the king and Saint-Florentin, having tired of the "impropriety" of the court's obstructionism, traveled to the Palace of Justice in Paris for a surprise session with the magistrates. There the king scolded the judges, reminding them that "sovereign power resides in my person only." "The rights and interests of the nation," the king asserted, "are necessarily united with my rights and interests, and repose in my hands alone."[26]

This ceremonial flagellation of the *parlement* did not permanently silence the magistrates, but it did open the way to a provisional resolution of the La Chalotais case. (He was exiled to Saintes and eventually spent time in the dungeon of Loches.)[27] The session also offered the clearest, most aggressive, and most memorable statement of the French monarchy's claim to "absolute" authority in the two decades before the French Revolution. In this politically fraught context, which had reminded Louis XV once again that "bonds of obedience" could be broken all too easily, he and his ministers would have had little inclination to devote new energy and attention to their continuing failure in the Midi.[28] The wife of a cabaret-keeper in Reims had been arrested in December for publicly announcing that "she would rather see the king die than the dauphin," and the government was in no mood to provide new occasions for insolent speech.[29] The embarrassment in this case would only have been compounded by memories of the previous fall, when the royal gun-bearer had been celebrated as a conqueror, and the beast—by all appearances—had been successfully tamed. To start all over again in the Gévaudan would have required a public revision of recent history, and that idea surely never had a chance.

Added to the government's desire to avoid all threat of political embarrassment in early 1766 was an honest belief in the effectiveness of the approach it now embraced. In the laboratory of their long experience with the Gévaudan, Saint-Florentin and L'Averdy had gradually become convinced of two things: wolves posed a widespread threat to public safety, and they had finally happened upon the most sound and cost-efficient strategy for dealing with the problem. In view of the great abundance of moving targets dispersed throughout the realm, the prospect of continuing a centralized strategy directed at the elimination of the most troublesome animals—on a one-by-one basis, and at the hands of an expert commissioned by the court—had little appeal. Only an information campaign aimed at equipping locals with the initiative and know-how to address their own problems seemed to offer hope for long-term success. Around Verdun, Delisle de Moncel had used a combination of traps, poisons, and relentless hunting to eliminate some three dozen wolves, "most of them of a foreign breed," between November and the middle of February. He had thus provided a model that could be emulated by others.

In the circular with which he distributed recipes for poisons, as well as in-structions in the use of traps, L'Averdy had urged the intendants to encourage local *gentilshommes* to rouse themselves to action. The same thought echoed in the *Courrier d'Avignon*'s long article devoted to the exploits of Delisle de Moncel in April 1766. "[The authorities] are convinced that if every seigneur led frequent wolf hunts on their own lands, in the end they would at least suc-ceed in destroying a great number of these dangerous animals."[30]

Over the next several years the crown's favored procedures became more entrenched. In response to perceived demand, in 1768 the royal printer pub-lished Delisle de Moncel's handbook for wolf-killing, a text based on the fruit of his own experiences. He would elaborate his prescriptions with a supple-mental text of 1771.[31] By 1770, the effectiveness of the Method—the word was consistently capitalized—seemed so incontestable that Bertin, the secretary of state, whose portfolio now included the maintenance of French agriculture, simply repeated the measures taken by L'Averdy several years earlier. "The suc-cess of this Method," attested by many, had persuaded him to print new cop-ies. He asked Saint-Priest to "please have it distributed in your *généralité*."[32] Meanwhile in the northeast of France, by the middle 1770s the royal wolf-hunting stable had provided Delisle de Moncel a form letter to use whenever the presence of wolves required new activity on his part. The document au-thorized him to organize public hunts and to deploy his methods in all juris-dictions affected by the menace of harmful wolves.[33] In 1786 the new minister of the king's household, the baron Louis-Charles-Auguste de Breteuil, took another step toward routinization of wolf-hunting techniques when he an-nounced that all wolf hunts would henceforth be carried out under the aus-pices of the royal wolf-hunting stables, of which various branches had been established in the provinces.[34]

In retrospect we can see, in the twenty years after 1765, the gradual forma-tion of a state policy to contain the dangers of wolf populations through a combination of education, encouragement, and consultative assistance. In 1787, in a cost-cutting measure prompted by the financial crisis of the so-called "pre-Revolution," the monarchy closed the royal wolf-hunting stables, but the signs of wolf infestation that followed that relaxation of vigilance led to a redoubling of efforts in the middle 1790s.[35] In 1799–1800 alone—the year for which the most accurate aggregate figures exist—over 5,000 wolves were destroyed on French territory, most of them killed by private individuals en-couraged by prize money offered by the government. That impressive number points to the existence of a robust and state-assisted wolf-hunting effort operative at the end of the eighteenth century, an effort that carried into the Napoleonic era. This coordinated state program, its roots in the bureaucratic procedures set in place after the experience endured by the Gévaudan, quelled a new surge in violent incidents in the early nineteenth century, a surge that would count as the "last significant episode" of wolf attacks on humankind in French history.[36]

For a host of personal, political, and administrative reasons, Saint-Florentin and L'Averdy thus allowed 1 October 1765 to stand as an irrevocable dividing line in the Gévaudan's, and the nation's, relationship with its beast. Future hunts for voracious animals would be conceived through a new and far less sensationalizing lens, and they would be carried out by largely autonomous local agents who performed their work well beyond public view. The ministers made these decisions, moreover, without ever announcing them as such. They preferred not to draw attention to the continuities between the experiences of 1765 and those of 1766, and they had no desire either to embarrass the king or to endanger the status of the achievement of Antoine, who after all had served capably and loyally. For them, the hunt for the "beast of the Gévaudan" represented a closed book—one to be placed on a hard-to-reach shelf.

In Languedoc and Auvergne, reactions to the renewed violence varied. The intendants and at least some of their subdelegates saw no compelling reason to contest the emerging interpretation of the ministers. In late March the Estates of the Gévaudan assented to Lafont's plans to continue with poisons, and they even agreed that the province should defray the expenses of the new operations.[37] Closer to the danger, however, many voiced opinions diametrically opposed to those of the ministers at Versailles. Local curés, in particular, resisted the crown's instinct to move on. Perhaps because they heard the insistent pleas and day-to-day worries of their peasant parishioners, or perhaps because they had taken to heart the alarmed and alarming *mandement* of the bishop of Mende, they continued to suspect that mysterious forces lay behind the killings. Long after October of 1765, many (though not all) local priests articulated, and intentionally propagated, fantastic theories of the beast's identity.[38] In doing so, they highlighted an emerging opposition between local and national perspectives, a structural opposition that would provide a foundation for the modern meanings of the beast.

The curé of Lorcières, Jean-Baptiste Ollier, regarded the monarchy's officials as gullible not because they had once believed strange stories, but because they had come to be persuaded that the beast of the Gévaudan was a mere wolf. In the last days of 1765, Ollier drafted a letter in which he reminded the subdelegate Montluc of a conversation they had had weeks earlier. Evidently pondering the outcome of Antoine's hunts, Ollier had insisted at the time that the beast "was not dead and that it was not a wolf." Antoine and others had erred "by hunting for a wolf, and not for a voracious and wild animal that is truly a monster by nature." In evoking the "monstrous" character of the beast, Ollier insisted on a meaning for the animal that was implied by the French Academy's dictionary definition of the term monster—a being "contrary to the order of nature." The curé expressed his irritation over the reports alleging that the beast was nothing other than a wolf, for these reports had "fooled both the court and the people."[39]

Ollier went to great lengths to fortify his case in the days to come. He drafted a new "Description of the man-eater" that contained the familiar hall-marks of the "black stripe along the back," the "wide forehead," the "redoubt-able talons," and a "strong resemblance" to engravings produced in Mende, but he also composed a narrative outline that helpfully reconnected the dots for those who had lost sight of important continuities.[40] Ollier's "Sincere and exact relation of the horrible events that occurred in the course of the year 1765" provided a month-by-month account of all casualties suffered in Lor-cières and adjoining regions. He included sightings and attacks from as late as 21 October—long after the destruction of the great wolf at Les Chazes—and he represented November of 1765, the period when "we thought we were en-joying peace and tranquility," as the only sustained break in the action. The calm "did not last long," for in early December the beast "unfortunately made itself known once again in this country that is so filled with misery."[41] For Ol-lier, then, the story of the beast of the Gévaudan represented a single, undif-ferentiated experience that continued into 1766, an experience in which An-toine's hunt at Les Chazes figured as an unhealthy distraction.

Other inhabitants of the region heard the curé's message and shared his convictions. We know that Ollier relayed his thoughts both to the subdelegate Montluc and to a tax collector in Saint-Flour, and Montluc would claim at the end of January that "all individuals [of Lorcières] who have seen the ani-mal on numerous occasions swear that it is still the same animal that commits all the ravages . . . and that it is not a wolf." Montluc admitted that he had begun to wonder about the truth himself, and he reported that he had heard rumors echoing the thoughts of the insistent curé "in several places in the Gévaudan."[42]

Beyond Lorcières others expressed ideas consistent with those of Ollier. Few shared their neighbor's boldness. An indignant Ollier would write to Ballainvilliers, and eventually to L'Averdy himself, beseeching charity on behalf of his flock, in view of the afflictions of "the monster that has ravaged my parish and that ravages it still."[43] But less forceful personalities also signaled their belief in the extraordinary creature still at large. Fournier, the curé in Bessyre-Saint-Mary who reported on the attacks of 2 December, had needed little convincing, and several burial notices that he composed over the course of the next year attributed the death of young shepherds in his corner of the Gévaudan to "the ferocious beast that ravages the world."[44]

One letter written in the summer of 1766 openly contemplated the specter of witchcraft. The anonymous author complained that "they have been looking in the woods" for a wolf recently spotted near Brioude, when in fact "they should be looking in houses." The coincidental timing of a great number of unfortunate recent events—"so much disruption of the seasons," "so much snow in some areas, while there is none in others," "so many storms," "so many ravines filled with falling rocks," "so many wolves entering into homes"—had convinced this observer that "the world is swarming with witches." The king himself should be alerted to this emergency, since the activities of witches might lie behind "all that troubles the state" as well as the many "murders that desolate our realm."[45]

In appealing to the king for a remedy, however wistfully, the would-be witch-hunter departed from the consensus view of his compatriots. Ollier, though happy to petition higher authorities for financial relief, specifically asked Ballainvilliers to ensure that no more "foreign persons" would be sent southward by the king. *Etrangers* were expensive, they inflicted damage on the countryside, and "they hunt for a wolf, and not a ferocious beast." Better, then, to commission local seigneurs to lead hunts involving local residents—people who knew the land and could guess "where such monsters might take refuge."[46] On this point, there seemed to be little debate. In 1766 and 1767 the king received no other requests, official or unofficial, for additional direct assistance in conducting the hunt for the beast. Royal reticence and local resentment had joined to produce a mutually acceptable conclusion: the residents of the Gévaudan and Auvergne should now be left to their own devices.

The region thus of its own volition turned inward, and the changed dynamics in the localities had consequences not only for the immediate quest to eliminate the monster but also for the remembrance of the story in the generations to come. The evidentiary base for the entire post-1765 phase of the story of the beast is frustratingly thin when compared to the documentary riches of 1764–1765. The lacunae are an unfortunate by-product of national, and journalistic, indifference. (The *Courrier d'Avignon* had tried mightily to revive the story of the beast in March and April of 1766, but even Morénas's rhetoric had cooled by late May of that year.[47]) The existing sources nevertheless offer revealing glimpses into the collective determination of a population convinced that it would now have to save itself from the tyranny of a cruel enemy.

The use of poison proved effective—no fewer than ninety-nine wolves died between April 1766 and March 1767—but not effective enough.[48] Fortunately, the pace of the beast's attacks had slowed since its reappearance. The twenty-four known human fatalities between December of 1765 and June of 1767 amounted to fewer than half of the fifty-nine suffered in the previous eighteen-month period beginning in July of 1764. But the spring of 1767 brought a horrifying rash of killings that refocused the efforts of the inhabitants of the Margeride. The shock of five deaths in one ten-day period in April and early May of 1767 inspired a fiercely concentrated campaign to bait the beast with slaughtered dogs and livestock laced with poison. When continued casualties, including three from the hard-hit area between Nozeyrolles and Bessyre-Saint-Mary, revealed the failure of that stratagem, the locals resolved to stage new hunts in the same region.[49] In June, residents of the Margeride appear to have participated in pilgrimages to local shrines, and in the hours after one of these events the marquis d'Apcher organized a group of about three hundred men for a hunt that led eventually to the foot of Mont Mouchet.[50] There, in the woods of La Ténazeyre just to the northwest of Auvers, on the morning of 19 June, one of the residents of nearby Bessyre-Saint-Mary—none other than Jean Chastel, the trickster who had run afoul of Antoine and his troop in August of 1765—killed a large wolf just as it emerged from a dense thicket. At 109 pounds, this wolf did not equal Antoine's wolf in size, but it apparently impressed the people of the region as unusual in its build and its appearance.

In the wake of this event, the locals not only celebrated the death of a large wolf, but consciously mimicked the procedures of late September 1765, when officials had moved to verify the monstrous status of Antoine's animal.

At the Apcher estate north of Saugues, the royal notary Roch-Etienne Marin helped to lay the foundations for a counternarrative of the conquest of the beast of the Gévaudan, one that seemed to crystallize the simmering local resentments toward haughty northerners that had flared up repeatedly in the previous two years—from Malzieu and the banks of the Truyère to La Panouse and the bog at Montchauvet. The new narrative, as first captured in Marin's deposition, offered the animal of La Ténazeyre as a replacement for the Les Chazes beast and put local heroes in the place of Antoine.

The marquis d'Apcher, committed to eliminating the animal that had visited terrible ravages "for several years" on the frontier region between Auvergne and the Gévaudan, had moved into action late in the evening of 18 June after hearing of another attack. After Apcher's men had beaten the bushes along the Margeride seemingly without interruption for nearly twelve hours, Chastel was given his opportunity the next morning, and he did not waste his chance. Marin confirmed that the local marksman had indeed killed a wolf at La Ténazeyre, but "several hunters and many knowledgeable people" agreed that the animal was "quite different in shape and proportion from the wolves normally seen in this country." Its head was "monstrous," and its eyes—would the secret of their sparkling character finally be revealed?—had a "singular membrane" buried beneath the orbital bone that the wolf could apparently extend over the eyeballs "at will." The animal's coat had a mix of colors—red, grey, white—that "the hunters had never seen on wolves" before, and Marin remarked on one other feature that clinched the animal's status as a monster equal if not superior to the one at Les Chazes. Its skeleton was arranged in such a way that it had "the freedom to turn around with ease," whereas the bones of the wolf "did not permit this facility."[51]

This last observation about skeletal flexibility attests to the strength of local recollection and to the desire and willingness of the region's inhabitants to offer resistance to a familiar narrative. Chastel's animal was examined, after all, by the same surgeon from Saugues who had performed the first assessment of Antoine's wolf—the man who had seen "nothing indicating that this animal had eaten human flesh."[52] The royal notary Marin ordinarily performed his services, ironically enough, at the abbey of Les Chazes. They would have been acutely aware of the discrepancy between the experiences of their terror-stricken compatriots and the "public transcript" that related Antoine's climactic triumph, a narrative that, however convenient for the powers that be, had been contradicted by subsequent events.[53] In any case, the actions of local authorities in the immediate wake of the Chastel kill suggest a deliberate intent to rewrite the conclusion to the painful story they had known and lived.

In addition to their textual replication of the single strangest characteristic ascribed to Antoine's "hyena," they brought in a parade of witnesses to verify their animal's predatory identity. Shattering precedent, and signaling broad community awareness of the need to get the story "right," they talked to more than three hundred people. They claimed that a scar on the animal reflected a wound suffered at the hands of a local glassmaker in February of 1765—thus linking their beast to an earlier history and effectively denying the beastly identity of Antoine's creature.[54] They also drafted an official deposition that recorded complete measurements of their wolf's body parts, and they prepared to send the animal's carcass on to Ballainvilliers in Auvergne's capital. On learning that the intendant "was not currently present" in Clermont, the Apchers decided to make their own arrangements for the animal, with help from the surgeon of Saugues.

The story of the dead wolf's subsequent peregrinations—a story surely closer to fable than to reality—would reinforce in later memory the distinction between the resolve and heroism demonstrated by Chastel and his countrymen, on the one hand, and the indifference of the faraway central government, on the other. According to local lore, as transmitted by the beast's nineteenth-century historians, Chastel and one of the marquis d'Apcher's domestic officers traveled north with their own impressive trophy in August 1767. They arrived at Versailles and managed against all odds to secure a royal audience, whereupon the king promptly insulted Chastel and ordered the swift burial of his rotting and odoriferous creature. In the middle of the nineteenth century, the abbé Pourcher would later report, the aging mayor of Saugues, M. Estaniol, would recall hearing old men of ancient memory make the claim that only "intrigue at court" had deprived Jean Chastel "of the honor of victory and the prize money promised to the man who vanquished" the beast of the Gévaudan.[55]

Antoine's brusque treatment of Chastel and his sons after the heated confrontation at Montchauvet in 1765 had thus prefigured the final "injustice" that Jean Chastel had to endure. Despite local consensus that the ravages of the beast had finally come to an end at the close of summer 1767, and despite Chastel's receiving a modest prize for his efforts from the Estates-General of Languedoc, he would never be celebrated by king and country as the "liberator of two provinces." That distinction belonged only to the king's gun-bearer Antoine, who lived out his remaining days with an unsullied reputation as a beast-hunter extraordinaire.[56]

Taming (and Unleashing) the Beast

The cross-generational memories of the mayor of Saugues show that the distinctive regional perspective that took shape in 1766–1767 had a long and rich afterlife. The events at La Ténazeyre and their aftermath yielded a robust shadow history of the beast of the Gévaudan, the first documentary traces of which are found in a narrative cobbled together by the curé of Aumont in 1767 or 1768.[57] The locals' history featured a monstrous creature and ravaged victims, but also local self-reliance, native heroes who succeeded where royal officials had failed, and a parallel trip to Versailles that ended—at least in some versions—with a humble hero's unwarranted humiliation. The sources of lingering resentment embodied in this narrative ensured that the ravages of the beast would resonate deep in the soil of the region for many years to come. Pourcher, a native of the area who could recall the details of his own great-grandfather's alleged sighting of the beast, would remark that the reputation of Jean Chastel remained "alive on every hearth" as late as the 1880s.[58]

As was already apparent in Ollier's agitated reflections of early 1766, the fascination and proud mythologizing that marked the Gévaudan's continuing relationship to its infamous beast achieved its defining characteristics in contrast to—indeed, partly in opposition to—national indifference. A widely shared attitude of detached nonchalance set in suddenly in late 1765 and lasted at the national level for more than a century. The crown's decision to deny or ignore the special character of the Gévaudan's affliction after 1 October 1765, and its desire to refocus attention elsewhere, certainly explains much of the change. The absence of any coverage of the Gévaudan's later travails in the *Gazette de France* and other Parisian publications probably reflected a deliberate decision taken by Choiseul and others at court. The public's impatience to find new diversions may have been reinforced by news of the crown's systematic treatment of an acknowledged wolf problem covering the entire realm. And the continuing political fireworks of the late 1760s and early 1770s provided a series of distractions for the crown's subjects—as well as sources of serious concern for the agents of the crown. Finally, the sheer logic of the lingering official narrative about the beast of the Gévaudan, complete with its grand climax and quiet denouement in October of 1765, sent a powerful signal that it was time to move on.

Nevertheless, the strategic disregard of government officials cannot fully account for the veil of silence that descended on the phenomenon of the beast in the late 1760s and after. Equally important was a diffuse and generalized embarrassment arising from the entire episode, especially among elites who wondered if they should have known better. Premonitory signs of coming regret can be found as early as the middle of 1765. In August Jean-François Antoine had already said of the royal ministers themselves that "they no longer believe in [d'Enneval's] Beast." The composer of a manuscript news journal who expressed amused interest in the news from the Gévaudan early in the year apparently had his mind changed by the more outlandish accounts of late winter and spring. By the end of September he stared in disbelief at the outpouring of details on the "so-called hyena" that had committed the ravages in the Gévaudan. By reporting these details, he averred, the journals of the day only "besmirched themselves." The fanciful tales of this "chimerical beast" had taken in many an unsuspecting observer, however, even among the high and mighty. "We have seen the extent to which the government was deluded into accepting its existence, and the paternal care that His Majesty showed in trying to destroy the creature." Officials had allowed themselves to be carried away, the writer asserted, even though "reasonable people have recognized for a long time that [this beast] was only a wolf of a type slightly stronger than normal, a wolf that multiplied" but continued to garner sole credit for all the terrors inflicted on the Gévaudan.[59]

In a culture where avoidance of shame acted as a strong motive force for all public behavior, open disavowals of earlier "delusions" came rarely. Traces of regret do emerge, nonetheless, from contemporary writing on the saga. Magné de Marolles found that the sickeningly familiar news arriving from the Gévaudan in the spring of 1766 had transformed the meaning of the story he had chronicled for a year. In a postscript to his spellbinding history he expressed feelings similar to those of a speculator who has witnessed the sudden collapse of the stock market. "After having gone to so much trouble to pull together all the details of an event that I had regarded as quite extraordinary, on the assumption that [the story] concerned a sole and unique beast," he faced the fact that his efforts had gone largely to waste. "It is clear today that we were wrong to attribute to a single wolf all the ravages committed in the

Gévaudan . . . I confess now that I have some regret over the time and labor that this collection has cost me, and especially this historical précis, which has now been proven false, at least in part." He, too, had fallen prey to the "then-reigning prejudice about a ferocious Beast of an unknown or foreign species."[60] Twenty years later, the poor man was still kicking himself. In a treatise extolling the pleasures of hunting with firearms, he noted regretfully that he had recorded the details of the famous episode in the Gévaudan "practically day by day."[61]

The form of embarrassment evinced by Magné de Marolles—"it is clear today that we were wrong"—became a general if only semiconscious state of mind in the years after Antoine's grand finale. A regretful impulse to turn away from the whole dizzying episode found reinforcement in the cresting influence of the Enlightenment, a new post-Calas and post-Jesuit atmosphere that militated against religious fanaticism and its expressions, and the desire of many onlookers, casual and otherwise, to distance themselves from a phenomenon now subjected to questioning and outright mockery. Voltaire fired a first public shot across the bow of the beast's legend in the late summer of 1765 with his *Questions on Miracles.* There he assimilated the tale of the beast to other faith-stretching stories such as that of Jonah in the whale's belly and the "fable" of Mohammed and his Koran. Others would soon adopt the same disdainful perspective on the alleged monster of the Gévaudan and the fears to which it had given rise.[62]

Fortunately, for all who wished to save face and wipe clean the memories of their own indiscretions, contemptuous condemnation of the more glaring excesses of 1764–1765 could be used to brush aside a multitude of lesser indulgences of the marvelous, of which many could have been proven guilty. Better yet for all literate males, the entire phenomenon of superstitious exaggeration could be retrospectively blamed on rustics and women, whose rational faculties were still widely impugned in the eighteenth century, despite vigorous proto-feminist arguments by a handful of authors of both sexes.[63] Thus Regnault could scoff at peasant fears of an "Evil Spirit" even as he ignored the alchemy that had turned a wolf into a hyena in the elegant surroundings of an intendant's residence in September of 1765.

Long before Regnault's dismissive jibe, Labarthe *fils* had already anticipated the convenient casting of blame. In a letter of 1764 that poked fun at contemporary rumors that the beast smoked, talked, and made itself invisible, Labarthe contemptuously remarked that "every peasant, every woman, has her story." He did this even as he asserted—and in the same text—that the beast ranged over "immense distances" in a day and apparently had the ability to scare victims to death.[64] Frederick II of Prussia, a masterful synthesizer of Enlightened thought, and one who had taken more than a passing interest in the story of the beast, would have recognized and approved of Labarthe's condescension. In a 1770 discussion of the baron d'Holbach's *Essay on Prejudices,* he regretted the "irresistible penchant for the marvelous" that one invariably found among "the people." Sunk in "invincible ignorance," and lacking "the time to think or reflect," laboring people possessed no "reason" at all beyond their own simple prejudices.[65]

Immanuel Kant had developed an argument strikingly similar to that of Frederick as early as 1766, and he had used the recent phenomenon of the beast of the Gévaudan to illustrate the head-shaking challenges that lay ahead for those determined to explore "the frontiers between folly and understanding." In his *Dreams of a Spirit-Seer Elucidated by Dreams of Metaphysics,* Kant lamented that "certain absurdities have found acceptance even among rational people." He announced, for example, that the time had come to let go of the idea that biological oddities could be produced through "the operation of the imagination of pregnant women." The frustrating persistence of such muddled thinking, Kant believed, could be blamed in part on the powerful if unacknowledged influence of the simple-minded. Voltaire had asserted, in the *Encyclopedia,* that the "weak minds" of "the ignorant" were particularly vulnerable to the distortions of a runaway "imagination," and Kant worried that the rational could not always be insulated from the contagious foolishness of the lower sort. Recent French experience had shown how easily "common country folk," including "children and women," could induce "a substantial number of intelligent men to take a common wolf for a hyena, and that in spite of the fact that any sensible person could see that there are not likely to be any African predators prowling around the forests of France."[66]

The reassuring idea that sane and right-thinking men had been victimized by superstitious women, overimaginative children, and credulous peasants provided convenient cover for male embarrassment. The useful fiction of the temporary and unfairly induced lapse of judgment also provided a powerful incentive to avoid occasions for dredging up memories of the beast and of the excited reactions its mysterious workings had once elicited. When word of the beast entered the public arena in the last thirty years of the eighteenth century, it did so not as a subject of serious reflection but only as a punch line for jokes—either dismissive throwaway lines or political name-calling. In his declining years the sage of Ferney himself, remarking on the tiresome stream of curiosity-seekers who flocked to his home, was said to have compared his situation to that of the fascinating monster turned into a spectacle. "If only they could be told I'm not home. What do they take me for, the beast of the Gévaudan?"[67]

The beast *qua* beast gained new life as a metaphor to be applied to unsavory or undesirable political actors. After the chancellor René-Nicolas de Maupeou finally made an end of resistance by the *parlements* to crown fiscal policy by abolishing them outright in 1771, one so-called "patriot" opponent of the coup composed a satirical piece in which he had the dastardly chancellor reassuring an accomplice that he would survive the political storm. "So my friend, when you hear them say that I'm a villain, a Mandrin, an ogre, a man-eater, the Beast of the Gévaudan, a vampire . . . look unfazed, and tell yourself, 'These Parisians squawk, but that's as far as they'll go.'"[68] On the eve of the Revolution, Marie-Antoinette and her coterie were compared to a pack of maneating animals that, "having inundated the woods and the plains," had now taken possession of the court itself. The characterization of the queen would have sounded familiar to those with memories dating to 1764. This destructive foreign import was suspected of being a "panther" escaped "from the court of Germany." Strong, powerful, and with "flaming eyes," the animal had committed great "ravages."[69] During the decade of the Revolution, the most notorious architects of the Reign of Terror (1793–1794), including Maximilien Robespierre and Jean-Baptiste Carrier, earned comparison to the bloodthirsty beast of yore.[70] And later, in the period of the Restoration, royalists would use the metaphor of the beast, "who brought evil everywhere," to stigmatize Jacques-Antoine Manuel, a charismatic leader of the hated liberal faction in the Chamber of Deputies.[71]

As a term of opprobrium that could reliably elicit smiles or scorn, the pejorative label "beast of the Gévaudan" thus held a secure if marginal position in late-eighteenth- and early-nineteenth-century political rhetoric. The actual beast and its story, however, receded ever further from consciousness. It retained significance only in the minds of those who wished to indulge their own self-congratulatory myths about the coming of modernity and the ineluctable march of progress. For them the phantom beast of the 1760s served as a convenient symbol that separated an age of rationalist triumph from a bygone era in which the Enlightenment's victory over darkness and peasant superstition had remained sadly incomplete.

This sharply dichotomous perspective on the Age of Reason and its discontents had already gained form by the 1790s. Its impact on the meanings ascribed to the story of the beast—suggested indirectly in 1799 by Goya's indelible aphorism "the sleep of reason produces monsters"—is perhaps best seen in a writing informed by generational hindsight.[72] In a popular and imitated work on "error and prejudice" that went through multiple editions between 1810 and 1828, Jacques-Barthélemy Salgues sought to expose the long and destructive history of human credulity, whose end was finally coming into sight.[73] Salgues did not offer unqualified praise for the religious skeptics of the Enlightenment, whose scorn for the church had been carried to excess and had helped prepare the way for the extremist delusions of the Revolution. But Salgues approved the philosophes' long campaign against fanaticism and irrationality, which he repositioned within a historical narrative fully consistent with Christian orthodoxy.

Adam and Eve had been unable to bequeath to their children "philosophy and the Cartesian method," gifts that would have prevented "so many idiocies and misfortunes." Adam, who had "relied unwisely on his wife," had unfortunately earned a punishment that crippled the critical faculties of his race, leaving his progeny at the mercy of "false prophets, false religions, false mysteries, [and] false miracles."[74] Happily, Salgues explained, time and experience had slowly peeled the scales from the eyes of the benighted. The author—an opponent of the Jesuits, an admirer of Voltaire's campaign for religious toleration, and a critic of the absolutist rigidity that had led to the coup against the *parlements* in 1771—represented the 1760s as the critical threshold beyond which the "contagion of philosophy" could not be contained. With the completion of the *Encyclopédie* in 1765, the "torrent became difficult to resist," even for kings and rulers with a stake in the status quo.[75] In the future, Salgues observed, proper respect for religion would need to be retained, and "the philosophers of '93" should be dismissed as lunatics, but as long as "true philosophy" continued to make progress, humanity in the nineteenth century could look forward to the prospect of eliminating any errors left over from the eighteenth.[76]

Salgues identified the episode of the beast as one of the last and most egregious examples of embarrassing idiocy in "a century that liked to call itself the century of Enlightenment."[77] That wolves, "tormented by hunger," some-times emerged from their lairs "to throw themselves on women and children" should have been an incontestable fact recognized by all. But when this expe-rience interacted with rustic ignorance, it gave vent to undisciplined imagina-tions. "Since the art of reasoning is rare in villages, peasants—especially the peasants—will assume that [many] wolves are one," and that the woods where attacks take place "are occupied by some extraordinary animal." An outbreak of lupine violence in the not-too-distant past, an episode that had "occupied all of France," provided the classic example of the phenomenon. Salgues pro-ceeded to exaggerate the "rumors" about the beast that were supposedly broad-cast by a gullible press ("it eats only the brains of women," it "prefers light meals," it "had designs on the capital"). He did this to accentuate the "ridicu-lous" character of the fears aroused by the beast and the inevitability of the story's sudden end. Wise men such as Buffon, he asserted, had warned of the dangers of exaggeration, and the story faded quickly after people were aston-ished to find "nothing extraordinary" in the animal paraded at court.[78] Fortu-nately, his book suggested, such flights of collective irrationality would occur less frequently in the future.

In the later eighteenth and early nineteenth centuries, dismissive repre-sentations of the beast and its story thus served as a useful cleansing agent in the construction of a triumphal narrative of modernization. Self-styled ratio-nalists discomfited by recent evidence of widespread credulity, and eager to place themselves on the right side of history, distanced themselves from the embarrassing story of the beast. They did so by reducing the story to cari-cature and by limiting responsibility for its popularity to the inventions of people supposedly steeped in ignorance—women, children, and peasants. By "blotting out" from memory the evidence of elite involvement in the con-struction of the beast's image, writers of the period freed themselves to form an uncomplicated picture of a traditional world left behind by rational mod-erns. Selective amnesia facilitated a periodization of past and present that pre-disposed learned elites either to downplay or ignore the beast of the Gévaudan and its once-powerful allure.[79]

The beast's effective relegation to local spaces and the realm of fantasy, where "reason" slumbered and enchantment held its dominion, nevertheless gave rise to a second narrative tradition that exoticized the memory of the beast and made its image available for new purposes. This imaginative ap-proach to the story of the beast made its first mark in the public sphere in the only text from the revolutionary generation that actually showed some appreciation for the details of the story it revisited. In a three-act play of 1809 the beast reemerged, with many of the fabulous features of its original story still intact, to entertain audiences at Paris's Théâtre de l'Ambigu-Comique. The audience for Maurin de Pompigny's *Beast of the Gévaudan* would have learned that the dreaded animal had been smuggled into France by "an African." A character who heard it described said of the beast that there was "nothing in the world more frightening, more abominable, more terrifying." The animal fused the characteristics of "a wild bull, a wolf, a boar, and a rabid dog," with eyes like "glowing coals," and a head "as large as a pumpkin." It climbed like a cat, skipped like a billygoat, and was alleged to have "wings on its legs."[80]

None of the dramatis personae from 1765 reappeared in this theatrical version of the story, however, because the events unfolded on a stage far removed from familiar reality. Horace Walpole had once suggested that the beast properly belonged in a gothic romance, but it was Pompigny who first placed the famous animal in an antiquated and partly mythic French past. The Gévaudan that suffered from this beast's ravages was a late-medieval principality riven by romantic and political intrigue. The "beast" in the title of the play functioned once again partly as metaphor, because the true scoundrel of the drama turned out to be a human being "more frightening than the monster I have purged from the earth," according to Prince Gaston, the eventual conqueror of the four-footed creature. The scheming courtier Bertolas had engineered the beast's release into the forests around Mende and then used the pretext of the animal's uncontrolled ravages to foment armed rebellion against the sovereign, the generous and just king, Alphonse. Gaston, having barely escaped the seductive trap set for him by the treacherous Bertolas, ordered the body of the slain animal delivered "to the feet of [the] sovereign"—an echo from the original event. But in this case the monster's delivery to the king's quarters was meant to serve only as "a sign of the tranquility that will now reign in our estates." With both public enemies safely out of the way, Gaston and his half-brother Raoul repaired their strained relations and pledged their fealty to their father, Alphonse, who returned triumphantly to his capital in Mende.[81]

In view of the date of its composition, this play from the Napoleonic era inevitably reads like an allegory of France's painful political history of the previous twenty years. The "beast" of revolutionary agitation, let loose by malign conspirators, was defeated just as the prospect of wide destruction reached its greatest height. Fratricidal conflict came to an end and social solidarity returned to face down a foreign threat—all under the rule of a unifying figure who welcomed former rebels back into the political fold. The beast had been "a monster, a monstrous monster," but political tranquility beckoned at last.[82] The emperor would have found little reason to quarrel with this lightly coded political message.

By displacing current political anxieties onto a remote time and place where exotic monsters roamed, Pompigny's *Beast of the Gévaudan* gave expression to the developing gothic imagination of the early nineteenth century, which migrated from England in the 1790s and would acquire a secure literary foothold during the Restoration (1815–1830). In a time of wrenching social transformations and disorienting breaks with the past, fantastic monsters enabled authors and their various audiences to project onto foul beings in remote settings the unresolved anxieties that accompanied the dissolution of traditional structures of culture and society. The English pioneered the gothic form, and Mary Shelley's *Frankenstein* (1818) stands as its most famous example, but Charles Nodier's nightmarish tale *Smarra, or The Demons of the Night* (1821) offered a reading experience fully as haunting and transgressive as those of Shelley or Ann Radcliffe. The French "frenetic novels" of the late 1810s and 1820s, as Nodier himself noted disapprovingly, also specialized in "monstrous extravagances."[83]

After about 1830, the romantic gothic mood became a central impulse driving French (and European) literary production, and it is no exaggeration to say that the genre's maturation paralleled, if only coincidentally, the story of the beast of the Gévaudan itself. The genre was born in the same historical moment inhabited by the beast—Walpole is generally credited with inventing the literary gothic style. It arguably reached its nineteenth-century apex with *The Strange Case of Dr. Jekyll and Mr. Hyde* (1886), a novel that Robert Louis Stevenson wrote only a few years after his exploratory travels through the Cévennes in 1878. There Stevenson had encountered the tale of the beast, and he reported reading a fictionalized treatment of the story that offered a new explanation for the uncertainty that had arisen from the monster's trail of destruction. In this novel of 1856 the ravages of the beast were the result of diabolical teamwork between an enormous wolf and a terrifying wolf-man who had raised and trained the ferocious animal. The lycanthrope Jeannot-

Grands-Dents was represented, and described himself, as "a hideous degrada-
tion of the human species," a "maniac" worthy of the later Hyde, one who always "comes back at night, when others sleep."[84]

While traveling through the Cévennes and the Gévaudan, Stevenson had
clearly absorbed at least some of the atmospherics of Elie Berthet's *The Beast of
the Gévaudan*, one of two fanciful treatments of the story that appeared in
France around mid-century.[85] Berthet's stylized characters lacked three dimensions, and Stevenson himself said of the novel that "[I] do not wish to read it
again." Still, the book is representative of the beast's passage into the realm
of fantasy because it combined recognizably authentic historical detail with
unrestrained fictionalizing. Portefaix and the bishop of Mende make appearances, d'Enneval is subjected to merciless mocking, and the action is set in the
middle of the eighteenth century, but gothic motifs abound. Dark forests,
heavy mists, and dilapidated castles frame the beast's ravages, and scary nocturnal scenes merge with elements of fairy-tale romance and cloak-and-dagger
suspense. The hero Léonce, an orphan raised by his uncle, suffers a terrifying
attack in the darkest reaches of the Mercoire forest near Langogne, and he
comes away convinced that the beast is human. After the wolf-man conveniently falls to his death in a cascading waterfall, Léonce, with one successful
thrust of his knife at the tale's conclusion, sees his life transformed. In reward
for killing the great wolf, Léonce wins renown and a new bride (the young
mistress of an ancient chateau), and he learns that he is a nobleman who
stands to inherit great wealth. Neither Antoine nor Ballainvilliers could have
crafted a better ending for the tale.

The impulse to fantasize about the beast, unleashed in part by the story's
exclusion from purportedly rational public spaces, thus found new outlets in
the postrevolutionary era. A powerful and widespread fascination for fictionalized monsters kept the story of the beast alive for all who found meaning
in dark mystery. (The rage for fictional monsters contrasts with the period's
treatment of the biological monster, which faded as a category of scientific
analysis in the later eighteenth century and came to be fully normalized by
anatomists of the 1820s and after.)[86] In the Gévaudan and its environs, oral
traditions that had long upheld the existence of an extraordinary or supernatural beast, and rejected the "official" narrative about the conquest at Les
Chazes, found room to flourish and expand. Peasant suspicions about the
presence of *loups-garous* in the Gévaudan even seem to have percolated up to
the published literature of the nineteenth century. The "monster" Bertolas,

whose malevolent complicity with the beast lay behind countless deaths, and the hideous Jeannot-Grands-Dents, whose lycanthropy may or may not have been delusional, could trace their imaginative lineage to rumors of werewolves present in the Gévaudan back to 1765 and beyond.

The abbé Pierre Pourcher (1831–1915) stood at the confluence of the two narrative traditions that stretched from the late 1760s to his own era. His interpretive instincts found reinforcement both in the nineteenth century's attraction to fanciful monsters and in a local inclination to insularity that had fostered distrust of the tidy "public transcript" about the beast propounded since the days of Antoine. Other developments specific to his own era—secularization and its reception by zealous Catholics, the invention of folklore as a mode of scholarly inquiry, and a new valorization of rural "tradition"—helped to insure that when Pourcher reintroduced the beast to the attention of the nation in the burgeoning Third Republic, its story became emblematic of a lost and lamented culture largely defined by mystery.

Modern Mutations of a Marvelous Beast

The critical perspective that the abbé Pourcher brought to bear in his seminal history of the beast of the Gévaudan was a product of its time. Like many clerics, Pourcher was bothered by the slow march of secularization, which he and others saw as a consequence of the French Revolution of 1789 and its nineteenth-century aftershocks. He regarded with suspicion the modern forces that undermined Catholic authority in the lives of the faithful, and he shared with Joseph-Frédéric Saivet, bishop of Mende in the 1870s, a belief that "the true cause of our problems is modern society's official rupture with God."[87]

Everywhere in Europe the church felt itself under siege throughout much of the nineteenth century. An agitated Pius IX condemned even "moderate rationalism" in his *Syllabus of Errors* of 1864, and the First Vatican Council's provocative declaration of papal infallibility appeared in 1870, just one year before Otto von Bismarck asserted secular superiority over the German church through his controversial policy of *Kulturkampf.* In France the environment had seemed to grow more hostile toward religious authority after the elections of 1880, which finally put genuine "republicans" in charge of the fledgling Third Republic. A law of 1880 overturned the longtime ban on working on Sundays. The pivotal Ferry laws of 1881–1882 rendered public education free and mandatory, but also secular. The permissible delay between birth and baptism, once set at twenty-four hours, was extended to eight days in 1887.[88]

Pourcher watched these developments with growing alarm, and he reacted by condemning the spiritual legacy of the French Revolution, the sordid details of which he laid out in a three-volume history of the French episcopacy.[89] In Pourcher's view even the initial challenge to royal authority in 1789 had been illegitimate—the Bastille had fallen to "the dregs of humanity"— and soon the clergy found themselves at the mercy of scoundrels "who became the premier administrators of France, making the Revolution according to their own interests."[90] Pourcher's history prominently featured lists of "priests martyred during the Revolution," for whom he obviously felt a strong affinity. "In my opinion," he wrote, "today's clergy are in the same position as those of that epoch. They like to throw stones at us, though happily they always miss."[91]

The tale of persecuted virtue that Pourcher shared in his episcopal history had a distinctly local flavor, reflecting his strong attitude of regional pride. Pourcher expressed sympathy for the "poor vicars of the Lozère" (the modern administrative department, created in the Revolution, that corresponds to the old region of the Gévaudan). They were "full of faith" and, for that very reason, "hounded by certain patriots." He took special pride in the courage of the bishop of Mende, Jean-Arnaud de Castellane, who refused to swear the clerical oath and tragically fell into the hands of a vengeful mob during the infamous September days of 1792. He thus became one of only four bishops martyred for rejecting the Civil Constitution of the clergy.[92] In Pourcher's hands, the history of the postrevolutionary church became a sad but inspiring story of patient perseverance through an age of reckless reform and contagious godlessness. In the unfolding of that story, Mende and the region of the Gévaudan had played a proud role.

In his suspicion toward the policies of the Third Republic, his nostalgic look back at a time of prerevolutionary stability, and his association of that Edenic state with the enduring values of his provincial community, Pourcher gave expression to the broad cultural and political geography of France in the second half of the nineteenth century. Until the official separation of church and state in 1906, many French clerics, and perhaps most, fought to reverse the tide of secularization that they associated with the integrative nationalist policies pushed by politicians in Paris. A defiant church became the "core and the inspiration" of resistance to the Third Republic by the late 1870s, when voters began to remove from the national legislature deputies with monarchist sympathies.[93] In the south, the bishops of Rodez and Mende became known for their intransigent defense of tradition. They worked, according to the republican prefect of Aveyron in 1879, for "the subordination of civil power to theological power."[94] Pourcher's own hostility toward modern secularization even found its way into the pages of his history of the beast. Remarking the many signs of impiety that had tainted the era of Voltaire, he asked, "Have we changed today? The unfortunate times we live through, are they not punishment for our forgetfulness toward God and scorn for religion? . . . Let us pray that God will save France."[95]

The clerical politics of the late nineteenth century encouraged both an appreciation for cultural traditions and a regional patriotism that stood in contrast to a nationalist and republican patriotism associated with the great urban centers, and especially cosmopolitan Paris. In this respect, reactionary political sensibilities merged with and reinforced a more general cultural nostalgia that gained new salience in the second half of the nineteenth century. The cascading forces of modernity that invaded the French countryside over the course of the century—an integrated market economy, democratic politics, national educational norms and mandatory schooling, a network of railroads, eventually the telegraph—threatened to efface distinctive local identities and customs. For the more self-conscious promoters of modernization in France, this counted as a good thing. Many residents of cities and agents of the central government had looked down their noses at the "rude, coarse, and savage ways" of the peasantry since early in the century.[96]

Notwithstanding the condescension expressed by many republican civilizers, the specter of modernization also renewed appreciation for a fading rural culture. In some cases the celebration of endangered customs and traditions could serve political purposes. By mid-century, for example, Catholic bishops had begun to look favorably on the continued existence of local patois, once seen as an unwanted barrier to doctrinal uniformity. The persistence of local languages now struck many as a useful "*cordon sanitaire* against the flood of subversive ideas" broadcast in French texts that emanated from Paris and other cities.[97] But the valorization of tradition was not specifically linked to any one political constituency or program. Evidence of a growing awareness or heightened perception of change could be found across the political and social spectrum in the last decades of the nineteenth century. Local learned societies, which proliferated after about 1830, showed a keen interest in archaeology, as well as the history of provincial customs and the premodern past.[98] Even pilgrims like Stevenson perceived a shifting landscape. Impressed by the rusticity of the Gévaudan and the Cévennes, he nevertheless glimpsed a transformation on the horizon. Noting that the construction of a railway station in Mende was nearing completion in 1878, he observed, "a year or two hence and this may be another world."[99]

This widespread sensitivity to passing traditions framed the rise of folkloric studies in the second half of the nineteenth century. Even the word *folklore* was a product of the period, having first appeared in a letter of 1846 by the Englishman William Thoms, a student of popular legends. French scholars soon picked up the term and applied it to their own growing ethnographic interest in the resilient traditions of "the people." French folklore, writes one of its twentieth-century historians, sounded "the song of the regions in peril," the song of "the countryside, revealing its archaic and authentic riches." Motivating most folklorists in the last decades of the century was the ideal of a "permanent peasant civilization," one that now seemed to offer "through the upheavals of the times the final images of an original purity."[100]

A sense of urgency guided the first practitioners of folklore in France. Armand Landrin, who became the chief curator of the ethnographic museum installed at the Trocadero palace in Paris in 1878, wrote of the need to preserve "all that has some connection to the everyday life of former times, which is in the process of being modified or disappearing."[101] The journalist Edmond Villetard called for a museum devoted specifically to regional French cultures, complaining that "it's already a little late; within a few years, [such study] will amount to an archaeological enterprise." Landrin's frequent collaborator, Paul Sébillot, founder in 1885 of the Société des Traditions Populaires, echoed his partner's concerns about the irreversible modifications overtaking the lives of rural folk. He announced the need to look for cultural "survivals" amid "the changes that have occurred since the beginning of this century."[102]

As local museums began to dedicate temporary exhibits to traditional folkways in the late 1880s and 1890s, Sébillot and Landrin advised them to collect and display forms of dress, agricultural and artisanal implements, and evidence of "popular arts, beliefs, and superstitions." Sébillot himself, a native of Brittany, became the first great specialist of Breton customs and legends, though he also studied Auvergne and the Pyrénées, and he published several important anthologies of French folklore.[103] Throughout France, what Paul Delarue has called the "golden age" for the collection of folktales, myths, and legends began around 1870 and continued right up to the First World War.[104] Versions of many of these collected tales appeared in the pages of Sébillot's groundbreaking journal, the *Revue des Traditions Populaires*. The first "International Congress on Popular Traditions," held at the Trocadero in 1889, devoted displays to myths and beliefs, oral literature, and popular verse and song. Louis Lambert's collection of tales from Languedoc rolled off the presses in 1899, featuring a tale titled *Le Loup-Garou*.[105]

Pierre Pourcher had no direct contact with Sébillot or his circle of folklorists, and he received no training as an ethnographer, but when he began writing the first well-documented history of the beast of the Gévaudan in the late 1880s, he did so within an increasingly tradition-conscious political and intellectual milieu. And like the scholars who sought to preserve and promote the vestiges of a fading way of life, Pourcher associated tradition with a timeless rural culture defined by its opposition to cities, to modernity, and to a process of national homogenization with various technological, pedagogical, and political dimensions. The resentments he carried as a defiant Catholic, and his familiarity with and loyalty toward a venerable oral tradition of the beast of the Gévaudan, combined with the folkloric mania of the times to produce a narrative that encouraged both regional solidarity in the face of outside threats and a belief in the Gévaudan's enduring cultural distinctiveness.

Pourcher constructed his history of the beast around two interrelated themes that gave tangible form to the locals' long-gestating counternarrative of the story. He argued, in effect, that the peasants had been right all along. The beast had indeed exerted a sort of magic over its terrain, a magic finally defeated only with divine assistance. The monarchy, meanwhile, in the person of Antoine, had deviously conspired to dupe the provincials into believing it had solved a problem that resisted all human solutions. Mindful of the contemporary value of his strong message to keep the faith, Pourcher sent a draft of his work to the Roman See in 1887.[106] Perceived through the lens of nineteenth-century frictions between Paris and the provinces, his story also underscored the duplicitous ways of government agents from the north, whose designs had always to be regarded with suspicion.

Pourcher's extensive use of quotations from the archival corpus is partly explained by the thoroughness with which the sources documented the inexplicable behavior of the beast. The abbé consistently accented, and used for his own purposes, the sense of wonder conveyed by eighteenth-century eyewitnesses. To account for the mysteries, he simply returned to the original interpretation offered by the bishop of Mende himself, whose problematic Jansenism never entered into the discussion. For Pourcher, as for his eighteenth-century predecessor in priestly interpretation, the beast had been a "scourge" sent by God. "God's providence enters into everything, presides over everything," he wrote. Although the beast consistently frustrated experienced hunters, "they did not want to believe that it was a punishment of God." "This beast was not a wolf," but the educated had refused to face reality.[107] Worse, they used their misreading of the situation as a pretext to cast aspersions on the wiser locals. The "foreigners" assumed that "terror had deprived of their reason all the sensible people of the Gévaudan, [and] that these mountain people were so unskilled and so stupid that they simply did not know how to deliver themselves from the monster that devoured them."[108]

Despite Pourcher's evident resentment of intrusive and uncomprehending outsiders, he did not leave the inhabitants of the region entirely blameless. In the face of obvious evidence of divine action in the world around them, the people of the time had shown little interest in trying "to appease [God's] anger." Nor did they try "to find the causes of [their] affliction." They failed to see the writing on the wall, curiously enough, even though they all "believed in a supernatural event."[109] Later in his text, in what seems to have been a clear allusion to the troubling innovations of his own day, Pourcher speculated that the eighteenth-century modification of the traditional Roman liturgical calendar and the abolition of the feast of St. Severian, the legendary first bishop of Mende, had been responsible for provoking God's ire.[110]

Deliverance from the scourge of God had come only in 1767, after the performance of appropriate gestures of humility on the part of faithful locals. Parish priests had organized a mass pilgrimage to the ancient chapel of Beaulieu, a sacred place of miracles perched between Vachelerie and Brassalière, at the foot of Montchauvet. There, according to Pourcher, Jean Chastel had prepared for the hunt at La Ténazeyre by seeking a priest's blessing for his musket and for the lead balls that he would soon launch against the region's nemesis. Later, when the beast fortuitously entered his sights in the forest, "Chastel was saying the litanies of the Holy Virgin, which he knew quite well, and because of pious sentiments and confidence in the Mother of God, he wanted to finish his prayers. After he finished, he closed his book, folded his glasses, which he placed in his pocket, took up his musket and instantly killed the beast." The monster, in a clear signal of the presence of the divine, actually waited for Chastel to finish his prayers.[111]

This account of Chastel's behavior reflected the broad European devotion to the cult of the Virgin Mary in the second half of the nineteenth century, which became especially intense in France after the apparitions at Lourdes in 1858.[112] Pourcher even acknowledged that he knew of Chastel's encounter with the beast only because the story had been passed down through family tradition. He hardly saw this as a disqualifying condition of his narrative, however. Pourcher represented the one other known account of the killing—a brief sketch devoid of spiritual overtones and told by the local archivist Auguste André—as equally the product of a loosely organized oral tradition. In his telling of the story, the abbé even reinforced the sacral character of Chastel's achievement by closing his book with the history of his own intriguing recovery of a cherished relic—the very weapon thought to be the instrument of the beast's destruction.[113]

Chastel's semisacred character contrasted most markedly, in Pourcher's history, with the conniving dishonesty of Antoine. A close reading of the events that stretched from Les Chazes to Versailles indeed yields evidence of the gun-bearer's complicity in making the wolf of Les Chazes into an extraordinary creature. As demonstrated in Chapter 7, however, Antoine's arguably mild form of dishonesty had been provoked by the wide and growing suspicion that the beast of the Gévaudan amounted to nothing more than a wolf or wolves. His own unquenchable desire for honor, and the impelling force of a cultural script that demanded cathartic resolution at center stage, led Antoine to participate in an exercise of rhetorical legerdemain of which he and his co-conspirators may have been less than fully conscious.

From Pourcher's perspective, however, Antoine's guilt stemmed from a far greater crime. With malice aforethought, Antoine had conspired to pose as the liberator of the Gévaudan. He had done this not because he felt compelled to rescue a dying legend whose continued existence would prove useful to his honor. On the contrary, Antoine had conspired to deceive the public, in premeditated fashion, because he knew that he faced an unconquerable beast. The gun-bearer hoped to collect prizes and honors and then quietly slip away to leave the pitiful residents of the Gévaudan to fend for themselves.

The gun-bearer, wrote Pourcher, "like many others, had laughed from afar at the lack of success of the hunts carried out in the Gévaudan; but once he arrived, he recognized the difficulties he faced, and he began to search immediately for a way to escape the morass into which he had been thrown. For this reason, he spoke only of the tracks and paws of a wolf . . . [He] never ceased claiming that these were voracious wolves committing all the ravages, [and he thus] prepared for the moment when he could make a grand exit and abandon the country."[114] Nowhere in the abbé's history does the reader learn about Antoine's open-mindedness about the challenge he confronted, or about the gun-bearer's enduring habit of referring to "the Beast or wolves" in his correspondence. Instead the man from court plays his assigned role as a polite but condescending schemer.

In Pourcher's book, the dramatic altercation involving the Chastels, Pélissier, and La Chesnaye in August of 1765 thus acquired new meaning. Antoine, "ashamed of the fruitlessness of his hunts," which he tried to explain away by citing lack of support and "the great number of wolves" in the area, anticipated through his treatment of Chastel and sons the reception that the true "liberator" would receive at the hands of "enemies at court" in 1767. Jealous of a man who might usurp their glory, and "worried by his skill at the hunt, which was far superior to theirs," Antoine and his like-minded friends from Versailles turned Chastel into an object of derision. The maneuver formed part of their master plan to "toss aside" the beast and its story like yesterday's sweepings—once it no longer served a useful purpose. They enacted this scheme even though the beast had once "excited the curiosity of a great number of men."[115]

The strands of skepticism that abounded in 1765 occupy only the tiniest corner of Pourcher's canvas, and for the abbé their appearance figured not as evidence of evolving attitudes toward the veracity of public rumors but as predictable expressions of the hard-heartedness of the unfaithful. God decided to hide from the eyes of the court—and "especially from the savants"—the "true nature of this scourge." Thus, the transfer of the Les Chazes beast to Louis XV's court is represented in Pourcher's history not as a staged finale arranged with nods and winks, designed to provide closure, but as proof of the final success of Antoine's great deception. Antoine "tricked the court," and the ministers "allowed themselves to be seduced out of fear of attracting the king's ill will." Not "knowing how, not daring, not being able" to contradict Antoine's account of the felling of the beast of the Gévaudan, Saint-Florentin and L'Averdy affirmed that wolves lay behind all subsequent attacks, and they thereby prepared the ultimate "injustice for the country's true liberator." The gun-bearer and his son, meanwhile, enriched themselves at the expense of the truth. Pourcher cited wild rumors that Antoine *fils* had raked in a profit of 200,000 livres at public showings of the putative beast.[116]

The abbé published his *Beast of the Gévaudan* at his home in Saint Martin-de-Boubaux in the southeastern corner of the Gévaudan using his own printing press. The print run cannot have been large. Among local historians alert to the beast and its legend, however, Pourcher's heavy tome soon became the indispensable guide to the event. Certainly by 1901, when the abbé François Fabre wrote his own history that focused on the Auvergnat dimension to the whole experience, Pourcher's analysis stood as the founding model that other local historians sought to complement, embellish, or refine. Fabre, another clergyman native to the region, wrote his book in order to fill out with new archival materials the general narrative already established by Pourcher, who had ignored relevant manuscripts stored in the Puy-de-Dôme.[117]

Outside local circles, Pourcher's text seems to have attracted little attention from historians, despite its archival density. Because of the disciplinary concerns and habits that had shaped their field since the early years of the century, professional historians would not have been inclined to see the value of the abbé's book.[118] Inspired by philosophical historians such as François Guizot and Jules Michelet, and generally sympathetic to republican politics, throughout most of the nineteenth century the trained historians of the Ecole Normale and the Parisian universities focused their efforts on pedagogy and the construction of an integrative national narrative about the French past. They focused especially on constitutional and administrative history, the history of governmental regimes, and the gradual emergence of French nationhood.[119] Local and regional history attracted relatively little attention from the professionals until the early years of the twentieth century, by which time local history was being mobilized for overarching purposes.[120] Influential theorists of historical method, such as Henri Berr, urged the historical discipline to "abandon its minute, parochial preoccupations, and seek to discover the empirical laws that underlie human progress."[121] In light of this emphasis on the grand sweep of human history, and a powerful imperative to associate French history with progress and the rise of scientific rationalism (a patriotic imperative strengthened by the loss of the Franco-Prussian War in 1870), the beast's story was bound to hold little appeal.[122]

The beast's failure to register in the minds of cosmopolitan elites was well captured, ironically enough, in a brief essay ostensibly devoted to its history. In 1898, Victor Jacquemont du Donjon paid attention to the legend of the beast only long enough to express astonishment at its longevity in local memory. In a contribution to *La Nouvelle Revue* he lamented that although the image of "this animal recovered from fable" remained vivid in the department of the Lozère, where fear of the beast was still kept alive in traditions of popular song, the achievements of the fourteenth-century pope Urban V, "pride of the Gévaudan," had practically vanished from modern memory. The beast's tale, like the traditional belief in werewolves, would no doubt be passed "on to posterity." For Jacquemont, however, the contrasting fates of Urban V and the beast stood as a blemish on contemporary society. Playing with the double meaning of the French term *bête* ("beast" but also "idiot"), Jacquemont made the sad announcement that "the future belongs to the *Bêtes,* and the present too."[123]

By evoking popular song, ageless fables, and rural superstition ("today we would be more incredulous," he told his readers), Jacquemont du Donjon alluded to the most likely reason for historians' passive neglect of the beast at the end of the nineteenth century. The abbé Pourcher's lavish retelling of the tale had reflected and reaffirmed developing ideas about French rural culture and its meaning for the modern world. As Isabelle Collet has noted, by the dawn of the twentieth century the "rustic classes" had come to be defined by their "spatial and temporal alterity." The construction of "tradition" and its various expressions (dress, lore, song), and the filtering contrasts of archaic/modern and rural/urban, had transformed the inhabitants of pastoral communities into an exotic and timeless "other." Early practitioners of folklore, Collet observes, perceived "no real difference" between the critical perspectives directed toward "extra-European" societies and those needed to understand the French "peasant world."[124] In 1889, the year of Pourcher's *Beast,* the *Revue des Traditions Populaires* juxtaposed French beliefs, folksongs, and regional cuisine to examples of Japanese proverbs and the superstitions of the East Indies. Sébillot himself contributed a piece on New Year's greetings of the French Gironde, which were then compared to those common among the "blacks of Louisiana."[125]

In constructing a narrative about a divinely empowered beast, and in validating and codifying a distinctly local form of remembrance for the saga, Pourcher's text helped to define the beast and its legend as remnants of an archaic and nearly irretrievable French past. Pourcher thus performed an intriguingly symmetrical "blotting out" that recalled the dismissive narratives constructed by elites of the late-eighteenth and early-nineteenth centuries. Like Kant or Salgues, who had ignored elite participation in the creation of the beast's image so as to imagine for their own convenience an uncomplicated bygone age of superstition and rustic ignorance, Pourcher took possession of the beast with a narrative that focused on peasants' centrality to the beast's story, and to its eventual conquest. Also like his elite predecessors in historical invention, Pourcher reified a traditional world, one where monsters appeared in unusual stories in distinctive settings. But for Pourcher and his appreciative readers, this tradition, far from representing an embarrassing past that needed to be escaped, constituted a golden age characterized by simple faith, popular heroism, and the occasional supernatural event (or, at least, unjaded belief in such events).

As vital insignia of rural tradition and regional identity, the beast and its story, as revivified by Pourcher, thus resisted appropriation by the developing historical discipline. Historians' alleged "methodological malady" prevented them from engaging with living oral traditions and the socially integrative functions they performed—especially when those traditions were emblems of a lamentable provincial backwardness that hardly required explanation.[126] The beast of the Gévaudan and its legend thus found their natural home in folklore, and within an essentially folkloric understanding of France's rural past.[127] Paul Sébillot, in a massive anthology of "traditions, legends, tales, and songs" published in 1898, linked the popular story of "The Werewolf Lord" to the modern oral traditions of the beast of the Gévaudan.[128] Arnold Van Gennep placed the beast within his discussion of the traditional *loup-garou* and followed Sébillot in linking the werewolf "lord of Montsuc" to what he termed "traits from the theme of *The Beast of the Gévaudan.*"[129]

Van Gennep, who played an important coordinating role for folkloric research in the first decades of the twentieth century, collaborated with the Auvergne native Henri Pourrat, who assisted the master in the collection and analysis of stories and legends from Auvergne and its environs. A young enthusiast who had told Van Gennep in 1911 of his desire to recover the "fashions of feeling and of thinking among the people of Auvergne," Pourrat would later go on to produce a sprawling anthology of folk tales often described as the French answer to the work of the Brothers Grimm.[130] Even before he published the first volumes of that memorable collection, however, Pourrat published, in 1946, a *Faithful History of the Beast of the Gévaudan* redolent of the mountain culture that had framed the original events.[131]

In a revealing expression of his regional sympathies and his scholarly and literary sensibilities, Pourrat asserted in his opening pages that "only those from the mountains" were inclined to delve into stories such as those of the beast, which "would not be welcomed elsewhere."[132] He casually referred to the "hundred years and more" during which old men had told the beast's story around a fire, and Pourrat himself proceeded to offer a rendition of the story that, although informed by the research of Pourcher, focused on a variant of local belief downplayed by the pious abbé.[133] The *Faithful History* attributed the beast's ravages not to the hand of an angry God but rather to a werewolf, a phenomenon whose reality is "more than the cityfolk of today can understand." Pourrat's readers learned that the peasants in the mountains, in contrast to sophisticated urbanites, had recognized the reality of wolf-men since "time out of mind."[134] Here Pourrat gave expression to a belief current among inhabitants of "mountain" regions since the late nineteenth century, namely, that if werewolves no longer roamed around their fields and streams, their grandfathers had nevertheless known such creatures, and they had left the region only "about the time of the French Revolution."[135]

This tendency to represent the beast's story as an authentic expression of ancient rural belief, a tendency that first took form in the late nineteenth century and reached a creative peak with the novelistic treatment of Pourrat, remains alive and well.[136] But perhaps the most important, if unintended, consequence of the gradual folkloricization of the beast's tale in the nineteenth century was the fungible status it acquired as it became further separated from the conditioning contexts that framed the events behind the story. In a process that James Fentress and Chris Wickham have called the "decontextualization" of social memory, accounts of the past, especially when first preserved through oral tradition, can become severed from "the accompanying contexts that would put the information into perspective" and thus serve as a check on the narrative freedoms of later conveyors of the story. If not counteracted quickly, the drift away from the moorings of the historical record can become permanent, for "mnemonic reinforcement decontextualizes the information as it preserves it."[137] In the case of the beast, the gradual decontextualization of its story meant that it eventually became available for "recontextualization" in new narrative genres that reflected contemporary concerns or offered the possibility of entertaining reinterpretation of a story with fantastic appeal.

The most powerful of the new narrative genres with which the beast became associated emerged around the turn of the twentieth century: the true crime story. An anomalous handful of deranged killers (for example, Vlad the Impaler) had dotted Europe's vast premodern landscape, but the anonymous psychotic who eliminates victims wantonly struck European perception as an unwelcome innovation of the late nineteenth and early twentieth centuries. The phenomenon seemed to many a natural product of the social forces characteristic of modernity—mass migration, enormous urban spaces, the loss of stable communities, the plasticity of personal identity, and the alienation that accompanies social dislocation. The sensational murders perpetrated by Jack the Ripper in London in 1888 gave vivid shape to contemporary anxieties about class, criminality, and the pathologies lurking within modern social spaces.[138] The crimes of the Ripper also forced the category of the serial killer into the European cultural imagination.

In France, concerns about the modern condition and its connection to the presence of psychotic killers would reach a pinnacle in 1921, with the arrest of Henri Désiré Landru, an ex-convict who swindled and killed at least ten widows after using false promises of marriage to lure them to his villa on the outskirts of Paris. Even before the spectacular trial of the "human monster" Landru, however, France had already been introduced to the shocking reality of serial murder.[139] In the mid-1890s, a series of randomly selected victims had fallen at the hands of a wandering psychotic who inspired an unprecedented manhunt. Joseph Vacher, an army veteran who escaped from an asylum and wandered the rural southeast, eventually confessed to strangling and mutilating at least eleven teenaged shepherds and farm hands. The spreading word of his revolting murders inspired a media sensation, and popular songs compared him to "the werewolf of legend."[140] His capture and confession in 1897 brought frenzied newspaper coverage and extended commentary on the sources of criminal deviance. Vacher became known in France as the "Ripper of the Southeast," and his execution in 1898 took place amid "the cheers of would-be spectators" gathered outside the walls of his prison.[141]

Within the context of these distinctly contemporary anxieties, a doctor from Montpellier, Paul Puech, intervened in discussions about the beast of the Gévaudan with an article that absorbed the beast into a topical narrative about "monstrous criminals." Although there had never been a "medico-legal inquest" into the events, Puech lamented, he argued in an essay of 1912 that the existing evidence established a homology between the killings visited upon the Gévaudan between 1764 and 1767 and shocking crimes of recent vintage, such as "those of Jack the Ripper and Vacher." The victims had all been women and children, "precisely the ordinary victims of sadistic crimes." The incidence of decapitation and pointless mutilation seemed to point to the presence of a human assailant. Most suggestively, Puech identified the similar ravages com-

mitted in the Soissonnais in the winter of 1765 as the work of a copycat criminal. "It is not too bold to assume that this bloody sadist . . . had imitators,"
killers whose unbalanced psyches would have responded to the strong impressions emanating from the Gévaudan. Their desire to reenact horrific crimes,
Puech suggested, merely anticipated the notorious Vacher, who had clearly
emulated the work of London's famed Ripper.[142]

Puech's hypothesis of the beast as psychotic killer had ripple effects plainly
visible today. Following upon the conspiratorial musings of the abbé Pourcher,
whose status as the most cited expert on the story would never be challenged,
Puech's thesis consummated the beast's transformation into an object of speculative theorizing untethered by firm rules of evidence. In 1930 François Fabre
would release a second, expanded, edition of his work of 1901 partly in an effort to refute Puech's ahistorical argument, but the thesis of the "sadistic mad-
man" *(fou sadique)* took its place in the twentieth century amid the favored
explanations of the enduring "mystery" of the beast's identity. The beast's association with this narrative genre only added to the stigma that continued to
repel serious historical interest in its story. Even the novelist Abel Chevalley,
whose *Beast of the Gévaudan* appeared in 1936, and the folklorist Pourrat, both
of whom shifted blame for the killings to an individual werewolf identified as
a local malevolent actor (one of the sons of Jean Chastel!), contributed to the
century's fixation on the hypothesis of the beast-as-serial-killer.[143]

In France new nostalgia for the culture of *la France profonde* emerged after World War II. Pourrat's collection of folk tales was symptomatic of a broad
folkloric revival, as "popular tradition" came increasingly to signify "national
tradition," and in the new tellings of the beast's tale that eventually emerged,
the argument first introduced by Puech mutated uncontrollably.[144] Marguerite Aribaud-Farrère asserted that the beast was really a depraved aristocrat
from Paris, relocated to a southern abbey where he could wreak havoc in disguise. René de Chantal, after pondering the long list of hypotheses offered
about the beast's identity, including an extraterrestrial and a tyrannosaurus,
carefully considered the evidence for and against the presence of a "great sexual pervert." R. F. Dubois wrote of a diabolical hybrid led by a psychotic local.
Pierre Cubizolles claimed to prove "in undeniable fashion" the culpability of a
"man disguised as a beast." André Aubazac suggested ex-soldiers turned into
itinerant cannibals on the road home from war. The filmmaker Christophe
Gans, meanwhile, showed his audience an armored beast guided by a sinister religious cabal.[145] All of these modern students of the tale, inspired by

the speculations of Puech and by the atmosphere of suspicion cultivated by Pourcher, offered variations on the theme of the unhinged killer set against an early-modern landscape.

The reverberations of the decontextualization (and recontextualization) of the beast's story continue to be felt. In the most pressing current debates about the events of two centuries ago, contemporary ecological issues have crept to the foreground. After falling into extinction in the 1930s, wild wolves reappeared on French territory in the early 1990s, having migrated across the Italian Alps. Because of the Bern Convention on the Conservation of European Wildlife, which in 1979 accorded the wolf status as a "strictly protected species," France's new wolf population was permitted to grow without even limited culling. This development provoked an outcry from sheep farmers worried about their flocks. Debates about wolves' environmental impact have thus provided a backdrop for much recent writing about the beast.

Environmentalists eager to rescue the reputation of the wolf, and to allay anxieties about the animal's potential threat to humans, have seen an opportunity in the uncertainties that allegedly envelop the identity of the beast. They have proposed a variety of alternative explanations for the mysteries surrounding the killings in the Gévaudan. The wolf advocate Gérard Ménatory, the driving force behind the opening of the Gévaudan's glorious wolf park near Marvejols in the 1980s, argued forcefully that the beast could not have been a wolf, given the timid habits of the modern species. He opted instead for the hyena, one probably led by a trainer.[146] Many followed Ménatory's lead. Hervé Boyac, author of an impassioned "defense" of the wolf, proposed that the beast was a wolf-dog hybrid led by a sinister trainer and "outfitted with a protective covering to repel the blows of firearms [and] bayonets." (Boyac, ironically, apologized for disappointing readers who had expected a "fabulous animal, terribly strange.") The subtitle to Michel Louis's well-timed contribution to the debate over the beast in 1992 announced the broad purpose of his book: "innocence of the wolves." Like Boyac, Louis detected in the beast's ravages the fingerprints of a malicious human actor leading some sort of hybrid creature. Roger Oulion would add to this interpretive tradition by identifying the ringleader of the "organized crime" inflicted on the Gévaudan. In the pages of Oulion's slender tome, the chief facilitator of the attacks turns out to have been none other than the comte de Morangiès.[147] Cryptozoologists, meanwhile, have come to the aid of wolf lovers by adding to the repertoire of strange animals that might explain the eyewitness accounts from the eighteenth century. One such author, noting that "no terrestrial animal" combined the features of the dog, the bear, and the hyena—as the beast was alleged to have done—found an intriguing alternative to all known quadrupeds. He identified the beast as a "hemicyon," an ursid said to have survived the disappearance of its original habitat in the Miocene era of 25 million years ago.[148]

The environmentally conscious defenders of wolves and the purveyors of the other theories that would serve to exonerate the lupine species have long had to contend with the great number of other writers who have insisted—in the tradition of Fabre's retort to Puech—that the beast of the Gévaudan could be none other than a wolf or wolves.[149] As one commentator observed in the late 1980s, contemporary disputes over the species of the beast of the Gévaudan had come to define the field. "We find ourselves in the presence of two schools," which R. F. Dubois grandiloquently described as the "Cartesian" (those who weighed the evidence and pointed to wolves) and the "Lorenzist" (those oriented to the study of animal behavior, in the manner of the Austrian ethologist Konrad Lorenz, and who cast blame on any actors other than wolves). All historians of the beast, Dubois noted, seem preoccupied by one dilemma above all: "the Beast had to be a wolf, or, the Beast cannot have been a wolf."[150] Although convincing evidence demonstrating the responsibility of wolves has accumulated rapidly in recent years—thanks especially to the work of Jean-Marc Moriceau—the absence of an arbiter acknowledged by all parties has meant that the "debate" has continued. It will not be resolved soon.

The origins of this odd and constricting interpretive impasse can be found, I have suggested, in the evolution of the two opposing narrative traditions that began to take shape already by 1766. From the inkwells of government officials and embarrassed elites and from the soil of the Gévaudan sprang two competing understandings of the events that unfolded between 1764 and 1767. The first version aimed at the taming, and ultimately the silent interment, of the legend of the beast of the Gévaudan. One of the long-term effects of this perspective was to insure that most of the illuminating historical context for the beast's story came to be forgotten or suppressed. The other view, originating in local memories of native heroism and official treachery, and later reinforced by folklorists and nostalgic champions of tradition, made the monstrous beast and its story into an emblem of rustic culture and timeless lore. A critical effect of this perspective was to complete the decontextual-ization of the narrative of the beast, thus enabling its repackaging for audi-ences nurturing their own attractions to mystery, the supernatural, or the stubbornly inexplicable. Between these two perspectives, largely obscured by the narrowness of their purview, lay a rich and multilayered story that con-tained elements far more fascinating, and historical lessons far more revealing, than the form and habits of an intriguingly mysterious beast.

Conclusion

The Beast in History

While conducting research in Paris in the summer of 2007, I shared an eye-opening lunch on the Place de la Sorbonne with a French academic friend. As we exchanged news about our teaching and research experiences, we eventually arrived at the subject of the beast of the Gévaudan. When I admitted to feeling some trepidation about the likely reception my gestating book would receive in France, and especially among French historians, my friend responded with a telling warning. "Yes, you do need to be careful," he offered sympathetically. He feared that the book would not be "taken seriously" by historians because the subject was so firmly associated with the realm of popular entertainment. If I wanted to avoid supercilious stares, he seemed to say, the book would need to be so encrusted in conventional expressions of academic wisdom that no one would mistake it for yet another "theory" about the beast of the Gévaudan.

Time will render its own verdict on the value of scholarly research about monsters in the Gévaudan, but on the path toward the book's completion I encountered more than one intellectual skeptical of the significance of the beast and its story. Perhaps Henri Pourrat, the mid-twentieth-century novelist and student of folk beliefs, was more right than he knew, for as the high proportion of local authors in literature devoted to the beast shows clearly, "only those from the mountains" have been disposed to pay close attention to the events of 1764–1767.[1] Largely unrecognized is the fact that this curious division of intellectual labor, and professional historians' inclination to dismiss the phenomenon of the beast as unserious and unimportant fare, actually emerged from a nineteenth-century historical conjuncture that objectified rural tradition in ways that proved debilitating. The gradual transformation of the decontextualized beast into an icon of ageless lore or entertaining fantasy discouraged if it did not prohibit the meticulous and purposeful unpacking of a phenomenon rich with historical meaning.

As noted in Chapter 1, the few professional historians who have discussed the events of the Gévaudan in the 1760s have generally explained the broad fascination for the beast's escapades by interpreting it as a magnification of peasant superstitions. For Le Roy Ladurie the phenomenon represented the accidental nationalization of just another local werewolf story. For Christophe Pincemaille the entire episode stemmed from the peasantry's ancestral beliefs and "taste for the fantastic." Jean-Marc Moriceau, writing at greater length in his recent *Beast of the Gévaudan,* helpfully set out to disprove the imagined singularity of the beast by placing its ravages in the "environmental context" of early-modern French history, a context characterized by widespread lupine violence. To explain the beast's disproportionate impact on eighteenth-century imaginations, however, Moriceau resorted to the same stereotypes present in elite discourse since the age of Voltaire. He cited the impact of the "collective fears" and the "collective psychosis" of the peasants of the Gévaudan, "who were well inscribed in the popular culture of their epoch." The perspective of the rustics, he noted, contrasted with that of the lettered elites and "people of the city, most of whom scoffed" at the superstitious state of mind. The stubborn uncertainties that surrounded the killings formed a combustible mixture with the "irrational core" of the local population, whose fundamental human instinct to irrationality can still be detected in "a part of public opinion today."[2]

This propensity to compartmentalize responsibility for the frenzied attention devoted to the beast reflects an enduring desire to demarcate the phenomenon and set it off from the experience of the modern world, where human "irrationality" is meant to be repressed or exiled to certain sectors of suspect public opinion. This analytical tendency, which echoes the polarizing contrast between modernity and tradition foregrounded in learned discourse of the 1890s, as well as the older condescension expressed by Kant, covers up the abundant evidence of elite complicity in the making of the beast. To grasp the full dimensions of the metastasizing public phenomenon that was the beast of the Gévaudan, and to understand how the perspectives of French elites both shaped and were shaped by the story, one needs to consider the events in light of the roiling volatility of French culture and society in the early and middle 1760s. The story of the beast, in other words, has long called out for one more act of "recontextualization," this one intended to reposition the story within the boundaries of its original historical context.

When viewed from the perspective of long-term developments in the early-modern era, the phenomenon of the beast can still look surprising and anomalous. Exhausting religious conflict and the experimental work of natural philosophers gradually "disenchanted" the operations of nature over the course of the seventeenth and eighteenth centuries.[3] The educated developed an attitude of amused condescension toward expressions of alleged irrationality. From the publication of Perrault's *Tales of Past Times* in 1697 through the heyday of the published French fairy tale in the middle of the eighteenth century (the canonical *Beauty and the Beast* appeared in 1757), salon-goers and other members of high society appropriated oral tales and rural superstitions as artifacts suitable for polite diversion and moral instruction. Elite writers and their readers thus learned to savor and refine popular culture even as they infantilized the "people" whose traditions of belief they borrowed and reformulated.[4] More generally, the strengthening of the Enlightenment, beginning with Voltaire's aggressive championing of *lumières* in the 1730s, also encouraged elites to mock, dismiss, or find amusement in the assumptions and beliefs associated with the popular classes and their experiences.

Elites of the middle decades of the eighteenth century may have begun to awaken to the seemingly exotic foreignness of the peasantry, but on the subject of the natural world the mental habits of elites and the peasants they liked to mock were not starkly dissimilar. The everyday assumptions and self-image of many nobles and other members of literate society reserved space for forms of wonder, amazement, and even magical thinking. Thus, despite a growing skepticism toward the marvelous, and toward peasant testimony of all sorts, the monstrous rumors emanating from the Gévaudan steadily acquired new strength throughout late 1764 and 1765. And despite modern impressions to the contrary, elites worked in conjunction with the uncultivated, and often took the lead, in every phase of the story's mutation from local emergency to uncontrollable public sensation.

Facing reports of an intriguingly mysterious natural form, elites, not unlike the peasants closest to the action, remained open to extraordinary theories. The suggestions of hybridity that surrounded the creature, as well as the alleged characteristics of sparkling eyes and a repellent odor, seem to have held equal appeal to those on the lookout for sorcery, on the one hand, and those anticipating natural discovery, on the other. In any case, fear of and fascination for natural mystery had grown organically from the anxious atmosphere that prevailed at this historical moment, one in which the character and classification of natural phenomena, the boundaries between the religious and the magical, the efficacy of royal power, the mechanics of publicity, and the civic health and direction of the polity itself had been opened to questioning. The unsettled context in which the calamity of the Gévaudan first arrested their attention conditioned elites' participation in the making of the beast's spectacular career.

An inclination to listen to unusual soundings grew not only from the persistence of traditional folk beliefs and educated readers' growing interest in them, but also from the writings of the educated, who had lately stimulated new interest in the fascinations of nature. From the wide-ranging naturalist Buffon, whose *Natural History* came to function as a kind of field guide for monsters in 1764–1765, to the overseas travelers Lafitau and Bougainville, and from the human porcupine Edward Lambert to Claude-Nicolas Le Cat's "monstrous fetus" of 1764, learned discourse in the middle of the century reflected and elicited a mounting curiosity about exotic creatures, unfamiliar or ill-defined species, and the location of the line separating natural from unnatural forces. Some early reports from and about the Gévaudan suggested that the beast might be a foreign import escaped from a menagerie or smuggled into France through a Mediterranean port. Others maintained that the beast combined characteristics of multiple species and even suggested that it might be a product of species cross-mixing, controlled examples of which had recently begun to generate commentary in learned journals and the writings of naturalists. Among an educated reading public primed for such alerts, conflicting rumors about the beast's form and habits would have been enough to attract interest in the movements of an odd creature in a faraway land. To be sure, skeptical voices could be heard throughout the episode, but the skeptical perspectives existed on a continuum of natural curiosity where strange beings consistently attracted serious attention and where uncertainty inspired informed (and relatively uninformed) efforts to distinguish the likely from the unlikely. For every Grimm there was a Labarthe *fils,* for every Walpole a Fréron.

This existing predisposition to show interest in the story grew into hypnotic fascination between late 1764 and the middle of 1765. In that period the beast gained new allure thanks to the interventions of an array of institutions and individuals, virtually all from the upper tiers of the social and political hierarchy, who discovered their own reasons to accept, or promote belief in, the existence of an extraordinary predator. The bishop of Mende, his thoughts conditioned by the raging war between the Jesuits and the Jansenists, saw the beast's presence as a dramatic demonstration of the necessity of efficacious grace, and of the power of divine anger toward the ungodly. Although his *mandement* of 31 December decried the superstitious belief in the power of humans to perform magic, he wished to leave little doubt among the faithful that the beast possessed abilities imparted by the divine will itself. Throughout the Gévaudan and beyond, the bishop's terrifying invocation of the judgment of providence contributed to the developing impression that the beast exerted a form of magic over its hapless victims.

In the secular sphere, two other individuals had begun to make their mark on the image of the beast by late 1764. Burdened by the weight of deficits left over from the late and lamented Seven Years' War—a deficit in sales figures for one, a nagging moral deficit for the other—they moved as if in tandem to enhance the spectacular reputation of an animal whose prowess promised to fill aching voids. For François Morénas, primary chronicler of the beast's accomplishments, the events in the Gévaudan occurred at just the moment when the details of a compelling "human interest" story were most welcome in the pages of his *Courrier d'Avignon.* A talented innovator in the developing genre of the journalistic *fait divers,* and an adaptable editor who wished to retain his newspaper's profitable status in the volatile postwar market for the printed word, Morénas seized on the trauma of the Gévaudan with entrepreneurial gusto. By transmitting suspect rumors, publishing letters from the region, and inventing color and detail whenever the occasion called for it, Morénas kept the beast consistently in his readers' sights. His instinct to embellish reality established a template for reporting that would be widely imitated by journalists and printmakers in the course of 1765, as the story strengthened its grip on the imaginations of readers and listeners in Europe and beyond.

The experience of Captain Duhamel mirrored that of Morénas not only in its great impact on the image of the beast but also in its representativeness. Morénas may have been uniquely talented, but his resourceful exploitation of the story of the beast exemplified journalism's rapid growth after mid-century as well as journalists' growing sensitivity to the demands of the reading public. (By the 1760s this sensitivity became apparent even in the offices of the *Gazette de France*.) Duhamel, too, was a unique individual with his own concerns and his own complex emotional investment in the outcome of his mission. But the captain's sensitivities and vulnerabilities mark him as a prototypical sufferer from the malaise that settled over France as the scope of its loss to the English and the Prussians became clear. Signs of wounded pride and mounting anxiety dot the cultural and political landscape between the late 1750s and 1766. The crown became more sensitive to subversive words and intentions, even as magistrates and anonymous pamphleteers adopted deliberately subversive arguments about the need for reform. The army retreated in disgrace to reflect on its defeat. Overcompensating expressions of patriotic feeling and royal or national pride saturated literature of all genres. *The Siege of Calais* became an unexpected runaway hit. The beast, inevitably, became a metaphor for war, and even for "Mr. Pitt" himself.

The atmosphere of insecurity and self-doubt affected many thousands, including the Gévaudan native Morangiès, and it weighed heavily on the dragoon captain. Duhamel's anxieties found clear expression in his persistent concern for honor and reputation, his eagerness to please his disgraced commander and social superiors, and a desire to found his "glory" on the defeat of a troublesome animal. So that the dimensions of the beast would match the importance of the mission in his own mind, Duhamel channeled local rumor and combined it with his own fertile imagination to produce a picture of the beast that he knew would meet or exceed the expectations of a curious public. He boasted to his friend Roussel that "no one is in a better position than I, sir, to provide you an exact account of the terrifying ravages" of the beast, and he repeatedly used his purportedly privileged knowledge about the monster to solidify and enhance its status in public opinion.[5] By inflating the image of the seemingly unbeatable beast, Duhamel created a handy explanation for his failure to bring it down, but he also earned a disproportionate share of the responsibility for the mythologizing that infused reports about the beast throughout the first half of 1765.

The bishop of Mende, Morénas, and Duhamel made their greatest impact on the story of the beast between late December and the middle of February. This concentrated period can be seen as marking the second phase in the making of the beast of the Gévaudan (after the first potent interactions, in autumn of 1764, between wild rumor and receptive imaginations in places like Paris). The third phase of the phenomenon had less precise chronological borders, since the forces at work during this period were also in evidence at earlier and later moments in the saga. Between roughly mid-February and the end of June in 1765, however, publicity-seekers and publicity-makers made their most powerful contributions to the creation of the beast of the Gévaudan. They did so by simultaneously making and unmaking heroes who had been sent (or were selected by fate) to do battle with the beast.

The noble hunters d'Enneval, father and son, passed through the crucible of publicity that formed in response to the early alarm created by the beast's ravages. Having arrived on the scene in February shrouded by an aura of invincibility created through boasts, excited rumors, and classical analogies, they emerged from that crucible in June with their image in tatters and their word lacking all credibility. Their behavior, consisting of equal parts arrogance, duplicity, and incompetence, crystallized the conflicting values that separated locals from *étrangers*. Their ostentatious plumage and their foreign ways also made visible the contrast between the actual local experience of events and the naïve fantasies about those events that were fueled by newspaper stories and the rapid proliferation of dramatic prints. Through their failure and embarrassment, and later efforts to exonerate themselves by exaggerating the challenges they faced, the d'Ennevals made lasting contributions to the legend.

Running parallel to the long and demoralizing experience of the d'Ennevals was another publicity phenomenon that inspired faith in new heroes. The construction of heroic narratives featuring Jacques Portefaix and Jeanne Varlet reflected the influence of a whole range of interests and anxieties that motivated the many elites (and nonelites) drawn to their affecting stories. Following the war, French subjects felt a heightened need to hear stories of patriotic courage and virtuous resilience. Such needs found multiple literary, philosophical, and political expressions in the 1760s, and they informed the almost reverential accounts of the events at Villeret and Bessière. The low status and unlikely place of origin of the principal players, which made the patriotic resonance of their acts all the more powerful, also excited new and widening journalistic appreciation for a good story. The editors of the *Gazette de France* endowed the humble heroes of the Gévaudan with extraordinary if not supernatural abilities, thus turning them into paragons of rustic virtue. Their example was soon followed in various French and foreign publications whose interest in the Gévaudan had been intermittent or nonexistent before that time. The attention paid to the young Portefaix by Louis XV himself from February to April not only provided another clear marker of the growing importance of both patriotism and publicity in 1765, but also ratified governmental interest in, and concerns about, the seemingly extraordinary story unfolding in the hills of the Massif Central. By the time popular and official excitement for Portefaix and the *femme* Jouve had run its course in late spring, the beast of the Gévaudan had reached its imaginative peak in the minds of a large and spellbound audience.

The stories of Portefaix and *femme* Jouve, as well as representations of other events that seemed to defy credulity, increased levels of skepticism in the course of late spring and early summer. In fact, a deep ambivalence evident both in the bureaus of the monarchy and in the wider public sphere framed and helped to define the fourth and last phase of the story of the beast of the Gévaudan in 1765. Between June and September some ventured that the beast might be a simple wolf after all. Signs of flirtation with this idea can be found among a wide range of journalists, officials, and huntsmen, including most prominently the royal gun-bearer François Antoine himself. The indications of a collective change of heart only underscore the decisive role played by elites in the final act of the making of the beast during the last days of September.

A mix of thoughts and motivations must have run through the minds of those implicated in the destruction and display of the monster from Les Chazes. The need to defend or claim honor, a burning desire to be fascinated, distaste at the thought of confronting and explaining a collective over-reaction, a sudden compulsion to complete a long-developing narrative of heroic conquest: the documentary record transmits traces of all these psychological forces. Whatever the precise combination of impulses, and whatever the degree of self-conscious intent, François Antoine and a large group of collaborators revived a terrible beast of the unconscious, one that had seemed on the verge of expiring. In the woods of the abbey of Les Chazes the royal gun-bearer killed a wolf and immediately breathed new life into a monster.

The allegedly fabulous character of the animal Antoine had defeated would be affirmed and corroborated by a variety of voices. In the space of ten frenzied days, Antoine received critical assistance from a series of actors who had their own reasons to help him: relieved (but perhaps intimidated) peasants corralled at the chateau of Besset, an intendant transported by his own imaginative fancies, an imperfectly informed doctor extrapolating from the work of famed naturalists, journalists and printmakers only too happy to convey the animal's allegedly gigantic size, royal ministers eager for a clean and correct ending, a vindicated king happy for a cause to celebrate. All of these people, and more, joined Antoine and his son in rushing to the rescue of the faltering legend in the Gévaudan. Doubters there were—Walpole, Voltaire, and perhaps also the courageous *Pucelle*. Other voices of mild skepticism would be heard in the first weeks of October, but by the time Antoine arrived at Fontainebleau in early November to receive official congratulations for a job well done, the die had been cast. Official France, and much of an exhausted nation, had tacitly agreed to recognize the animal from Les Chazes as the terrible beast of the Gévaudan. By equally common if unacknowledged consent, they also quietly moved to put to rest both the beast and their own complex involvement in its long and confusing story.

The two-year aftermath of the killing at Les Chazes saw the fifth phase in the making of the terrible beast. Suspicious of uncomprehending "foreigners" and of all external authorities, and grappling with the vexing return of unprovoked violence in their fields, the locals of the Gévaudan and Auvergne remade the fabulous beast according to familiar specifications. They gave it new meaning, however, by changing the circumstances and locale of its conquest. They kept alive a legend that would pass through underground corridors into the modern and contemporary eras.

The period 1766–1767 also saw the early formation of an uncoordinated conspiracy of silence among elites at all levels of French society, including government officials. Confirmed in their own long-building suspicions that the beast of the Gévaudan had been something of a fiction, they were unwilling to contemplate the existence of a fabulous heir. Convinced that the crown's policy of gradual wolf elimination would prove effective against the problem of widespread rural terror, and newly persuaded of the need to maintain a sober skepticism toward evidence of the unusual, elites inside and outside government adopted one of two postures toward monsters and the rumors that swirled about them. They met them with silence, or they scoffed at such notions. Among the local population of the Gévaudan and Auvergne, the full legacy of the extraordinary or enchanted beast of the 1760s would live on, together with valued myths about malicious accomplices, brave victims,

and local heroes. But Parisian onlookers and other elites, including participants in the events but also many others once gripped by news of the atrocities, contrived to forget a troubling and embarrassing episode. The former
lead huntsmen were especially conspicuous by their silence, but the impulse
to forget was shared widely, if not universally, among French elites.[6] Through
their scorn they allowed peasants and women to take full blame for any unfortunate misunderstandings. Through their persistent silence they allowed that
reading of events to solidify into a self-evident truth.

Establishing cause and effect is the historian's most difficult challenge,
and one would be hard pressed to make the case that an event as singular as
the hunt for the beast actually laid down a temporal dividing line separating
before and after. Many other events that occurred between 1756 and 1771—the
Seven Years' War, the Brittany Affair, the Maupeou coup—would seem to be
likelier candidates for causative status. Nevertheless, the long duration of the
search for the beast and the speedy evaporation of publicity in the aftermath
of the hunt's apparent resolution mark this period as a transformative nexus in
the evolution of lay attitudes toward nature. As rumors and representations of
the beast became part of the cultural landscape, readers, listening audiences,
and participants in the actual hunts had ample time to linger over and to
interrogate the assumptions that fed the reports and the variance between
known facts and patterns of speculation. Skepticism, when it appeared belat-
edly, arrived with shivers of embarrassment. Significantly, after the events of
the 1760s, no putatively supernatural creature ever again provoked the wide
and socially heterogeneous delirium that had been associated with the beast of
the Gévaudan. The absence of similar agitations in later years signals changes
in the conceptual environment that have long invited historical investigation.

In past readings of the phenomenon of the beast of the Gévaudan, however, modern historians have unwittingly inherited and reactivated the disdain
evinced by the self-consciously rationalist elite males of the late eighteenth
and early nineteenth centuries. The eighteenth-century elites who affected
disdain for peasant superstitions threw up a wall of forgetfulness between
themselves and the excitement that had once surrounded the beast. That wall
enabled self-styled rationalists to sanitize their own recollections of the events
of the mid-1760s and to shield themselves, at the time and ever since, from
association with popular credulity or impolitic suspensions of disbelief. Those
atavistic mental habits became defining features of some prior stage in the de-

velopment of modern civilization. The fantastic and decontextualized itera-
tions of the story that have appeared in profusion since the nineteenth century
have further thrown historians off the scent of historical evidence for the
beast's tale.

The elites long shielded by the protection of selective memories about the
beast in fact belonged to the same expansive and disorderly conceptual environment inhabited by the peasants of the Gévaudan and their monster. The
list of contributors to the beast's making includes, at minimum, Choiseul-
Beaupré, Duhamel, Morénas, Ballainvilliers, Saint-Priest, Reinchard, Jaladon,
Saint-Florentin, the d'Ennevals, Fréron, the comte de Brioude, the brothers
Lafont, Montluc, the comte d'Eu, Moncan, L'Averdy, the Antoines, Louis XV,
and a host of minor players. (And why was the famed naturalist Buffon content to look on silently from the sidelines?) These were sensible people, well
educated and well positioned. Without their active promulgation of the tale
or at least openness to its extraordinary features, the story of the beast would
never have penetrated far beyond the crests of the Massif Central. The images
they created, transmitted, or sustained helped to fertilize minds throughout
France and beyond, igniting a cultural conversation that resonated with surprising depth.

A student of monstrous images and of their relationship to the societies
that produce them has suggested that the *monster* should be understood as "an
embodiment of a certain cultural moment—of a time, a feeling, and a place."[7]
The sixth, seventh, and many subsequent "makings" of the beast of the Gévaudan in the modern and contemporary periods provide proof for that postu-
late. The mutations experienced by the story of the beast offer indisputable
evidence of the connection between social context and the contours of the
monsters imagined by the creative and the anxious. In 1809 Pompigny placed
his beast in a safely distant era that just happened to be confronting the challenges of political reconciliation. A few decades later, Berthet's fictional beast
roamed in a darkly gothic setting inhabited by werewolves and ancient castles.
Pourcher then resuscitated the "scourge of God" at a moment when irreligion
and the specter of secularization had come to haunt the dreams of tradition-
minded clerics. Sébillot and Pourrat found a unique beast that signified rustic
belief and lore. Doctor Puech redefined the beast of the Gévaudan as a psychotic serial killer only a decade after France's first enervating confrontation
with random mass homicide in the late 1890s. Ménatory, Louis, and others
have been moved to imagine a panoply of nonlupine monsters of the Gévau-

dan precisely because of their own embeddedness in environmentalist or animal rights movements that only emerged in the second half of the twentieth century.

The monsters that invaded the Gévaudan in 1764–1765 must also be understood as vivid creations of a context—the fraught and combustible context of France after the Seven Years' War. The tensions and creative energies peculiar to France in the early and middle 1760s yielded an array of anxieties that activated monstrous imaginations and filled heads with fears waiting to be projected. Foreign animals, uncontrollable hybrids, and products of uniquely monstrous births were not the only entities troubling minds in these years. Although no one literally mistook the beast for Mr. Pitt, the Prussian cavalry, secretive Protestants, a faltering monarchy, lost honor, or threats to civic virtue, the presence of these and other worries made the French vulnerable to the insinuation that a malevolent "public enemy" had taken possession of the southern countryside. A craving for national and moral rebound also inclined them to simplify the nature of the contest as a one-on-one clash between good and evil, and it made them determined to secure a smashing victory.

The fears distilled and generated by the beast affected people from across the social and political spectrum, and in this way, too, the monster was a product of its time. As the episode of the Gévaudan unfolded, some skeptics reiterated longstanding prejudices against the irrationality of ignorant rustics and the urban riff-raff (the *canaille*). In the extended aftermath of the story, a bottomless fount of antipopular prejudice would be used to wash the hands, and memories, of elites and to recast the phenomenon of the beast as an emanation of popular foolishness.

The evidence from 1764–1765 reveals a different story, however. The sources of wonder and anxiety that fed the creation of a beast were multiple, and few were connected specifically to popular traditions. The literate and the unlearned alike stood watch on the borders of the unthinkable. Cultivated citizens of the last third of the eighteenth century would trade in the myth of an extraordinary beast for a new myth that projected their own forever-disenchanted rationality.[8] The new myth helped guide their passage, and the passage of their heirs, into the cultural world bequeathed by the French Revolution. There they would encounter the beast and other terrifying creatures only as fictions or as figments of folklore. Evidence of modern forgetfulness comes laced with poignancy, however, for it marks the middle 1760s as one of the last moments in French history when a cross-section of educated elites, as well as the humble, could openly confront extraordinary monsters as something other than make-believe expressions of the unconscious. Monstrous habitats still had a place in the interpretive toolkit with which thinking people deciphered and made sense of an often unsettling reality.

D'Enneval, "since his return to Normandy, continues to insist on the existence of an extraordinary Beast in the Gévaudan; someone of my acquaintance told me this, having heard . . . that he had seen it from about two hundred paces, and that it had a prominent stripe on its back and a tail as thick as an arm."[9] The context in which d'Enneval imagined his mysterious and maddening enemy has now vanished, but the record shows that in 1764–1765 a great configuration of elites, skeptics among them, took the beast and its world very seriously indeed. Students who wish to understand the French *ancien régime,* and the shape of the modern world that emerged from it, should follow their lead.

Notes

Note on Place Names

Note on Sources

Acknowledgments

Index

Notes

Abbreviations

AD	Archives Diplomatiques
ADH	Archives Départementales de l'Hérault
ADHL	Archives Départementales de la Haute-Loire
ADL	Archives Départementales de la Lozère
ADPD	Archives Départementales du Puy-de-Dôme
AESC	*Annales: Economies, Sociétés, Civilisations*
AL	*Année Littéraire*
AM	*Annales du Midi*
AN	Archives Nationales
BEP	*Boston Evening Post*
BHVP	Bibliothèque Historique de la Ville de Paris
BM	Bibliothèque Mazarine
BNF	Bibliothèque Nationale de France
CL	*Correspondance Littéraire*
CA	*Courrier d'Avignon*
FHS	*French Historical Studies*
GA	*Gazette d'Amsterdam*
GC	*Gazette de Cologne*
GF	*Gazette de France*
GL	*Gazette de Leyde*

HWC   *The Yale Edition of Horace Walpole's Correspondence*
  JE   *Journal Encyclopédique*
 JMH   *Journal of Modern History*
  LC   *London Chronicle*
  MF   *Mercure de France*
  MS   *Mémoires Secrets*
RGCC   *Revue du Gévaudan des Causses et des Cévennes*
RHMC   *Revue d'Histoire Moderne et Contemporaine*
SHAT   Service Historique de l'Armée de Terre
  SJC   *Saint James's Chronicle*

Introduction

1. Jean-Baptiste Duhamel to unidentified, [24–30 Nov.] 1764. See Marius Balmelle, "Lettres inédites du Capitaine Duhamel sur la Bête du Gévaudan (octobre 1764–avril 1765)," *RGCC* 13 (1967): 96–120, esp. 108.

2. *CA,* 23 Nov. 1764 (report from Paris, 15 Nov.). Because the *Courrier d'Avignon,* unlike other papers, frequently included multiple reports on the beast in the same issue, I will identify in parentheses the date and place of origin of the story cited.

3. The French box-office champion of 2001 quickly rose to the top ten among French cinematic exports. See Charlie Michael, "French National Cinema and the Martial Arts Blockbuster," *French Politics, Culture, and Society* 23 (2005): 55–74. Among the liberties taken by the screenwriters: an American Indian character, schooled in the martial arts, who serves as the companion of the story's hero, a naturalist supposedly sent from Versailles; a monstrous animal, covered in armor, raised and trained with the assistance of a secret religious society; a vast and labyrinthine brothel in Mende that doubles as a sort of witches' coven.

4. Exemplary cases include Carlo Ginzburg, *The Cheese and the Worms: The Cosmos of a Sixteenth-Century Miller,* trans. John and Anne Tedeschi (Baltimore, 1980); Emmanuel Le Roy Ladurie, *Carnival in Romans,* trans. Mary Freeney (New York, 1979); Alain Corbin, *Village of Cannibals: Rage and Murder in France, 1870,* trans. Arthur Goldhammer (Cambridge, Mass., 1992); Jan Goldstein, *Hysteria Complicated by Ecstasy: The Case of Nanette Leroux* (Princeton, 2010).

5. The number of notable works written by natives of the Gévaudan (or an adjoining territory) is extraordinary: Auguste André, "La Bête du Gévaudan: Notice Historique," *Bulletin de la Société d'Agriculture, Industrie, Sciences et Arts du Département de La Lozère* 35 (1884): 189–210; Pierre Pourcher, *La Bête du Gévaudan: Véritable Fléau de Dieu* (Saint-Martin-de-Boubaux, 1889); François Fabre, *La Bête du Gévaudan* (Paris, 1930); Henri Pourrat, *Histoire Fidèle de la Bête en Gévaudan* (Clermont-Ferrand, 1946); Xavier Pic, *La bête qui mangeait le monde en pays de Gévaudan et d'Auvergne* (Paris, 1971); Guy Crouzet, *Quand Sonnait le Glas au Pays de la Bête* (Clermont-Ferrand, 1985) and *La Grande Peur du Gévaudan* (Saint-Amand-

Montrond, 2001); Serge Colin, *Autour de la Bête du Gévaudan* (Le Puy-en-Velay, 1990); Pierre Cubizolles, *Loups-Garous en Gévaudan: le martyre des innocents* (Brioude, 1995); Roger Oulion, *La bête du Gévaudan: Nouvelles révélations sur un crime organisé au XVIIIe siècle, en Gévaudan* (Roure, 2006). Jean Richard, who oversaw the republication of Fabre's classic work in 2001 and was a principal founder of the marvelous Musée Fantastique de la Bête du Gévaudan in Saugues, is also a native.

6. Alain Bonet has constructed a particularly useful website at http://labetedugevaudan.com. Readers find an overview of the main events, a list of most of the individuals who played roles in the search for the beast, capsule summaries of the principal "theories" of the beast's identity, many transcribed documents from archives and contemporary publications, a bibliography of modern works on the beast, and links to the annual newsletter, "Gazette de la Bête."

7. See Chapter 8.

8. Even the well-informed account of Jean-Marc Moriceau, one of the only university historians in France to offer an analysis of the events, is constrained by that perennial but limiting question—was it a wolf or was it not? See my Conclusion for further discussion of Moriceau. Jean-Marc Moriceau, *La Bête du Gévaudan* (Paris, 2008). Also see his impressive *Histoire du Méchant Loup: 3000 attaques sur l'homme en France, XVe–XXe siècle* (Paris, 2007).

9. Duhamel left behind a rich cache of letters. In addition to the letters contained in the departmental archives in Montpellier and Puy-de-Dôme, I have drawn extensively from Marius Balmelle's published collections of the Duhamel correspondence. Based on manuscripts in Amiens, Balmelle's publications appeared in sequence in the late 1960s (building on several earlier publications of the 1950s). The three principal publications, from the *Revue du Gévaudan des Causses et des Cévennes* in 1967, 1968, and 1969, will be given their full bibliographical citations with their first appearance in each chapter, and will be identified thereafter by short title and with the year of publication placed in brackets.

10. Even many Anglophone historians of eighteenth-century France know little or nothing about the beast, though the amateur British historian Derek Brockiss has tried to spread the word. In addition to his contributions to websites, he published a translation of the abbé Pourcher's foundational work: *The Beast of Gévaudan* (Bloomington, Ind., 2006). The only other full account in English, Richard H. Thompson, *Wolf-Hunting in France in the Reign of Louis XV: The Beast of the Gévaudan* (Lewiston, N.Y., 1991), is lively, readable, and reasonably well informed. But the author favors generalizations, he perpetuates myths, he mischaracterizes some of the figures and forces involved, and his research is based almost entirely on secondary sources, which are accepted uncritically and put in the service of various playful assertions.

11. To be sure, the existing literature provides slices of context. Elisabeth Claverie and Pierre Lamaison provide a vivid analysis of Gévaudanois' material culture in *L'Impossible Mariage: Violence et Parenté en Gévaudan, XVIIe, XVIIIe, et XIXe siècles* (Paris, 1982), 303–341. Serge Colin usefully highlights the demographic context in *Au-*

tour de la Bête du Gévaudan (Le Puy-en-Velay, 1990). Yannick Séité provides an over-view of journalistic coverage in "La Bête du Gévaudan dans les Gazettes: du Fait Div-ers à la Légende," in *Les Gazettes européennes de langue française (XVIIe-XVIIIe siècles),* ed. Henri Duranton, Claude Labrosse, and Pierre Rétat (Saint-Etienne, 1992), 145–153. Still, full-scale accounts that seek to relate the beast to its historical setting are nonexistent. The one near-exception is Robert Poujade, "La Bête du Gévaudan: Contribution à l'Histoire d'un Mythe," *RGCC* (1985): 25–53. Poujade's effort to posi-tion the story at the confluence of cultural nostalgia and emergent modernism pro-vided a model of analysis that invited elaboration. To date, no one has followed the lead.

1. Sounding the Alarm

1. Few details are known about the first killings. The victims lived in remote ar-eas with few literate inhabitants and no one outside the affected regions was yet pay-ing attention. For chronicles of the deaths, see Pierre Pourcher, *La Bête du Gévaudan: Véritable Fléau de Dieu* (Marseille, 2006), Boulet at 18; François Fabre, *La Bête du Gévaudan,* ed. Jean Richard (Clermont-Ferrand, 2001), Boulet at 1.

2. P. A. Albert, "La 'Bête du Gévaudan' en Ardèche," *RGCC* 12 (1966): 99–102. The curé wrote, "on the first of July in the year 1764 was buried Jeane boulet [sic], without sacraments, having been killed by the savage beast." Use of the definite ar-ticle suggests that the priest referenced a known animal. Albert cites other circum-stantial evidence placing a dangerous wolf in the Vivarais by April of 1764.

3. The news had clearly spread among the locals that a deadly creature was on the prowl. The curé who buried a boy killed near the forest in Saint-Flour-de-Mercoire, for example, blamed the calamity on "the ferocious beast." ADL EDT 150 GG 1, 16 Sept. 1764.

4. In addition to Fabre's Tableau des victimes, see the account in Xavier Pic, *La bête qui mangeait le monde en pays de Gévaudan et d'Auvergne* (Paris, 1971), 17.

5. The *comté* of the Gévaudan only came under the definitive tutelage of the kings of France in 1258, when Louis IX acquired it from the king of Aragon in ex-change for territories in the Pyrenees. In this untamed area, however, the monarch's "regalian rights" were alienated to the bishop/comte of the Gévaudan (a transfer of rights formalized by charter in 1307), in exchange for the comte's loyalty. The bishop's authority over the region would rival that of kings to the end of the eighteenth cen-tury. See Paul vicomte de Lescure, *Armorial du Gévaudan* (Lyon, 1929), 7–9; and *Doc-uments historiques sur la province de Gévaudan,* ed. Gustave de Burdin (Toulouse, 1847), 1: 13–23. On the city of Mende's later struggles against the vast jurisdictional claims of the bishop see Rémy Chastel, "Les luttes des Mendois pour la conquête du pouvoir municipal sous l'Ancien Régime," *RGCC* 2 (1996): 65–81.

6. Vivian R. Gruder, *The Royal Provincial Intendants: A Governing Elite in Eighteenth-Century France* (Ithaca, N.Y., 1968), 37, 53.

7. Biographical details for Lafont have been gleaned from Lescure, *Armorial du Gévaudan,* 918; and Michel Bourrier, *Trophime Lafont, Soldat de la Révolution: La vie aventureuse du citoyen Lafont, volontaire de La Lozère* (Nice, 1989), 11–12.

8. On the long early-modern process by which elites negotiated their opposing provincial and emerging national identities and the languages through which those identities were expressed, see Paul Cohen, "Courtly French, Learned Latin, and Peasant Patois: The Making of a National Language in Early Modern France" (Ph.D. diss., Princeton University, 2001).

9. Lafont was nominated for this honor by the bishop of Mende, who praised his integrity and loyal service in letters to the minister Saint-Florentin. See Saint-Florentin to Saint-Priest, 15 May 1766; Cardinal de Choiseul to Saint-Florentin, 22 May 1766; Saint-Priest to Lafont, 30 May 1766. ADH C 1994.

10. Lafont to Saint-Priest, 30 Oct. 1764. ADH C 43.

11. Duhamel to Moncan, 1 Nov. 1764, in Marius Balmelle, "Lettres inédites du Capitaine Duhamel sur la Bête du Gévaudan (octobre 1764–avril 1765)," *RGCC* 13 (1967): 96–120, esp. 101; Morangiès to Lafont, 26 Oct. 1764. ADH C 44, folder "1764," no. 108.

12. Lafont to Saint-Priest, 14 Nov. 1764. ADH C 43.

13. Moncan to Duhamel, 14 Oct. 1764, in Marius Balmelle, "Un recueil inédit sur la Bête du Gévaudan (octobre 1764–avril 1765)," *Actes du Quatre-Vingtième Congrès des Sociétés Savantes* (Paris, 1955): 101–112, esp. 102.

14. Morangiès to Lafont, 26 Oct. 1764. ADH C 44, no. 108.

15. Duhamel to Lafont, 29 Oct. 1764, in Balmelle, "Lettres inédites du Capitaine Duhamel" [1967], 98.

16. *Dictionnaire de l'Académie Française,* 4th ed. (Paris, 1762).

17. *CA,* 23 Nov. 1764 (report from Paris, 15 Nov.)

18. Emmanuel Le Roy Ladurie, Jean Jacquart, and Hugues Neveux, *L'Age Classique des Paysans, de 1340 à 1789* (Paris, 1975), 540.

19. An indirect sign of this new self-consciousness had appeared in an anonymous essay published in the *Mercure de France* in March 1755. Titled "Doubts on the existence of a public," its author feared that the great profusion of published works, and of powerful publishers and publicists, in the previous twenty years had actually diluted "the authority of the public" in matters of taste and discernment. See *MF,* March 1755, 32–40.

20. Jean-Marc Moriceau, *Histoire du Méchant Loup: 3000 attaques sur l'homme en France* (Paris, 2007), 237–243.

21. Ibid., 10–11. For his careful and still conservative estimates, see 240–241; on the "dogma," see 19.

22. Jacques-Louis Ménétra, *Journal of My Life,* ed. Daniel Roche, trans. Arthur Goldhammer (New York, 1986), 96.

23. On the tale's likely roots in werewolf legends, see Jack Zipes, ed., *The Trials and Tribulations of Little Red Riding Hood* (New York, 1993), 20.

24. Moriceau, *Histoire du Méchant Loup,* 38–39 (for the Gâtinais), 118–151 (Touraine, Limousin, Auxerrois).

25. For the Limousin see De la Chateigneraye to D'Ormesson, 26 March 1744. ADPD 1 C 1729. On the Lyonnais see Moriceau, *Histoire du Méchant Loup,* 163–167.

26. Untitled *mémoire,* January 1764. ADPD 1 C 1730.

27. Moriceau, *Histoire du Méchant Loup,* 241.

28. Le Roy Ladurie, *L'Age Classique,* 539. Yannick Séité, in an otherwise insightful and informative essay, likewise attributes the legend of the beast almost entirely to the manipulations of journalists. See "La Bête du Gévaudan dans les Gazettes: du Fait Divers à la Légende," in *Les Gazettes européennes de langue française (XVIIe-XVIIIe siècles),* ed. Henri Duranton, Claude Labrosse, and Pierre Rétat (Saint-Etienne, 1992), 145–153.

29. Christophe Pincemaille, "La vérité sur la bête du Gévaudan," *L'Histoire* 101 (1987): 58–63.

30. Voltaire, *Epître à l'auteur du livre des trois imposteurs* [1769], in *Oeuvres complètes de Voltaire,* ed. Louis Moland (Paris, 1877–1885), 10: 403.

31. Fabre, *La Bête du Gévaudan,* Tableau des victimes.

32. *Relation de la Figure & des Désordres commis par une Bête féroce qui ravage le Gévaudan depuis plusieurs mois; avec la Description d'un Combat remarquable que plusieurs Enfans soutinrent contre ce cruel Animal,* 5 March 1765. In "Recueil factice de pièces relatives à la bête du Gévaudan, formé par Gervais-François Magné de Marolles," BNF M-1915, fol. 34r.

33. Lafont to Saint-Priest, 30 Oct. 1764. ADH C 43.

34. Emmanuel Le Roy Ladurie, *Les Paysans de Languedoc* (Paris, 1966), 1: 96.

35. Serge Colin, *Autour de la Bête du Gévaudan* (Le Puy-en-Velay, 1990), 49.

36. On seigneurial power and parish organization in the Gévaudan and the greater Massif Central, see P. M. Jones, "Parish, Seigneurie, and the Community of Inhabitants in Southern Central France in the Eighteenth and Nineteenth Centuries," *Past and Present* 91 (1981): 74–108. On land tenures in the Massif Central, and the various ways in which seigneurs exploited their advantages over the peasantry, see Olwen Hufton, "Social Conflict and the Grain Supply in Eighteenth-Century France," *Journal of Interdisciplinary History* 14 (1983): 303–331.

37. On the preponderance of marshes and the poor yield of the soil, see Elisabeth Claverie and Pierre Lamaison, *L'Impossible Mariage: Violence et Parenté en Gévaudan, XVIIe, XVIIIe, et XIXe siècles* (Paris, 1982), 41, 305–307; on diet see R.-J. Bernard, "L'Alimentation paysanne en Gévaudan au XVIIIe siècle," *AESC* 24 (1969): 1449–1467; on population see Colin, *Autour de la Bête du Gévaudan,* 49; for the quotation on population density see Michel Péronnet, ed., *Mémoires sur le Languedoc suivis du Traité sur le Commerce en Languedoc de l'Intendant Ballainvilliers (1788)* (Montpellier, 1989), 218.

38. Conscription statistics from the early nineteenth century show that the hilly

zones of the lower Massif Central "produced the puniest, and the highest percentage of rickety or deformed recruits." See Hufton, "Social Conflict and the Grain Supply," 308.

39. Ballainvilliers, *Mémoires sur le Languedoc,* 222.

40. The provincial syndic Joubert complained, in a letter to Lafont in April of 1765, that the spinners of cotton "continue to multiply," doing great harm to the native woolen industry. See Joubert to Lafont, 15 April 1765. ADH C 8251.

41. Burdin, ed., *Documents historiques sur la province de Gévaudan,* 2: 125.

42. On transhumance see R. J. Bernard, "L'élevage du mouton dans le Nord-Est du Gévaudan au XVIIIe siècle," *RGCC* 15 (1969): 94–116; Jean-Marie Miossec and Alain Saussol, "A Propos de la Transhumance Languedocienne vers La Lozère," *Bulletin de la Société Languedocienne de Géographie* 5 (1971): 455–467; Le Roy Ladurie, *Les Paysans de Languedoc,* 1: 112–114; Claverie and Lamaison, *L'Impossible Mariage,* 322–327.

43. Ballainvilliers, *Mémoires sur le Languedoc,* 226.

44. François Antoine, "Observations présentées à Monseigneur le comte de Saint-Florentin, Ministre et Secrétaire d'Etat, à Messieurs les Commandants et Intendants des Provinces de Languedoc et d'Auvergne par le Sr Antoine," [July 1765]. ADPD 1 C 1735.

45. Paul Sébillot, *Gargantua dans les Traditions Populaires* (Paris, 1883), 275; see also Claverie and Lamaison, *L'Impossible Mariage,* 304.

46. Claverie and Lamaison, *L'Impossible Mariage,* 304–305.

47. On forests as places where "society's conventions no longer hold true," see Jack Zipes, *The Brothers Grimm: From Enchanted Forests to the Modern World* (New York, 2002), 45. On the liminal nature of forests see also Bruno Bettelheim, *The Uses of Enchantment: The Meaning and Importance of Fairy Tales* (New York, 1976), 94.

48. When Robert Louis Stevenson, lost and wandering near the village of Fouzilhac in 1878, mustered the courage to ask a native to guide him toward civilization, he was disappointed to hear that the villager would not "cross the door," for "you see, it is black outside." Stevenson himself acknowledged the "roaring blackness" and remarked that "I have been abroad in many a black night, but never in a blacker." Robert Louis Stevenson, *Travels with a Donkey in the Cévennes,* ed. Christopher Maclachlan (New York, 2004), 27–28.

49. For the panoply of creatures from the animal kingdom often credited with rural destruction in "oral, peasant, and medieval" culture see Moriceau, *Histoire du Méchant Loup,* 299–340.

50. *CA,* 23 July 1765 (report from Paris, 13 July).

51. For discussion of the various magical characteristics attributed to animals in French rural folklore, see Paul Sébillot, *Le Folklore de France,* vol. 3 (Paris, 1906), 24, 28, 43–44.

52. This belief was widespread throughout rural France. The English naturalist

Thomas Pennant, traveling through the countryside of Burgundy in 1765, noted the local peasants' preoccupation with wolves, and he reported matter-of-factly that "loup garou is one which kills children." In the lower Dauphiné, glassmakers apparently came under special suspicion of lycanthropy because the high temperatures of their ovens required an unending supply of powerful fuel—including, it was speculated, the fat of local children. Louis Lambert, who in the 1890s published one of the first collections of the traditional folktales of Languedoc, shared the popular story of "Le Loup Garou," whose unrestrained hunger for children's flesh finally led to his demise. See, respectively, Thomas Pennant, *Tour on the Continent, 1765,* ed. G. R. De Beer (London, 1948), 39; Raymond Moyroud, "Loups et loups-garous autour des verreries en Bas-Dauphiné sous l'Ancien Régime," *Le Monde Alpin et Rhodanien* 30 (2002): 125–134; Louis Lambert, *Contes Populaires du Langudeoc* (Carcassonne, 1985), 19–20.

53. Jean de Nynauld, *De la Lycanthropie, Transformation et Extase des Sorciers,* ed. Nicole Jacques-Chaquin and Maxime Préaud (Paris, 1990), 80. Nynauld's work, a refutation of Jean Bodin's *De la Démonomanie des Sorciers* (Paris, 1580), was first published in 1615.

54. Jean Beauvoys de Chauvincourt, *Discours de la Lycanthropie,* ed. Patrick Sbalchiero (Grenoble, 2009), 105–106; *Relation de la Figure & des Désordres commis par une Bête féroce,* in "Recueil factice," fol. 34v.

55. Chauvincourt, *Discours de la Lycanthropie,* 110–120.

56. For more on the physical and behavioral characteristics of the werewolf, see Nicole Jacques-Lefèvre, "Such an Impure, Cruel, and Savage Beast: Images of the Werewolf in Demonological Works," in *Werewolves, Witches, and Wandering Spirits: Traditional Belief and Folklore in Early Modern Europe,* ed. Kathryn A. Edwards (Kirksville, Mo., 2002), 181–197; Caroline Oates, "The Trial of a Teenage Werewolf: Bordeaux, 1603," *Criminal Justice History* 9 (1988): 1–29.

57. Buffon had said of the wolf, in vol. 7 of the *Histoire Naturelle,* that its eyes "sparkle, and shine in the dark." Here I take Buffon's discussion of the wolf from an eighteenth-century English translation, *Natural History, General and Particular, by the Count de Buffon,* trans. William Smellie (London, 1791), 4: 201.

58. See Pierre de Lancre, *Tableau de l'Inconstance des Mauvais Anges et Démons: Où il est amplement traité des sorciers et de la sorcellerie,* ed. Nicole Jacques-Chaquin (Paris, 1982), 221.

59. Stevenson, *Travels with a Donkey in the Cévennes,* 25.

60. Philippe Salvadori, *La Chasse sous l'Ancien Régime* (Paris, 1996), 20–23. Olwen Hufton notes, however, that better-off communities, concentrated especially in the southern part of Languedoc, often disregarded these strictures with impunity. See "Attitudes towards authority in eighteenth-century Languedoc," *Social History* 3 (1978): 281–302, esp. 285–291.

61. Morangiès to Lafont, 26 Oct 1764. ADH C 44, folder "1764," no. 108.

62. Balmelle, "Un recueil inédit sur la Bête du Gévaudan," 103. Even Moncan betrayed concerns by specifying that Duhamel would have the authority to regulate the use and distribution of firearms. On the fears of criminality, see Chapter 4.

63. Saint-Priest to Lafont, 6 April 1765. ADH C 43. Saint-Priest demurred by claiming, truthfully, that any loaning of firearms from an armory in the region would require authorization from the minister of war, Etienne-François, duc de Choiseul.

64. Antoine to Ballainvilliers, 21 Aug. 1765. ADPD 1 C 1736. Referring to the victims, virtually all of whom had been guarding flocks or herds, Antoine said that "if they had had loaded guns [*fusils*], they undoubtedly would have killed this cruel beast."

65. Montluc to Ballainvilliers, 24 April 1765. ADPD 1 C 1732.

66. Ribeyre to Ballainvilliers, 24 Oct. 1764, with accompanying "Relation." ADPD 1 C 1731.

67. Montluc to Ballainvilliers, 29 Dec. 1764. ADPD 1 C 1731.

68. Saint-Priest to Saint-Florentin, 22 Oct. 1764. ADH C 44, folder "1764," no. 104.

69. Moncan's views must have been shaped at least partly by Duhamel. On 14 October Moncan acknowledged receiving from Duhamel a letter "on the subject of the leopard that has been roaming for some time in your environs" and he thanked him "for the offer you have made" to find and destroy the creature. In publicly announcing Duhamel's assignment, Moncan later identified the beast as a "monster or leopard." See Balmelle, "Un recueil inédit sur la Bête du Gévaudan," 103.

70. Lafont to Saint-Priest, 30 Oct. 1764. ADH C 43.

71. As cited in Albert, "La 'Bête du Gévaudan' en Ardèche," 101.

72. Duhamel to Moncan, 24 Dec. 1764. In Balmelle, "Un recueil inédit sur la Bête du Gévaudan," esp. 108–109.

73. *CA,* 30 Nov. 1764 (report from Paris, 22 Nov.).

74. G.-F. Magné de Marolles, "Précis Historique des ravages de la Bête féroce qui a désolé si longtemps le Gévaudan et l'Auvergne, des chasses et battues qui ont été faites, et des divers moiens qu'on a tentés pour la détruire depuis son apparition au mois de Juin 1764, jusqu'à sa prise par M. Antoine Lieutenant des Chasses et Port-arquebuse de S. M. Le 20 Septembre 1765," in "Recueil factice," 66r.

75. The inaccuracy of the musket accounts for European infantries' reliance on line formations. Massive volleys compensated for inaccuracy, though not always particularly well. See Christopher Duffy, *The Military Experience in the Age of Reason* (New York, 1987), 208. Some hunters, especially in central and northern Europe, used the more accurate rifle, named for the deep-grooved rifling on the interior of the barrel which propelled the ball toward its target with greater reliability. The precise model of firearm is rarely mentioned in the documents from the Gévaudan, but until the end of the century the French infantry relied on the smoothbore musket, with which an experienced shot could hope but not expect to hit a man or large animal at

one hundred yards. See H. L. Petersen, "The Eighteenth Century and the End of the Flintlock," in *Pollard's History of Firearms,* ed. Claude Bair (Middlesex, 1983), esp. 106–143.

76. Lafont to Saint-Priest, 30 Oct. 1764. ADH C 43.

77. *CA,* 30 Nov. 1764 (report from Paris, 22 Nov.).

78. Near Verdun, in the spring of 1766, a lieutenant of the *grande louveterie* reported that, among the dozens of wolves he had killed in a two-month period, several were "of foreign species." See Magné de Marolles, "Précis Historique des ravages de la Bête féroce," in "Recueil factice," fol. 79v. Also see the long account in *CA,* 15 April 1766 (report from Paris, 5 April).

2. Monsters Real and Imagined

1. The "cardboard" is borrowed from Stephen Jay Gould, who memorably discredited the triumphalist accounts of geological science that still shaped geology textbooks through the middle of the twentieth century. See *Time's Arrow, Time's Cycle: Myth and Metaphor in the Discovery of Geological Time* (Cambridge, Mass., 1986), 4–7.

2. In France the 1760s saw the publication of J.-J. Rousseau's *Social Contract* and his astoundingly popular didactic novels *Julie* and *Emile* (all in 1761–1762), the completion of Denis Diderot's influential philosophic *summa,* the *Encyclopedia* (1765), the appearance of Voltaire's *Essay on Tolerance* (1763) and his public crusades on behalf of the persecuted families of Calas and Sirven (1763–1766), as well as the political and cultural ascendancy of the path-breaking laissez-faire economists known as physiocrats (1763–1768).

3. Herbert Butterfield, *The Whig Interpretation of History* (London, 1931). In recent years historians of the Enlightenment have consistently highlighted the irrationalities, errors, and contradictions contained within the age of reason. See Robert Darnton, *Mesmerism and the End of the Enlightenment in France* (Cambridge, Mass., 1968); David W. Bates, *Enlightenment Aberrations: Error and Revolution in France* (Ithaca, N.Y., 2002); Julia V. Douthwaite, *The Wild Girl, Natural Man, and the Monster: Dangerous Experiments in the Age of Enlightenment* (Chicago, 2002); Harold Mah, *Enlightenment Phantasies: Cultural Identity in France and Germany, 1750–1914* (Ithaca, N.Y., 2003); Jessica Riskin, *Science in the Age of Sensibility: The Sentimental Empiricists of the French Enlightenment* (Chicago, 2002).

4. Lorraine Daston and Katherine Park, *Wonders and the Order of Nature, 1150–1750* (Cambridge, Mass., 1998), esp. 21–66.

5. As cited in Daniel Mornet, *Les Sciences de la Nature en France au XVIIIe Siècle: Un Chapitre de l'Histoire des Idées* (Paris, 1971), 13.

6. See Michael R. Lynn, *Popular Science and Public Opinion in Eighteenth-Century France* (Manchester, U.K., 2006), 22, 31. For Rousseau's comment, see 32.

7. For earlier examples of this widely held belief, see Daston and Park, *Wonders and the Order of Nature,* 189, 198.

8. On Malebranche see Jacques Roger, *Les Sciences de la Vie dans la Pensée Française du XVIIIe Siècle: la génération des animaux de Descartes à l'Encyclopédie* (Paris, 1963), 399; Eller is discussed and cited in Georges Canguilhem, "La monstruosité et le monstrueux," in *La Connaissance de la Vie* (Paris, 1975), 171–189, esp. 176.

9. Darnton, *Mesmerism and the End of the Enlightenment;* J. B. Shank, *The Newton Wars and the Beginning of the French Enlightenment* (Chicago, 2008), 286–288, 311, 321–342.

10. The material for much of the following paragraph comes from Mornet, *Les Sciences de la Nature,* 15–17.

11. Gabriel-François Coyer, *Suite des Bagatelles Morales* (London, 1769), 167.

12. For the Maillet quote see Roger, *Les Sciences de la Vie,* 523. The texts in question: Benjamin Martin, *Philosophical Grammar; Being a View of the Present State of Experimental Physiology, or, Natural Philosophy* (London, 1748); Benoît de Maillet, *Telliamed, ou Entretiens d'un Philosophe Indien avec un Missionaire Français sur la Diminution de la Mer, la Formation de la Terre, etc.* (Amsterdam, 1748). On Le Cat's text, and the discussion it generated in the *Mercure de France,* see Mornet, *Les Sciences de la Nature en France,* 17. On Le Cat's elevated, perhaps overblown, reputation, see Gérard Hurpin, "Claude-Nicolas Le Cat, ou de la notoriété médicale au XVIIIe siècle," *Histoire des Sciences Médicales* 35 (2001): 151–162. On his correspondence with Voltaire, see 159.

13. As cited in Roger, *Les Sciences de la Vie,* 398. For the details of the debate over anatomical monsters, especially for the first half of the eighteenth century, see Patrick Tort, *L'Ordre et les Monstres: Le débat sur l'origine des déviations anatomiques au XVIIIe Siècle* (Paris, 1980).

14. John Locke, *A Discourse of Miracles,* in *The Works of John Locke,* 10 vols. (London, 1823), 9: 256. Cited in Lorraine Daston, "Marvelous Facts and Miraculous Evidence in Early Modern Europe," *Critical Inquiry* 18 (1991): 93–124, esp. 117.

15. Beliefs about a divinely or demonically enchanted world continued to percolate in various "underworld" locations even among the educated, however. See, for example, Lynn Mollenauer, *Strange Revelations: Magic, Poison, and Sacrilege in Louis XIV's France* (University Park, Pa., 2007), esp. 71–95.

16. On public dissections at the Academy of Sciences see Jacques Roger, *Buffon: A Life in Natural History,* ed. L. Pearce Williams, trans. Sarah Lucille Bonnefoi (Ithaca, N.Y., 1997), 69. On Duverney's reputation see Anita Guerrini, "Duverney's Skeletons," *Isis* 94 (2003): 577–603.

17. For explorations of both perspectives, see Roger, *Les Sciences de la Vie,* 325–418; Alan Kors, "Monsters and the Problem of Naturalism in French Thought," *Eighteenth-Century Life* 21 (1997), 23–24.

18. Voltaire, *Des Singularités de la Nature* [1768], in *Oeuvres Complètes de Voltaire,* ed. Louis Moland (Paris, 1877–1885), 27: 183. On the eighteenth century's pivotal role

in turning the monster into an instrument and not merely an object of science, see Canguilhem, "La Monstruosité et le Monstrueux," 179–184.

19. Patrick Graille, "Portrait scientifique et littéraire de l'hybride au siècle des Lumières," *Eighteenth-Century Life* 21 (1997): 70–88, esp. 71. On Maupertuis's own distinctive theory of generation and the role of monsters in generating the theory, see Michael H. Hoffheimer, "Maupertuis and the Eighteenth-Century Critique of Preexistence," *Journal of the History of Biology* 15 (1982): 119–144.

20. For helpful discussion of Linnaeus's changing taxonomy, see Douthwaite, *Wild Girl*, 14–17.

21. "Hence this child, monstrous as it is, demonstrates the circulation of the blood from the mother to the foetus, and from the foetus to the mother again, which some moderns deny, and others endeavor, at least, to render doubtful." Le Cat's demonstration was notable enough to have been reported to the English Royal Academy. "A Monstrous Human Foetus, Having Neither Head, Heart, Lungs, Stomach, Spleen, Pancreas, Liver, nor Kidnies. By Claude Nicolas Le Cat, M.D., Professor and Demonstrator Royal in Anatomy and Surgery; Perpetual Secretary to the Academy of Sciences at Rouen, F. R. S. etc. Translated from the French by Michael Underwood, Surgeon to the British Lyingin Hospital in London," *Philosophical Transactions (1683–1775)* 57 (1767): 1–20, esp. 16.

22. Jean-Baptiste Robinet, *Considérations Philosophiques de la Gradation Naturelle des Formes de l'Etre ou les Essais de la Nature qui apprend à faire l'homme* (Paris, 1768), 198. See Michel Duval, "Un littérateur encyclopédiste au siècle des Lumières: Jean-Baptiste Robinet (1735–1820)," *Bulletin et Mémoires de la Société Archéologique et Historique d'Ille-et-Vilaine* 58 (2004): 87–96; Canguilhem, "La Monstruosité et le Monstrueux," 179.

23. Denis Diderot, *Le Rêve de d'Alembert,* ed. Colas Duflo (Paris, 2002), 112. Diderot would have doctor Bordeu explain to Mademoiselle de Lespinasse that all animal organisms are but the developed product of an original soft substance consisting of filaments, "unformed, fibrous, more analogous to a bulb or the root of a plant than to an animal" (116).

24. Judging by the holdings of private libraries, in any case. See Daniel Mornet, "Les enseignements des bibliothèques privées (1750–1780)," *Revue d'Histoire Littéraire de la France* 18 (1910): 449–496, esp. 460. The book also cracked the top ten among English readers. See G. S. Rousseau, "Science books and their readers in the eighteenth century," in *Books and Their Readers in Eighteenth-Century England,* ed. Isabel Rivers (New York, 1982), 197–255, esp. 222.

25. Roger, *Buffon,* 292. On Buffon's understanding of nature, and his dispute with Linnaeus, see 81–92, 126–150, 288–335.

26. Ibid., 327; Graille, "Portrait scientifique et littéraire de l'hybride," 74. On the "Degeneration," see Paul Lawrence Farber, "Buffon and Daubenton: Divergent Traditions within the *Histoire Naturelle,*" *Isis* 66 (1975): 63–74, esp. 69–70.

27. Charles Bonnet, *Contemplation de la Nature* (Amsterdam, 1764). On Bonnet's interest in hybridity see Léon Poliakov, "Le fantasme des êtres hybrides et la hiérarchie des races aux XVIIIe et XIXe siècles," in *Hommes et Bêtes: Entretiens sur le racisme*, ed. Léon Poliakov (Paris, 1975), 167–181, esp. 170; and Graille, "Portrait scientifique et littéraire de l'hybride," 72; René-Antoine Ferchault de Réaumur, *Art de faire éclore et d'élever en toute saison des oiseaux domestiques de toutes espèces, soit par le moyen de la chaleur du fumier, soit par le moyen de celle du feu ordinaire* (Paris, 1749).

28. Buffon referred specifically to the phenomenon of intermixing. See Claude Blanckaert, "Of Monstrous Métis? Hybridity, Fear of Miscegenation, and Patriotism from Buffon to Paul Broca," in *The Color of Liberty: Histories of Race in France,* ed. Sue Peabody and Tyler Stovall (Durham, N.C., 2003), 42–71, esp. 46.

29. Jean-Louis Fischer, "Lafitau et l'Acéphale: Une Preuve Tératologique du Monogénisme," in *Naissance de l'ethnologie? Anthropologie et missions en Amérique, XVI–XVIIIe siècle* (Paris, 1985), 91–105.

30. As cited in Louise E. Robbins, *Elephant Slaves and Pampered Parrots: Exotic Animals in Eighteenth-Century Paris* (Baltimore, 2002), 172.

31. Ibid., 69.

32. Saint-Florentin to M. Alliot, 9 May 1765. AN O1 *407. For biographical details on the dwarf Bébé, whose birth name was Nicolas Ferri, see Ernest Martin, *Histoire des Monstres depuis l'Antiquité jusqu'à nos Jours* (Paris, 1880), 342–345.

33. Parrots, for example, were acquired by grocers, hatmakers, bakers, saddlers, and café owners. See Robbins, *Elephant Slaves,* 136–138.

34. Pennant, *Tour on the Continent 1765,* ed. G. R. De Beer (London, 1948), 31.

35. Ibid., 10. On the Asian rhinoceros see Robert M. Isherwood, *Farce and Fantasy: Popular Entertainment in Eighteenth-Century Paris* (Oxford, 1986), 45; on the exotic more generally see Robbins, *Elephant Slaves,* 68–99, esp. 88.

36. *CA,* 2 April 1765 (report from Paris, 23 March).

37. Isherwood, *Farce and Fantasy,* 46–47.

38. Delisle de Sales first achieved fame for *De la Philosophie de la Nature* (Amsterdam, 1770–1774). See Pierre Malandain, *Delisle de Sales: Philosophe de la Nature* (Oxford, 1982). Both the porcupine man and the recollections of Delisle de Sales are discussed in Douthwaite, *Wild Girl,* 19–20, 209.

39. Voltaire, *Des Singularités de la Nature* [1768], in *Oeuvres Complètes,* 27: 186. See also Graille, "Portait scientifique et littéraire de l'hybride," 76.

40. Darnton, *Mesmerism and the End of the Enlightenment,* 30–32.

41. Paula Findlen, *Possessing Nature: Museums, Collecting, and Scientific Culture in Early Modern Italy* (Berkeley, 1994), 3, 36, 55.

42. Daston and Park, *Wonders and the Order of Nature,* 316–360.

43. On the "preternatural" see Daston, "Marvelous Facts and Miraculous Evidence," 97.

44. See Anne Carol's introductory chapter in *Le 'Monstre Humain': Imaginaire et*

Société, ed. Régis Bertrand and Anne Carol (Aix-en-Provence, 2005), 15, 11. Carol cites the "process of triage" that began to separate "true monsters, now objects of study," from "fables and popular superstitions" in the eighteenth century.

45. Lynn, *Popular Science and Public Opinion.* On the "schools of physics," an observation by Jean-Baptiste Pujoulx, see 6; on the "singular, amazing" demonstrations of Nollet, 25.

46. *CA,* 16 Nov. 1764 (report from Paris, 8 Nov.) and 23 Nov. 1764 (report from Paris, 15 Nov.).

47. Magné de Marolles, "Précis Historique," in "Recueil factice," fol. 65r.

48. *CA,* 23 Nov. 1764 (report from Paris, 15 Nov.) and 30 Nov. 1764 (report from Paris, 22 Nov.).

49. *CA,* 23 Nov. 1764 (report from Paris, 15 Nov.).

50. *CA,* 30 Nov. 1764 (report from Paris, 22 Nov.).

51. Lafont to Saint-Priest, 30 Oct. 1764. ADH C 43.

52. Duhamel to Ballainvilliers, 20 Jan. 1765. ADPD 1 C 1731.

53. *GA,* 8 Feb. 1765; Magné de Marolles, "Précis Historique," in "Recueil factice," fol. 63v.

54. *GF,* 23 Nov. 1765.

55. "Relation et figure de la bête féroce qui ravage le Languedoc," ADL EDT 009 GG 4. The "Relation" is undated but it brings readers up to date on events through January of 1765.

56. Blanckaert, "Of Monstrous Métis?," 44–46.

57. *CA,* 30 Nov. 1764 (report from Paris, 22 Nov.).

58. Micheline Cuénin, ed., *Mémoires du Comte de Forbin (1656–1733)* (Paris, 1993), 172–173.

59. Moriceau discusses the case of the Lyonnais, *Histoire du Méchant Loup,* 333–334. The naturalist in question only published his findings in 1765. See Jean-Louis Alléon-Dulac, *Mémoires pour servir à l'Histoire Naturelle des Provinces de Lyonnais, Forez et Beaujolais* (Lyon, 1765).

60. Buffon, *Histoire Naturelle, Générale et Particulière; Avec la description du Cabinet du Roi,* vol. 9 (Paris, 1761), 277–278.

61. Ibid., 280.

62. AL (1765), vol. 1, 311–329, esp. 321. In the *Courrier d'Avignon's* issue of 19 February 1765, a letter sent from "the Gévaudan" on 7 February echoed the thoughts of Duhamel, as he expressed them in a personal letter to the comte de Lastic (see "Lettres inédites du Capitaine Duhamel sur la Bête du Gévaudan (octobre 1764–avril 1765)," *RGCC* nouvelle série 14 [1968], 147–149). The author of the letter in the *Courrier* explained: "It was thought, at the beginning, that [the beast] was a hyena; but the stories that have come in now have us convinced that it's an indefinable monster," one with "fire" in its eyes, and whose "talons terrify all who see them up close." The exact identity of the letter-writer cannot be determined, but Lafont's name and movements are the only ones specified in the letter, and the subdelegate would down-

play the likelihood of the hyena in his presentation to the Estates of the Gévaudan a few weeks later in March. The *Courrier*'s reliance on Lafont-supplied information on 22 November 1764 (when it related the beast's favored mode of attack) and 2 February 1765 (when it described the heroism of a local boy in Villeret) makes it safe to assume that Lafont was the source of the new skepticism on the hyena published by the *Courrier* on 19 February.

63. Robbins, *Elephant Slaves and Pampered Parrots,* 188.

64. Stanley J. Idzerda, ed., *Lafayette in the Age of the American Revolution: Selected Letters and Papers, 1776–1790* (Ithaca, N.Y., 1977), 1: 6.

65. *Histoire Naturelle, Générale et Particulière, Avec la Description du Cabinet du Roi,* 90 vols. (Paris, 1752–1805). For details of the publication history of Buffon's opus see Jacques Roger and E. Genet-Varcin, "Bibliographie de Buffon," in *Oeuvres philosophiques de Buffon,* ed. Jean Piveteau (Paris, 1954), 513–575, esp. 525.

66. Lafont to Saint-Priest, 30 Oct. 1764. ADH C 43.

67. Ballainvilliers to Saint-Florentin et al., 24 Sept. 1765. ADPD 1 C 1736. Elie Fréron, in his *Année Littéraire,* drew openly from Buffon in published correspondence from the spring of 1765. He wrote to a friend, "I have read, Monsieur, the article 'Hyena' in M. de Buffon's excellent *Natural History. . .*" See *AL* (1765) vol. 1, 323. For other references see Yannick Séité, "La Bête du Gévaudan dans les Gazettes: du Fait Divers à la Légende," in *Les Gazettes européennes de langue française (XVIIe–XVIIIe siècles),* ed. Henri Duranton, Claude Labrosse, and Pierre Rétat (Saint-Etienne, 1992), 145–153, esp. 152.

68. Morangiès to Lafont, 26 Oct. 1764. ADH C 44, folder "1764," no. 108.

69. "Extrait des délibérations des Etats du Gévaudan," 26 March 1765. ADL C 806.

70. Lafont to Saint-Priest, 30 Oct. 1764. ADH C 43.

71. *CA,* 30 Nov. 1764 (report from Paris, 22 Nov.).

72. Duhamel to unknown, late Nov., 1764, in Balmelle, "Lettres inédites du Capitaine Duhamel" [1967], 107.

73. *CA,* 23 Nov. 1764 (report from Paris, 15 Nov.).

74. Magné de Marolles, "Précis Historique," in "Recueil factice," fol. 66r.

75. Gabriel-Florent de Choiseul-Beaupré, "Mandement de monseigneur l'évêque de Mende pour ordonner des prières publiques à l'occasion de l'animal anthropophage qui désole le Gévaudan. Année 1764," in Pourcher, *La Bête du Gévaudan,* 55–59. All quotations from the *mandement* come from the Pourcher text.

76. Serge Colin, *Autour de la Bête du Gévaudan* (Le Puy-en-Velay, 1990), 81.

77. The attitudes of Pincemaille and Le Roy Ladurie have been noted. R. F. Dubois identified the bishop as the first in an unending line of individuals who forced their own interpretations on the phenomenon (Dubois, *Vie et Mort de la Bête,* 7); Xavier Pic faulted the bishop for invoking the supernatural and thus fueling belief in "an imaginary beast" (Pic, *La Bête qui Mangeaient le Monde,* 29); Jean-Marc Moriceau admonished the bishop for failing to bring "rationality" to the situation (*Histoire du Méchant Loup,* 184.) Richard H. Thompson accused "the aged prelate" of falling

into "the error of superstition," calling his *mandement* a "horrendous document." See *Wolf-Hunting in France in the Reign of Louis XV: The Beast of the Gévaudan* (Lewiston, N.Y., 1991), 77.

78. Such was d'Alembert's characterization of all who could be regarded as "Jansenists" in 1766. See *Sur la Destruction des Jésuites en France* (Paris, 1843), 35.

79. For representative examples in the last third of the century see Nigel Aston, *The End of an Elite: The French Bishops and the Coming of the Revolution, 1786–1790* (Oxford, 1992), 15–17.

80. Maurice Pezet, *L'Epopée des Camisards: Languedoc, Vivarais, Cévennes* (Paris, 1978).

81. Between 1726 and 1760 Protestants convened six national synods in the south of France; the largest and most threatening had occurred in lower Languedoc in 1744. *Histoire des Protestants en France: De la Réforme à la Révolution,* ed. Philippe Wolff (Toulouse, 2001), 205. On the alarm expressed by Languedoc's bishops see also James N. Hood, "Catholic-Protestant Relations and the Roots of the First Popular Counter-Revolutionary Movement in France," *JMH* 43 (1971): 245–275, esp. 253.

82. On their wide political influence, despite their constitution's prohibition of "meddling" in political affairs, see Harro Höpfl, *Jesuit Political Thought: The Society of Jesus and the State, c. 1540–1640* (Cambridge, 2004), esp. 53–63.

83. On Jansenist morals, and their critique of the Jesuits' "two-tiered system of natural and supernatural morality," see Dale K. Van Kley, *The Damiens Affair and the Unraveling of the Ancien Régime, 1750–1770* (Princeton, 1984), 83; and Van Kley, *The Jansenists and the Expulsion of the Jesuits from France, 1757–1765* (New Haven, Conn., 1975), 6–11.

84. Louis XV's prime minister Fleury nervously noted in 1734, for example, that "there are only too many links between Jansenists and Protestants." See John Mc-Manners, *Church and Society in Eighteenth-Century France* (Oxford, 1998), 2: 450.

85. Gabriel Florent Choiseul-Beaupré, *Lettre Pastorale de Monseigneur L'Evêque de Mende, adressée aux Ecclésiastiques de son Diocèse: pour justifier, contre un Libelle anonyme, la doctrine des Conférences de son Diocèse, sur la Grace efficace par elle-même, la Predestination gratuite, les Caractères de la Nouvelle Alliance, etc.* (Mende, 1761), 122–125. The first edition of this work had appeared in 1759.

86. McManners, *Church and Society,* 2: 40, 49.

87. Ibid., 51–53, esp. 51. On the controversial "convulsionaries" and the debates around them in the 1730s see Catherine Maire, "Les querelles jansénistes de la décennie 1730–1740," *Recherches sur Diderot et sur l'Encyclopédie* 38–39 (2005): 71–92.

88. On the association between natural prodigies and divine anger, see Daston and Park, *Wonders and the Order of Nature,* 177–190.

89. See Jean Beauvoys de Chauvincourt, *Discours de la Lycanthropie,* ed. Patrick Sbalchiero (Grenoble, 2009), 99–101. In 1615 Jean de Nynauld, who sought to counteract the demonological theories of Jean Bodin, stressed the illusory character of werewolf beliefs, but he also insisted that "God has reserved to himself the preroga-

tive of creating and transforming creatures into other species." Jean de Nynauld, *De la Lycanthropie, Transformation et Extase des Sorciers,* ed. Nicole Jacques-Chaquin and Maxime Préaud (Paris, 1990), 120.

90. As described in *Nouvelles Ecclésiastiques, ou Mémoires pour servir à l'Histoire de la Constitution Unigenitus, pour l'année 1765* (20 March 1765).

91. Van Kley, *The Damiens Affair,* 58.

92. Van Kley, *The Jansenists and the Expulsion of the Jesuits,* 9.

93. That the bishop read the tragic events of 1764 as an affirmation of timeless theological principles is shown in the opening lines of his provocative *mandement,* where he highlighted again—just as he had done in a 1761 treatise on grace—the instructive humility of King David, whose feelings of hopeless abandonment found expression in the book of Psalms. "*For how long, Lord, will you show an eternal anger? For how long will your wrath burn like fire?* To whom does this grief-stricken language apply," the bishop asked his listeners in 1764, "if not to us, on whom God's hand now weighs so heavily?" Cf. *Lettre Pastorale,* 4.

94. Van Kley, *The Damiens Affair,* 65–70, and *The Jansenists and the Expulsion of the Jesuits,* 65–71; McManners, *Church and Society,* 2: 542–546. On the likely role of Choiseul see Julian Swann, *Politics and the Parlement of Paris under Louis XV, 1754–1774* (Cambridge, 1995), 206–217.

95. For an account of the riot, see BM, ms. 2378, "Recueil d'anecdotes littéraires et politiques, 1765," 4 Jan. 1765.

96. See "Tableau Historique des évenemens politiques, militaires et intérieures des différentes cours de l'Europe, depuis la Paix de Paris du 10 fevrier 1763 jusqu'à la mort de Louis Quinze du 10 May 1774." AD, Mémoires et Documents, France, 560, fols. 214–220, esp. 218r.

97. *Nouvelles Ecclésiastiques,* 20 March 1765.

98. On the predominance of the clerical profession in the Gévaudan see Patrick Cabanel, *Cadets de Dieu: vocations et migrations religieuses en Gévaudan, XVIIIe–XXe siècle* (Paris, 1997), 93.

99. David D. Bien, *The Calas Affair: Persecution, Toleration, and Heresy in Eighteenth-Century Toulouse* (Princeton, 1960). The "spasmodic hostility" is mentioned on 28, though Bien emphasizes the more general "toleration by indifference" that characterized relations in Toulouse.

100. See, for example, the "Amendes contre les Nouveaux Convertis, année 1765." ADH C 387.

101. Hood, "Catholic-Protestant Relations," 253–254.

102. Saint-Florentin to Saint-Priest, 28 Feb. 1764. ADH C 451, no. 316.

103. Saint-Priest to Saint-Florentin, 8 April 1765. ADH C 452.

104. [Jean-Pierre Sers] to Saint-Priest, 10 Oct. 1765. ADH C 407, no. 68; "Interrogatoire," 14 Oct. 1765. ADH C 407, no. 60.

105. Saint-Priest to Saint-Florentin, 21 Oct. 1765. ADH C 407, no. 50. For his remark about guns, see Bossignac to Lafont, 4 March 1765, in ADH C 407, no. 55.

106. The prince de Conti, who conspired to rebel against his cousin Louis XV in the mid-1750s, entered into discussion with the English and with Protestants of the south of France, and Pitt had been led to believe that Huguenots would rise in rebellion if the English launched an attack on Rochefort. The Protestants of La Rochelle opposed the English in the end, but a significant number of Languedocian Protestants had favored the plan for rebellion. See John D. Woodbridge, *Revolt in Prerevolutionary France: The Prince de Conti's Conspiracy against Louis XV, 1755–1757* (Baltimore, 1995), esp. 55–66, 86, 99–116.

107. Hood, "Catholic-Protestant Relations," 258. Another sign of the relaxation of attitudes is the growing sensitivity to the demographic drain caused by persecutions. In the spring of 1764, Saint-Priest ordered all of his subdelegates to provide rough census figures on the Protestant population within their domains; he asked to be alerted to any correlation between population declines and repressive measures taken by the state. See ADH C 28, folder "1764."

108. Saint-Priest to Saint-Florentin, 11 Oct. 1765. ADH C 407, no. 54.

109. On the improved post-1763 atmosphere for Protestants see Wolff, ed., *Histoire des Protestants en France*, 206–231.

110. This is the interpretation of Catherine Velay-Vallantin, "Entre fiction et réalité: *Le Petit Chaperon Rouge* et la Bête du Gévaudan," *Gradhiva* 17 (1995): 111–126, esp. 118–119.

111. Serge Colin estimates that as many as one in six residents of the Gévaudan may have been Protestant, most found in communities of the Cévennes to the east and in the small western city of Malzieu. See Colin, *Autour de la Bête du Gévaudan,* 49–52.

112. The sensible subdelegate ultimately determined that the accusation grew out of a personal dispute between a Protestant minister and the embittered curé. See Degors to Saint-Priest, 25 July 1765. ADH 452, no. 2.

113. On the unpatriotic and disobedient tendencies that linked Protestants to Jesuits in the magistrates' eyes see Bien, *The Calas Affair,* 71.

114. *LC,* 2 Feb. 1765. A similar version of the story appeared in *The Gentleman's Magazine,* Feb. 1765, "Miscellaneous Articles from the Papers."

115. *CA,* 22 January 1765 (report from Mende, 9 Jan.).

3. Digesting Defeat

1. On the "crisis of confidence" see James C. Riley, *The Seven Years War and the Old Regime in France: The Economic and Financial Toll* (Princeton, 1986), esp. 192–222. See also Julian Swann, *Politics and the Parlement of Paris under Louis XV, 1754–1774* (Cambridge, 1995), 218–249.

2. Arlette Farge, *Dire et Mal Dire: L'Opinion Publique au XVIIIe siècle* (Paris, 1992), 272.

3. G-F. Magné de Marolles, "Précis Historique des ravages de la Bête féroce qui a

désolé si longtemps le Gévaudan et l'Auvergne, des chasses et battues qui ont été faites, et des divers moiens qu'on a tentés pour la détruire depuis son apparition au mois de Juin 1764, jusqu'à sa prise par M. Antoine Lieutenant des Chasses et Port-arquebuse de S. M. Le 20 Septembre 1765," in "Recueil factice de pièces relatives à la bête du Gévaudan, formé par Gervais-François Magné de Marolles," BNF M-1915, fol. 63v.

4. *CA,* 26 Feb. 1765 (report from Paris, 16 Feb.) and 5 March 1765 (report from Paris, 23 Feb.). The martial language is also highlighted in Yannick Séité, "La Bête du Gévaudan dans les Gazettes: du Fait Divers à la Légende," in *Les Gazettes européennes de langue française (XVIIe–XVIIIe siècles),* ed. Henri Duranton, Claude Labrosse, and Pierre Rétat (Saint-Etienne, 1992), 145–153.

5. Duhamel to Moncan, 24 Dec. 1764, in Marius Balmelle, "Un recueil inédit sur la Bête du Gévaudan (octobre 1764–avril 1765)," *Actes du Quatre-Vingtième Congrès des Sociétés Savantes* (Paris, 1955), 108–109.

6. *CA,* 1 Jan. 1765. On the early history of the *Courrier d'Avignon,* see René Moulinas, "Les journaux publiés à Avignon et leur diffusion en France jusqu'en 1768: contribution à l'histoire de la presse au XVIIIe siècle," *Provence Historique* 18 (1968): 121–138, esp. 126–127.

7. René Moulinas, *L'Imprimerie, la librairie et la presse à Avignon au XVIIIe siècle* (Grenoble, 1974), 297–305.

8. After a fitful but promising beginning in the seventeenth century, French periodical publishing, like book publishing, first took off in the early eighteenth century, with the 1730s serving as the launching pad. At least nine hundred new journal titles appeared in the course of the eighteenth century, compared to fewer than two hundred in the seventeenth. See Jean Sgard, "La multiplication des périodiques," in *Histoire de l'édition française: Le livre triomphant, 1660–1830,* ed. Roger Chartier and Henri-Jean Martin (Paris, 1990), 247–255.

9. For *Courrier* sales estimates, and its distribution schedule in 1733, see Moulinas, *L'Imprimerie, la librairie et la presse,* 347–350, 301; for sales comparisons see Gilles Feyel, "La diffusion des gazettes étrangères en France et la révolution postale des années 1750," in *Les Gazettes européennes de langue française,* ed. Duranton, Labrosse, and Rétat, 88.

10. Moulinas, *L'Imprimerie, la librairie et la presse,* 315–316, 319; for the sales figures of the *Gazette de France* see Gilles Feyel, *L'Annonce et la Nouvelle: La presse d'information en France sous l'Ancien Régime (1630–1788)* (Oxford, 2000), 543. On the possibility that the *Courrier*'s circulation estimates may have been inflated by competitors and resentful former employees of Giroud, see Feyel, *L'Annonce et la Nouvelle,* 530, n. 74.

11. Geneviève Bollème, *La Bibliothèque Bleue: Littérature Populaire en France du XVIIe au XIXe Siècle* (Paris, 1971); *La Bibliothèque Bleue et les Littératures de Colportage,* ed. Thierry DelCourt and Elisabeth Parinet (Paris, 2000).

12. Robert Favre, Jean Sgard, and Françoise Weil, "Le Fait Divers," in *Presse et*

Histoire au XVIIIe Siècle: L'Année 1734, ed. Pierre Rétat and Jean Sgard (Paris, 1978), 199–225, esp. 200.

13. Ibid., 200–201.

14. The authorities and their official organ the *Gazette de France,* writes Gilles Feyel, preferred not to countenance evidence of uncontained "social disorder." Feyel, *L'Annonce et la nouvelle,* 541. See also Françoise Weil, "Un épisode de la 'guerre' entre la *Gazette de France* et les gazettes hollandaises: l'échec du projet de transformation de la *Gazette de France* en 1762," in *Les Gazettes européennes de langue française,* 99–105, esp. 104. On the "subversive" potential of the eighteenth-century *fait divers* see Favre, Sgard, and Weil, "Le Fait Divers," 204.

15. The original title of the journal: *Le Courrier: Historique, Politique, Literaire Galant & Moral.* In his first paragraph Morénas signaled his desire to provide information of both the "useful and pleasing" varieties. See *Courrier,* 2 Jan. 1733.

16. *Courrier,* 30 Nov. 1734, quoted in Moulinas, *L'Imprimerie, la librairie et la presse,* 367, n. 8.

17. "The frequent accounts that come to us from the Gévaudan," he wrote in 1765, "are a sad supplement to the sterility of our other news." See *CA,* 26 Feb. 1765 (report from Paris, 16 Feb.).

18. Moulinas, *L'Imprimerie, la librairie et la presse,* 276.

19. Hans-Jürgen Lüsebrink, "Le tremblement de terre de Lisbonne dans des périodiques français et allemands du XVIIIe siècle," in *Gazettes et information politique sous l'Ancien Régime,* ed. Henri Duranton and Pierre Rétat (Saint-Etienne, 1999), 303–311, esp. 306, 308–309.

20. As cited in Moulinas, *L'Imprimerie, la librairie et la presse,* 360.

21. Moulinas, "Les journaux publiés à Avignon et leur diffusion en France jusqu'en 1768," 125; Feyel, *L'Annonce et la nouvelle,* 529.

22. Moulinas, *L'Imprimerie, la librairie et la presse,* 363. A publisher in Lyon moaned that the *Courrier* was in the process of "gaining the upper hand over the *Gazette* and ruining the realm by draining money away from the king and toward Avignon, for the benefit of a foreign publisher."

23. For the full history of this postal revolution, see Feyel, *L'Annonce et la nouvelle,* 691–706. Wide distribution and speedy delivery also became possible at mid-century because of the monarchy's efforts to improve roads and increase the political and commercial integration of the country. See Guy Arbellot, "La grande mutation des routes de France au milieu du XVIIIe siècle," *AESC* 28 (1973): 765–791.

24. Feyel, "La diffusion des gazettes étrangères en France," 97.

25. *CA,* 28 Sept. 1764 (report from Paris, 20 Sept.); 12 Oct. 1764 (report from Paris, 4 Oct.); 2 Nov. 1764 (report from Paris, 25 Oct.); 26 Oct. 1764 (report from Paris, 18 Oct.); 6 Nov. 1764 (report from London, 19 Oct.); 27 Nov. 1764 (report from Paris, 17 Nov.).

26. *CA,* 1 Jan. 1765.

27. The first story on "the beast" appeared in the issue of 16 Nov. 1764, the last in

the issue of 21 March 1766. On the total figures see Gérard Blanc, "Représentation du Gévaudan dans le 'Courrier d'Avignon' (1764–1765): de l'espace-information au territoire," in *Les Gazettes européennes de langue française*, 155–165, esp. 156.

28. *CA*, 15 Jan. 1765 (report from Mende, 2 Jan.).

29. *CA*, 18 Jan. 1765 (report from Marvejols, 2 Jan.).

30. *CA*, 12 March 1765 (report from Marvejols, 1 March). See also *Relation de la Figure & des Désordres commis par une Bête féroce qui ravage le Gévaudan depuis plusieurs mois; avec la Description d'un Combat remarquable que plusieurs Enfans soutinrent contre ce cruel Animal,* in "Recueil factice," fol. 34v. Morénas may instead have intended to confirm an observation made by Buffon, who had said of the wolf that its odor "excites such an aversion in the dog that he flies, and comes quivering to the feet of his master." Buffon, *Natural History, General and Particular, by the Count de Buffon,* trans. William Smellie (London, 1791), vol. 4, 198.

31. *CA*, 8 Jan. 1765 (report from Mende, 26 Dec. 1764).

32. *CA*, 18 Jan. 1765 (report from Marvejols, 2 Jan.).

33. *CA*, 29 Jan. 1765 (report from Mende, 18 Jan.). Italics added.

34. *CA*, 25 Jan. 1765 (report from Bas Languedoc, 12 Jan.).

35. *CA*, 26 Feb. 1765 (report from Paris, 16 Feb.) 26 March 1765 (report from Paris, 16 March).

36. Richard Waddington, *La Guerre de Sept Ans: Histoire Diplomatique et Militaire* (Paris, 1899), 1: 626.

37. Franz A. J. Szabo, *The Seven Years' War in Europe, 1756–1763* (Harlow, U.K., 2008), 98.

38. Waddington, *La Guerre de Sept Ans,* 1: 627.

39. Ibid., 636.

40. Abbé Bernis [to Choiseul-Stainville], 29 Nov. 1757. In François-Joachim de Pierre, cardinal de Bernis, *Mémoires et Lettres de François-Joachim de Pierre, cardinal de Bernis,* ed. Frédéric Masson (Paris, 1903), 2: 144.

41. Waddington, *La Guerre de Sept Ans,* 2: 31. On Clermont's long retreat see also Szabo, *The Seven Years' War,* 132–136, and Jonathan Dull, *The French Navy and the Seven Years' War* (Lincoln, Neb., 2005), 120.

42. Waddington, *La Guerre de Sept Ans,* 2: 37–40.

43. Ibid., 56–64. See also Serge Colin, "L'armée et la chasse à la Bête du Gévaudan: Le regiment de Clermont-Prince," *Bulletin Historique de la Société Académique du Puy-en-Velay et de la Haute-Loire* 80 (2004): 203–212, esp. 205.

44. For a review of French disappointments in North America, especially in the fateful year 1759, see Fred Anderson, *Crucible of War: The Seven Years' War and the Fate of Empire in British North America, 1754–1766* (New York, 2000), esp. 297–384.

45. On the wave of reforms that swept the military between 1763 and 1788, all inspired by the Seven Years' War, see Emile G. Léonard, *L'Armée et ses problèmes au XVIIIe siècle* (Paris, 1958), 239–257; Jay M. Smith, *The Culture of Merit: Nobility, Royal Service, and the Making of Absolute Monarchy in France, 1600–1789* (Ann Arbor, Mich.,

1996), 227–261; Rafe Blaufarb, *The French Army, 1750–1820: Careers, Talent, Merit* (Manchester, 2002), 16–45.

46. Abbé Bernis [to Choiseul-Stainville], 22 Nov. 1757 (for "cut to pieces") and 24 March 1758. In *Mémoires et Lettres,* 140, 193, 195–196.

47. The marquis de Caraman, as cited in Blaufarb, *The French Army, 1750–1820,* 16.

48. In his "Précis des Guerres de Frédéric II." See *Correspondance de Napoléon Ier,* ed. J. B. P. Vaillant (Paris, 1870), 32: 241.

49. The opinion is that of Horace Walpole. See Walpole to Lord and Lady Hertford, 9 March 1765, in *HWC,* ed. W. S. Lewis et al., vol. 38 (New Haven, Conn., 1974), 519. For the play's popular reception, and lukewarm critical reactions, see Edmond Dziembowski, *Un Nouveau Patriotisme Français, 1750–1770: La France Face à la Puissance Anglaise à l'Epoque de la Guerre de Sept Ans* (Oxford, 1998), 472–480; David A. Bell, *The Cult of the Nation in France: Inventing Nationalism, 1680–1800* (Cambridge, Mass., 2001), 63–65.

50. The play was performed at Versailles on 21 February, 7 March, and 21 March, with the famed Mademoiselle Clairon in the starring role. See AN O1 3013, "Année 1765, Versailles, Comédie Française."

51. Pierre Buirette de Belloy, *Le Siège de Calais, tragédie: Par M. de Belloy. Représentée pour la première fois, par les Comédiens Français ordinaires du Roi, le 13 Février 1765. Suivie de notes historiques* (Glasgow, 1765), 4. The original: *Malheur aux Nations qui, cédant à l'orage/Laissent par les revers avilir leur courage.*

52. SHAT Yb 656, 13, and 1 Yf 9292.

53. Duhamel to M. de Seuroin, secrétaire des commandemens de SAS Mgr le comte de Clermont, 20 March 1765, in Marius Balmelle, "Lettres inédites du Capitaine Duhamel sur la Bête du Gévaudan (octobre 1764–avril 1765)," *RGCC* 15 (1969): 118–135, esp. 121.

54. Duhamel to M. de Seuroin, 13 Feb. 1765, in Marius Balmelle, "Lettres inédites du Capitaine Duhamel sur la Bête du Gévaudan (octobre 1764–avril 1765)," *RGCC* 14 (1968): 136–158, esp. 152–154.

55. Duhamel to Clermont, undated, in Marius Balmelle, "Lettres inédites du Capitaine Duhamel" [1969], 128.

56. Duhamel to unidentified recipient, [24–30 Nov.] 1764, in Marius Balmelle, "Lettres inédites du Capitaine Duhamel sur la Bête du Gévaudan (Octobre 1764–Avril 1765)," *RGCC* 13 (1967), 107. On the specifications for the dragoon uniform, see Colin, "L'armée et la chasse à la Bête du Gévaudan," 209.

57. Duhamel to comte de Lastic, 12 Feb. 1765, in Balmelle, "Lettres inédites du Capitaine Duhamel sur la Bête du Gévaudan" [1968], 149.

58. "Diocese de Mende, Subdelegation de Mende." ADH C 60. This document, drafted in the mid-1770s, shows that the comte inherited seigneurial rights over at least eleven parishes in the diocese, containing scores of villages. The bishop of

Mende controlled more than twice as many, but no other secular lord rivaled Morangiès in standing or importance.

59. Paul vicomte de Lescure, *Armorial du Gévaudan* (Lyon, 1929), 58–59; see also Frédéric Dussaud, *Le Château de Morangiès et ses Seigneurs* (Nîmes, 2004), 66.

60. Jean-Marc Moriceau, *La Bête du Gévaudan* (Paris, 2008), 272–276.

61. Lafont to Saint-Priest, 30 Oct. 1764. ADH C 43. On the victim's identity, François Fabre, *La Bête du Gévaudan,* ed. Jean Richard (Clermont-Ferrand, 2001), Tableau des victimes.

62. Morangiès to Lafont, 26 Oct. 1764. ADH C 44, folder "1764," no. 108.

63. *CA,* 22 Jan. 1765 (report from Rodez, 9 Jan.). For "beauty of her canton," see comte de Brioude to Fréron in *AL* (1765), vol. 2, 107. For commentary on the age and gender of the victims see *CA,* 19 Feb. 1765 (report from the Gévaudan, 7 Feb.). For more examples of the attention given to the beauty of female victims, see *AL* (1765), vol. 3, 28; *CA,* 16 April 1765 (report from Marvejols, 6 April); 23 April 1765 (report from Marvejols, 14 April).

64. On male honor see George L. Mosse, *The Image of Man: The Creation of Modern Masculinity* (Oxford, 1996), 17–19. The imperative to protect and avenge informs the essence of male honor, for as J. K. Campbell writes: "Manliness implies not only the condition of being courageous but the ability of a man to do something efficient and effective about the problems and dangers which surround him." Campbell, "Honour and the Devil," in *Honour and Shame: The Values of Mediterranean Society,* ed. J. G. Peristiany (London, 1965), 141–170, esp. 145–146.

65. The episode is discussed in a later chapter. For Morangiès's visit, see *CA,* 26 March 1765 (report from Marvejols, 17 March).

66. Morangiès to Lafont, 26 Oct. 1764 and 28 Oct. 1764. ADH C 44, folder "1764," no. 108.

67. Morangiès to Lafont, 26 Oct. 1764 and 29 Oct. 1764. ADH C 44, folder "1764," no. 108.

68. Morangiès to Lafont, 28 Oct. 1764. ADH C 44, folder "1764," no. 108.

69. Lafont to Saint-Priest, 2 April 1765. ADH C 44, folder "avril 1765," no. 235. Lafont reported to Saint-Priest that Morangiès had communicated with the minister of war, and that Choiseul's *premier commis de la guerre,* Duboy, had supported the idea of putting Morangiès in charge, but that they had waited approximately two months for a definitive answer from Choiseul himself. The reference to "cruel animal" comes from Morangiès to Lafont, 26 Oct. 1764. ADH C 44, folder "1764," no. 108.

70. Colin, "L'armée et la chasse à la Bête du Gévaudan," 204–205.

71. On the efforts of the seigneur de La Coste of Pradelles, who lobbied for control over the hunts around Langogne in October of 1764, see Serge Colin, "Le Colonel des montagnes et la Bête du Gévaudan," *Société Académique du Puy-en-Velay et de la Haute-Loire* 81 (2005): 171–179.

72. On 14 October Moncan thanked Duhamel "for the offer you have made" to take charge of the hunt. See Balmelle, "Un recueil inédit sur la Bête du Gévaudan," 103; for Duhamel's reference to his request to Moncan see Duhamel [to Roussel], undated [January 1765], in Balmelle, "Lettres inédites du Capitaine Duhamel" [1967], 112. For "honored" and "gallant" see Duhamel to Moncan, 1 Nov. 1764, ibid., 99. The evidence for Roussel's patronage of Duhamel is circumstantial but strong. The captain mentioned to Roussel that his mother "is aware of all that I owe you" and regretted having recently missed the chance to visit in person to give her own thanks for his generosity. Duhamel also asked that his greetings be extended to Roussel's wife, who may have been the true power broker. Mme. Roussel can be seen, for example, intervening with Saint-Florentin on behalf of another client who sought the lieutenancy of the chateau of Vincennes in March of 1766. See Duhamel to Roussel in ibid., 111–114, and AN O1 589, folder "Minutes des Lettres du Ministre [de la Maison du Roi], 1766," 7 March 1766.

73. Duhamel to Lafont, 29 Oct. 1764, in Balmelle, "Lettres inédites du Capitaine Duhamel" [1967], 98; Lafont to Saint-Priest, 30 Oct. 1764. ADH C 43.

74. Duhamel to Moncan, 1 Nov. 1764, in Balmelle, "Lettres inédites du Capitaine Duhamel" [1967], 99–100.

75. Lafont to Saint-Priest, 4 Nov. 1764, in ADH C 43.

76. Duhamel to unidentified, 1 Nov. 1764, in Balmelle, "Lettres inédites du Capitaine Duhamel" [1967], 103. The recipient of the letter is not identified, but the governor is one of only two local dignitaries to whom the letter could conceivably have been addressed. The only other possible recipient is the bishop of Mende, but Duhamel would pay him a personal visit within days.

77. *Dictionnaire de l'Académie Française,* 4th ed. (Paris, 1762). The definitions of *galant* and *galant homme* included: "A man who has integrity, civil, sociable, of good company and agreeable conversation"; it was said of someone who gives "satisfaction" by his deeds, and it applied to "diverse things that are considered agreeable and respected in their way."

78. As, for example, in Duhamel to Moncan, 29 Nov. 1764, in "Lettres inédites du Capitaine Duhamel" [1967], 115–116, and Duhamel to Seuroin, 20 March 1765, in "Lettres inédites du Capitaine Duhamel" [1969], 120.

79. Duhamel to Choiseul-Beaupré, 19 Nov. 1764, in Balmelle, "Lettres inédites du Capitaine Duhamel" [1967], 106–107.

80. Duhamel to Morangiès, 13 Feb. 1765, in Balmelle, "Lettres inédites du Capitaine Duhamel" [1968], 150–151.

81. Moncan to Duhamel, 14 Oct. 1764, in Balmelle, "Un recueil inédit sur la Bête du Gévaudan," 103.

82. Duhamel [to Roussel], undated [January 1765], in "Lettres inédites du Capitaine Duhamel" [1967], 114.

83. Duhamel to Moncan, 19 Nov. 1764, in Balmelle, "Un recueil inédit sur la Bête du Gévaudan" [1955], 105.

84. For "cruel" and "dangerous," see Morangiès to Lafont, 28 Oct. 1764 and 26 Oct. 1764; for "Monster," "Africa," "lion," peasants, and "Beast," see Morangiès to Lafont, 26 Oct. 1764. ADH C 44, folder "1764," no. 108.

85. Duhamel to Lafont, 19 Nov. 1764. ADH C 43. Discussing an encounter related by a local grenadier, Duhamel told Lafont that the man "described it, and I found it similar to what has been depicted [by others]." Later in the same letter, he reported that a peasant's secondhand description of the beast, provided by a traveler passing through the region, "is exactly similar to that provided by all who have seen this animal."

86. Lafont to Saint-Priest, 23 Nov. 1764. ADH C 43.

87. Duhamel to unidentified, November 1764, in Balmelle, "Lettres inédites du Capitaine Duhamel" [1967], 107. Again it seems likely that the recipient was the comte d'Eu, governor of Languedoc and highest ranking dignitary in the province. Duhamel closed the letter by declaring, "you will be the first to know" when "my wishes have been granted."

88. Duhamel to Moncan, 19 Nov. 1764, in Balmelle, "Un recueil inédit sur la Bête du Gévaudan" [1955], 104.

89. The details are culled from three letters: Duhamel to Choiseul-Beaupré, 30 Nov. 1764, in Balmelle, "Un recueil inédit sur la Bête du Gévaudan (octobre 1764–avril 1765)" [1955], 110; Duhamel to Moncan, 29 Nov. 1764, in Balmelle, "Lettres inédites du Capitaine Duhamel" [1967], 117; Duhamel to unidentified, [24–30 Nov.] 1764, in ibid., 107.

90. Morangiès to Lafont, 26 Oct. 1764. ADH C 44, folder "1764," no. 108.

91. For details of the Auvergne case, see Duhamel to Ballainvilliers, 25 Jan. 1765. ADPD 1 C 1731. For Javols, see Lafont to Saint-Priest, 16 Feb. 1765. ADH C 44, folder "janvier 1765," no. 121.

92. Duhamel to unidentified, [24–30 Nov.] 1764, in Balmelle, "Lettres inédites du Capitaine Duhamel" [1967], 108; Duhamel to Moncan, 29 Nov. 1764, ibid., 119.

93. Duhamel to Moncan, 29 Nov. 1764, in Balmelle, "Lettres inédites du Capitaine Duhamel" [1967], 115, 118–119; Duhamel to unidentified, [24–30 Nov.] 1764, in ibid., 107.

94. Duhamel to Ballainvilliers, 24 Dec. 1764. ADPD 1 C 1731.

95. Duhamel [to Roussel], undated [early January 1765], in "Lettres inédites du Capitaine Duhamel" [1967], 112–115.

96. Saint-Florentin to Saint-Priest, 16 Dec. 1764. ADH C 44, folder "1764," no. 116; Saint-Florentin later noted in a letter to Ballainvilliers that experience had shown "what kind of success we can expect from the detachment of troops." See Saint-Florentin to Ballainvilliers, 31 Dec. 1764. ADPD 1 C 1731. In that same letter, he actually announced that "we have decided to recall the [detachment of troops]." For

some time Ballainvilliers himself believed that the orders had been given. See, for example, Ballainvilliers to Montluc, 30 Jan. 1765. ADPD 1 C 1731. Saint-Florentin evidently changed his mind after discussions with the military commandant of Languedoc.

97. Duhamel to the comte d'Eu, 24 Dec. 1764, in Balmelle, "Lettres inédites du Captaine Duhamel" [1967], 120.

98. Duhamel also reported to his friend Roussel that he and his dragoons were "mortified" at the thought that they would have to cease and desist without having finished the task. They would be willing to carry on, living off "bread and water" alone if necessary. He even requested permission from Moncan to continue on without compensation. See Duhamel [to Roussel], undated [early January 1765], in "Lettres inédites du Capitaine Duhamel" [1967], 115.

99. *CA*, 18 Jan. 1765 (report from Marvejols, 2 Jan.) and 25 Jan. 1765 (report from Bas Languedoc, 12 Jan.).

100. Duhamel to Lafont, 2 April 1765, in Balmelle, "Lettres inédites du Capitaine Duhamel" [1969], 124.

101. *Relation de la Figure & des Désordres commis par une Bête féroce qui ravage le Gévaudan depuis plusieurs mois; avec la Description d'un Combat remarquable que plusieurs Enfans soutinrent contre ce cruel Animal*, 5 March 1765, in "Recueil factice," fol. 34r. The author of the piece explained that Duhamel "would have massacred" the beast if not for bad luck.

102. Duhamel to Moncan, 24 Dec. 1764, in Balmelle, "Un recueil inédit sur la Bête du Gévaudan" [1955], 108–109.

103. Duhamel to comte de Lastic, 12 Feb. 1765, in Balmelle, "Lettres inédites du Capitaine Duhamel" [1968], 147.

104. Duhamel [to Ballainvilliers], 20 Jan. 1765. ADPD 1 C 1731.

105. Duhamel to [Roussel], undated [early January 1765], in Balmelle, "Lettres inédites du Capitaine Duhamel" [1967], 115.

106. The captain noted disapprovingly that "the artist in Mende never consulted me with regard to the copy he made of the engraving I had the honor of presenting to M. the bishop," in Duhamel to [the comte de Lastic], 12 Feb. 1765, in Balmelle, "Lettres inédites du Capitaine Duhamel" [1968], 147. Duhamel received thanks for the engraving from the governor, who nevertheless still awaited "the death of the original." See comte d'Eu to Duhamel, 2 Feb. 1765, in Balmelle, "Lettres inédites du Capitaine Duhamel" [1968], 142. On Ballainvilliers see Duhamel [to Ballainvilliers], 20 Jan. 1765. ADPD 1 C 1731. One can infer that Saint-Priest also received a copy, given the language of the comte d'Eu to Saint-Priest, 24 Feb. 1765. ADH C 44, folder "Jeune Portefaix," no. 4. (The comte d'Eu, whose full name was Louis-Charles de Bourbon, comte-pair d'Eu, signed in this instance, as he occasionally did, as the comte de Bourbon.) On Roussel and the comte de Clermont, "to whom I wanted to send a copy," see Duhamel [to Roussel], in Balmelle, "Lettres inédites du Capitain Duhamel" [1967], 115.

107. Comte de Bourbon [comte d'Eu] to Saint-Priest, 24 Feb. 1765. ADH C 44, folder "Jeune Portefaix, 1765–1785," no. 4.

108. Caylus to père Paciaudi, 3 March 1765. Anne Claude Philippe de Tubières, comte de Caylus, *Correspondance inédite du comte de Caylus avec le P. Paciaudi, Théatin (1757–1765): suivie de celles de l'abbé Barthélemy et de P. Mariette avec le même,* ed. Charles Nisard (Paris, 1877), 98.

109. Duhamel [to Ballainvilliers], 20 Jan. 1765. ADPD 1 C 1731.

110. *CA,* 18 Jan. 1765 (report from Marvejols, 2 Jan.); *GL,* 1 Feb. 1765.

111. Duhamel to comte de Lastic, 12 Feb. 1765, in Balmelle "Lettres inédites du Capitaine Duhamel" [1968], 147.

112. On Duhamel's severity, which included forced billeting, and his use of traps see Duhamel to Moncan, 20 Jan. 1765, in Balmelle, "Lettres inédites du Capitaine Duhamel" [1968], 137; complaints, and justifications, for Duhamel's severe tactics are detailed in Montluc to Ballainvilliers, 26 Jan. 1765 (ADPD 1 C 1731), and Lafont [to Saint-Priest], 16 Feb. 1765. ADH C 44, folder "février 1765," no. 123.

113. Early in February the governor complained to Duhamel, hyperbolically, "for a century, I have heard no news from you!" See comte d'Eu to Duhamel, 2 Feb. 1765, in Balmelle, "Lettres inédites du Capitaine Duhamel" [1968], 142.

114. Duhamel [to Saint-Priest], 20 Jan. 1765, in Balmelle, "Lettres inédites du Capitaine Duhamel" [1968], 136.

115. Duhamel to Moncan, 20 Jan. 1765, in Balmelle, "Lettres inédites du Capitaine Duhamel" [1968], 137. The February tensions are discussed below. Duhamel's willingness to dress his dragoons in women's costume, and the expectations of success that he imputed to the local peasantry, suggest that he may have tapped into a tradition of disguise that villagers had deployed against wolves or other predators in earlier generations. The existence of such a tradition would provide another perspective on the so-called "war of the demoiselles"—rural protests that involved males dressed as women—that took place in the Pyrenees in 1829–1831. For an account of that later episode of male masquerade, one that focuses especially on the persistent belief in "white fairies" of the woods, see Peter Sahlins, *Forest Rites: The War of the Demoiselles in Nineteenth-Century France* (Cambridge, Mass., 1994).

116. *GF,* 18 Feb. 1765, and *GL,* 26 Feb. 1765. The correspondent for the *Gazette de France* observed, after detailing the plan of the dragoons-in-disguise, "let us hope that all of these measures . . . will deliver us from this terrible animal whose ferocity and audacity seem to grow by the day."

117. The dragoons had been placed at Aumont, Pueche, Beauregard, Termes, Albaret-le-Comtal, Prunières, Escaires, and Reymes. A thirteen-year-old boy was attacked near Termes on 6 February, but this was not the incident reported by Duhamel. See Duhamel to Lastic, 12 Feb. 1765, in Balmelle, "Lettres inédites du Capitaine Duhamel" [1968], 148.

118. Ballainvilliers to Saint-Florentin, 2 Feb. 1765. ADPD 1 C 1731.

119. For an overview of the November hunts, and Duhamel's early tactics, see Moriceau, *La Bête du Gévaudan,* 44–48.

120. Lafont to Saint-Priest [undated]. "Objets des lettres de M. Lafont qu'il convient de remettre sous les yeux de M. l'Intendant pour qu'il se determine sur les ordres qu'on luy demande." ADH C 44, folder "janvier, 1765," no. 119; on the firearms and other specifications see also the ordinance drafted for Montluc's subdelegation in Auvergne, 1 Feb. 1765. ADPD 1 C 1732. Montluc asked all the "Gentilshommes" nominally in charge of their subjects to "allow muskets only to those with long experience using them."

121. The general hunt gathered people from seventy-three parishes of the Gévaudan, twenty of Auvergne, and a handful of others from neighboring Rouergue to the west.

122. This is the inference drawn from Montluc's initial orders, which had the hunters of Auvergne converging at La Garde, just east of Saint-Just and northwest of Malzieu. See 1 Feb. 1765, ADPD 1 C 1732; a report from Malzieu relayed in the *Courrier d'Avignon* of 26 February placed the point of convergence just west of the river Truyère.

123. Most of what follows comes from Lafont's detailed account of the hunt. See "Objets des lettres de M. Lafont," 16 Feb. 1765. ADH C 44, folder "janvier, 1765," no. 119.

124. Ibid. For news coverage of the vicar, see *GF,* 15 March 1765, and *GL,* 22 March 1765; for the comments of Magné de Marolles, see "Précis Historique," in "Recueil factice," fol. 68v.

125. For the friction between Duhamel, Brun, and their respective supporters in Malzieu see the "Objets des lettres de M. Lafont," and Lafont to Saint-Priest on 16 Feb. 1765. ADH C 44, folder "février, 1765," no. 121.

126. Saint-Florentin to Saint-Priest, 10 March 1765. ADH C 44, folder "mars 1765," no. 183.

127. Lafont, "Objets des lettres." The girl was characterized as "young and pretty" in an April letter from Tardieu de Labarthe (Labarthe *fils*), a notable of Marvejols, to Elie Fréron, publisher of the *Année Littéraire.* See *AL* (1765), vol. 3, 28.

128. *AL* (1765), vol. 3, 29.

129. Lafont, "Objets des lettres." Lafont mentions his delay in Lafont to Saint-Priest, 16 Feb. 1765. ADH C 44, folder "janvier, 1765," no. 121.

130. Duhamel to M. de Seuroin, 13 Feb. 1765, in Balmelle, "Lettres inédites du Capitaine Duhamel" [1968], 152.

131. Duhamel to comte de Lastic, 12 Feb. 1765, in ibid., 147–149.

132. Ibid., letter of 13 Feb. 1765 to Morangiès, 150–151.

133. *CA,* 12 March 1765 (report from Marvejols, 1 March).

134. *CA,* 19 Feb. 1765 (report from Mende, 8 Feb.).

135. The alleged werewolf Jean Grenier had testified to the fact in 1603. See Pierre de Lancre, *Tableau de l'Inconstance des Mauvais Anges et Démons: Où il est amplement*

traité des sorciers et de la sorcellerie, ed. Nicole Jacques-Chaquin (Paris, 1982), 215. A judge from the period, Henry Boguet, also reported that "the clothing of children that [werewolves] have killed and eaten was found whole and undisturbed in the fields, as if a person had undressed them." See Michel Meurger, "L'Homme-Loup et son Témoin: Construction d'une Factualité Lycanthropique," in Jean de Nynauld, *De la Lycanthropie, Transformation et Extase des Sorciers,* ed. Nicole Jacques-Chaquin and Maxime Préaud (Paris, 1990), 143–179, esp. 154–155.

136. *CA,* 26 Feb. 1765 (report from Paris, 16 Feb.). For the "tender flesh," see report from Marvejols, 17 Feb.

137. *CA,* 26 Feb. 1765 (report from Marvejols, 17 Feb.).

138. *CA,* 22 Feb. 1765 (report from Marvejols, 11 Feb.).

139. *CA,* 1 March 1765 (report from Paris, 21 Feb.).

140. *CA,* 23 April 1765 (report from Avignon, 22 April).

141. Duhamel to Lastic, 1 March 1765, in Balmelle, "Lettres inédites du Capitaine Duhamel" [1968], 156; also Duhamel to Seuroin, 20 March 1765, in Balmelle, "Lettres inédites du Capitaine Duhamel" [1969], 118.

142. Duhamel to Clermont, undated [late March], in Balmelle,"Lettres inédites du Capitaine Duhamel" [1969], 128.

143. Duhamel to comte de Lastic, 12 Feb. 1765, in Balmelle, "Lettres inédites du Capitaine Duhamel" [1968], 147; also Duhamel to Moncan, 2 April 1765, in Balmelle, "Lettres inédites du Capitaine Duhamel," [1969], 123.

144. Horace Walpole to Horace Mann, 26 March 1765, in *HWC,* vol. 38 (New Haven, Conn., 1974), 289.

145. As he admitted to Lafont. See Duhamel to Lafont, 2 April 1765, in Balmelle, "Lettres inédites du Capitaine Duhamel" [1969], 124.

146. *CA,* 23 April 1765 (report from Avignon, 22 April). This letter, dated 9 April, was intended in part as a vindication of Duhamel, whose "intelligence and zeal" had not received their due. Morangiès wished to set the record straight by correcting misattributions (in which he had been given credit for actions taken by Duhamel) from earlier issues of the *Courrier.*

147. See Lafont's defense of Duhamel in Lafont to Saint-Priest, 16 Feb. 1765. ADH C 44, folder "février, 1765," no. 121. Duhamel himself also reported on kind words by the lawyer Bès de la Bessière. See Duhamel to Lafont, 29 March 1765, in Balmelle, "Lettres inédites du Capitaine Duhamel" [1967], 105.

148. Duhamel to Lastic, 12 Feb. 1765, in Balmelle, "Lettres inédites du Capitaine Duhamel" [1968], 148.

4. A Star Is Born

1. Benedict Anderson, *Imagined Communities: Reflections on the Origin and Spread of Nationalism* (London, 1991).

2. *Dictionnaire de l'Académie Française,* editions of 1694, 1762, 1798, and 1832.

3. Jürgen Habermas, *The Structural Transformation of the Public Sphere: An Inquiry into a Category of Bourgeois Society,* trans. Thomas Burger (Cambridge, Mass., 1991).

4. Paul Benhamou, "La lecture publique des journaux," *Dix-huitième siècle* 24 (1992): 283–295; and "Inventaire des instruments de lecture publique des gazettes," in *Les Gazettes européennes de langue française (XVIIe–XVIIIe Siècles),* ed. Henri Duranton, Claude Labrosse, and Pierre Rétat (Saint-Etienne, 1992), 121–129, esp. 127. On libraries and reading rooms, see also Roger Chartier, *The Cultural Uses of Print in Early-Modern France,* trans. Lydia Cochrane (Princeton, 1987), 209–218. On Nantes, see 211.

5. As cited in Benhamou, "La lecture publique des journaux," 284–285.

6. The almanachs, in particular, devoted more space to news over the course of the eighteenth century. See Pierre Rétat, "Gazette et almanach: l'année 1727," in *Presse et Evénement: Journaux, Gazettes, Almanachs (XVIIIe–XIXe Siècles),* ed. Hans-Jürgen Lüsebrink and Jean-Yves Mollier (New York, 2000), 79–95; and Rolf Reichardt and Christine Vogel, "Textes et Images: Evénements visualisés dans les *Messagers Boiteux* Franco-Allemands (1750 à 1850)," in *Presse et Evénement,* 207–274. For examples of specific borrowings by popular almanachs, see Lüsebrink's discussion of the legend of Louis Mandrin, "Des 'Messagers Boiteux/Hinkinde Boten' à la Bibliothèque Bleue: Filiations Textuelles et Rapports Interculturels," in *La Bibliothèque Bleue et les Littératures de Colportage,* ed. Thierry DelCourt and Elisabeth Parinet (Paris, 2000), 267–280, esp. 271–273.

7. Mme. Doublet's newssheet repeated the *Gazette de France* almost word for word in one instance in 1749. See Robert Darnton, "Mademoiselle Bonafon and the Private Life of Louis XV: Communication Circuits in Eighteenth-Century France," *Representations* 87 (2004): 102–124, esp. 110. See also Françoise Weil, "Les Gazettes Manuscrites avant 1750," in *Le Journalisme d'Ancien Régime: Questions et Propositions,* ed. Pierre Rétat (Lyon, 1982), 93–100; François Moureau, "Pour un Dictionnaire des Nouvelles à la Main," in *Le Journalisme d'Ancien Régime,* 21–26.

8. Frederick II to d'Alembert, 24 March 1765. *Oeuvres de Frédéric le Grand,* ed. J. D. E. Preuss (Berlin, 1854), 24: 437. Grimm noted in his April newssheet, "The *Gazette de France* has busied itself, for several months, detailing in all their splendor the exploits of a new species. With each issue, one finds a moving narrative of the ravages of the wild beast of the Gévaudan." *CL,* ed. Maurice Tourneux (Paris, 1878), 6: 254–255.

9. Magné de Marolles acknowledged that the *Courrier's* "truthfulness is not that well established in the minds of a lot of right-thinking people," but he was nonetheless "convinced" that the journal "can be believed in this matter." See "Précis Historique," in "Recueil factice de pièces relatives à la bête du Gévaudan formé par Gervais-François Magné de Marolles," BNF M-1915, fol. 63v.

10. *CA,* 15 Jan. 1765 (report from Mende, 2 Jan.). Cf. *GA,* 29 Jan. 1765. To see the

pattern compare the *Courrier*'s editions of 14 May and 18 June with those of the *Gazette d'Amsterdam* on 24 May and 2 July.

11. *GL,* 12 Feb. 1765. The *St. James's Chronicle* was open about its parasitic ways. After its account of the episode at the Darissatis bridge, the editors added: "We think it high time to acquaint our readers, that all the accounts relating to this animal, are taken originally from the Brussels Gazette." *SJC,* 12 Feb. 1765. The adventurer and publicist-for-hire Jean-Henri Maubert de Gouvest, who acquired the privilege for the *Gazette de Bruxelles* in 1759, supposedly made the paper "proverbial for want of veracity"; in England, at least, the paper was called "Maubert's lying Brussels Gazette." See *The General Biographical Dictionary,* ed. Alexander Chalmers (Oxford, 1815), 21: 475.

12. Alain Nabarra, "Le journalisme à la recherche de lui-même au XVIIIe siècle: Les modalités de l'information," *Cahiers de l'Association internationale des études françaises* 48 (1996): 21–41, esp. 27.

13. Two of his lower officers had given chase, "mais un maudit marais impraticable les força d'abandonner leur proye." Duhamel to [Roussel], undated [January 1765], in Marius Balmelle, "Lettres inédites du Capitaine Duhamel sur la Bête du Gévaudan (octobre 1764–avril 1765)," *RGCC* 13 (1967), 113. See also Duhamel to Ballainvilliers, 24 Dec. 1764. ADPD 1 C 1731.

14. A citizen of Saint-Chély, where the dragoons were stationed, identified this dragoon as a lower officer named Dulaurier. See the account of M. Bès de la Bessière in Auguste André, "La Bête du Gévaudan: Notice Historique," *Bulletin de la Société d'Agriculture, Industrie, Sciences et Arts du Départment de La Lozère* 35 (1884): 189–210, esp. 192–193.

15. *GA,* 8 Feb. 1765; *LC,* 11 Feb. 1765; *Relation de la Figure & des Désordres commis par une Bête féroce qui ravage le Gévaudan depuis plusieurs mois; avec la Description d'un Combat remarquable que plusieurs Enfans soutinrent contre ce cruel Animal,* 5 March 1765, in "Recueil factice," fol. 34r.

16. *Relation Générale et circonstanciée de tous les Désordres commis par la Bête qui ravage le Gévaudan & les Pays circonvoisins.* ADH C 44, folder "1764," no. 10.

17. *GA,* 8 Feb. 1765; on the light touch, see *CA,* 5 Feb. 1765 (report from Marvejols, 27 Jan.). See also Frederick II to d'Alembert, 24 March 1765, in *Oeuvres,* vol. 24, 437.

18. Montluc to Ballainvilliers, 13 Feb. 1765. ADPD 1 C 1732. See the burial notice for Marie Pounhet, in the parish of Fontans, in ADL 4 E 063 1.

19. *JE* (March 1765), vol. 2, pt. 3, 165.

20. *GA,* 22 March 1765. The same incident was reported in the *GF,* 15 March 1765.

21. *JE,* May 1765, vol. 3, pt. 3, 166.

22. For "rather significant," see *AL* (1765), vol. 3, 28; on "passing erect," see *SJC,* 16 March 1765.

23. *SJC,* 5 March 1765.

24. *AL* (1765), vol. 1, 314.

25. *LC,* 27 March 1765.

26. Walpole took a close interest in the beast during his long stay in France in 1765. With the same tone of wry detachment found in the *Chronicle,* he kept his English friends apprised of new developments. In an incriminating letter to Horace Mann on 26 March—one day before publication of the *Chronicle's* story—he compared the beast to the dragon of Wantley. See *HWC,* ed. W. S. Lewis et al., vol. 38 (New Haven, Conn., 1974), 289.

27. See AD, Mémoires et Documents, Fonds Divers Angleterre, 59, fols. 4–7, 55–60, 63–65, 69–70. In one article that complained about Great Britain's premature (and overly generous) peace terms with the French in 1763, the writer explained that the opposition party in Parliament wanted citizens to believe that "England is going to exterminate France" (fol. 4).

28. BM, ms. 2378, "Recueil d'anecdotes littéraires et politiques, 1765, vol. 1," 14 April 1765. According to François Moureau, this particular newssheet was destined for Charles de Brosse, a *président* in the *parlement* of Burgundy. See Moureau, *Répertoire des Nouvelles à la Main: Dictionnaire de la presse manuscrite clandestine, XVIe-XVIIIe siècle* (Oxford, 1999), 303.

29. *CA,* 26 April 1765 (report from Paris, 18 April).

30. Gabriel-François Coyer, *Suite des Bagatelles Morales* (London, 1769), 167.

31. *CA,* 3 Jan. 1766.

32. See *CA,* 12 Feb. 1765 (report from Mende, 31 Jan.); 19 Feb. 1765 (report from Paris, 9 Feb.); 1 March 1765 (report from Paris, 21 Feb); 26 March 1765 (report from Paris, 16 March).

33. Magné de Marolles wrote in the margins of the first page of his collection that he believed the dossier might "prove useful to the government" should any similar event occur in the future. "Recueil factice," fol. 1r. On the d'Enneval correspondence, see fol. 63r.

34. On the growing presence of the popular *complaintes* among the materials distributed by *colporteurs,* see Chartier, *The Cultural Uses of Print,* 233–234.

35. Créquy engages in a lengthy discussion of the origins of the tune and lyrics of the popular ditty. See *Souvenirs de la Marquise de Créquy: 1710–1802,* ed. Maurice Cousin de Courchamps (Paris, 1834), 62–64.

36. "*Sur la Bête Monstrueuse et Cruelle du Gévaudan,*" in "Recueil factice," fols. 93–96. The original reads:

Falloit-il que l'enfer eût vomi de son sein
Ce Monstre abominable, exécrable, inhumain!
N'est-ce pas incarné quelque Démon sur Terre
Lequel au genre humain déclare ainsi sa guerre
Qui, même avant le règne, un jour de l'Antechrist
Exerce par avance ici-bas son esprit?

37. We know that Walpole was a frequent attendee of the salon of his friend Du Deffand, and Walpole juxtaposed Catherine II and the beast on more than one occa-

sion. See *HWC*, 31: 56 and 31: 61–62. The king of Poland, in a response to a letter from Mme. de Geoffrin, reported in March of 1765 that he had "laughed until I cried at the mention of the beast that still roams here, there, and everywhere"; context makes clear that Geoffrin referenced Catherine II, whose wildness could be controlled if only she had a Fénelonian "mentor." Claude de Moüy, ed., *Correspondance inédite du Roi Stanislas-Auguste Poniatowski et de Madame de Geoffrin (1764–1777)* (Geneva, 1970), 144.

38. Clairon seems not to have pressed hard for Fréron's imprisonment until mid-February, giving added plausibility to the chronology offered here. Bachaumont's *Mémoires Secrets* instantly saw Clairon as the target of Fréron's January commentary on Olligny. See *MS*, vol. 2 (London, 1777), 167. When protesting his innocence to Clairon's protector the Duc de Richelieu in March of 1765, after he had also described the beast, a contrite Fréron offered the suggestive but inconclusive defense that "I never had any intention of depicting this celebrated actress." Whether the "depiction" was found in the language about the beast or in words about the dissolute morals of most actresses is unknown. See Fréron to Richelieu, 2 March 1765, in *Revue Rétrospective, ou Bibliothèque Historique, contenant des Mémoires et Documents Authentiques, Inédits et Originaux* 2nd ser., vol. 10 (1837), 144. For the original pieces in the *Année Littéraire* see *AL* (1765), vol. 1, 120 and 323–325. For the rhythm of Fréron's publishing schedule—his commentary on Olligny appeared in the second and the description of the beast appeared in the fifth issue of 1765—see Philippe Van Tieghem, *L'Année Littéraire (1754–1790): comme intermédiaire en France des littératures étrangères* (Geneva, 1966), 5–6. The belief that Clairon's resentments focused particularly on the beast certainly has a long pedigree, though the assertion has not been carefully documented. See Charles Maurice, *Le Théâtre-français: monument et dépendances* (Paris, 1860), 80; Jean Dorsenne, "Une nouvelle bête du Gévaudan," *Gringoire: Le Grand Hebdomadaire Parisien, Politique, Littéraire*, 22 November 1935, 3; Jean Susini, "Autour de la Bête du Gévaudan," *Lou Païs* (November, 1970), 183; and Jean Richard, in his "Complément Bibliographique" for François Fabre, *La Bête du Gévaudan* (Paris, 2001; 1st ed., Paris, 1930).

39. Buffon to the abbé Le Blanc, 22 Sept. 1765. Georges Leclerc, comte de Buffon, *Correspondance Générale,* ed. H. Nadault de Buffon (Geneva, 1971), 1: 138.

40. On the bleeding see *CA,* 20 Sept. 1765 (report from Paris, 12 Sept.). Saint-Florentin was back to work by 3 October, when his personal correspondence resumed. In a letter of 22 Oct., Saint-Florentin reported that he hoped his wound would close "in the course of this week." For the resumption of activity see Saint-Florentin to comte de Tressan, 3 Oct. 1765. AN O1 *407, 392. For the closing wound see Saint-Florentin to Duc de Randonneau, 22 Oct. 1765. AN O1 589. On the mechanical hand, see *GC,* 22 Oct. 1765. For "ordinary gaiety" see *GC,* 24 Sept. 1765.

41. On the minister's pursuit of dragon's blood (a medicinal herb) see Saint-Florentin to L'Averdy, 15 Oct. 1764. AN O1 *406, 407–408.

42. L'Averdy to Saint-Priest, 14 April 1765. ADH C 44, folder "avril 1765," no. 230.

Also L'Averdy to Ballainvilliers, 27 Jan. 1765. ADPD 1 C 1731. On the lectures, rendered "free and open" by a royal declaration of 1673, see Anita Guerrini, "Duverney's Skeletons," *Isis* 94 (2003), 577–603, esp. 597.

43. The following discussion of fiscal debates and their impact draws liberally from Michael Kwass, *Privilege and the Politics of Taxation in Eighteenth-Century France* (Cambridge, 2000), 158–193, and Julian Swann, *Politics and the Parlement of Paris under Louis XV, 1754–1774* (Cambridge, 1995), 156–192.

44. The words are those of James C. Riley, *The Seven Years War and the Old Regime in France: The Economic and Financial Toll* (Princeton, 1986), xix.

45. Both cited in Kwass, *Privilege and the Politics of Taxation,* 173–174.

46. For emphasis on the politically pivotal nature of the year 1763, see Antonella Alimento, *Réformes fiscales et crises politiques dans la France de Louis XV: De la taille tarifée au cadastre général* (Brussels, 2008).

47. Joël Félix, *Finances et Politique au Siècle des Lumières: Le ministère L'Averdy, 1763–1768* (Paris, 1999), 124.

48. As cited in Kwass, *Privilege and the Politics of Taxation,* 185.

49. John D. Woodbridge, *Revolt in Prerevolutionary France: The Prince de Conti's Conspiracy against Louis XV, 1755–1757* (Baltimore, 1995), 135–136.

50. Thomas E. Kaiser, "Louis *le Bien-Aimé* and the Rhetoric of the Royal Body," in *From the Royal to the Republican Body: Incorporating the Political in Seventeenth- and Eighteenth-Century France,* ed. Sara E. Melzer and Kathryn Norberg (Berkeley, 1998), 131–161.

51. This incident from 1728 is discussed in ibid., 142. My thanks to Tom Kaiser for bringing it to my attention.

52. Swann, *Politics and the Parlement of Paris,* 197, 236.

53. As cited in Kwass, *Privilege and the Politics of Taxation,* 175.

54. On the propaganda campaign, see David A. Bell, *The Cult of the Nation in France: Inventing Nationalism, 1680–1800* (Cambridge, Mass., 2001), 63–68; Edmond Dziembowski, *Un Nouveau Patriotisme Français, 1750–1770: La France Face à la Puissance Anglaise à l'Epoque de la Guerre de Sept Ans* (Oxford, 1998), 423–486; Keith Michael Baker, "Controlling French History: The Ideological Arsenal of Jacob-Nicolas Moreau," in *Inventing the French Revolution: Essays on French Political Culture in the Eighteenth Century* (Cambridge, 1990), 59–85.

55. Arlette Farge and Jacques Revel, *The Vanishing Children of Paris: Rumor and Politics before the French Revolution,* trans. Claudia Miéville (Cambridge, Mass., 1991).

56. Lisa Jane Graham, *If the King Only Knew: Seditious Speech in the Reign of Louis XV* (Charlottesville, Va., 2000), 208. The words are actually those of the *parlement* of Paris.

57. BNF, manuscrit Joly de Fleury 2075, "Mauvais Discours," fols. 95–106, esp. 97, 102–103.

58. Ibid., fol. 98.

59. On physiocratic doctrine, which anticipated Smithian free market theory, the

standard works remain Georges Weulersse, *Le Mouvement Physiocratique en France (de 1756 à 1770)*, 2 vols. (Paris, 1968); Elizabeth Fox-Genovese, *The Origins of Physiocracy: Economic Revolution and Social Order in Eighteenth-Century France* (Ithaca, N.Y., 1976).

60. Grain riots had already occurred in Caen by October, as reported in *CA*, 2 Nov. 1764 (report from Paris, 18 Oct.). On the disturbances in Languedoc see H. Bourderon, "La lutte contre la vie chère dans la généralité de Languedoc au XVIIIe siècle," *AM* 66 (1954): 155–170, esp. 162. On L'Averdy and the freeing of the grain trade, see Félix, *Finances et Politique au Siècle des Lumières*, 187–205; Steven L. Kaplan, *Bread, Politics, and Political Economy in the Reign of Louis XV*, 2 vols. (The Hague, 1976), 1: 121–163, esp. 140–142.

61. On the Britanny affair, see Swann, *Politics and the Parlement of Paris*, 250–283, esp. 253–254; John Rothney, ed., *The Brittany Affair and the Crisis of the Ancien Régime* (Oxford, 1969).

62. At the end of December Saint-Florentin did authorize Ballainvilliers to offer 1,200 livres in recompense to the beast's killer, but he soon cautioned the intendant about giving rewards to those who had fought with the beast: "it could happen that, in order to collect a similar prize, someone could come and say that he too had battled the beast, even giving himself light wounds so as to be believed more readily." See Saint-Florentin to Ballainvilliers, 31 Dec. 1764. ADPD 1 C 1731. Also Saint-Florentin to Ballainvilliers, 30 Jan. 1765. AN O1 *461, fol. 17v.

63. L'Averdy to Ballainvilliers, 27 Jan. 1765. ADPD 1 C 1731. The quotations are from the *ordonnances* of both Saint-Priest and Ballainvilliers. For Saint-Priest, see *CA*, 19 Feb. 1765 (report from Montpellier, 12 Feb.); for Ballainvilliers, see ADH C 44, folder "mai 1765," no. 245.

64. Jean-Marc Moriceau, *La Bête du Gévaudan* (Paris, 2008), 67. The typical reward for the head of a wolf: six livres.

65. Saint-Priest to L'Averdy, undated. ADH C 44, folder "Jeune Portefaix, 1765–1785," no. 46.

66. *CA*, 19 Feb. 1765 (reports from Bas Languedoc, 11 Feb., and Montpellier, 12 Feb.).

67. The prediction was actually made two weeks before the royal announcement, when word reached Nîmes that the provincial Estates-General had decided to offer a reward of 2,000 livres. See Ginhoux to Joubert [syndic of the Estates], 12 Jan. 1765. ADH C 8251.

68. Labarthe *fils* to Fréron, *AL* (1765), vol. 3, 26–27.

69. Ballainvilliers to Saint-Florentin, 2 Feb. 1765, and Saint-Florentin to Ballainvilliers, 8 Feb. 1765. ADPD 1 C 1731.

70. Albert Grimaud and Marius Balmelle, *Précis d'Histoire du Gévaudan, rattachée à l'Histoire de France* (Paris, 1925), 333.

71. Jacques-Louis Ménétra, *Journal of My Life*, ed. Daniel Roche, trans. Arthur Goldhammer (New York, 1986), 96.

72. Duhamel to Moncan, 20 Jan. 1765, in Marius Balmelle, "Lettres inédites du Capitaine Duhamel sur la Bête du Gévaudan (octobre 1764–avril 1765)," *RGCC* 14 (1968): 136–158, esp. 138.

73. The troubles had begun in the first half of 1764, as Laforest's semi-annual reports to the intendant make clear. See Laforest to Saint-Priest, 27 Feb. 1764. ADH C 88. See also his semi-annual reports dated 27 June 1763, 5 January 1764, 6 July 1764, and 4 January 1765. ADH C 1585. On the "contagion" see both Laforest to Saint-Priest, 4 Jan. 1765 (ADH C 1585), and Laforest to Saint-Priest, 6 Jan. 1766 (ADH C 1586, no. 63). By July of 1768 the subdelegate could concede that "for some time, there have been fewer crimes committed in the region, though there are still some that remain hidden and about which we cannot collect information." See "Etat des Crimes," 10 July 1768. ADH C 1587, no. 60.

74. Laforest's pleas reached highest volume in the second half of 1765. See Laforest to Saint-Priest, 6 Jan. 1766. ADH C 1586, no. 64. On the "disarmament" see Saint-Priest to R.-C. de Maupeou, 20 March 1765 (ADH 1585); on his answer to Lafont, see Saint-Priest to Lafont, 6 April 1765. ADH C 43.

75. *Documents historiques sur la province de Gévaudan,* ed. Gustave de Burdin (Toulouse, 1847), 107, 119.

76. [Illegible] to Saint-Priest, 28 Feb. 1783. ADH C 43.

77. "Etat des Crimes," 24 April 1764. ADH C 1585. Also Lafont to Saint-Priest, 23 Nov. 1764. ADH C 43.

78. See "Projet de mémoire pour servir à dresser l'avis de M. de St. Maurice sur l'Etat des sénéchaussées, sièges présidiaux, et autres Justices Royalles." ADH C 71, no. 3. Also see "Projet pour le Rétablissement de Differents Sièges Royaux de la Province de Languedoc." ADH C 71, no. 372. Also see petition of the "Officiers de la sénéchaussée et siège présidial" of Puy. ADH C 71, no. 625.

79. *CA,* 22 March 1765 (report from Saugues, 11 March); Lafont worried aloud to Saint-Priest that "everyone is armed," including new outsiders who showed up every day. Lafont to Saint-Priest [undated], in "Objets des lettres de M. Lafont." ADH C 44, folder "janvier 1765," no. 119.

80. Lafont to Saint-Priest [undated], in "Objets des lettres de M. Lafont." ADH C 44, folder "janvier 1765," no. 119.

81. Lafont to Saint-Priest, 2 April 1765. ADH C 44, folder "avril 1765," no. 235.

82. Duhamel to Seuroin, 20 March 1765, in Marius Balmelle, "Lettres inédites du Capitaine Duhamel sur la Bête du Gévaudan (octobre 1764–avril 1765)," *RGCC* 15 (1969): 118–135, esp. 118–119.

83. As detailed in a complaint sent from Labarthe *fils* to Saint-Priest in February. Cited in Xavier Pic, *La bête qui mangeait le monde en pays de Gévaudan et d'Auvergne* (Paris, 1971), 66–67.

84. Lafont to Saint-Priest, 2 April 1765. ADH C 44, folder "avril 1765," no. 235.

85. M. Robin, from Bordeaux, offered to share with Saint-Priest his "secret" weapon for trapping "all sorts of animals," providing that the intendant award him

some part of the announced recompense, at the level "you judge appropriate." Robin to Saint-Priest, 2 April 1765. ADH C 44, folder "avril 1765," no. 226. A "poor" curé with another inspired "secret"—straw likenesses of women, stuffed with calves' liver—expressed in February his hope that God would see that "I am given some part of His Majesty's recompense." See [Pouvel to Saint-Priest], 23 Feb. 1765. ADH C 44, folder "février 1765," no. 131. Lespinasse de Mongibaud, a "poor man in his sixties, not in good health," offered to make the trip to the Gévaudan himself—in exchange for an advance. See [Lespinasse de Mongibaud to Saint-Priest], undated. ADH C 44, folder "juin 1765," no. 281.

86. *AL* (1765), vol. 4, 46–47.

87. [Hébert], 30 March 1765. ADPD 1 C 1732. Hébert's plan was perhaps not as outlandish as it seems two hundred years later. In February, Lafont suggested to Saint-Priest the possibility of deploying effigies of women and children in the Gévaudan's fields. See Lafont to Saint-Priest [undated], in "Objets des lettres de M. Lafont." ADH C 44, folder "janvier 1765," no. 119.

88. Montluc to Ballainvilliers, 20 April 1765. ADPD 1 C 1732.

89. *AL* (1765), vol. 2, 286. Hébert was not mentioned by name in the letter, but the details parallel Hébert's plan. Fréron's correspondent cannot be precisely identified because at any one time there were at least ten men who claimed the title "chanoine-comte de Brioude." Attached to the basilica of Saint-Julien-de-Brioude was a noble chapter of canons which conferred honorific status on select representatives of the most distinguished noble families of Auvergne. The letter-writer, in identifying himself as comte de Brioude, may have wished to remain anonymous even as he sought to command respect by signaling his noble standing.

90. Boucainville even cited his sources. "M. Nicolle, in his geography, volume two, page 391, 1758 edition, says that these animals would be quite harmful to the inhabitants [of Yucatan] if they did not feed on young wild calves, which exist in abundance" on the peninsula. The curé refers to Nicolle de La Croix, author of *Géographie moderne. Tome second précédée d'un petit traité de la sphere & du globe, ornée de traits d'histoire naturelle & politique, & terminée par une géographie ecclésiastique, où l'on trouve tous les archevêchés & evêchés de l'Eglise catholique, & les principaux des églises schismatiques* (Paris, 1758; first ed. 1752).

91. [Boucainville], 25 March 1765. ADH C 44, folder "mars 1765," no. 191.

92. D'Enneval to Ballainvilliers, 17 April 1765. ADPD 1 C 1732.

93. [Duparquet], undated. ADH C 44, folder "avril 1765," no. 154.

94. Saint-Priest to Duparquet, 7 April 1765. ADH C 44, folder "août 1765," no. 361.

95. [Lespinasse de Mongibaud to Saint-Priest], undated. ADH C 44, folder "juin 1765," no. 281.

96. Montluc wrote to Ballainvilliers: "I take the honor of sending back to you the *mémoire* composed by M. Rodier; M. Duhamel assured me that he read it." Montluc to Ballainvilliers, 20 April 1765. ADPD 1 C 1732.

97. [Rodier], undated. ADH C 44, folder "avril 1765," no. 180,

98. Papoux to Saint-Priest, 2 May 1765. ADH C 44, folder "mai 1765," no. 268.

99. D'Enneval to M. de Fontaine, Maître particulier des Eaux et Forêts d'Alençon, 27 Feb 1765, in "Recueil factice," fol. 46r. D'Enneval also described an engraving provided by Ballainvilliers.

5. The Perils of Publicity

1. The exact channels of communication are a mystery, as Moriceau has shown. See Jean-Marc Moriceau, *La Bête du Gévaudan* (Paris, 2008), 120–122. We know, however, that the comte d'Eu headed to the capital in the first week of February, where he stayed at the Parisian *hôtel* of the intendant of Alençon, who would soon assist L'Averdy's negotiations with the Norman hunters. The governor had instructed Duhamel to send him a letter at the residence of the intendant, informing him "what becomes of the beast." We also know that d'Enneval, before his departure for the south, traveled to Versailles where he met with Cromot du Bourg and unsuccessfully sought a meeting with L'Averdy. See comte d'Eu to Duhamel, 2 Feb. 1765, in Marius Balmelle, "Lettres inédites du Capitaine Duhamel sur la Bête du Gévaudan (octobre 1764–avril 1765)," *RGCC* 14 (1968), 142; d'Enneval to Lallemant de Lévignen, 29 March 1765, in "Recueil factice de pièces relatives à la bête du Gévaudan, formé par Gervais-François Magné de Marolles," BNF M-1915, fol. 46v.

2. L'Averdy to Lallemant de Lévignen [intendant of Alençon], 5 Feb. 1765. ADH C 44, folder "février 1765," no. 138. On "celebrity," Magné de Marolles referred not to the d'Ennevals in particular, but to the many hunters drawn to the Gévaudan after the first of the year. He compared the entire phenomenon to the "Heroic" age, when the finest huntsmen of ancient Greece competed to defeat the Erymanthian Boar. See "Précis Historique," in "Recueil factice," fol. 70r.

3. Magné de Marolles, "Précis Historique," in "Recueil factice," fol. 69r.

4. *AL* (1765), vol. 2, 104.

5. *CA,* 8 March 1765 (report from Paris, 28 Feb.); 12 March 1765 (report from Paris, 2 March); 15 March 1765 (report from Paris, 7 March).

6. *CA,* 12 March 1765 (reports from Paris, 2 March, and Marvejols, 1 March); 15 March 1765 (report from Marvejols, 9 March). Whatever their zeal for the public good, they also paid careful attention to finances while in the Gévaudan. The younger d'Enneval immediately submitted claims for travel reimbursement upon arrival. They were paid 720 livres, largely for travel and lodging, on 18 March. See BNF, manuscrits français 7847, fols. 13, 60.

7. *AL* (1765), vol. 2, 214. In this letter of 16 March, the comte de Brioude already revealed signs that d'Enneval's engagement was not going as planned.

8. Saint-Priest to Lafont, 2 March 1765. ADH C 43.

9. L'Averdy to Alençon, 5 Feb. 1765. ADH C 44, folder "février 1765," no. 138.

10. D'Enneval to Ballainvilliers, 21 Feb. 1765. ADPD 1 C 1732. Also d'Enneval to

Ballainvilliers, 9 March 1765. ADPD 1 C 1732. The departure date is given in R. Guillemain d'Echon, *La Chasse du Loup: Les Gentilhommes Louvetiers de Normandie et du Maine* (Alençon, 1926), 12.

11. D'Enneval to M. de Fontaine, Maître particulier des Eaux et Forêts d'Alençon, 27 Feb. 1765. "Recueil factice," fol. 46r.

12. In a letter to Saint-Priest on 13 June, the Norman detailed his movements: *"Nous nous rendîmes à six heures à la chapelle beaulieu dans la margere [at the place] nous indiqués, ou nos gens firent raport qu'ils avoient connaissance d'un animal qu'ils soupçonnoient etre la beste."* ADH C 44, folder "juin 1765," no. 276. In February he announced his arrival at Massiac in a letter to Ballainvilliers also typical in its formality (especially when making excuses). He told the intendant that he would stay at Massiac *"jusqu'a ce que j'en sache des nouvelles d'ailleurs."* ADPD 1 C 1732.

13. Ballainvilliers's subdelegate Montluc noted on 20 March that the d'Ennevals "have abandoned Saint-Chély to M. Duhamel, who is there with his dragoons." Montluc to Ballainvilliers, 20 March 1765. ADPD 1 C 1732.

14. Duhamel to comte de Lastic, 1 March 1765. In Balmelle, "Lettres inédites du Capitaine Duhamel" [1968], 156–157; the claim about "two weeks" was detailed in Duhamel to Seuroin, 20 March 1765, in Balmelle, "Lettres inédites du Capitaine Duhamel sur la Bête du Gévaudan (octobre 1764–avril 1765)," *RGCC* 15 (1969), 118–119.

15. *"[Il] est fort malhonnette et veut jouer l'important."* Duhamel to Seuroin, 20 March 1765, in Balmelle, "Lettres inédites du Capitaine Duhamel" [1969], 120.

16. D'Enneval [to Ballainvilliers], 4 March 1765. ADPD 1 C 1732.

17. D'Enneval [to Ballainvilliers], 9 March 1765. ADPD 1 C 1732.

18. Lafont to Saint-Priest, 19 March 1765. ADH C 44, folder "mars 1765," no. 200.

19. Duhamel to Seuroin, 20 March 1765, in Balmelle, "Lettres inédites du Capitaine Duhamel" [1969], 120.

20. Lafont to Saint-Priest, 19 March 1765. ADH C 44, folder "mars 1765," no. 200.

21. Ibid. Lafont's exact words: *"Ces Messieurs semblent avoir la plume légère."*

22. L'Averdy to Saint-Priest, 26 March 1765. ADH C 44, folder "mars 1765," no. 198. Saint-Priest had indicated to L'Averdy on 18 March that he was inclined to leave Duhamel in place, with the two hunters covering distinct territories, a proposal to which L'Averdy—by then well primed by d'Enneval—had responded that "I confess that I cannot entirely share your opinion on the need to leave things as they are." Moncan had assured Duhamel that he, too, found the behavior of the d'Ennevals "strange." See Saint-Priest to L'Averdy, 18 March 1765. ADH C 44, folder "mars 1765," no. 202. Also Duhamel to Seuroin, 20 March 1765, in Balmelle, "Lettres inédites du Capitaine Duhamel" [1969], 120.

23. Duhamel [to Lafont], March 1765, in Marius Balmelle, "Lettres inédites du Capitaine Duhamel" [1967], 104.

24. Montluc to Ballainvilliers, 20 March 1765. ADPD 1 C 1732. "They give credit to M. Duhamel for having expended much effort and good will to destroy this monster," Montluc generously conceded, "but unfortunately [the beast] always eluded him and did much damage, devouring two persons in Auvergne this month."

25. Montluc to Ballainvilliers, 24 April 1765. ADPD 1 C 1732. Montluc reported to the intendant that his own brother had recently gone off to join the d'Ennevals in the field, a fortuitous event without which "I would not be any better informed than someone living a hundred leagues from here."

26. *Procès-verbaux des délibérations des états du Gévaudan,* ed. Ferdinand André (Mende, 1881), 7: 548.

27. *GL,* 3 May 1765.

28. Montluc to Ballainvilliers, 20 April 1765. ADPD 1 C 1732. The hearsay about the d'Ennevals's imminent departure was reported by Duhamel on the eve of his own departure from Saint-Chély. See Duhamel to Moncan, 2 April 1765, in Balmelle, "Lettres inédites du Capitaine Duhamel" [1969], 123.

29. "Lettre d'un Picqueur de M. le comte de Montesson à son maître," 22 April 1765. "Recueil factice," fol. 48r.

30. "Lettre d'un Picqueur de M. le comte de Montesson à son maître," 22 April 1765, fol 47v; d'Enneval to Lallement de Lévignen, 11 April 1765, fol 47r; d'Enneval to Lallement de Lévignen, 29 March 1765, fol. 46v. All from "Recueil factice."

31. BHVP, ms. 637 [Nouvelles à la main], fol. 126v.

32. D'Enneval to Lallement de Lévignen, [25–30 April 1765]. "Recueil factice," fol. 48v.

33. See, respectively, Lafont to Saint-Priest, 2 April 1765 (ADH C 44, folder "avril 1765," no. 235); "Lettre de M. Breuguière, curé de Langogne en Gévaudan en réponse à M . . . qui lui avait écrit au sujet de la Bête féroce," 28 April 1765 ("Recueil factice," fol. 50v); Dulignon fils [to Saint-Priest], 20 April 1765 (ADH C 8251); [Joubert] to Lafont, 15 April 1765 (ADH C 8251).

34. *GF,* 1 April 1765. *"[Elle] continue ses entreprises & ne cesse de répandre l'allarme & la consternation dans tous les lieux exposés à ses incursions."*

35. Lafont to Saint-Priest, 19 March 1765. ADH C 44, folder "mars 1765," no. 200.

36. Duhamel to Choiseul-Beaupré, 13 March 1765, in Balmelle, "Lettres inédites du Capitaine Duhamel" [1968], 158.

37. *CA,* 9 April 1765 (report from Paris, 30 March).

38. Abbé Trémoulet of Javols to Duhamel, 2 April 1765. In Ferdinand André, "Les Ravages des Loups en Gévaudan," *Annuaire administratif, statistique, historique & commercial du département de La Lozère pour 1872* 41 (1871), 3–46, esp. 29.

39. *CA,* 9 April 1765 (report from Paris, 30 March).

40. Lafont to Saint-Priest, 19 March 1765. ADH C 44, folder "mars 1765," no. 200.

41. Lafont reported twice to Saint-Priest that the seigneurs around Mende were

pressing for a general hunt to take place before the end of April. D'Enneval at first gave evasive answers and resisted "without giving a satisfactory explanation." See Lafont to Saint-Priest, 2 April 1765, and Lafont to Saint-Priest 13 April 1765. ADH C 44, folder "avril 1765," nos. 235 and 239.

42. The Lafayettes were publicly discussed by Brioude in a letter of 16 March, *AL* (1765), vol. 2, 215. No relation to the marquis of revolutionary fame, these Lafayettes are exceedingly hard to identify. The d'Ennevals' helper seems most likely to have been Jean de Lafayette-Vieille, perhaps accompanied by one or more nephews. Jean, born in 1699, was approximately the age of the elder d'Enneval, and his age and status would explain why the Lafayette name might have been used to identify the company as a whole. We know that these Auvergnats were not wealthy because d'Enneval paid them for their time. See d'Enneval to Lallemant de Lévignen, 29 March 1765. "Recueil factice," fol. 47r. On the Lafayette-Vieilles, see Albert de Ramacle, *Dictionnaire Généalogique: Familles d'Auvergne* (Clermont-Ferrand, 1995), 2: 288.

43. *GL,* 1 May 1765.

44. D'Enneval to Lallement de Lévignen, [25–30 April 1765]. "Recueil factice," fol. 48r. Also Lafont to Saint-Priest, 24 April 1765. ADH C 44, folder "avril 1765," no. 244.

45. All agreed on this accounting of the basic details. See Jean-François d'Enneval to Lallemant de Lévignen, "Recueil factice," fol. 48v–49v.

46. Morangiès to Lafont, 3 May 1765. ADH C 44, folder "mai 1765," no. 269.

47. Morangiès to Lafont, 18 May 1765. ADH C 44, folder "mai 1765," no. 258.

48. Lafont to Saint-Priest, 23 May 1765. ADH C 44, folder "mai 1765," no. 264.

49. In his draft response to Lafont's complaint about the d'Ennevals, sent in the first week of June, Saint-Priest initially suggested that it would be good strategy to have all the aggrieved communities "take their own complaints to the minister," but this suggestion was deleted before the letter was sent. The intendant instead took the matter into his own hands. See Saint-Priest to Lafont, [June 1765]. ADH C 44, folder "juin 1765," no. 279. Comte de Scordeck to Saint-Priest, 27 May 1765. ADH C 44, folder "mai 1765," no. 266.

50. [Saint-Priest] to Antoine, 3 June 1765. ADH C 44, folder "juin 1765," no. 299. On Saint-Florentin's assessment of the "very urgent" circumstances, see Saint-Florentin to L'Averdy, 7 June 1765. AN O1 *407, 216. For a list of disbursements throughout the summer see AN O1 638, fol. 2v.

51. Lafont to Saint-Priest, 24 May 1765. ADH C 44, folder "mai 1765," no. 271; d'Enneval to Ballainvilliers, 13 June 1765. ADPD 1 C 1733; Antoine to Ballainvilliers, 18 July 1765. ADPD 1 C 1734. "M. d'Enneval, following the orders of the court, left this morning."

52. Antoine wrote similar, though not identical, letters about this meeting to the intendants Ballainvilliers and Saint-Priest. See Antoine to Ballainvilliers, 18 July 1765. ADPD 1 C 1734. Also Antoine to Saint-Priest, 18 July 1765. ADH C 44, folder "juillet 1765," no. 327.

53. For Lafont's reference to "recriminations" see Lafont to Saint-Priest, 20 July 1765. ADH C 44, folder "juillet 1765," no. 335. The certificate is dated 18 July 1765. ADH C 44, folder "août 1765," no. 375.

54. Lafont to Saint-Priest, 23 Nov. 1764. ADH C 43.

55. Magné de Marolles would write that d'Enneval, even after his return to Normandy, "continues to insist on the existence of an extraordinary Beast in the Gévaudan." See "Précis Historique," in "Recueil factice," fol. 79v.

56. Duhamel to Lafont, 2 April 1765, in Balmelle, "Lettres inédites du Capitaine Duhamel" [1969], 124.

57. "Like so many others, these gentlemen believed, especially with their dogs who are said to be so excellent, that they would take this beast within two weeks; three weeks have passed and their hunts have gotten them nowhere." Duhamel to Seuroin, 20 March 1765, in Balmelle, "Lettres inédites du Capitaine Duhamel" [1969], 118–119.

58. Morangiès and d'Enneval had one more strained encounter in mid-May, and circumstantial evidence suggests that Morangiès deserved his share of blame. D'Enneval threatened to complain to the ministers that the peasants of the comte's parish of Saint-Alban had refused to join him in his hunts of 12 and 16 May. Morangiès's sensitivity to the charge, and his earlier prediction that some parishes "would refuse to march" if called on again suggest at least indirectly that the comte had ordered the peasants not to cooperate with his enemy. Morangiès to Lafont, 18 May 1765. ADH C 44, folder "mai 1765," no. 258.

59. *CA,* 12 March 1765 (report from Paris, 2 March).

60. Duhamel to Lafont, 2 April 1765, in Balmelle, "Lettres inédites du Capitaine Duhamel" [1969], 125.

6. Heroes and Skeptics

1. For the "fabulous" see *CA,* 22 Feb. 1765 (report from Paris, 14 Feb.); for "novel" see LaBarthe *fils* to Fréron, 1 April 1765, *AL* (1765), vol. 3, 36.

2. The name of Jeanne Varlet has been the source of some confusion. She was most often referred to in public documents as the *femme* Jouve, or Jeanne Jouve. She was also known, however, as Jeanne Chastang. At the time and ever since, her last name has also been spelled as both Varlet and Marlet. I have opted for the spelling given in a notarial document drafted after her combat with the beast, in which she and her husband are identified as "Pierre Jouve and Jeanne Varlet . . . residents and tenants of La Bessiere in the parish of Saint-Alban, diocese of Mende." See BNF, manuscrits français (hereafter ms. fr.) 7847, "Dépenses," fol. 24.

3. [Reboul], *Essai sur les moeurs du temps* (London, 1768), 281. On the social profile of the "subaltern hero"—a term derived from the "subaltern" lower military offices who often outshone their superiors—see André Corvisier, "Les 'héros subalternes' dans la littérature du milieu du XVIIIe siècle et la réhabilitation du militaire,"

Revue du Nord 66 (1984): 827–838. For discussion of the patriotic resurgence of the post-war years, and its implications for the French social order, see Jay M. Smith, *Nobility Reimagined: The Patriotic Nation in Eighteenth-Century France* (Ithaca, N.Y., 2005), 143–181.

4. Antoine to Saint-Priest, 21 Aug. 1765. ADH C 44, folder "août 1765," no. 367.

5. Literary works of the 1760s continually reinforced the connection between a patriotic politics and the loving bonds of family and community. See Anastasia Lazakis, "*Le Coeur d'un Bon Citoyen:* The Sentimentalization of Classical Republicanism in Eighteenth-Century France," (Ph.D. diss., Duke University, 2007), esp. 145–202.

6. BM, ms. 2378, "Recueil d'anecdotes littéraires et politiques, 1765," 18 Feb. 1765.

7. The newspapers showed confusion over Portefaix's age, sometimes listing it at eleven years, sometimes at twelve. Lafont's close investigation of Portefaix's situation and background confirmed that the boy had turned twelve on 8 November 1764. See Lafont to Saint-Priest, 19 March 1765. ADH C 44, folder "avril 1765," no. 186.

8. *CA*, 12 Feb. 1765 (report from Mende, 31 Jan.).

9. Saint-Priest to L'Averdy, 8 Feb. 1765. ADH C 43.

10. Comte d'Eu to Saint-Priest, 24 Feb. 1765. ADH C 44, folder "Jeune Portefaix, 1765–1785," no. 4.

11. In fairness to the *Courrier,* it should be noted that Lafont's first letter to Saint-Priest on 2 February had included similar language, and Lafont may have been the source of the rhetorical embellishments. According to Lafont, Portefaix exhorted his friends to "deliver their comrade or they should all perish with him." Lafont to Saint-Priest, 2 Feb. 1765. ADH C 44, folder "février 1765," no. 144.

12. *BEP,* 15 July 1765; see also *MF* (April 1765), vol. 2, 184–186; *JE* (1765), vol. 2, pt. 3, 165; *AL* (1765), vol. 1, 327–329; *GC,* 5 March 1765; *GL,* 26 Feb. 1765; *SJC,* 23 Feb. 1765.

13. The *Gazette de France* ran one brief update on 14 January. Stories then ran on 18 February, 15 March, 1 April, 15 April, 10 May, 17 May, 3 June, and 10 June.

14. *CL,* ed. Maurice Tourneux (Paris, 1878), vol. 6, 255; see also the 2 April 1765 entry in [Louis Petit de Bachaumont], *MS* (London, 1777), vol. 2, 198.

15. Choiseul to Saint-Priest, 11 Aug. 1761. ADH C 43.

16. On the editorial experimentation of the 1760s, and the difficulties the *Gazette* faced in holding on to its readership, see Feyel, *L'Annonce et la nouvelle: la presse d'information en France sous l'Ancien Regime (1630–1788)* (Oxford, 2000), 744–759. The crown was still holding intendants' feet to the fire in 1767, when it reminded them of the need to send in "bulletins that will include everything capable of attracting the interest of the public." See Duc de Choiseul to Saint-Priest, 3 March 1767. ADH C 43. The mention of patriotic feats and examples of natural history came in a 1771 circular that repeated the admonitions of earlier years. [Emmanuel-Armand de Vignerot du Plessis de Richelieu, duc] d'Aiguillon to Saint-Priest, 31 Oct. 1771. ADH C 43. Cf. Choiseul to Saint-Priest, 11 Aug. 1761 (ADH C 43), which had mentioned "natural history" and "singular and extraordinary feats."

17. Saint-Priest to L'Averdy and Saint-Florentin, 8 Feb. 1765. ADH C 43. Saint-Priest either wrote a near-duplicate letter to the editors of the *Gazette* or they had the information conveyed to them by a minister. Most of the Portefaix details came from other sources, but other features of the *Gazette's* 18 February story parallel the letter. Saint-Priest had said of the beast, for example, that *"le 22 elle a coupé la tête d'une femme à Julianges en Gévaudan, frontière d'Auvergne."* The paper reported that *"Le 22 elle attaqua une femme à Julianges sur la frontière d'Auvergne."* On the subject of the beast's movement, the letter noted that its perambulations *"se prolongent d'une Etendue de 40 lieues dont le Gévaudan est toujours le centre."* In the *Gazette, "ses courses se font dans une étendue de pays de plus de 40 lieues, dont le Gévaudan est le centre."*

18. L'Averdy to Saint-Priest, 19 Feb. 1765. ADH C 44, folder "février 1765," no. 128.

19. BNF, ms. fr. 7847, "Dépenses," fol. 14. The words are those of Saint-Priest in his initial instructions to Lafont. Portefaix's one-time reward would later be turned into a yearly pension, paid in two semi-annual installments; see fol. 35. See also *CA,* 19 Feb. 1765 ("Extrait d'une lettre du Gévaudan," 7 Feb.).

20. Saint-Priest had praised the king's "paternal kindness" at the time of the announcement of the large royal reward. See Saint-Priest to L'Averdy, undated. ADH C 44, folder "Jeune Portafaix, 1765–1785," no. 46.

21. Montperoux to Saint-Priest, 28 Feb. 1765. ADH C 44, folder "février 1765," no. 129. The *Courrier d'Avignon* would report the death of the ambassador Montperoux in September. See *CA,* 27 Sept. 1765 (report from Paris, 19 Sept.).

22. *CA,* 22 Feb. 1765 (report from Paris, 14 Feb.).

23. L'Averdy to Saint-Priest, 19 Feb. 1765. ADH C 44, folder "février 1765," no. 128. The *Gazette de Cologne* conveyed news of the king's intentions (along with various inaccuracies) in its report "from France" of 1 March. See *GC,* 5 March 1765.

24. Lafont to Saint-Priest, 19 March 1765. ADH C 44, folder "mars 1765," no. 200; on the appearance of the poem, titled "Portefaix," see *CL,* vol. 6, 255.

25. Lafont to Saint-Priest, 19 March 1765. ADH C 44, folder "mars 1765," no. 186. On Serverette's importance as a weaving center, see Elisabeth Claverie and Pierre Lamaison, *L'Impossible Mariage: Violence et parenté en Gévaudan: XVIIe, XVIIIe, et XIXe siècles* (Paris, 1982), 329.

26. Lafont to Saint-Priest, 19 March 1765. ADH C 44, folder "mars 1765," no. 186.

27. Details of the arrangements are discussed in Choiseul to Saint-Priest, 27 July 1770. ADH C 44, folder "Jeune Portafaix, 1765–1785," no. 79.

28. As detailed in BNF, ms. fr. 7847, fol. 17. On Morangiès's interest, see "Extrait de la lettre écrite à M. l'intendant par M. le comte de Morangiès," March 1765. ADH C 44, folder "mars 1765," no. 164.

29. On Saturday, 13 April, the day of the party's arrival, the provincial syndic Joubert paid a visit to Saint-Priest's honored guest, who, in Joubert's estimation, "well

deserves that something be done for him." See Joubert to Lafont, 15 April 1765. ADH C 8251.

30. In July of 1770, Choiseul authorized Portefaix's admission to the artillery school at Bapaume in northern France. Because Bapaume was dedicated especially to the training of young nobles who aspired to commissions, Portefaix was soon transferred to Douai. On his initial appointment to Bapaume, see Choiseul to unidentified, 12 Oct. 1770. ADH C 44, folder "Jeune Portefaix, 1765–1785," no. 63. For Portefaix's presentation to Louis XV and Choiseul in 1770, and his name change, see Prince de Beauvau to Saint-Priest, 6 Dec. 1770. ADH C 44, folder "Jeune Portefaix, 1765–1785," no. 19. A letter to the controller-general, written by the director of the artillery school at Douai in 1772, confirmed Portefaix's steady progress. See Bréand to Terray, 13 Oct. 1772. ADH C 44, "Jeune Portefaix, 1765–1785," no. 16. On Portefaix's death in 1785, see *ordonnance* of Marie-Joseph-Emmanuel de Guignard de Saint-Priest, 26 Nov. 1785. ADH C 44, folder "Jeune Portefaix, 1765–1785," no. 30.

31. Lafont to Saint-Priest, 19 March 1765. ADH C 44, folder "mars 1765", no. 200.

32. *GF,* 1 April 1765; Magné de Marolles, "Précis Historique," in "Recueil factice de pièces relatives à la bête du Gévaudan, formé par Gervais-François Magné de Marolles," BNF M-1915, fol. 70r.; Labarthe *fils* to Fréron, 1 April 1765, *AL* (1765), vol. 3, 36–37.

33. The *Courrier* would provide two lengthy, and not entirely consistent, accounts: 26 March 1765 (report from Marvejols, 17 March) and 2 April 1765 (report from Marvejols, 24 March). The *Gazette de France* placed *femme* Jouve not in her home of Bessière but in the larger neighboring village of Le Rouget—literally a stone's throw from Bessière. (Even today Bessière often fails to register on road maps of the region.) See *GF,* 1 April 1765. The account from Leiden differed in subtle ways from both of the earlier accounts. See *GL,* 9 April 1765.

34. Béraud [of Saint Alban] to Choiseul-Beaupré, 14 March 1765. ADH C 44, folder "mars 1765," no. 205.

35. Ibid. The pregnancy was attested by the curé, but not mentioned explicitly in the newspapers.

36. *CA,* 26 March 1765 (report from Marvejols, 17 March).

37. Ibid. The *Relation Generale & circonstanciée de tous les Désordres commis par la Bête féroce qui ravage le Gévaudan & les pays circonvoisins,* in which the "Femme Jouve" featured prominently, was dated 11 April 1765. See "Recueil factice," fol. 35r–35v.

38. Lafont to Saint-Priest, 19 March 1765. ADH C 44, folder "mars 1765" folder, no. 200. The role of Morangiès is revealed in a letter from Saint-Florentin to Saint-Priest, 3 April 1765. AN O1 *461, fol. 100r. For the 25 April meeting with the notary see BNF, ms. fr. 7847, fol. 24 (in which a royal notary conveyed Saint-Priest's language).

39. *CA,* 2 April 1765 (report from Marvejols, 24 March).

40. Jean-Jacques Rousseau, *Julie, ou La Nouvelle Héloïse: Lettres de deux amants habitants d'une petite ville au pied des Alpes*, ed. René Pomeau (Paris, 1988), 691. My thanks to Mita Choudhury for first calling to my attention these Rousseauean echoes.

41. See Roger Chartier, *The Cultural Uses of Print in Early Modern France*, trans. Lydia G. Cochrane (Princeton, 1987), 215.

42. On readers' heartfelt responses to Rousseau and his heroine, see Robert Darnton, "Readers Respond to Rousseau: The Fabrication of Romantic Sensitivity," in *The Great Cat Massacre and Other Episodes in French Cultural History* (New York, 1984), 215–256. The contemporary source quoted here is from 245.

43. *CA*, see both 9 April 1765 (report from Paris, 30 March) and 12 April 1765 (report from Paris, 4 April). Compare Morénas's words with those of Mably, who had his Greek hero famously declare, in the *Entretiens de Phocion*, "One who is incapable of being a husband, a father, a neighbor, a friend, is incapable of being a citizen." [Gabriel Bonnot de Mably], *Entretiens de Phocion, sur le Rapport de la Morale avec la Politique* (Amsterdam, 1763), 44.

44. Magné de Marolles, "Précis Historique," in "Recueil factice," fol. 70r.

45. "Le Triomphe de l'Amour Maternel: Poëme Héroïque." The anonymous poem was one half of an extended celebration of the Gévaudan's two most famous heroes. *L'Hyenne Combattue, ou Le Triomphe de L'Amitié et de L'Amour Maternel, en Deux Poëmes Héroiques* (Amsterdam, 1765). The following quotations are from 13–15, 18–19.

46. *"Telle aussi la vertu, par éclat de son lustre/Sait tirer de l'oubli le nom le moins illustre/Et que je plains les coeurs qui n'ont jamais senti/Combien par cet éclat un nom est ennobli!"*

47. *CL*, vol. 6, 373. *"On peut bien dire aussi que tels héros, tels poëtes."* Grimm's notice appeared in September, suggesting that the poem had been published in late July or August.

48. [Champdevaux], *L'Honneur considéré en lui-même, et relativement au duel* (Paris, 1752), 93.

49. Denis Diderot, *Le Fils Naturel* (Paris, 1757) and *Le Père de Famille* (Paris, 1758); Michel Sedaine, *Le Philosophe Sans le Savoir* (Paris, 1765) and *Le Déserteur* (Paris, 1769); Louis-Sébastien Mercier, *L'Indigent* (Paris, 1772), *La Brouette du Vinaigrier* (Paris, 1775), and *Le Campagnard, ou le Riche Désabusé* (The Hague [Paris], 1779). For discussion of the more sympathetic portrayals of various non-noble social characters in the *drame*, see Felix Gaiffe, *Le Drame en France au XVIIIe Siècle* (Paris, 1910), 369–399.

50. *"Aux dons que sur ce coeur le Ciel a répandus/Il se plaît d'ajouter un triomphe de plus/Un Roi qui des vertus lui-même est le modèle/A transmis à la tienne une gloire nouvelle/Père d'un peuple heureux, ses regards bienfaisants/Dans ses moindres sujets lui font voir les enfans."*

51. Chevalier de Juilly-Thomassin, "A l'Auteur du Patriotisme," *MF* (April 1765), vol. 2, 47.

52. Pierre Buirette de Belloy, *Le Siège de Calais, tragédie: Par M. de Belloy. Représentée pour la première fois, par les Comédiens Français ordinaires du Roi, le 13 Février 1765. Suivie de notes historiques* (Glasgow, 1765), vi.

53. Louis de Basset de La Marelle, *La Différence du Patriotisme National chez les François et chez les Anglois* (Paris, 1766), 24.

54. *L'Hyenne Combattue,* 5, 10.

55. BM, ms. 2378, "Recueil d'anecdotes littéraires et politiques, 1765, vol. 1," 3 April 1765.

56. *CA,* 2 April 1765 (report from Marvejols, 24 March).

57. *CA,* 19 Feb. 1765 ("Extrait d'une lettre du Gévaudan," 7 Feb.) and 22 Feb 1765 (report from Paris, 14 Feb.); for the "pushed" and "hind legs," *GF,* 18 Feb. 1765.

58. D'Enneval had described the beast as having "a very long tail that it plays with like a cat about to pounce on its prey." D'Enneval to M. de Fontaine, Maître particulier des Eaux et Forêts d'Alençon, 27 Feb. 1765. In "Recueil factice," fol. 46r.

59. The last events recorded, in the caption beneath the engraving, occurred on 18 and 22 April, which suggests a May publication date. Had the image been published much later, the events at La Chaumette and the general hunts of early to mid-May would likely have been included.

60. As recounted in Chapter 2, the event at *La Baume* had begun when Duhamel, ready to fire on the cornered beast, was stunned by its unlikely escape—caused in large part by the sudden arrival of others in his party. A broadsheet published in the first week of March had said of the beast that "il fut investi dans un petit Bosquet" (caught in the midst of a copse of trees) before it made its escape. That language is repeated in the later engraving.

61. Grimm had announced his skepticism on the first of April, and at least one other composer of *nouvelles à la main* showed a clear change of direction in his reporting on the beast in early April. In February the compiler of the manuscript still entertained the thought that the beast might be a hyena or a "wolf of strange type," and he excitedly reported the departure of the great wolf hunter d'Enneval for the south. In March he appreciatively reported on one of the beast's great escapes, which "spreads terror in the region." By April he complained that news reports were "so removed from reality that one wonders about the judgment of the editors who announce their details." In May he apologized to the recipient of his manuscript for "outlandish details" concerning the beast. See BM, ms. 2391 [Nouvelles à la main], 8 Feb., 25 Feb., 5 March, 3 April, and 11 May, 1765.

62. *CA,* 16 April 1765 (report from Paris, 6 April).

63. *CA,* 16 April 1765 (report from Marvejols, 6 April); 23 April 1765 (report from Marvejols, 14 April).

64. On the wandering man see *CA,* 30 July 1765 (report from Langogne, 13 July). Also see the story of the girl who hid for days behind a rock, *CA,* 18 June 1765 (report from Marvejols, 6 June), and the story of the boy who "contracted a fever" after the beast looked him in the eyes, *CA,* 23 July 1765 (report from Paris, 13 July).

65. *GF,* 17 May 1765. Cf. *CA,* 14 May 1765 (report from Marvejols, 5 May).

66. Lafont to Saint-Priest, 4 May 1765. ADH C 44, folder "mai 1765," no. 274.

67. *MS,* vol. 2, 198; Horace Walpole to Lord and Lady Hertford, 26 March 1765, in *HWC,* ed. W. S. Lewis et al., vol. 38 (New Haven, Conn., 1974), 525. Walpole publicly admitted to authoring the novel only in 1765, but he saw connections between its success and the public's taste for the beast of the Gévaudan. "If I had known its history a few months ago, I believe it would have appeared in the *Castle of Otranto*—the success of which has, at last, brought me to own it."

68. Lafont to Saint-Priest, 4 May 1765. ADH C 44, folder "mai 1765," no. 274.

69. Lafont to Saint-Priest, 23 May 1765. ADH C 44, folder "mai 1765," no. 271.

70. Duhamel to Lafont, 11 Nov. 1764. ADH C 43. "It is well established [*bien constaté*] that there are two animals; several reports confirm it. They even say that they are almost always present together."

71. *CA,* 18 Jan. 1765 (report from Marvejols, 2 Jan.), and 11 June 1765 (report from Paris, 1 June). Vigier to Ballainvilliers, 2 Jan. 1765. ADPD 1 C 1731.

72. *CA,* 15 March 1765 (report from Paris, 7 March), and 2 April 1765 (report from Paris, 23 March). See also *GF,* 22 March 1765, and *GL,* 29 March 1765.

73. *GC,* 22 March 1765.

74. Trophime Lafont to Etienne Lafont, [May 1765], as cited in Pierre Pourcher, *La Bête du Gévaudan* (Marseille, 2006), 199. This letter appears to have vanished from the archives, though Pourcher cited it in 1889 as having come from the Archives Départementales de l'Hérault. In any case, Etienne Lafont referred to Trophime's report in his own correspondence, and the account provided in the *Gazette de France* shows familiarity with the contents of Trophime's letter.

75. *CA,* 14 May 1765 (report from Marvejols, 5 May); *GF,* 17 May 1765; *GA,* 24 May 1765; *GL,* 24 May 1765; *MF* (July 1765), 190–191.

76. *CA,* 18 Jan. 1765 (report from Marvejols, 2 Jan.). For the deer see *CA,* 22 March 1765 (report from Saugues, 11 March).

77. The phrase is adapted from Stuart Clark's magisterial *Thinking with Demons: The Idea of Witchcraft in Early Modern Europe* (Oxford, 1997). Clark shows the various ways in which acceptance of the existence of demons and witches became part of the intellectual firmament of the early-modern era—not only for religious figures but for natural philosophers, political thinkers, and social commentators of all kinds.

78. *CA,* 30 April 1765 (report from Marvejols, 21 April).

79. For indirect confirmation see Jean-François Antoine to François Antoine, [5 Aug. 1765]. ADH C 44, folder "août 1765," no. 369. Also Magné de Marolles, "Précis Historique," in "Recueil factice," fol. 79v.

80. Magné de Marolles, "Précis Historique," in "Recueil factice," fol. 70r. Horace Walpole used the same term. See Walpole to Horace Mann, 26 March 1765, in *HWC,* ed. W. S. Lewis et al., vol. 38 (New Haven, 1974), 289, fn.

81. "Extrait des délibérations des Etats du Gévaudan," 26 March 1765. ADL C 806. Also Lafont to Saint-Priest, 9 April 1765. ADH C 44, folder "avril 1765," no. 238.

82. Montluc to Ballainvilliers, 13 Feb. 1765. ADPD 1 C 1732. Cf. Montluc's printed announcement of the general hunt scheduled for 7 February. The document is dated 1 Feb. 1765, in ADPD 1 C 1732.

83. *AL* (1765), vol. 3, 25–40; *CA,* 16 April 1765 (report from Paris, 6 April).

84. He asserted, for example, that one local man had been frightened to death by the appearance of the beast. See Labarthe *fils* to M. Séguier, 31 Oct. 1764, in Léon Pélissier, "Nouveaux documents sur la bête du Gévaudan," *AM* 11 (1899): 69–83, esp. 74–76. The characterization of Labarthe as "Voltairean" is that of Pélissier, 73.

85. Unidentified to Ballainvilliers, 22 Jan. 1765. ADPD 1 C 1731. Also Pagès de Vixouse to Ballainvilliers, 14 Jan. 1765. ADPD 1 C 1731.

86. Ballainvilliers to Saint-Florentin and L'Averdy, 3 Aug. 1765. ADPD 1 C 1736. Ballainvilliers expressed his opinion in the margins of the letter, after noting that Antoine seemed "determined to conjecture that all these carnages have been done by wolves." On his fondness for modernity and *lumières* see René Rigodon, "Ballainvilliers (1758–1767)," *Bulletin Historique et Scientifique de l'Auvergne* 78 (1958), 69–80. The intendant patronized the arts, read the physiocrats, rewarded high-performing students in the *collèges,* and sought to beautify and modernize the city's architecture by removing medieval remnants and installing "regular and symmetrical structures."

87. ADH C 44, folder "juillet 1765," no. 330.

88. For "le poil hérissé" see, for example, *Relation de la Figure & des Désordres commis par une Bête féroce qui ravage le Gévaudan depuis plusieurs mois; avec la Description d'un Combat remarquable que plusieurs Enfans soutinrent contre ce cruel Animal, 5 mars 1765* (n. p., 1765), in "Recueil factice," fol. 34r; see also *CA,* 19 Feb. 1765 (report from the Gévaudan, 7 Feb.). On its catlike head see, for example, *CA,* 23 Nov. 1764 (report from Paris, 15 Nov.).

89. Reinchard to Saint-Priest, 4 Aug. 1765. ADH C 44, folder "août 1765," no. 363.

90. L'Averdy to Saint-Priest, 12 June 1765. ADH C 44, folder "juin 1765," no. 307.

91. Polluche Lumina to Ballainvilliers, 17 June 1765. ADPD 1 C 1734.

92. On rabies in the Soissonnais see anonymous letter to M. Molliand, intendant of Soissons, 15 June 1765. AN O1 *407, p. 225. The *Courrier d'Avignon* would begin reporting on "another species of Monster" attacking people around Verdun in August. See *CA,* 16 Aug. 1765 (report from Paris, 8 Aug.).

93. On 5 August, the king resolved to grant the elder d'Enneval "some marks of his satisfaction," including an annual pension of 350 livres. BNF, ms. fr. 7847, fol. 60.

94. J.-F. Antoine to François Antoine, [August] 1765. ADH C 44, folder "août 1765," no. 369.

95. Comte de Brioude to Fréron, 16 March 1765, in *AL* (1765), vol. 2, 214; Saint-Priest to Lafont, 6 April 1765. ADH C 43.

96. Saint-Priest to Lafont, 6 April 1765. ADH C 43. See also L'Averdy to Saint-Priest, 26 March 1765. ADH C 44, folder "mars 1765," no. 198. Also d'Enneval to Ballainvilliers, 4 March 1765. ADPD 1 C 1732. D'Enneval had complained of the hunts carried out by Duhamel that they *"affarouche cet animal, au point de ne le pouvoir*

approcher." L'Averdy told Saint-Priest that such hunts could *"effaroucher l'animal au point de n'en pouvoir plus approcher."*

97. *GF,* 15 April 1765.

98. In connection with the feats and recompense of *femme* Jouve, the *Boston Evening Post* assured its dubious readers that the editors of the *Gazette de France* were "too prudent, too well informed of what happens at the court of the king . . . to attribute to his Most Christian Majesty rewards for an action which never had an existence." *BEP,* 17 June 1765.

99. After reporting the news of Antoine's assignment, for example, Fréron's *Année Littéraire* went silent until the autumn. The *Journal Encyclopédique* published only one story in the summer, one that noted Antoine's arrival in Malzieu. The *Gazette d'Amsterdam* also published one story, in July, cribbed from various dispatches in the *Courrier d'Avignon.* Even the *Gazette de Leyde* slackened its pace in the summer, for the first time allowing an entire month to lapse with no news of the beast between July and August. The *Mercure de France,* which lagged behind general news publications in any case, added nothing after the news of *femme* Jouve was reported in early July. Its only other summer contribution was a poem, "Apology for the Ferocious Beast," that took as its subject a healthy by-product of the hunt for the "man-eating monster": the elimination of many wolves in the woods of the Gévaudan. *JE,* vol. 5, pt. 2 (15 July 1765), 163–164; *GA,* 2 July 1765; *CA,* 18 June 1765; *GL,* 16 July 1765 and 16 Aug. 1765; *MF,* August 1765, 38.

100. F. Antoine to Ballainvilliers, 11 July 1765. ADPD 1 C 1734.

7. Exaggerated Expectations and Extraordinary Endings

1. Lafont to Ballainvilliers, 12 July 1765. ADPD 1 C 1734. On 26 July he would declare that "the inhabitants killed most recently were killed by none other than wolves." F. Antoine to Ballainvilliers, 26 July 1765. ADPD 1 C 1734. The reference to Voltaire—Antoine regretted that he lacked Voltaire's wit—would come in September. Antoine to Saint-Priest, 16 Sept. 1765. ADH C 44, folder "septembre 1765," no. 387.

2. F. Antoine to Saint-Priest, 18 July 1765. ADH C 44, folder "juillet 1765," no. 327.

3. [F. Antoine], "Observations présentées à Monseigneur le comte de Saint-Florentin, Ministre et Secrétaire d'Etat, à Messieurs les Commandants et Intendants des Provinces de Languedoc et d'Auvergne par le Sr Antoine," [July 1765]. ADPD 1 C 1735.

4. F. Antoine to [Ballainvilliers], 27 July 1765. ADPD 1 C 1735. Also Lafont to Saint-Priest, 30 July 1765. ADH C 44, folder "juillet 1765," no. 344.

5. F. Antoine to Ballainvilliers, 24 June 1765. ADPD 1 C 1734.

6. [F. Antoine], "Observations," July 1765. ADPD 1 C 1735.

7. Labarthe *fils* to M. Séguier, 10 September 1765, in Léon Pélissier, "Nouveaux documents sur la bête du Gévaudan," *AM* 11 (1899), 69–83, esp. 83.

8. F. Antoine to Ballainvilliers, 11 July 1765. ADPD 1 C 1734. Also F. Antoine to Ballainvilliers, 27 July 1765. ADPD 1 C 1735. The second letter was a copy of a similar letter sent to Saint-Priest and Moncan, in which Antoine addressed all three: "C'est uniquement sur vos seules demandes à la Cour qu'il pourra réussir."

9. [Jean-François] Antoine to F. Antoine, 5 Aug. 1765. ADH C 44, folder "août 1765," no. 369.

10. He used this language when reporting to Ballainvilliers the nature of the message he had sent to Saint-Florentin. F. Antoine to Ballainvilliers, 27 July 1765. ADPD 1 C 1735. Antoine would report the arrival of the twelve dogs in a letter to the comte de Tournon, as reported in the *Courrier d'Avignon*. *"Le 16 Septembre au soir il nous arriva un levrier, deux limiers, huit chiens courants de la louveterie, & un bon limier de Fontainebleau, un valet de limiers avec un valet de chien pour les faire chasser."* See *CA*, 15 Oct. 1765 (report from Avignon, 14 Oct.).

11. Little is known about Tournon, but for a brief sketch see Marius Balmelle, "Le Comte de Tournon et la Bête du Gévaudan," *Revue du Vivarais* (1969), 170–172.

12. *GF*, 10 June 1765. The Gazette reported that Louis XV, "having been informed" that the beast's ravages continued unabated, had decided to send to the Gévaudan and Auvergne a "Lieutenant of His Majesty's Hunt" in order to give chase to this "formidable animal."

13. Lafont to Saint-Priest, 2 July 1765. ADH C 44, folder "juillet 1765," no. 340. Also Saint-Priest to F. Antoine, 3 Aug. 1765. ADH C 44, folder "août 1765," no. 365.

14. *CA*, 23 Aug. 1765 (report from Besset, 11 Aug.).

15. In a letter recording the events of July, Lafont made a point of emphasizing that Antoine "brings to his work the greatest exactitude in drafting depositions [*procès-verbaux*] of all events, signed by the curés, vicars, and consuls of the sites, by his son, his guards, my brother, and myself when I am there." Lafont to Saint-Priest, 30 July 1765. ADH C 44, folder "juillet 1765," no. 344.

16. F. Antoine to Ballainvilliers, 11 July 1765. ADPD 1 C 1734. Also [F. Antoine], "Observations," [July 1765]. ADPD 1 C 1735. Also F. Antoine to Ballainvilliers, 21 Aug. 1765. ADPD 1 C 1736.

17. Both the procession and the fireworks display are described in a detailed letter from Malzieu that the *Courrier* quoted in full. See *CA*, 1 Oct. 1765 (report from Avignon, 30 Sept.).

18. F. Antoine to Ballainvilliers, 29 July 1765. ADPD 1 C 1735.

19. F. Antoine to Ballainvilliers [and Saint-Priest and Moncan], 27 July 1765. ADPD 1 C 1735.

20. "Procès-verbal," 16 Aug. 1765. ADH C 44, folder "août 1765," no. 366.

21. F. Antoine [to the consuls of Saugues], 17 Aug. 1765. ADH C 44, folder "août 1765," no. 374. Also F. Antoine to Saint-Priest, 21 Aug. 1765. ADH C 44, folder "août 1765," no. 367.

22. F. Antoine [to the consuls of Saugues], 17 Aug. 1765. ADH C 44, folder "août 1765," no. 374.

23. F. Antoine to Saint-Priest, 21 Aug. 1765. ADH C 44, folder "août 1765," no. 367. See also F. Antoine to Saint-Priest, 16 Sept. 1765. ADH C 44, folder "septembre 1765," no. 387.

24. Baron du Roure de Paulin, "La Bête du Gévaudan dans les armoiries de la famille Antoine," *Bulletin Historique et Scientifique de l'Auvergne* (Clermont-Ferrand, 1906), 292–295, esp. 294. Paulin provides useful background, but he seems to have misidentified Antoine's father. If a Jean-Marc Antoine fathered a François Antoine, as Paulin contends, there would have been three François Antoines in the 1720s, all holding or aspiring to hold offices at court. On the movement across collateral lines: in 1713 François Antoine *père* resigned the position of gun-bearer in favor of his nephew Jean-Marc. See "Brevet d'assurance," 11 May 1713. AN O1 57, fol. 71.

25. An uncle of the gun-bearer, Jean Antoine, had earned nobility in 1704. See AN O1 48, fol. 22, Jan. 1704.

26. AN O1 38, fol. 308, 22 Dec. 1694. After assuming the office of *garçon de la chambre* upon his father's death, Antoine would use a portion of his wife's dowry to reimburse his brothers and sisters for the cost of the office. See AN O1 71, fol. 222, "Brevet d'assurance," 15 July 1727. Later, his second wife's dowry would help finance the purchase of the office of gun-bearer. For details of the contract, spelled out in the succession arrangements for his son, see AN O 1 102, fol. 432, 20 July 1758.

27. In 1770, for example, Jean-François would be named overseer and protector of the forest of Marcoussis, where poachers created "daily disorders." He received the honor not only because of his "knowledge and experience in hunting" but also for "the zeal that he has always demonstrated for the person and the service of His Majesty, in succession from father to son." "Brevet qui commet le S. Antoine pour la conservation du fauve dans la forêt de Marcoussis et de ses dépendances," 25 March 1770. AN O1 116, fols. 291–293.

28. [F. Antoine], "Observations," [July 1765]. ADPD 1 C 1735.

29. "Copie des affiches qui doivent etre imprimees pour la province du gevaudan, et que M. Antoine supplie Monsieur de Ballainvilliers d'en vouloir bien faire imprimer de pareilles pour la province d'Auvergne," July 1765. ADPD 1 C 1734. See also F. Antoine to Ballainvilliers, 11 July 1765. ADPD 1 C 1734.

30. Lafont to Saint-Priest, 30 July 1765. ADH C 44, folder "juillet 1765," no. 344. Antoine would refer to the "supernatural strength" of the beast in making the case that the defeated wolf of Les Chazes had been the Gévaudan's prime offender. See F. Antoine to Saint-Priest, 22 Sept. 1765. ADH C 44, folder "septembre 1765," no. 385.

31. F. Antoine to Ballainvilliers, 24 July 1765. ADPD 1 C 1734.

32. [Parish register], 25 July 1765. ADHL 6 E 164-1.

33. F. Antoine to Saint-Priest, 13 Aug. 1765. ADH folder "août 1765," no. 368. See also F. Antoine to Saint-Priest, 21 Aug. 1765. ADH C 44, folder "août 1765," no. 367. Also F. Antoine to Ballainvilliers, 13 Aug. 1765. ADPD 1 C 1736. See *CA*, 3 Sept. 1765 ("Extrait d'une lettre de Malzieu," 14 Aug.). The reference to the "heavens," and the request for recompense, are in Antoine to Ballainvilliers.

34. Antoine shared his personal recollection of the experience in a letter to the comte de Tournon, which soon made its way to the *Courrier d'Avignon*. See *CA*, 15 Oct. 1765 (report from Avignon, 14 Oct.).

35. "Procès-verbal" at Les Chazes, 21 Sept. 1765. ADH C 44, folder "septembre 1765," no. 377.

36. The weight range for *Canis lupus lupus L.,* the most common type of wolf in France, was between 35 and 65 kilograms (or approximately 77 and 143 pounds). Antoine's wolf weighed 130 pounds, putting it at the upper end of the normal range. See Alain Molinier and Nicole Molinier-Meyer, "Les loups et l'homme en France," *RHMC* 28 (1981): 225–245, esp. 225, n. 2.

37. In a letter to Saint-Priest in which he recapped the events at Les Chazes as he had heard them reported, Lafont cited the *Pucelle*'s testimony exclusively, noting only that she had seen "a good resemblance" between Antoine's wolf and the wolf that had attacked her. For his part, Lafont remained reserved. "So often fooled by false appearances," he added, "I am not getting my hopes up." Lafont to Saint-Priest, 29 Sept. 1765. ADH C 44, folder "septembre 1765," no. 386.

38. "Procès-verbal" at Les Chazes, 21 Sept. 1765. ADH C 44, folder "septembre 1765," no. 377.

39. It took the subdelegate Lafont to apprise Saint-Priest of this fact. See Lafont to Saint-Priest, 29 Sept. 1765. ADH C 44, folder "septembre 1765," no. 386.

40. F. Antoine to Saint-Priest, 22 Sept. 1765. ADH C 44, folder "septembre 1765," no. 385.

41. *CA,* 8 Oct. 1765 (report from the Gévaudan, 24 Sept.).

42. See Antoine's *procès-verbal* of a killing at La Vachelerie, 14 Sept. 1765. ADPD 1 C 1736.

43. F. Antoine to Saint-Priest, 22 Sept. 1765. ADH C 44, folder "septembre 1765," no. 385.

44. "Procès-verbal" at Les Chazes, 21 Sept. 1765. ADH C 44, folder "septembre 1765," no. 377.

45. Ballainvilliers to Saint-Florentin and L'Averdy, 3 Aug. 1765. ADPD 1 C 1736.

46. Ballainvilliers to L'Averdy, [undated]. ADPD 1 C 1735.

47. Ballainvilliers to L'Averdy, Saint-Florentin, Bertin, Maupeou, Choiseul, [24 Sept. 1765]. ADPD 1 C 1736. I have been unable to locate the royal letter in the archives, but it was cited by the archivist Auguste André in the 1880s and was later used by Pourcher. In his letter to the king, apparently written before the others, Ballainvilliers appears to have believed that the bayonet wound detected on Antoine's animal had been inflicted not by the *Pucelle* but by the illustrious Portefaix himself. See Auguste André, "La Bête du Gévaudan: Notice Historique," *Bulletin de la Société d'Agriculture, Industrie, Sciences et Arts du Département de La Lozère* 35 (1884): 189–210, esp. 199–200. Bertin had not long before played a key role in founding the Royal Veterinary School at Lyon in 1764. For a history of the veterinary school from 1761 to the nineteenth century, see Yvonne Poulle-Drieux, "A propos du bicentenaire de l'Ecole

vétérinaire de Lyon," *Revue d'Histoire des Sciences et de leurs Applications* 16 (1963): 227–232.

48. Ballainvilliers to L'Averdy, Saint-Florentin, Bertin, Maupeou, Choiseul, [24 Sept. 1765]. ADPD 1 C 1736.

49. Buffon, *Histoire Naturelle, Générale et Particulière: Avec la Description du Cabinet du Roy* (Paris, 1761), 9: 292.

50. Walpole to Anne Pitt, 8 Oct. 1765. *HWC,* ed. W. S. Lewis et al., vol. 31 (New Haven, Conn., 1961), 56.

51. Buffon, *Histoire Naturelle,* 9: 292–293.

52. Joannes Jonstonus, *A Description of the Nature of Four-Footed Beasts: with their figures en[graven in brass], written in Latin by Dr. John Johnston,* trans. J. P. (Amsterdam, 1678), plate LXXII. The surgeon Jaladon probably also derived slender corroborating evidence for the allegedly foul odor of the Les Chazes beast from the Latin name Jonstonus gave to his hyena: *Hyaena Odorata Africana.*

53. Charles Jaladon, "Procès-verbal," 27 Sept. 1765. ADPD 1 C 1736. Also Buffon, *Histoire Naturelle,* 9: 292.

54. Saint-Florentin to Ballainvilliers, 4 Oct. 1765. AN O1 *461, fol. 305r. The lines about the hyena were crossed out before the letter was sent, which happened three days after the beast's presentation to the court on 1 October. For the final version of the letter see Saint-Florentin to Ballainvilliers, 4 Oct. 1765. ADPD 1 C 1736.

55. *CA,* 10 Sept. 1765 (report from Paris, 31 Aug.).

56. Lafont to Saint-Priest, 27 Sept. 1765. ADH C 44, folder "septembre 1765," no. 386.

57. Ballainvilliers to Antoine, 23 Sept. 1765. ADPD 1 C 1736.

58. The full contents of the letter were published in *CA,* 15 Oct. 1765 (report from Avignon, 14 Oct.).

59. *MF,* Oct. 1765, 199.

60. F. Antoine to Ballainvilliers, undated [October 1765]. ADPD 1 C 1736.

61. No existing illustration followed Antoine's orders exactly to the letter, but the final image in this chapter seems to have captured most of what he wanted—including giant fangs, protruding tongue, and the bleeding wounds inflicted by Antoine. Reinchard stands passively at Antoine's side. There is no way to know whether the artist who crafted the image was commissioned by Ballainvilliers.

62. F. Antoine to Ballainvilliers, 23 Sept. 1765. ADPD 1 C 1736.

63. As noted in a letter, dated 12 Oct. 1765, published in the *Année Littéraire.* See *AL* (1765), vol. 8, 204–210.

64. Walpole to Henry Seymour Conway, 2 Oct. 1765, in *HWC,* ed. W. S. Lewis et al., vol. 39 (New Haven, Conn., 1974), 14.

65. Magné de Marolles, "Précis Historique," in "Recueil factice de pièces relatives à la bête du Gévaudan, formé par Magné de Marolles," BNF M-1915, fols. 77–78.

66. The showing at the Saint-Florentin residence is mentioned in BM, ms. 2379, "Recueil d'anecdotes littéraires et politiques," 2 Oct. 1765.

67. The details of the beast's demonstration are best revealed in the correspondence of Walpole. On the sheet see Walpole to Henry Seymour Conway, 2 Oct. 1765. *HWC,* ed. W. S. Lewis et al., vol. 39 (New Haven, Conn. 1974), 14.

68. Buffon's absence is shown by the dates of his correspondence from Montbard. See Georges Leclerc, comte de Buffon, *Correspondance Générale,* ed. H. Nadault de Buffon (Geneva, 1971), 1: 137–140.

69. Saint-Florentin to Ballainvilliers, 4 Oct. 1765. ADPD 1 C 1736.

70. BM ms. 2379, "Recueil d'anecdotes littéraires et politiques, 1765, vol. 2," 2 Oct. 1765.

71. William Cole, *A Journal of My Journey to Paris in the Year 1765,* ed. Francis Griffin Stokes (New York, 1931), 210–211.

72. Walpole wrote about the beast's presentation at Versailles in many letters from the first half of October. These comments are taken from Walpole to Henry Seymour Conway, 2 Oct. 1765, in *HWC,* ed. W. S. Lewis et al., vol. 39 (New Haven, Conn. 1974), 14; Walpole to Lady Hervey, 3 Oct. 1765, in *HWC,* ed. W. S. Lewis et al., vol. 31 (New Haven, Conn., 1961), 52–53; Walpole to Anne Pitt, 8 Oct. 1765, in *HWC,* ed. W. S. Lewis et al., vol. 31 (New Haven, Conn., 1961), 56; Walpole to John Chute, 3 Oct. 1765, in *HWC,* ed. W. S. Lewis et al., vol. 35 (New Haven, Conn., 1973), 113.

73. *GF,* 4 Oct. 1765. For a verbatim account see *JE,* 1765, vol. 7, pt. I, p. 161–162.

74. As reported in a letter of gratitude written to the intendant of Auvergne. F. Antoine to Ballainvilliers, undated [Oct. 1765]. ADPD 1 C 1736.

75. [Elisabeth Longy] to F. Antoine, 30 Sept. 1765. ADPD 1 C 1736.

76. *AL* (1765), vol. 8, 204–210. The letter is dated 12 Oct. 1765.

77. Thomas Pennant, *Tour on the Continent, 1765,* ed. G. R. De Beer (London, 1948), 9. Pennant visited the Quai at the end of February 1765.

78. William Cole, who purchased two prints, was among the paying customers who went to the Quai de la Ferraille. See Cole, *A Journal of My Journey to Paris in the Year 1765,* 211.

79. Antoine had signaled this intention in his published letter to Tournon. See *CA,* 15 Oct. 1765 (report from Avignon, 14 Oct.).

80. In folklore across cultures, David D. Gilmore notes, the presence of the monster inevitably calls forth the archetypal "Culture Hero" who engages in a climactic battle with a monstrous beast. See Gilmore, *Monsters: Evil Beings, Mythical Beasts, and All Manner of Imaginary Terrors* (Philadelphia, 2003), 5. Also see Catherine Delpy's commentary on fairy tales such as "Beauty and the Beast," where monstrous adversaries are never permitted "to compromise in any way the story's happy dénouement." Catherine Delpy, "'La Belle et la Bête': La figure du monstre dans le conte de fées littéraire des XVIIe et XVIIIe siècles," in *Le 'monstre humain': imaginaire et société,* ed. Régis Bertrand and Anne Carol (Aix-en-Provence, 2005), 191–202, esp. 195.

81. L'Averdy to Saint-Priest, 10 Oct. 1765. ADH C 44, folder "octobre 1765," no. 393.

82. *CL* vol. 6, 255.

83. F. Antoine to Saint-Priest, 29 Oct. 1765. ADH C 44, folder "novembre 1765," no. 403.

84. *New Hampshire Gazette and Historical Chronicle,* 20 Dec. 1765.

85. Antoine began collecting signed certificates of his good conduct before the end of 1765. For his second request to Ballainvilliers, where he asked for "a certificate signed in your hand," see F. Antoine to Ballainvilliers, 28 Dec. 1765. ADPD 1 C 1736. In this letter, Antoine mentioned having already received a similar document from Saint-Priest.

86. The words are from the formal grant of permission drafted by the *juge d'armes,* Louis-Pierre d'Hozier, as cited in Roure de Paulin, "La Bête du Gévaudan dans les armoiries de la famille Antoine," 293–294.

8. Narrative Echoes Past and Present

1. Only at the end of the eighteenth century and the beginning of the nineteenth did techniques of preservation allow the long-term maintenance of natural history collections. See Paul Lawrence Farber, "The Development of Taxidermy and the History of Ornithology," *Isis* 68 (1977): 550–566.

2. F. Antoine to Ballainvilliers, 20 Sept. 1765 ["Etat du grand loup tué le 19 septembre"]. ADPD 1 C 1736. This is one of several documents from late September carrying an incorrect date and written in Antoine's hand, a circumstance that has fueled conspiracy theories down to the present. See, for example, Abel Chevalley, *La Bête du Gévaudan* (Paris, 1936), esp. 137–147.

3. Ballainvilliers to F. Antoine, 23 Sept. 1765. ADPD 1 C 1736.

4. Charles Jaladon, "Procès-verbal," 27 Sept. 1765. ADPD 1 C 1736.

5. Guy Crouzet suggests that a hyena listed among the possessions of the Museum of Natural History in the early nineteenth century may have been the beast, but this seems more likely to have been a case of mistaken identity. The only written evidence is an allusive passage written more than fifty years after the events in the Gévaudan. See Guy Crouzet, *La Grande Peur du Gévaudan* (Saint-Amand-Montrond, 2001), 175–176. Virtually all of the records for the Jardin du Roi are missing for the 1760s, but much circumstantial evidence suggests that the beast never entered the collections. Buffon, who remained engaged in the management of the Jardin through the 1770s, never mentioned the beast. No letters from Saint-Florentin or the manager of the king's Menus Plaisirs to Buffon or other personnel at the Jardin survive, though Saint-Florentin wrote a brief letter thanking Ballainvilliers for the effigy and noting unenthusiastically that "I have shown it to the king." Documents from the Jardin du Roi never refer to the beast, though some other items (especially new acquisitions) are listed. Nor is the beast mentioned in contemporary documents of the royal menagerie, whose director complained in 1774 of the disrepair that had plagued the institution "for more than ten years, for lack of funds." An official at the Jardin made the same complaint about the collections in Paris in 1773, indicating the

crown's changing fiscal priorities at the close of the Seven Years' War. On the Jardin in the 1770s see AN O1 2124, esp. folder "Jardin des Plantes, 1773–1774," letter dated 7 Sept. 1773; on the menagerie, see AN O1 1805, esp. folder "Versailles-Chateau-Menagerie, 1704–1791," nos. 202, 208; on Saint-Florentin's correspondence in the fall of 1765, see AN O1 *460, *461, *407, *561, 589 (the letter to Ballainvilliers is from AN O1 589, 7 Oct. 1765); on papers of the Menus Plaisirs, see AN O1 3012, 3013.

6. [F. Antoine], "Observations," [July 1765]. ADPD 1 C 1735. Also F. Antoine to Ballainvilliers, 21 Aug. 1765. ADPD 1 C 1736.

7. Steven L. Kaplan, *Bread, Politics, and Political Economy in the Reign of Louis XV,* 2 vols. (The Hague, 1976), 1: 161. See also 2: 448.

8. John Rothney, ed., *The Brittany Affair and the Crisis of the Ancien Régime* (Oxford, 1969), 163–169; Julian Swann, *Politics and the Parlement of Paris under Louis XV, 1754–1774* (Cambridge, 1995), 254–281.

9. Lafont had earlier noted in a letter to Saint-Priest that "several people claim to have seen the ferocious beast," but he had been unable to verify their reports. See Lafont to Saint-Priest, 18 Oct. 1765. ADH C 44, folder "octobre 1765," no. 395. The "perfect tranquility" is from Lafont to Saint-Priest, 26 Nov. 1765. ADH C 44, folder "décembre 1765," no. 406.

10. Curé Fournier [to Montluc], 6 Dec. 1765. ADPD 1 C 1738. Also Montluc to Ballainvilliers, 1 Jan. 1766. ADPD 1 C 1738. For the Lorcières casualty, see the burial notice of the curé Ollier, as cited in Pierre Pourcher, *La Bête du Gévaudan* (Marseille, 2006), 336.

11. L'Averdy to Saint-Priest, 10 Dec. 1765. ADH C 44, folder "décembre [1765]," no. 404. Adding to the suspicious nature of the timing of this message is the date of the letter's arrival, which Saint-Priest or his secretary always marked in the upper margins: 29 December. Three weeks would have been an unusually long lag time. For example, letters from Saint-Florentin to Saint-Priest on 16 Dec. 1764 and 25 Feb. 1765 took ten days and eight days to arrive, respectively. It seems possible, if not likely, that L'Averdy wrote his letter in the middle of the month after he had heard the news from Bessyre-Saint-Mary—in a preemptive move to quash renewed talk about "the beast of the Gévaudan." For the Saint-Florentin letters see ADH C 44, folder "1764," no. 116; ADH C 452, no. 33.

12. Delisle de Moncel was not mentioned in the L'Averdy letter, but the details of his experiences, and their connection to the methods publicized by the minister, were later shared in the *Courrier d'Avignon,* 15 April 1766 (report from Paris, 5 April).

13. "Secret pour empoisonner les Loups, sans aucun risque pour tout autre animal." ADPD 1 C 1739.

14. One cooperative subdelegate informed his superior that "I will need at least twenty more copies [of L'Averdy's memoir] to hand out to the gentlemen in my jurisdiction." See Pagès de Vixouse [to Ballainvilliers], 20 Jan. 1766. ADPD 1 C 1739.

15. Saint-Priest to L'Averdy, 3 March 1766. ADH C 44, folder "1766," no. 411. See also Ollier et al., "Procès-verbal," 15 Feb. 1766. ADPD 1 C 1738.

16. D'Ormesson to Ballainvilliers, 15 Jan. 1766. ADPD 1 C 1738.

17. Comte de Bourbon [comte d'Eu] to Saint-Priest, 28 March 1765. ADH C 44, folder "1766," no. 408.

18. *CA,* 21 March 1766 (reporting from Marvejols, 1 March).

19. Saint-Florentin to Ballainvilliers, 18 Jan. 1766. ADPD 1 C 1738.

20. "Mémoire intéressant pour la province du Gévaudan," and "Suite d'un Mémoire concernant la Province du Gévaudan" [undated]. AN F10 476, dossier 1.

21. "Plan de chasse" [undated]. AN F10 476, dossier 1. The plan's actual author, consistently written about in the third person, remained unidentified, but in the margins of the document—a large annotated map depicting the Margeride—one reads that "the person who drafted this plan knows the exact distance between each parish."

22. L'Averdy to Saint-Priest, 24 March 1766. ADH C 44 folder "1766," no. 407.

23. Saint-Florentin to Ballainvilliers, 18 Jan. 1766. ADPD 1 C 1738. See also Saint-Florentin to Saint-Priest, undated [March 1766]. ADH C 43.

24. Saint-Florentin to Ballainvilliers, 14 June 1765. ADPD 1 C 1738. Also L'Averdy to Ballainvilliers, 15 June 1766. ADPD 1 C 1738.

25. Ballainvilliers to Saint-Florentin, 7 June 1765. ADPD 1 C 1738. The intendant wrote that recent descriptions gave the beast "a rusty coat with a black stripe on its back, which makes me presume that it is a voracious wolf."

26. From the official transcript, as quoted in Rothney, *The Brittany Affair,* 175–178.

27. Julian Swann, "Disgrace without Dishonor: The Internal Exile of French Magistrates in the Eighteenth Century," *Past and Present* 195 (2007): 87–126, esp. 106.

28. Rothney, *The Brittany Affair,* 178.

29. See Arlette Farge, *Dire et Mal Dire: L'Opinion Publique au XVIIIe Siècle* (Paris, 1992), 274.

30. *CA,* 15 April 1766 (report from Paris, 5 April).

31. Nicolas Delisle de Moncel, *Méthodes et projets pour parvenir à la destruction des loups dans le royaume, par M. de Lisle de Moncel* (Paris, 1768); *Résultat d'expériences sur les moyens les plus efficaces et les moins onéreux au peuple, pour détruire dans le royaume l'espèce des bêtes voraces* (Paris, 1771).

32. Bertin to Saint-Priest, 24 Aug. 1770. ADH C 43.

33. "De Par le Roi," [1775]. AN O1 977, folder "Papiers du Grand Ecuyer," no. 9.

34. "Arrêt" of the baron de Breteuil, undated [1786]. ADH C 1910, no. 125.

35. The National Convention's Committee on Agriculture claimed in 1794, with some hyperbole, that the menace of ravenous wolves extended to "the gates of Paris." The commissioners proposed raising the bounty for each destroyed wolf to two hundred livres, and they estimated that at least 2,000 animals would have to be eliminated. See "Observations du Comité d'Agriculture et des Arts" [Year II]. AN F10 459.

36. For the "last" episode, which included a "beast of the Cévennes" that killed as many as forty people between 1809 and 1817, see Jean-Marc Moriceau, *Histoire du*

Méchant Loup (Paris, 2007), 224. On 1799–1800, see Alain Molinier, "Une cartographie des loups tués en France et dans les territoires sous contrôle français vers 1800. Jalons pour une écologie des loups," *Le Monde Alpin et Rhodanien* (2002), 101–116, esp. 103, 108.

37. "Extrait des délibérations des Etats du Gévaudan," 24 March 1766. ADL C 806.

38. In the parish register of Dèges in June of 1767, for example, the presiding priest reported simply that "Jeanne Bastide, aged nineteen, was killed and devoured by a man-eating wolf [*loup carnacier*]." See entry for 17 June 1767. ADHL E dépot 147–2.

39. J.-B. Ollier [to Montluc], 28 Dec. 1765. ADPD 1 C 1738.

40. J.-B. Ollier, "Description de l'antropophage ou de l'animal feroce qui desole et ravage le pais des frontieres du Gevaudan et de l'Auvergne, que l'on caracterise de monstre en sa nature," undated [early Jan., 1766]. ADPD 1 C 1738.

41. J.-B. Ollier, "Relation sincere & exacte des evenemens facheux qui sont arrivés pendant le cours de l'année 1765 par La Bête feroce dans la paroisse de Lorcieres haute Auvergne Diocese de l'Election de Saint-Flour," 3 Jan. 1766. ADPD 1 C 1738.

42. Montluc to Ballainvilliers, 26 Jan. 1766. ADPD 1 C 1738. In his letter of 28 December, Ollier asked Montluc to share its contents with the *receveur des tailles*. J.-B. Ollier [to Montluc], 28 Dec. 1765. ADPD 1 C 1738.

43. J.-B. Ollier to Ballainvilliers, 30 Dec. 1765. ADPD 1 C 1738.

44. See, for example, the notice for the twelve-year-old Jean Pierre Ollier de Lasoucheyre, 2 Nov. 1766. The same rhetoric—"devoured by the ferocious beast"—was used for the burial of Marie Denty in May of 1767. See ADHL 6 E 28–1.

45. Anon. [to Ballainvilliers], 27 July 1766. ADPD 1 C 1740.

46. J.-B. Ollier to Ballainvilliers, 3 Jan. 1766. ADPD 1 C 1738.

47. A report from Rodez on 24 May noted only that "the ravenous wolves [*loups carnassiers*] that have caused so much alarm and so many awful ravages in diverse provinces of France . . . will be remembered from father to son down to the most distant posterity," and that Rodez's "turn has come" for its share of the horror. *CA,* 10 June 1766 (report from Rodez, 24 May).

48. The figure is from Jean-Marc Moriceau, *La Bête du Gévaudan* (Paris, 2008), 213. The following narrative of events, covering the period between April and June 1767, closely follows Moriceau, 233–237.

49. For the burial notices in Nozeyrolles, where the parish priest attributed the deaths to "a ferocious beast or man-eating wolf," see ADHL 6 E 164–1.

50. The pilgrimages are discussed by Pourcher, who drew from local memory and his own ancestral traditions, but they are not independently confirmed by other sources. Some of the details were almost certainly invented, but the pilgrimages themselves would have been consistent with local religious culture and earlier requests for divine intervention in 1765. See Pourcher, *La Bête du Gévaudan* (Marseille, 2006), 360–362.

51. "Rapport du notaire royal Marin sur la Bête tué par Jean Chastel, désignée comme la Bête du Gévaudan," as reproduced in Jean-Marc Gibert, *La Bête du Gévaudan. Les Auteurs du XVIIIe, XIXe, XXe siècle: historiens ou conteurs?* (Mende, 1993), 110–112.

52. See Lafont to Saint-Priest, 29 Sept. 1765. ADH C 44, folder "septembre 1765," no. 386.

53. On the contrast between the "public transcript" that supports those in power and the "hidden transcript" developed "off-stage" by subordinates who resist "official" scripts, see James C. Scott, *Domination and the Arts of Resistance: Hidden Transcripts* (New Haven, Conn., 1990), esp. 1–16.

54. Gibert, *La Bête du Gévaudan,* 111. The claims of the glassmaker, a local nobleman named Verny de La Vedrine, had been investigated and found wanting by the subdelegate Marie in early March of 1765. Ironically, Verny de la Vedrine had tried to use the Chastels as character witnesses. They had been unable to vouch for his story. See Marie to Ballainvilliers, 4 March 1765. ADPD 1 C 1732.

55. Auguste André, "La Bête du Gévaudan: Notice Historique," *Bulletin de la Société d'Agriculture, Industrie, Sciences et Arts du Département de La Lozère* 35 (1884), 189–210, esp. 204–205. The story gained further embellishment, including the memories of the mayor of Saugues and details about Chastel's meeting with Louis XV, in Pourcher, *La Bête du Gévaudan,* 363–364.

56. The title had been bestowed by a correspondent for the *Année Littéraire.* See *AL* (1765), vol. 8, 204–210. Antoine died in late September of 1771, after which his widow and children were given lifelong pensions in appreciation for the gun-bearer's sixty years of loyal service. See [Pensions], AN O1 638, fol. 7r. Also "Brevet de 1000 l pension en faveur du S. Chevalier Antoine," 13 Nov. 1771. AN O1 117, fol. 995.

57. The brief history of M. Trocellier, curé d'Aumont, is undated, but it combines notes made during the ravages of 1764–1765 with observations on the spring of 1767, including especially the "patriotic zeal" shown by the marquis d'Apcher, who comes through as the real hero of the tale. Trocellier contributed to the local process of mythification. Its early entries repeated all of the most spectacular rumors, and he said of the animal at La Ténazeyre that "it was not a wolf," and that "they judged it to be some sort of monster." Still, he later came back to his history after having had second thoughts. In final concluding remarks he asserted that the beast was simply "two wolves," and he regretted that longstanding rumors about the beast's abilities made it seem as though the Gévaudanois still lived "in times of ignorance, when people believed in witches." [Registre parroisial d'Aumont], ADL EDT 009 GG 4.

58. Pourcher, *La Bête du Gévaudan,* 363. For the anecdote involving his great grandfather, 22.

59. BM ms. 2379, "Recueil d'anecdotes littéraires et politiques, 1765, vol. 2," 30 Sept. 1765.

60. "Précis Historique," in "Recueil factice de pièces relatives à la bête du Gévaudan, formé par Gervais-François Magné de Marolles," BNF M-1915, fol. 79v.

61. Gervais-François Magné de Marolles, *La Chasse au Fusil* (Paris, 1788), 259, n. 1.

62. Voltaire, *Questions sur les Miracles* [1765], in *Oeuvres Complètes de Voltaire,* ed. Louis Moland (Paris, 1877–1885), 25: 388.

63. See Lieselotte Steinbrügge, *The Moral Sex: Woman's Nature in the French Enlightenment,* trans. Pamela E. Selwyn (New York, 1992), esp. 3–20.

64. Labarthe *fils* to M. Séguier, 31 Oct. 1764, in Léon Pélissier, "Nouveaux documents sur la bête du Gévaudan," *AM* 11 (1899), 69–83.

65. Frederick the Great, "Examen de l'Essai sur les préjugés," in *Oeuvres de Frédéric le Grand,* ed. J. D. E. Preuss (Berlin, 1848), 9: 152.

66. *Immanuel Kant: Theoretical Philosophy, 1755–1770,* ed. David Walford (Cambridge, 1992), 343. I first encountered Voltaire's reflections on the imagination in Jan Goldstein, *The Post-Revolutionary Self: Politics and Psyche in France, 1750–1850* (Cambridge, Mass., 2005), 36–37. I then consulted Voltaire's essay on "Imagination" in the eighth volume of the *Encyclopédie.* See *Encyclopédie, ou dictionnaire raisonné des sciences, des arts et des métiers,* ed. Denis Diderot and Jean le Rond D'Alembert. University of Chicago: ARTFL Encyclopédie Projet (Winter 2008 Edition), ed. Robert Morrissey, http://encyclopedie.uchicago.edu.libproxy.lib.unc.edu. For more on eighteenth-century anxieties about the "disorderly" and "anarchic" potential of the imagination, see Goldstein, *Post-Revolutionary Self,* 33–46, 61.

67. Voltaire was credited with this remark by several contemporary sources. See, for example, *L'Encyclopédiana, ou Dictionnaire Encyclopédique des Ana* (Paris, 1791), 944.

68. [Mathieu-François Pidansat de Mairobert], *Journal historique de la Révolution opérée dans la Constitution de la monarchie françoise par M. de Maupeou, chancelier de France* (London, 1774), 40.

69. *La Chasse aux Bêtes Puantes et Féroces, qui après avoir inondé les bois, les plaines, etc., se sont répandues à la Cour & à la Capitale* (Paris, 1789), 4.

70. The opera star Sophie Arnould used the language against Robespierre in a letter of 21 Feb. 1795. See Louis Lacour, *Affaire du collier: Mémoires inédits du comte de Lamotte-Valois sur sa vie et son époque (1754–1830), publiés d'après le manuscrit autographe avec un historique préliminaire, des pièces justificatives et des notes* (Paris, 1858), 92; on Carrier, see 27 Dec. 1794 entry in *Réimpression de l'ancien Moniteur,* ed. A. Ray (Paris, 1862), 23: 50.

71. One opponent composed a song comparing the wolfish followers of the "beast" Manuel (who had earned royalist enmity by insulting the Bourbon monarch of Spain) to the "loyal dogs" whose solidarity eventually forced Manuel's ouster from the Chamber. See "La Bête du Gévaudan, Complainte Traduite du Languedocien," in *L'anti-libéral, ou le chansonnier des honnêtes gens,* ed. Charles-Joseph Rougemaïtre (Paris, 1823; 2nd ed.), 112. I wish to thank Max Owre for this reference. For penetrating discussion of the divisive political rhetoric of the Restoration period, see Maximilian Paul Owre, "United in Division: The Polarized French Nation, 1814–1830" (Ph.D. diss., University of North Carolina at Chapel Hill, 2008).

72. Francisco de Goya, "El sueño de la razón produce monstruos," etching from *Los Caprichos* (1799). The aphorism served as a caption to a haunting image of a sleeping man whose dreams are tormented by the presence of bats, owls, and other creatures of the night.

73. J.-B. Salgues, *Des Erreurs et des préjugés répandus dans les dix-huitième et dix-neuvième siècles,* vol. 2 (Paris, 1828). Earlier editions of the work—sometimes represented as added volumes—had appeared in 1810, 1811, 1813, 1815, 1818, and 1823–30. The work's first title had been *Des Erreurs et des préjugés répandus dans la société.* Louis Figuier drew from Salgues in his own *Histoire du Merveilleux dans les temps modernes* (Paris, 1860), and Eusèbe Salverte, *Des Sciences Occultes, ou Essai sur la Magie, les Prodiges, et les Miracles* (Paris, 1829), sought to portray belief in magic and miracles as an historical phenomenon specific to the pre-modern age.

74. Salgues, *Des Erreurs et des préjugés répandus,* 2: 1–2.

75. Ibid., 2: 64–67.

76. Ibid., 2: 10, 105.

77. Ibid., 2: 111. Salgues highlighted just two other moments from the prerevolutionary era: the musical quarrel between the "Gluckistes and the Piccinistes" in the 1770s and the Mesmerism craze of the 1780s.

78. Ibid., 2: 106–108.

79. On the phenomenon of "blotting out," and its function in helping people to conceptualize memories that are "transformed into a story," see James Fentress and Chris Wickham, *Social Memory* (Oxford, 1992), 73–77. On amnesia and the useful periodization of the past, see Eviatar Zerubavel, *Time Maps: Collective Memory and the Social Shape of the Past* (Chicago, 2003), esp. 86–93.

80. Maurin de Pompigny, *La Bête du Gévaudan: Melodrame en Trois Actes, en Prose, et à Grand Spectacle* (Paris, 1809), 10–11.

81. Ibid., 51.

82. Ibid., 10.

83. Nodier distinguished his own works from those in the "frenetic" style. See Anthony Gilnoer, "Du monstre au surhomme: Le Roman frénétique de la Restauration," *Nineteenth-Century French Studies* 34 (2006): 223–234. On Nodier and the "vogue" for the gothic after 1830, see Joan Kessler's introduction to *Demons of the Night: Tales of the Fantastic, Madness, and the Supernatural from Nineteenth-Century France* (Chicago, 1995), xi–li, esp. xiv–xxi. For other examples of the French literary fascination for monsters in the nineteenth century, which affected Alexandre Dumas, Théophile Gautier, and Guy de Maupassant among others, see *Vampires de Paris,* ed. Francis Lacassin (Paris, 1981). On the characteristics of the gothic, see Jerrold E. Hogle, "Introduction: The Gothic in Western Culture," in *The Cambridge Companion to Gothic Fiction,* ed. Jerrold E. Hogle (Cambridge, 2002), 1–20.

84. Elie Berthet, *La Bête du Gévaudan* (Paris, 1862), 123, 125. For Stevenson's comments, see Robert Louis Stevenson, *Travels with a Donkey in the Cévennes,* ed. Christopher Maclachlan (New York, 2004), 22–23.

85. The other story formed a chapter of M. Mary-Lafon's 1859 book of folk tales and historical vignettes. See M. Mary-Lafon, "La Bête du Gévaudan," in *Moeurs et Coutumes de la Vieille France* (Paris, 1859), 89–128.

86. Georges Canguilhem, "La monstruosité et le monstrueux," in *La Connaissance de la vie* (Paris, 1975), 184. On the declining interest in monsters among eighteenth-century natural philosophers, see Javier Moscoso, "Monsters as Evidence: The Uses of the Abnormal Body during the Early Eighteenth Century," *Journal of the History of Biology* 31 (1998), 355–382, esp. 359–360. On the development of "teratology" in the 1820s, see Evellen Richards, "A Political Anatomy of Monsters, Hopeful and Other-wise: Teratogeny, Transcendentalism, and Evolutionary Theorizing," *Isis* 85 (1994), 377–411.

87. See Jacques Gadille, *La Pensée et l'Action Politique des Evêques Français au Dé-but de la IIIe République, 1870–1883* (Paris, 1967), 1: 140. Saivet served only three years in Mende, but he was succeeded by Julien Costes, a protégé of the ultra-conservative bishop of Rodez. Costes became an avowed enemy of "republican" prefects and, ac-cording to one of those prefects, unabashedly "involved himself in political contests." See Gadille, 1: 175–176.

88. Eugen Weber, *Peasants into Frenchmen: The Modernization of Rural France, 1870–1914* (Stanford, 1976), 344, 360.

89. Pierre Pourcher, *L'Episcopat Français et Constitutionnel et le Clergé de la Lozère durant la Révolution de 1789: Le tout tiré des authentiques* (Saint-Martin-de-Boubaux, 1895–1900). For another contemporary history of the modern church, written by someone resentful of the clergy's "constant hostility to the political will of the French people," see Antonin Debidour, *L'Eglise Catholique et l'Etat sous la Troisième Répub-lique (1870–1906)* (Paris, 1906). For the "constant hostility," see vol. 1, vi.

90. Pourcher, *L'Episcopat Français*, 1: 6. For Pourcher's summary of the Revolu-tion, and the "dregs," see 1: 184–190.

91. Ibid., 1: 13.

92. Ibid., 1: 5, 13.

93. Weber, *Peasants into Frenchmen*, 361; see also Joseph F. Byrnes, *Catholic and French Forever: Religious and National Identity in Modern France* (University Park, Penn., 2005), 92.

94. As cited in Gadille, *La Pensée et l'Action Politique*, 1: 132.

95. Pourcher, *La Bête du Gévaudan*, 267.

96. The "coarse and savage" comes from the report of an inspector general of edu-cation in the Morbihan in 1880, as cited in Weber, *Peasants into Frenchmen*, 5.

97. Pim den Boer, *History as a Profession: The Study of History in France, 1818–1914*, trans. Arnold J. Pomerans (Princeton, 1998), 27.

98. Ibid., 18–31.

99. Stevenson, *Travels with a Donkey*, 37. The inhabitants of the Gévaudan may only have begun to feel integrated into the metropole in the last years of the nine-teenth century. As Weber has observed, bandits still used the area to escape the

clutches of the law in the middle of the century, a barter economy thrived into the 1880s, only about half of schoolchildren spoke French well, and roads frequently proved impassable for six months out of the year even in the 1890s. See *Peasants into Frenchmen,* 35, 55, 70, 199. Some suggest, though, that Weber overstated the instinctive cultural opposition between cities and country. See Jean-Pierre Jessenne, *Les campagnes françaises entre mythe et histoire (XVIIIe–XXIe siècle)* (Paris, 2006).

100. Jean-Claude Bouvier et al., *Tradition Orale et Identité Culturelle: Problèmes et Méthodes* (Paris, 1980), 11.

101. Isabelle Collet, "Les premiers musées d'ethnographie régionale, en France," in *Muséologie et Ethnographie,* ed. Ministère de la Culture et de la Communication (Paris, 1987), 68–97, esp. 77. The following two paragraphs are heavily indebted to Collet's illuminating essay. I thank Dan Sherman for bringing it to my attention.

102. Ibid., 75, 71, 73.

103. Paul Sébillot, *Littérature Orale de la Haute-Bretagne* (Paris, 1881); *Traditions et Superstitions de la Haute-Bretagne* (Paris, 1882); *Coutumes Populaires de la Haute-Bretagne* (Paris, 1886). See also *Littérature Orale de l'Auvergne* (Paris, 1898); *La Chanson Populaire et la Vie Rurale des Pyrénées à la Vendée* (Bordeaux, 1912); *Le Folklore de France,* 4 vols. (Paris, 1904–1907).

104. Paul Delarue, *Le Conte Populaire Français,* vol. 1 (Paris, 1957), 30.

105. Louis Lambert, *Contes Populaires du Languedoc* (Carcassonne, 1985), 19–20. On the International Congress, see Collet, "Les premiers musées d'ethnographie régionale," 69–70.

106. Pourcher published a letter from the Roman See acknowledging receipt of the work in July of that year. See Pourcher, *La Bête du Gévaudan,* 5.

107. Ibid., 284, 31, 70.

108. Ibid., 96.

109. Ibid., 110.

110. Ibid., 181, 267. The irony in Pourcher's explanation is that it would have been rejected by Choiseul-Beaupré, who embraced liturgical form as a kind of primitivist purification.

111. Ibid., 361–362.

112. See Michael P. Carroll, *The Cult of the Virgin Mary: Psychological Origins* (Princeton, 1986); Eugen Weber, "Religion and Superstition in Nineteenth-Century France," *Historical Journal* 31 (1988): 399–423, esp. 405–409. For a well-documented and carefully narrated account of Marian devotion in the 1870s, when German Catholics endured the *Kulturkampf,* see David Blackbourn, *Marpingen: Apparitions of the Virgin Mary in a Nineteenth-Century German Village* (New York, 1993). For the general European context, and the special importance of the French shrine at Lourdes, see *Marpingen,* 27–41. See also Detmar Klein, "The Virgin with the Sword: Marian Apparitions, Religion, and National Identity in Alsace in the 1870s," *French History* 21 (2007): 411–430.

113. Pourcher, *La Bête du Gévaudan,* 369–372.

114. Ibid., 258.

115. Ibid., 284.

116. Ibid., 337, 312.

117. François Fabre, *La Bête du Gévaudan en Auvergne* (Saint-Flour, 1901).

118. In 1898, however, one regional historian trained at the Ecole des Chartes cited Pourcher in a brief discussion of the beast's story. See Alfred Leroux, *Le Massif Central: Histoire d'une Région de la France,* vol. 1 (Paris, 1898), 79.

119. For the breakdown of topics treated in published historical work toward the end of the century, see Pim den Boer, *History as a Profession,* 13. On the influence of Guizot and Michelet, see William Keylor, *Academy and Community: The Foundation of the French Historical Profession* (Cambridge, 1975), 48–49.

120. Pierre Caron's call to action in 1902 evoked an earlier period of relative neglect: "The importance of works of local history is recognized today by all historians." Pierre Caron, "L'Organisation des études locales d'histoire moderne," *La Révolution Française: Revue d'Histoire Moderne et Contemporaine* 42 (1902), 481–510, esp. 481.

121. Keylor, *Academy and Community,* 130.

122. On the patriotic and republican nationalism of the historical profession in the last quarter of the nineteenth century, see Keylor, *Academy and Community,* 90–100.

123. Victor Jacquemont du Donjon, "La Bête du Gévaudan," *La Nouvelle Revue* 113 (1898), 296–302, esp. 302.

124. Collet, "Les premiers musées d'ethnographie régionale, en France," 88, 78. On the "othering" of rural tradition, see also Bouvier et al., *Tradition Orale et Identité Culturelle,* 10–11.

125. P. S., "Souhaits de Bonne Année," *Revue des Traditions Populaires* 4 (1889): 55–56. See also G. H. Murray Aynsley, "Moeurs et Superstitions comparées des Indes Orientales et de l'Europe," 19–24; and Félix Régamey, "Le Fantastique Japonais," 14–18. The application of similar tools of analysis in metropolitan and colonial contexts would become quite self-conscious by the 1930s, when Marcel Marget, a curator at France's Musée National des Arts et Traditions Populaires, sought to eliminate the distinction between "peoples ethnographic and ethnographicable." See Daniel J. Sherman, "'Peoples Ethnographic': Objects, Museums, and the Colonial Inheritance of French Ethnology," *FHS* 27 (2004): 669–703, esp. 671.

126. This specific allegation about methodology was leveled by Arnold Van Gennep, the most important folklorist in France in the first half of the twentieth century. See Nicole Belmont, *Arnold Van Gennep: The Creator of French Ethnography,* trans. Derek Coltman (Chicago, 1979), 116. The remark about historians' deficiencies needs to be taken with a grain of salt, as Van Gennep and folklorists struggled throughout the early twentieth century to obtain the kind of institutional support and legitimacy long accorded their counterparts in the historical profession.

127. Delarue, *Le Conte Populaire Français,* 1: 161–162. By crediting the beast's demise to a faithful warrior carrying a blessed weapon, Pourcher's story may even have

reflected the power of a widely broadcast folktale theme involving an "invincible arm" wielded against a magical creature; the prototype of the tale was *Le Chasseur Adroit.*

128. Paul Sébillot, "Le Seigneur Loup-Garou," in *Les Littératures Populaires de Toutes les Nations: Traditions, Légendes, Contes, Chansons, Proverbes, Devinettes, Superstitions,* vol. 35, *La Littérature Orale de l'Auvergne* (Paris, 1898), 228–232, esp. 232.

129. Arnold Van Gennep, *Contributions au Folklore des Provinces de France,* vol. 5, *Le Folklore de l'Auvergne et du Velay* (Paris, 1942), 320–321.

130. Van Gennep, *Le Folklore de l'Auvergne,* 349.

131. Henri Pourrat, *Le Trésor des Contes,* 13 vols. (Paris, 1948–1962). See Jack Zipes, *The Brothers Grimm: From Enchanted Forests to the Modern World* (New York, 2002), 135–137.

132. Henri Pourrat, *Histoire Fidèle de la Bête en Gévaudan* (Clermont-Ferrand, 1946), 11.

133. Ibid. Pourcher is cited on 105.

134. Ibid., 109.

135. Eugen Weber explains that "storytellers" had perceived the change by the latter part of the nineteenth century, and that they consequently began to treat "fairies and goblins and werewolves only as past realities: their grandfathers knew them, yes, but they left the region about the time of the French Revolution." See Weber, "Fairies and Hard Facts: The Reality of Folktales," *Journal of the History of Ideas* 41 (1981): 93–113, esp. 113.

136. See, for example, Claude Seignolle, *Contes, Récits, et Légendes des Pays de France* (Paris, 1997), 3: 549–567; Daniel Fabre and Jacques Lacroix, eds., *Histoire et Légendes du Languedoc Mystérieux* (Paris, 1970), 268–275; *Légendaire du Languedoc-Roussillon: enquête ethnographique menée par les élèves du Lycée Technique d'Etat de Montpellier,* [ed. André Combes], (Montpellier, 1972), 33.

137. Fentress and Wickham, *Social Memory,* 79–80.

138. For analysis of the story's embeddedness in its own cultural moment, see Judith Walkowitz, *City of Dreadful Delight: Narratives of Sexual Danger in Late-Victorian London* (Chicago, 1992).

139. On Landru see Robin Walz, *Pulp Surrealism: Insolent Popular Culture in Early Twentieth-Century Paris* (Berkeley, 2000), 76–113, esp. 81.

140. Pierre Deloux, *Vacher l'Assassin: Un Serial Killer Français au XIXe Siècle* (Paris, 1995), 26–27.

141. According to one historian, the consensus of the time held that Vacher's form of criminality was facilitated and enabled not by dislocation or social misery but rather by generous public assistance. See Timothy B. Smith, "Assistance and Repression: Rural Exodus, Vagabondage, and Social Crisis in France, 1880–1914," *Journal of Social History* 32 (1999), 821–846. For the "cheers" and the "bloody sadist," the latter a quote from medical testimony at the trial, see 822. On the Ripper moniker, Deloux, *Vacher l'Assassin,* 23.

142. P. Puech, "La Bête du Gévaudan," *Aesculape: Revue Mensuelle Illustrée* 2 (1912): 9–12.

143. Chevalley, *La Bête du Gévaudan* (Paris, 1936); Pourrat, *Histoire Fidèle*.

144. In fact, the folkloric revival pre-dated the war and can be linked to the Paris meeting of the International Congress of Folklore in 1937. The attendees, writes Catherine Velay-Vallantin, "manifested the resurgence of romantic passion for a simple folklore, purified of all corruption." "Le Congrès International de Folklore de 1937," *Annales: Histoire, Sciences Sociales* 54 (1999): 481–506, esp. 482–483. See also Sherman, "'Peoples Ethnographic.'"

145. Marguerite Aribaud-Farrère, *La Bête du Gévaudan identifiée* (Béziers, 1962); René de Chantal, *La Fin d'une Enigme: La Bête du Gévaudan* (Paris, 1983), 11, 315–337 (Chantal eventually concludes that an animal is the more likely suspect); R. F. Dubois, *Vie et Mort de la Bête du Gévaudan* (Liège, 1988), 314; Pierre Cubizolles, *Loups-Garous en Gévaudan: le martyre des innocents* (Brioude, 1995), 213; André Aubazac, *La Bête du Gévaudan: les faits, l'effet, les fées, des mots pour des maux, dé-mo . . .* (La Roche Blanche, 2009); Christophe Gans, *Le Pacte des Loups* (theatrical film, 2001).

146. Gérard Ménatory, *La Bête du Gévaudan: Histoire, Légende, Réalité* (Mende, 1976).

147. Hervé Boyac, *La Bête du Gévaudan: plaidoyer pour le loup* ([Saint-Auban], 2004), 239; Michel Louis, *La Bête du Gévaudan: L'innocence des loups* (Paris, 1992), and a second edition, *La Bête du Gévaudan* (Paris, 2003); Roger Oulion, *La bête du Gévaudan: Nouvelles révélations sur un crime organisé au XVIIIe siècle, en Gévaudan* (Polignac, 2006), 70.

148. Pascal Cazottes, *La bête du Gévaudan: enfin démasquée?* (La Motte d'Aigues, 2004), 114–116.

149. In addition to the work of Jean-Marc Moriceau, discussed in the introduction and Chapter 1, see François Fabre, *La Bête du Gévaudan;* Xavier Pic, *La Bête qui Mangeait le Monde en pays de Gévaudan et d'Auvergne* (Paris, 1971); Felix Buffière, *La Bête du Gévaudan: une énigme de l'histoire* (Toulouse, 1987); Guy Crouzet, *La Grande Peur du Gévaudan;* Serge Colin, *Autour de la Bête du Gévaudan* (Le Puy-en-Velay, 1990).

150. R. F. Dubois, *Vie et Mort de la Bête du Gévaudan* (Liège, 1988), 7–8.

Conclusion

1. Henri Pourrat, *Histoire Fidèle de la Bête en Gévaudan* (Clermont-Ferrand, 1946), 11. On the local authors, see the Introduction.

2. Jean-Marc Moriceau, *La Bête du Gévaudan* (Paris, 2008), 95, 248, 251, 97, 265.

3. For a thorough and regretful overview of the process see Morris Berman, *The Reenchantment of the World* (Ithaca, N.Y., 1981), 25–132; see also Lorraine Daston and Katherine Park, *Wonders and the Order of Nature, 1150–1750* (Cambridge, Mass., 1998), 329–363; for specific attention to the political implications of the process, see Marcel

Gauchet, *The Disenchantment of the World: A Political History of Religion*, trans. Oscar Burge (Princeton, 1997).

4. Marc Soriano, *Les Contes de Perrault: Culture Savante et Traditions Populaires* (Paris, 1989), 88–98; Raymonde Robert, *Le conte de fées littéraire en France, de la fin du XVIIe à la fin du XVIIIe siècle* (Nancy, 1981), 7–9, 381–428; Jack Zipes, *Beauties, Beasts, and Enchantment: Classic French Fairy Tales* (New York, 1989), 1–12. Salon-generated fascination for the moral lessons embedded in popular folk tales would produce not one but two published renditions of "Beauty and the Beast" in the middle of the eighteenth century. Gabrielle-Suzanne de Villeneuve's *Belle et la Bête,* from 1740, was followed by the better-known version written by Jeanne-Marie Leprince de Beaumont in 1757. See Catherine Delpy, "'La Belle et la Bête': La figure du monstre dans le conte de fées littéraire des XVIIe et XVIIIe siècles," in *Le 'Monstre' Humain: imaginaire et société,* ed. Régis Bertrand and Anne Carol (Aix-en-Provence, 2005), 191–202.

5. Duhamel to [Roussel], [Jan. 1765], in Marius Balmelle, "Lettres inédites du Capitaine Duhamel sur la Bête du Gévaudan (octobre 1764–avril 1765)," *RGCC* 13 (1967), 112.

6. The bishop of Mende and the gun-bearer François Antoine would both be dead within a few years after the conclusion of the events in the Gévaudan, but others would have had opportunities to provide commentary or reflections on the meaning of the story, and they chose to remain silent. Officials such as Saint-Priest, Ballainvilliers, and Lafont studiously avoided the subject. The comte de Morangiès would go on to achieve notoriety in the 1770s for profligate spending and a high-profile financial scandal in Paris, but neither he nor his many public defenders ever thought to use his engagement in the hunt for the beast as evidence of his creditable character. The d'Ennevals had good reasons to ignore their history in the Gévaudan, but one can at least imagine Duhamel finding excuses to revisit the story and its meaning. He survived the ordeal intact and went on to a long career as an officer in dragoon and cavalry regiments. Eventually made a knight of the order of Saint-Louis, he was also awarded a 400-livre annual gift by Louis XVI's minister of war in 1779 (even though "I do not have the honor of being known [personally] by His Majesty"), and he ended his forty-year career only on the eve of the French Revolution, in 1788. He retired with a quite respectable annual pension of 1,400 livres. Nonetheless, in the quarter-century (or more) that Duhamel lived after his experience in the Gévaudan, he breathed not a word of the story of the beast or of his own close involvement in it—at least not in ways that would become known to the public. On the Morangiès scandal see John Renwick, *Voltaire et Morangiès, 1772–1773, ou, Les lumières l'ont échappé belle* (Oxford, 1982), and Sarah Maza, *Private Lives and Public Affairs: The Causes Célèbres of Prerevolutionary France* (Berkeley, Calif., 1993), 19–20, 39–51. On Duhamel's career, see SHAT Yb 656 and 1 Yf 9292.

7. Jeffrey Jerome Cohen, ed., *Monster Theory: Reading Culture* (Minneapolis, 1996), 4.

8. But as Joshua Landy and Michael Saler have noted in their own survey of the

alleged "disenchantment" that characterized the nineteenth century, "the progressive disenchantment of the world was . . . accompanied, from the start and continually, by its progressive re-enchantment." Joshua Landy and Michael Saler, eds., *The Re-Enchantment of the World: Secular Magic in a Rational Age* (Stanford, 2009), 2. For powerful expressions of the phenomenon, particularly relevant for the history of the beast, see Maiken Umbach, "The Modernist Imagination of Place and the Politics of Regionalism: Puig i Cadafalch and Early Twentieth-Century Barcelona" (81–101); and Joshua Landy, "Modern Magic: Jean-Eugène Robert-Houdin and Stéphane Mallarmé" (102–129).

9. Magné de Marolles, "Précis Historique," in "Recueil Factice de pièces relatives à la bête du Gévaudan, formé par Gervais-François de Marolles," BNF M-1915, fol. 79v.

Note on Place Names

The names of local villages and towns took various forms in the eighteenth century. I have opted to use the identifier and the spelling most commonly used in the contemporary sources. When variations in spelling or other disagreements in the sources made identification difficult, I relied on the great Cassini map of France, watercolor versions of which were prepared for Marie-Antoinette in the 1780s. A searchable version of this map is available at http://cassini.ehess.fr/cassini/fr/html/index.htm. To prevent confusion for readers who may wish to find the sites of some of the events described, I list in parentheses the modern place names and spellings for sites identified differently on the maps or in the text:

Arzenc (Arzenc-de-Randon)
Aumont (Aumont-Aubrac)
Buffeirettes (Buffeyrettes)
Clermont (Clermont-Ferrand)
Les Chazes (Saint-Julien-des-Chazes)
Malzieu (Le Malzieu-Ville)
Nozeyrolles (Nozerolles)
Paulhac (Paulhac-en-Margeride)

Le Puy (Le Puy-en-Velay)
Ruines (Ruynes-en-Margeride)
Saint-Alban (Saint-Alban-sur-Limagnole)
Saint-Chély (Saint-Chély-d'Apcher)
Saint-Denis (Saint-Denis-en-Margeride)
Ubac (Les Hubacs)

Note on Sources

Complete references for all sources cited in the book, including the published material from the eighteenth century, are available at http://history.unc.edu/faculty/smith.html. The nature of the key primary sources deserves comment. The central sources for research on the beast of the Gévaudan were pulled together by nineteenth-century archivists working at the Archives Départementales de l'Hérault (Montpellier) and the Puy-de-Dôme (Clermont-Ferrand). A nineteenth-century fire destroyed many critical documents held at the Archives Départementales de la Lozère in Mende, but both that institution and the Archives Départementales de l'Haute-Loire in Le Puy-en-Velay still have valuable records for baptisms, marriages, and burials—the *état civil*. The most telling indicator of the size and wealth of the evidentiary treasure trove gathered in the nineteenth century is the fact that a single carton in Montpellier—C 44 for the *intendance de Languedoc*—contains over four hundred documents arising from the hunt for the beast, most of it correspondence involving the key players in 1764–1765. There is only a single folder devoted to the beast in carton C 43, but the scores of documents it contains are equal in quality to those in C 44. For the contextualizing purposes of this book, the documents from C 43 and C 44 were supplemented by many others detailing the administrative business of the intendant Saint-Priest and his subdelegates, all contained in series C.

Similarly concentrated riches await in Clermont-Ferrand. Series 1 C 1729–1740 *(intendance d'Auvergne)* offers hundreds more letters, depositions, and printed ordinances surrounding the beast, as well as fascinating material on earlier wolf infestations from the 1740s through the early 1760s. Many of these documents were recently made available online at http://www.archives-departementales.puydedome.com. Additional correspondence of the minister Saint-Florentin and information on François Antoine and his background are held in series O1 *(Maison du roi)* of the Archives Nationales in Paris. Series F10 *(Agriculture)* at that institution also contains revealing material on later efforts to combat wolf infestations.

At the Bibliothèque Nationale de France, the "Recueil factice de pièces relatives à la bête du Gévaudan," compiled by Magné de Marolles, is a precious source that brings together scores of manuscript letters, engravings, broadsheets, newspaper extracts, and the author's history of the event, all available for consultation on microfilm (M-1915). Other sources—including the *Gazette de France* and many other contemporary newspapers—are held in the Bibliothèque Nationale's print and microform collections. Their manuscripts collection also contains assorted documents connected to the hunt for the beast—mainly statements of expenses, receipts, and reimbursements, but also some related correspondence (manuscrits français 7847). Most of the book's illustrations come from either the "Recueil factice" or from the Bibliothèque Nationale's *Cabinet des Estampes.*

Manuscript newssheets that include rich material for 1765 were consulted at the Bibliothèque Mazarine (manuscrits 2378–2379, 2391) and the Bibliothèque Historique de la Ville de Paris (manuscrit 637). Consultation of different slices of the *Courrier d'Avignon* took place over a period of years at (or through the generous lending policies of) the University of Kentucky, the Widener Library at Harvard University, and the Médiathèque Emile Zola in Montpellier. The mother lode, where I was able to address small gaps in coverage from the other collections, is located at the Médiathèque Ceccano in Avignon. Other useful commentary on journalistic coverage of political events in the 1760s, and commentary on the events themselves, can be found at the Archives Diplomatiques at La Courneuve (in the collections labeled "France" and "Fonds Divers Angleterre").

Several valuable primary source collections, comprised of documents

scattered through libraries and municipal archives across France, were published by the archivists Ferdinand and Auguste André in the late nineteenth
century, and by Marius Balmelle in the 1950s and 1960s. References to their
collections are found in the book's bibliography. Secondary works devoted to
the beast are also listed there in a separate category.

Acknowledgments

The publication of a book long in the making normally sets off celebrations, but the culmination of this particular project brings a touch of sadness. The prospect of finally releasing my grip on the beast and surrendering all excuses to return to the Gévaudan would have been hard enough. But I also have to face the termination of the remarkably wide social and intellectual network that my pursuit of *la Bête* constructed over time. The "making" of this beast of a book felt, from the beginning, like a refreshingly collective endeavor. I will miss the lively little society that formed around the beast.

Early on, the question I generally encountered from other historians of France—"you're working on *what?*"—always gave way to curious queries, usually followed by offers of help. Fellow specialists provided bibliographical suggestions, thoughtful musings on the beast's meaning, reactions to drafts of my chapters as they became available, random suggestions that arrived in my inbox without forewarning, and signs of curiosity that I found encouraging. Don Reid often sent wolves, or readings about them, in my direction. With Michael Kwass I exchanged sensational crime stories and the occasional reference to wolf attacks or other depredations. François-Joseph Ruggiu alerted me to the vital, and then-forthcoming, work of Jean-Marc Moriceau. Max Owre provided unexpected and invaluable bibliographical assistance on the nineteenth century, and Sarah Farmer, Sarah Maza, and Dan Sherman provided essential tips for the twentieth century.

Other friends and colleagues helped mainly through conversation—but what conversation! Matt Adkins and Liana Vardi treated me to very different, but equally scathing, critiques of *Brotherhood of the Wolf.* Natasha Naujoks introduced me to the fictional lives of southern French vampires, and in the Office of Undergraduate Curricula at the University of North Carolina (UNC), Stephanie Medwid kept me honest with her surprising expertise on North American wolves. The "Mosswood Mafia" (you know who you are) explored various storytelling strategies and the great dramatic possibilities of fear. At weekly and then monthly meetings with my fellow Leadership Fellows in UNC's College of Arts and Sciences—Jane Danielewicz, Peggye Dilworth-Anderson, Beth Grabowski, Kevin Guskiewicz, Roberto Quercia, and Andrew Reynolds—I had the benefit of continuing moral support and sympathetic questioning.

For their careful readings of draft chapters, I especially wish to thank Joseph Bryan, Eve Duffy, Tom Kaiser, Lloyd Kramer, Keith Luria, Lynn Mollenauer (whose lengthy e-mail message, with bibliography, I am still digesting), Julia Osman, and Dan Sherman. The results of their thoughtful critiques should be obvious to them. Mita Choudhury, Doina Harsanyi, Natasha Naujoks, and John Rutledge all read the entire manuscript in one or another of its incarnations, and they provided valuable feedback, suggestions, and encouragement. Rutledge, in addition to peppering me with references from his office in UNC's Davis Library, subjected the manuscript to editorial rigor the likes of which I had not experienced since graduate school. Drafts of chapters, or partial chapters, were also discussed in two interdisciplinary environments as stimulating as they were congenial. In the fall of 2008, members of the Triangle French Studies Seminar at the National Humanities Center treated me to a thorough and productive grilling after I offered them an early version of my ideas. At UNC's Institute for the Arts and Humanities in the fall of 2009, the director John McGowan, associate director Julia Wood, and my fellow Faculty Fellows—Sarah Dempsey, Minrose Gwin, Dorothy Holland, Alan Shapiro, Jane Thrailkill, and Mayron Tsong—dissected the events at Les Chazes with gusto, offering helpful suggestions and references along the way. My thanks, too, to audiences and fellow panelists at meetings of the Society for French Historical Studies (in Houston and St. Louis) and to the participants in the 2009 UNC-NUS symposium on popular culture and national identity at the National University of Singapore who responded helpfully and critically to presentations of work in progress. The readers for Harvard University Press (the no-longer-anonymous Orest Ranum and one other) also gave the manuscript close readings and made a variety of sensible suggestions, all of which I acted upon in one way or another. Ranum has been consistently encouraging in a variety of ways. All of these readers, friends, colleagues, and critics made this a better book.

Colleagues outside of French history, and from other disciplines or other sectors of my university, also came into my orbit (or I into theirs) while I worked on the book, and they were helpful in more ways than I can recall. My rewarding experience at UNC's Institute for the Arts and Humanities has been mentioned, but I also got valuable help from nonspecialists closer to home in my own Department of History. John Sweet told me about American newspapers of the eighteenth century, Jim Leloudis invited me to introduce the beast to the smart and eager students of the UNC Honors program that he directs, and Chad Bryant encouraged me by discussing the book with Kathleen McDermott at Harvard University Press. My colleague Richard Talbert generously put at my disposal the rich resources of the Ancient World Mapping Center, and his deputy Brian Turner put in many hours drafting the book's superbly crafted maps of France and the Gévaudan. Beyond these helpful individuals of the history department, I have received other valuable support, both intellectual and material. While I worked in curricular matters, the senior dean, Roberta (Bobbi) Owen, helped finance a side trip to Widener Library at Harvard University and was largely responsible for my selection as a Leadership Fellow in the spring of 2008. Trips to France in the summers of 2005, 2007, and 2009 were made possible by grants from the American Philosophical Society and the UNC Vice Chancellor's Office for Research and Development, by the Leadership Fellows' program, and by research funds provided jointly by the College of Arts and Sciences and the Department of History. I was then able to combine semester leaves granted by the Department of History and the Institute for the Arts and Humanities to complete a full draft of the manuscript in the calendar year 2009. I am deeply grateful for the many forms of assistance provided through the sprawling institutional network of UNC and its College of Arts and Sciences.

Individuals working at a range of institutions outside of Chapel Hill also proved instrumental to the research process. In addition to the steady assistance provided by Rutledge and others at UNC's Davis Library, specialists at other institutions facilitated searches and gave me access to protected sources. A special word of thanks goes to Mary Molinaro, Director of Preservation and

Digital Programs at the University of Kentucky Libraries. I also wish to thank librarians at Duke University, Widener Library, the New York Public Library, the Bibliothèque Historique de la Ville de Paris, the Bibliothèque Mazarine, the Bibliothèque Nationale de France, the Médiathèque Emile Zola (in Montpellier), and the Médiathèque Ceccano (in Avignon).

Gilbert Bodinier saved me a trip to Vincennes by tracking down the personnel files for Captain Duhamel, and my former student Julia Osman, with more important things to worry about, took the time to e-mail digital copies of key documents. In Montpellier, the director of the Archives Départementales de l'Hérault, Vivienne Miguet, as well as several of her helpful staff —Luce Lebart, Bernadette Mukandoli, Laurent Pascal, and Carole Renard —scrambled about on very short notice to find documents and secure valuable reproductions. At Harvard University Press, Kathleen McDermott shepherded the manuscript through the production process with patience and efficiency, and Kate Brick provided thoughtful editorial guidance. I thank them all.

Reaching the end of this particular road is especially hard because the research that underlies the book is associated in my mind with pleasant family excursions through the south of France. I recall the small town pleasures of medieval Malzieu; the bustling commerce of old Mende; the wonderful wax figures of the Musée Fantastique de la Bête du Gévaudan in Saugues; the statue of *la Pucelle* at Auvers; sheep grazing by a rolling stream at Bessyre-Saint-Mary; beautiful September nights in Montpellier. These images provide vivid reminders of engrossing days spent in archives, but also of weekends and evenings spent making history come alive—trite though it may sound. The beast offered a story picturesque enough to hold the attention of children (my daughter, Alyssa, was the first to read a chapter, and my son, Connor, keeps agitating for a return to Saugues), and intriguing enough to cast spells on some adults, starting with my wife, who are left cold by conventional narratives of a dead past. Debbie shared in my discovery of many of the beast's precious narrative fragments, but in return for her attention she was then forced to facilitate the reassembling of those fragments through a writing process that lasted longer than promised. I can hope that future projects require smaller doses of energy, and I can hope to start making more reasonable promises, but I know I can never hope to find another project as rewarding, and as endlessly alluring, as this one turned out to be.

Index